VISIONING AUGUSTINE

D1073242

Challenges in Contemporary Theology

Series Editors: Gareth Jones and Lewis Ayres
Canterbury Christ Church University College, UK, and University of Durham, UK

"Challenges in Contemporary Theology" is a series aimed at producing clear orientations in, and research on, areas of "challenge" in contemporary theology. These carefully coordinated books engage traditional theological concerns with mainstreams in modern thought and culture that challenge those concerns. The "challenges" implied are to be understood in two senses: those presented by society to contemporary theology, and those posed by theology to society.

Published

VISIONING AUGUSTINE

John C. Cavadini
with a Foreword by Mark Therrien

WILEY Blackwell

This edition first published 2019
© 2019 John Wiley & Sons Ltd

All rights reserved. No part of this publication may be reproduced, stored in a retrieval system, or transmitted, in any form or by any means, electronic, mechanical, photocopying, recording or otherwise, except as permitted by law. Advice on how to obtain permission to reuse material from this title is available at http://www.wiley.com/go/permissions.

The right of John C. Cavadini to be identified as the author of this work has been asserted in accordance with law.

Registered Office(s)
John Wiley & Sons, Inc., 111 River Street, Hoboken, NJ 07030, USA
John Wiley & Sons Ltd, The Atrium, Southern Gate, Chichester, West Sussex, PO19 8SQ, UK

Editorial Office
9600 Garsington Road, Oxford, OX4 2DQ, UK

For details of our global editorial offices, customer services, and more information about Wiley products, visit us at www.wiley.com.

Wiley also publishes its books in a variety of electronic formats and by print-on-demand. Some content that appears in standard print versions of this book may not be available in other formats.

Limit of Liability/Disclaimer of Warranty
While the publisher and authors have used their best efforts in preparing this work, they make no representations or warranties with respect to the accuracy or completeness of the contents of this work and specifically disclaim all warranties, including without limitation any implied warranties of merchantability or fitness for a particular purpose. No warranty may be created or extended by sales representatives, written sales materials or promotional statements for this work. The fact that an organization, website, or product is referred to in this work as a citation and/or potential source of further information does not mean that the publisher and authors endorse the information or services the organization, website, or product may provide or recommendations it may make. This work is sold with the understanding that the publisher is not engaged in rendering professional services. The advice and strategies contained herein may not be suitable for your situation. You should consult with a specialist where appropriate. Further, readers should be aware that websites listed in this work may have changed or disappeared between when this work was written and when it is read. Neither the publisher nor authors shall be liable for any loss of profit or any other commercial damages, including but not limited to special, incidental, consequential, or other damages.

Library of Congress Cataloging-in-Publication Data

Names: Cavadini, John C., author.
Title: Visioning Augustine / John C. Cavadini ; with a foreword by Mark Therrien.
Description: Hoboken : Wiley, 2019. | Series: Challenges in contemporary theology | Includes bibliographical references and index. |
Identifiers: LCCN 2018039796 (print) | LCCN 2018041932 (ebook) | ISBN 9781119105763 (Adobe PDF) | ISBN 9781119105749 (ePub) | ISBN 9781119105718 (hardcover) | ISBN 9781119105732 (pbk.)
Subjects: LCSH: Augustine, of Hippo, Saint, 354–430.
Classification: LCC BR65.A9 (ebook) | LCC BR65.A9 C29 2019 (print) | DDC 270.2092–dc23
LC record available at https://lccn.loc.gov/2018039796

Cover Design: Wiley
Cover Image: © traveler1116/iStock.com

Set in 11.5/13pt Bembo by SPi Global, Pondicherry, India
Printed in Singapore by C.O.S. Printers Pte Ltd

10 9 8 7 6 5 4 3 2 1

Dedicated to
the Memory of So Many Great Teachers

Contents

About the Author

John C. Cavadini is Professor of Theology at the University of Notre Dame. He also serves as McGrath-Cavadini Director of the McGrath Institute for Church Life. His scholarship and teaching is focused on the theology of the Church Fathers, Origen and Augustine in particular. Appointed by Pope Benedict XVI, he has served one term on the International Theological Commission. He was also the 2018 recipient of the Monika Helwig Award for Outstanding Contributions to Catholic Intellectual Life, from the Association of Catholic Colleges and Universities. Among other publications, he is the author of *The Last Christology of the West: Adoptionism in Spain and Gaul, 785–820*; the editor of *Gregory the Great: A Symposium* and also of *Explorations in the Theology of Benedict XVI*; and co-editor, with Danielle Peters, of *Mary on the Eve of the Second Vatican Council*.

Foreword

A Quarter of a Century with a Theologian for All Centuries: An Introduction to John C. Cavadini's Visioning Augustine

Mark Therrien

Genius tends to be doubly rare – in its occurrence on the one hand, and in its being understood on the other. The rarity of the latter is too often the case for St. Augustine, the greatest of the Latin Fathers. I remember my introduction to this great Churchman. I learned that he was to blame for his pessimism regarding original sin, guilt, and sex; for his presumptuous psychological speculations on the Trinity; for his Platonist intellectualizing of the Gospel; and, finally, for his supposed genesis of later theories of double predestination (inter alia). But then, when I actually read Augustine under the tutelage of the author of the current collection of essays, I found myself encountering a very different Augustine. Far from a bleak pessimist, Prof. Cavadini helped me to discover an exegete who believed in the essential goodness of creation and who preached a God who freely made man, even while knowing that this same man would send him to the cross. Instead of someone suffering from a neurosis about human intimacy, I found, with Prof. Cavadini's help, a preacher whose vision of Christian marriage and sex was profound – indeed, who knew them to be so lofty that he also realized the extent to which the tragedy of sin had marked them and thus required redemption by Christ. Rather than a navel-gazer discovering the divine essence through audacious reflections on his own "self," Prof. Cavadini led me to see a priest, on his knees, gazing at the wounds that he knew himself to have inflicted. Far from a philosopher dreaming about Platonic ideas in the ether, we met a theologian who spoke powerfully of history – and of the fact that, in Jesus Christ, God had entered into it. And, finally, I did indeed find the *massa damnata* of the *City of God*. However, with Prof. Cavadini, I also found a broken but redeemed pastor who knew from his own experience the power of grace to transform even the hardest of hearts, and who in his homilies tries passionately to persuade the members of his flock to accept this grace so that they might find themselves in the City and not with the *massa* – even as he himself realized the full gravity of the Gospel's teaching about the narrow way, and that all of them might not make it.

Prof. Cavadini's Fall 2015 Seminar on Augustine was thus a formative moment in my graduate career, and one for which I remain grateful. In what follows, then, it is my honor to provide a synopsis of and intro-duction to the chapters in this volume, in which Prof. Cavadini has set out for us a new framework for reading Augustine – thus adding his voice to the symphony of scholarly efforts to recover the theology of this great *pater patrum* of the Church Universal.

I History Has Meaning: Augustine's Development as a Theologian of the Incarnation

The chapters in this volume start off in the early 1990s with much on *De Trin.*, a work that was not really in vogue then. As noted in the first chapter, titled "The Structure and Intention of Augustine's *De Trinitate*," few at the time wanted to deal with this work, because it was, supposedly, too speculative and abstract: it was read as being about how to make a philosophical (in particular, Plotinian) ascent to God. On the one hand, this reading is correct. *De Trin.* is about this kind of ascent in a way, but not as many have understood it. *De Trin.* is indeed about making an ascent, but what Augustine shows is that our attempts to ascend on our own (i.e. that which philosophy attempts to do) are totally futile. There are, in fact, two attempts to make an ascent in *De Trin.* – both of them fail. These failures are not accidental, but rather the point of the work, as Augustine himself says in the com-ments that he added to the beginning of the work later on. Through these failed attempts at a philosophical ascent, Augustine shows us that we cannot ascend on our own, but rather need Christ as our way to reach God as our goal. But what Augustine also realizes by the time of *De Trin.* is not only that Christ is the way by which we come to God, but also the goal himself. Christ is God incarnate, and therefore the goal of our ascent is not a God of metaphysical speculation – an essence somewhere behind and beyond the Trinity – but rather the real God: the God who is eternally Love, and who is made known to us only through the historical, temporal economy of our incarnate Lord, Jesus Christ. Thus, in *De Trin.*, Augustine shows a stronger interest in the historical and temporal. As he shows, we do not have to flee from that which is temporal in order to know God (as Augustine seems once to have thought). Rather, we come to know God *in* the temporal and historical. God has acted in history, and so history has meaning such that it cannot be sloughed off as we ascend to some impersonal divine heights.

This change in perspective is key for understanding Augustine and his development as a theologian. It is also something that helps us to understand his other works. In this vein, the second chapter, titled "The Sweetness of the Word: Salvation and Rhetoric in Augustine's *De doctrina christiana*," shows how this transformed perspective shapes Augustine's soteriology. In his earlier works, Augustine was mostly concerned with Christ as a teacher of interior knowledge – even when, as is the case in one early work, he does speak about Christ's passion. By the time of *De doctrina*, however, Augustine is concerned with the ins and outs of daily life, we might say; namely: the transformation of human affect or emotion, which takes place through the transformation of the human will. This transformation happens only through the grace of Christ, by means of looking to his passion and cross. The same theme is discussed in Chapter 3, titled "The Quest for Truth in Augustine's *De Trinitate*," which also expands upon how Augustine thinks about the relation of the human being to his or her culture. Our transformation in Christ is not something that matters for us alone. Rather, all human experience is cultural. In *De Trin.*, Augustine traces the roots of culture back, first of all, to our pre-linguistic inner word, and shows how our will shapes this word either in pride or love, such that its exterior expression leads to a culture that is either truly bound together in charity or perverted by pride. We are not reducible to our cultures, but are in fact the generators of culture. On the other hand, the wrong "encoding" of our inner word in its exterior forms generates cultures that are marked by ungodly pride, which ensnare us in turn. For Augustine, it was for this reason that the Word became incarnate: so that we could be conformed to his example and so that he could persuade us by his blood. In his earlier works, Augustine perhaps thought too readily that the disciplines of the liberal arts and philosophy could be used to ascend to God. By the time of

De Trin. and *De doctrina*, however, he realizes that these disciplines themselves are (in their current states) generated from our sinfully disposed wills, and thus require healing. To be sure, Augustine does not write culture off as meaningless. Rather, he realizes more acutely that it needs healing through Christ, to whatever extent this healing is possible in this life.

II   Reading Scripture: Augustine on the Re-Creation of the Person in the *Totus Christus*

In *De Trin.*, Augustine's new focus on Christ as the goal *and* as the end of our journey led him to emphasize the perpetual validity of the historical economy as that wherein God has worked our salvation. Within this perspective, Christ as a historical agent becomes central in Augustine's thought. Christ saves us not only by living and dying for us, but also by providing us with a model of godly human life. But to know what we must become in Christ, we must also see that from which Christ has rescued us. In this vein, Chapter 4, titled "Augustine's Book of Shadows," on Book Two of the *Conf.*, shows how, for Augustine, Scripture's narrative is also our own narrative. This book, which is prima facie about Augustine's sexual improprieties and his infamous theft of pears, has been the subject of much psychologizing on Augustine. Is not its rhetoric just too much? No, in fact, for what Augustine narrates is not chiefly his acts of licentiousness or thievery (although he does tell us of them), but rather his own descent into shadowy nothingness. He is thus, paradoxically, narrating a non-narrative of "total" insubstantiality, which is only possible by virtue of the fact that he actually has a *real* story now; namely, that of receiving God's grace and mercy, and so being given back himself. Book Two of the *Conf.*, beyond tales of sex and pears, is Augustine's exegesis of Genesis in light of his own life viewed from the perspective of Christ's story, according to which Christ obliterates the fallen solidarity of Genesis and restores humanity into a new solidarity with and in himself. This understanding of Genesis and its narrative of the Fall as key to understanding the person and work of Christ, and thus our own lives, is a key feature of Augustine's theology. Understanding what was lost in the Fall is particularly important for Augustine – not because of a gloomy pessimism, but rather so that we can know more truly both that from which Christ saves us, and also that which Christ has transformed in his death for our sake.

For Augustine, then, the Genesis narrative provides a key to understanding the human person and his need for Christ. Our need to engage in scripture is a constant focus of Augustine, in fact. In this regard, Chapter 5, titled "Simplifying Augustine," shows that, whether Augustine is writing a treatise for the more learned or preaching to the unlearned, his basic intention in either case is the same. He is not giving his audience pre-packaged doctrine that they must blindly accept. Rather, he is inviting his readers and listeners to make a journey together with him, in faith, to a greater understanding of the economy of Christ so as to come to know God. If in his early works Augustine thought that the liberal arts and philosophy could help one to make the ascent to God, by the year 400 he simply does not. Rather, the way to ascend is to look in faith to the Crucified, and to meditate on Scripture so as to come to a deeper understanding of the mercy and love of God for us that are narrated in them.

It is precisely this mercy which alone can transform our lives – including those aspects of them that are affected most deeply by the Fall, as we discover in Chapter 6, titled "Feeling Right: Augustine on the Passions and Sexual Desire." In thinking about sexual pleasure in marriage, Augustine turns to consider what man is supposed to be. In paradise, sex would have been by our totally unhindered free will and without lust – that is, without that unwilled, impulsive sexual desire which goes against our rational nature, and which seeks to have intercourse for the sake of power and for the sake of gratifying one's own perverse *libido dominandi*. Many would criticize Augustine and say that such a view is too cold and unemotional. But Augustine does not think that, in paradise, we would have been unfeeling or inhuman; in fact, he criticizes the *apatheia* of the Stoics precisely as inhuman and unfeeling. Rather, he distinguishes between emotions (which are neutral in themselves) and passions (which are emotions that are "pathologized" and thus become sicknesses). Sex in paradise would not have been characterized by unruly and irrational passion, but that does not mean that it would have been emotionless. Rather, it would have been *truly* emotional. How would that have even looked? We can only speculate from our post-fallen position, but for Augustine, following his insights about the full significance of the incarnation and the full humanity of Christ as the model for what our genuine humanity looks like, Christ again provides the key to understand *real* human psychology. As Scripture shows, Christ willed his emotions out of solidarity with us. They were felt truly by his own free willing of them, and thus they became a sign of his compassion for us, and so give us a model to imitate in turn. And again, exegesis of Scripture is key in this regard. For Augustine, the *locus theologicus* for understanding what *real* human emotion looks like, as shown by Christ, is the psalms, in which we find the whole Christ (Head and Body) speaking to us. What and who we are as human beings – as our real "selves," if we were to use this term (more on which, later) – is really known only in and through Christ. This point is absolutely key for Augustine, and is emphasized especially in Chapter 7, titled "The Darkest Enigma: Reconsidering the Self in Augustine's Thought." As this chapter shows, many people have imported into Augustine notions of the "self" that are modern. In fact, Augustine never discusses "the self" expressly. Modern theories tend to think of the "self" as an individual cut off from all others. In such understandings, the "self" is taken to be some sort of private center of being that is interior and inaccessible to all others. Bluntly put, Augustine does not think of the self in this way. Rather, according to Augustine, who we are can be understood only with respect to the incarnation as revealed to us in Scripture. The only identity that we have is not some permanently stable center that we must somehow access through interior speculation, but rather our perpetually restless heart that is continually being recreated by Christ. Therefore, it is not by becoming more interior that we become our real "selves," but rather by turning to him. We have no real identity apart from him. Rather, apart from him, we would have only non-identity, non-being, non-subsistence – that is, the state of shadowy un-reality discussed in *Conf.* book two. We never have a stable "self," even eschatologically, for in fact Augustine thinks that, the more we love God, the "more intense" our search for him becomes. Furthermore, this transformation in Christ is not some private encounter, but rather essentially communal and ecclesial. This point comes across especially in how Augustine thinks about the relationship of intimacy between man and woman in marriage, as shown in Chapter 8, titled "The Sacramentality of Marriage in the Fathers." Whereas some ancient Christian writers thought that the husband's task was to educate his wife in a philosophical or ascetical manner, Augustine understands marriage to be the place where

Christians are transformed in Christ by means of their mutual participation in the life of Christ, as that life is experienced in the Church.
Thus, we cannot divorce Augustine's teaching on marriage from his
ecclesiology. For Augustine, Christians encounter the transformative
love of Christ first of all in the Church, and then in marriage – in that
order. In his view, marriage mediates the love of Christ for his Body
the Church to the married couple, and *thus* transforms them; it is in
that sense that marriage is a sacrament in a real way, even if Augustine
does not theorize on it as a later scholastic might do. It is for this reason that marriage can be the place where one's healing in Christ takes
place: not principally through the husband's "educating" of his wife,
but rather through their shared participation in Christ's love. Thus, for
Augustine, the chief locus for our growth and reform in Christ is
always the Church. This idea is stressed especially in Chapter 9, titled
"Eucharistic Exegesis in Augustine's Confessions." In Augustine's
view, we are re-created through the mercy shown to us in Christ,
which mercy leads us to know God the Trinity (because God *is*
mercy). Therefore, we are re-created in the Church, especially through
that sacrament which is the memory of Christ's mercy shown to us
on the cross – namely, the Eucharist. We are re-created through Christ,
but since Christ has a body that includes many members, we are also
re-made, in some way, through the lived examples of their lives in
him. Not only Christ, but they too show us what it means to be
human beings made in the image and likeness of God, as God intended
us all to be from the beginning.

III   The Self-Sacrifice of Mercy and the Pride of the World: The City of God and its Shadow

The mystery of our re-creation in Christ is thus fundamentally ecclesial for Augustine. Correlatively, and as Augustine highlights in *City of
God*, there is a connection between the kind of persons that we are
and the kind of society that we will have, as Chapter 10, titled "Spousal
Vision: A Study of Text and History in the Theology of Saint
Augustine," shows especially. In his evaluation of the Roman Empire
and its character as a society, Augustine again turns to Genesis as a key
text. As he sees it, the Roman Empire is a society dominated by its
own lust for power (*libido dominandi*). The empire is in a state of being

thoroughly "confused" – a confusion with its roots in Adam and Eve as those who became *confusi* because of the Fall. In choosing to worship himself in his own pride, Adam brought about the fall of our original human solidarity. In choosing himself and in forgetting God (that is to say, in willing into being a perverse state of affairs wherein he made himself out to be God), Adam destroyed our original, spousal solidarity. It is this solidarity that Christ came to restore. Importantly, the key to understanding this solidarity is, for Augustine, the real value of the historical as that within which God acts, and thus also the reality of embodiment. Christ restores our broken solidarity in himself because he enters into history, thus taking upon himself a narrative in which we can also partake by grace. His story is one of mercy, inasmuch as he became weak and emptied himself for our sake. We can become partakers of his narrative now through our membership in his Body, the Church, and through partaking of the sacraments. But the fact that we become members of him does not mean that, ipso facto, we should look for the reality of a perfected society in this world. Augustine does indeed correlate the transformation of the human person and his society, but Augustine's eschatological perspective is also essential to note. Since Christ chose to come into our company, sinful though it was (and sinful though it will remain), we cannot expect to have a pure Church in this world. Belonging to this new society does not mean that we should look for perfection in this life, but rather that we should learn to see everything from the perspective of his mercy and compassion.

If we were to locate any single theme that forms a hermeneutical key for Augustine, it would in fact be "mercy." Chapter 11, titled "Trinity and Apologetics in the Theology of St. Augustine," brings this idea to the fore. This chapter highlights how we must look at the *City of God* in order to understand *De Trin.*, especially in regard to considering the apologetic context of the former as that which must shape our reading of the latter. In both texts, Augustine speaks of many of the same issues, and even in the same order. One issue that is particularly important is the question of worship. In book 10 of the *City of God*, Augustine speaks about philosophers such as Porphyry who seem to be closest to the Christian proclamation inasmuch as they do appear to know the true God. But if that is so, then why do they still allow for the worship of many gods? In fact, Augustine shows that, although it seems that these philosophers come near to the

Christian proclamation, they are also the farthest from the Gospel in other ways. Although it would seem that Porphyry (for example) knows the real God, in fact Augustine shows how Porphyry actually rejects Christ and the mercy that he shows, because he rejects the humility of the cross. But this is key, for the real God is the God of the cross. The key issue is that Porphyry does not know *what kind* of God the real God is, and this makes for all the difference. The real God is the God who is humble mercy – the mercy that is made manifest in the incarnation and passion of the Christ. Thus, in spurning this mercy, Porphyry spurns the Trinity.

Mercy is thus not accidental to God. This mercy *is* God. God is this mercy, because, from all eternity, God has willed the salvation of those called to his City. God has a *plan*, which even involved his ultimate act of foolishness on the cross. The last chapter, titled "God's Eternal Knowledge According to Augustine," highlights the foolishness of God that is wiser than men, and thus further explores Augustine's critique of philosophy. Even though it may seem that philosophy may offer some understanding of God that approaches the biblical proclamation, what Augustine shows is that the difference between the two is ever greater. The key to understanding Augustine in this regard is his reading of Paul and his understanding of Wisdom. The philosophers reject the cross because it makes manifest the lowliness of God in an utterly unique historical and personal way. In rejecting it, however, they also show themselves to have missed out on the true Wisdom of God, which in the eyes of this world is simply stupidity or folly (as the Apostle says). This is the real tragedy of philosophy. As Augustine shows, the philosophers (e.g. the Platonists) do understand some attributes of God, such as his immutability. As Paul points out in Romans 1, however, they still do not worship him but rather allow for the worship of multiple gods, because (they think) it is only through theurgy that most people can get to the divine – a union that they themselves achieve (or so they think) by philosophical means. But this is wrong. They have deceived themselves, because, in fact, we cannot attain unto God apart from the economy of the incarnation. What the philosophers do not understand is that the God who is the goal of our ascent is the same God who became involved in history and time, and who became the way by which we come to himself as goal. Put otherwise, for Augustine, the fact that the goal of our journey is Christ is key. The God who became incarnate is the same God to whom we

are to ascend. Therefore, one cannot truly know God apart from his
historical economy – apart from the fact that he, remaining immutable and without change, entered into time (*factus est!*) and now has a
narrative of real solidarity with us. The philosophers cannot imagine
a God who could enter into temporality in this way. Thus, they treat
God as if he needs to be protected (*sc.*, by them) from history and
time. But God does not require protection from history and time.
Rather he is the God who knows all things that transpire within
them – indeed, he has even *willed* them. Because God's knowing and
willing of all things are one and the same, the temporal economy is
not accidental, but rather planned from all eternity. Creation is freely
willed, and so created things reflect this freedom. History therefore
has significance. This is made most apparent in the fact that Christ
died and rose again from the dead. In contrast with the theories of the
philosophers who claim that time is cyclical, Christ's death is unique
and unrepeatable. The Platonists are right, then, when they say that
the divine nature does not change. But they also miss out on this fact:
"Some*one*" divine does in fact have a narrative. And it is from this
perspective of God entering into solidarity with us and taking a story
into himself that we understand everything else about him, including
his freely willed decision to create. What Scripture reveals, then, is not
only the cross as a moment of God's folly in time, but the eternal
foolishness of God, inasmuch as the cross has always been intended by
God and tells us about everything else that God has done for us in
turn. The real God is the one who, from all eternity, deigned to offer
his blood as the price for his free creation. In facing any free act
within history, therefore, we are faced with his eternal love in willing
to die for us. This love is what makes our freedom possible. In seeing
the freedom of the historical economy, then, we are faced with God's
eternal foolishness for our sake.

Preface

The essays presented in this volume have all appeared to the reading public before, some more recently than others. They are only lightly edited to bring the notes up to date, especially those notes that involve cross-references among themselves. Other than that, to avoid discrepancies between different published versions of the same article, the essays are, so to speak, "as is."

I have collected these studies at the request of students and colleagues who have, intermittently, asked me to consider collecting some of them. I have, equally intermittently, resisted collecting them. For one thing, readers can easily find scholarship on Augustine that they would read more profitably than my own. I feel the words of St. Benedict coming to mind, as he closes his *Rule*, directing the attention of those aspiring to perfection to the giants of monastic life and their teachings, the "teachings of the holy Fathers." For "what book," he asks, "of the holy catholic Fathers does not resoundingly summon us along the true way to reach the Creator? Besides the *Conferences* of the Fathers, their *Institutes* and their *Lives*, there is also the rule of our holy father Basil."[1] It would be easy to paraphrase here, for those aspiring to the perfect mastery of Augustinian studies, substituting modern names for Benedict's ancient ones – "for what book of theirs would not more resoundingly summon us along the true way?" – and the list, were I to populate it, would of course be longer by far, even embarrassingly longer, than St. Benedict's short list!

In view of this, the only defense for publishing, perhaps, would also be inspired by St. Benedict, when he says in the same chapter that he had written "a very little rule, for beginners." Perhaps one or two of the "very little" studies contained herein might serve as entry points into the study of Augustine for many readers who are beginners and would not have come across these smaller-sized essays otherwise. Of course, I could also echo St. Augustine himself and his own defense for writing on a topic others have covered, he says, quite adequately before him. In Book 3 of *On the Trinity*, acutely aware that his predecessors who had written in Greek had already said "everything we might properly wish to know on the subject," and yet also aware that not everyone will have mastered Greek enough to read them, he goes on to say that the more books there are written on the subject of the Trinity, "the more likely a reader is to find what they are looking for" (3.1).[2] It would be especially gratifying if some of these essays served to encourage beginners in the reading and interpreting of Augustine to "take a second look," so to speak, at someone whom they may have dismissed on the basis of the caricatures and negatively stereotyped readings of Augustine that unfortunately still circulate despite their repeated unsaying and dismantling in so many excellent studies of others. Perhaps they will be pleasantly surprised by the startling sophistication and subtlety of thought, which urges itself upon the reader at almost every turn in one's travels through such a vast and luxurious textual landscape as Augustine is continually painting for us.

Another reason I had resisted collecting some of my essays is that a such collection could be taken to imply that each essay does not stand on its own, but rather is part of a logical sequence of parts that could then serve as "chapters" in a book. In fact, though they are thematically connected, each of these essays was conceived independently as a self-contained meditation on the Augustinian texts they consider. They are invitations to the reader to engage in a similar meditation. They do not so much aspire to contributing to a settled body of knowledge called "Augustinian studies" as to serve, so to speak, as moments of encounter. But, fair warning, to encounter Augustine is not to encounter an inert element, one that is easy to reify as a stable object of study. Augustine, as a skilled *rhetor*, was trained to inspire, persuade, move, and maybe most of all, to unsettle. Our hearts may be "restless" but usually not restless enough. Instead, they harbor treasured complacencies that keep us from examining some of our heart's deepest commitments – treasured complacencies about our sex lives (including complacencies of those who renounce sex) that hide commitments to ingratitude; treasured complacencies regarding the quest for status and prestige that hide commitments to social structures of deception and of contempt for truth; and treasured complacencies about our own freedom that hide commitments to self-righteousness and, even more deeply, an addiction to incoherence. Our contemporary prophets of suspicion – Marx, Nietzsche, Freud, Durkheim – seem not to touch these complacencies very deeply by comparison. Alert to the pathologies of social structures, of intellectual endeavor even (and especially!) at its highest level, of passion and emotion, of the will to dominate, Augustine finds something even deeper at the base of them all, something discernible only from a perspective outside of the concentric circles of our own complacency, that is, from the perspective of revelation, and that is what he calls "pride," or *superbia*, the desire to compete with and to replace God with ourselves, to assert a mythos of absolute self-sufficiency, a fiction that we can generate meaning out of the nothing of ourselves independent of God. Pride is the "original" sin, and thus the original hermeneutic of suspicion, as deployed by Augustine.

Perhaps the reason why Augustine can afford to be so deeply suspicious is that he believes that healing is possible, and his rhetoric of unsettling is intended to disturb us enough so that we might, against all odds, be open to the healing that is available if we are humble enough to receive it. Are we open to the Church – so unlikely and seemingly unsuitable a prospect for anything much to speak of – as a kind of sacrament of the sources of true human solidarity? Are we open to Scripture as the two-edged sword, the Word of God, that Augustine's heart-searching rhetoric so searingly depends upon and deploys? Are we open to the sacraments as defying human attempts to achieve righteousness or communion as an accomplishment of our own, instead of as a gift? Are we open to the poor, enough to see in them trustworthy deposits of our hard-earned wealth? How open? Augustine keeps asking. Reading Augustine is exposing oneself to the hope that healing is available to us by these means, perhaps the most unsettling of all of Augustine's unsettling rhetoric, because implicitly we are asked, do we believe we need healing? Do we believe we can be healed? Do we want it? It is not easy to encounter Augustine because, if we read in a way that hopes to understand him, it means reading our own hearts as well, and it may be that a scholar (like myself) is the last person likely to read this way, and rather more likely to generate a scholarship of resistance or of cultivated distance.

In his brilliant and beautiful chapter on the *Confessions*, Peter Brown famously concludes that, "Like a planet in opposition, [Augustine] has come as near to us, in Book Ten of the *Confessions*, as the vast gulf that separates a modern man from the culture and religion of the Later Empire can allow."[3] Perhaps, Augustine might comment, it is not only the vast gulf that separates us from Antiquity that is responsible for Augustine's coming no nearer than a planet in opposition. Perhaps, Augustine might comment, it is because he is allowed to come no closer, because that vast gulf is what separates "modern man" from our own hearts, and Augustine asks us to cross it. And it might therefore be true that, ironically, to truly treat Augustine historically means not to "study" him and objectify his thought as something frozen in the past, but to allow the encounter with Augustine to engage us in dialogue and thus in the development of his thought. The dichotomy between "history" and "theology" seems especially self-effacing in the encounter with an ancient theologian who refuses to remain conveniently in the past.

It is tempting in writing about Augustine to re-voice him, to "speak" him in a Thomistic language, or in a Lutheran language, or a Calvinist language, or even in the Nietzschean language of the death of God. I have tried my best to learn, out of an encounter with Augustine, to "speak Augustinian," to think of the patient exposition of Augustinian texts as learning a kind of language, and to invite others to learn to speak Augustinian. Of course, one can ever and always speak only one's own language. Learning to "speak Augustinian," though, is perhaps learning to allow one's own speaking, one's own language, to be transformed in the reception to the Word that Augustine's writing is always trying to mediate. If so, learning to speak Augustinian would be a lifelong project! Nevertheless, it would be the truest "historical" approach that is possible. Even an actor is most convincing when you can sense that the voice speaking any given part is truly his own, having been so open to the experience of the character that its own speaking has become an act of generosity that is inalienable.

And finally, another thing one learns, and something which perhaps ties these essays together as invitations to an encounter, is that encountering Augustine, the Christian theologian – and this may be surprising – is anything but narrowly parochial. Augustine's theology allows revelation to overflow the banks of the Church, without thereby relativizing these banks – and in fact, another irony, by featuring them. Perhaps then, just as Augustine is a good witness against attempts to interpret him that are overly "historicizing," it may be that he is a good enough theologian to inspire the theological reader to avoid making the theological mindset narrower than it has to be. Yet he does that not by denying its specificity and its particularity as Christian and ecclesial, but by embracing it.

I owe many a debt of thanks in bringing this Foreword to a close. Lewis Ayres first suggested, and then paved the way, for this collection of essays to be published. Mark Therrien provided labor-intensive and characteristically intelligent assistance in selection and editing, and he provided the ultimate in spurring on the project by writing an Introduction that tries to show some of the connections among the essays, despite their quasi-self-standing nature. Other debts are mentioned in the notes to the essays themselves. I do not remember who taught me to love Augustine, though I know I did not have the good sense to turn to him on my own. I would like to remember at least the late Stephen Crites, Professor of Religion at Wesleyan University, who introduced me to the *City of God* when I was an undergraduate; and the late Jaroslav Pelikan, who, in some mysteriously unobtrusive but efficacious way, taught me to love Augustine by resisting simplification of his thought. I do not believe I have lived up to their hopes as I should have, but my gratitude is nevertheless undiminished.

Notes

1   *The Rule of St. Benedict in Latin and English With Notes,* Timothy Fry, O.S.B., ed. (Collegeville, MN: The Liturgical Press, 1981), chapter 73, pp. 295, 297.

2   St. Augustine (1991) *"The Trinity."* In *The Works of St. Augustine: A Translation for the 21st Century,* Part I, Vol. 5, Edmund Hill, O.P., trans. (Brooklyn, NY: New City Press), pp. 127–28.

3   Peter Brown (2000) *Augustine of Hippo,* new edition. (Berkeley and Los Angeles: University of California Press), p. 175.

Abbreviations

BA	Bibliothèque Augustinienne
CCSL	Corpus Christianorum Series Latina
CSEL	Corpus Scriptorum Ecclesiasticorum Latinorum
FC	Fathers of the Church
WSA	*The Works of St. Augustine: A Translation for the 21st Century*

Abbreviations of Works of St. Augustine (taken from the *Augustinus-Lexikon*, as also used by the periodical *Augustinian Studies*)

Acad.	*Contra academicos tres libri.* In CCSL 29, edited by W. M. Green and K. D. Daur, 3–61. Turnhout: Brepols, 1970.
an. quant.	*De animae quantitate liber unus.* In CSEL 89, edited by W. Hörmann, 131–231. Vienna: Verlag der Österreichischen Akademie der Wissenschaften, 1986.
b. coniug.	*De bono coniugali.* In CSEL 41, edited by J. Zychi, 187–231. Prague/Vienna: F. Tempsky; Leipzig: G. Freytag, 1900.
b. uid.	*De bono uiduitatis.* In CSEL 41, edited by J. Zychi, 305–343. Prague/Vienna: F. Tempsky; Leipzig: G. Freytag, 1900.
beata u.	*De beata vita.* In CCSL 29, edited by W. M. Green and K. D. Daur, 65–85. Turnhout: Brepols, 1970.

c. Faust.	*Contra Faustum Manicheum libri triginta tres.* In CSEL 25.1, edited by J. Zycha, 251–797. Prague/Vienna: F. Tempsky; Leipzig: G. Freytag, 1891.
cat. rud.	*De catechizandis rudibus liber unus.* In CCSL 46, edited by I. B. Bauer, 121–178. Turnhout: Brepols, 1969.
ciu.	*De civitate Dei libri uiginti duo.* CCSL 47 and 48, edited by B. Dombart and A. Kalb. Turnhout: Brepols, 1955. More recently: *De civitate Dei libri uiginti duo.* BA 33–36, edited by G. Bardy. [Paris]: Desclée de Brouwer: 1959–1960.
conf.	*Confessionum Libri XIII.* CCSL 27, edited by Lucas Verheijen, O.S.A. 2nd edition. Turnhout: Brepols, 1990.
cont.	*De continentia liber unus.* In CSEL 41, edited by J. Zychi, 141–183. Prague/Vienna: F. Tempsky; Leipzig: G. Freytag, 1900.
doctr. chr.	*De doctrina christiana libri quattuor.* CCSL 32, edited by K. D. Daur and J. Martin, 1–167. Turnhout: Brepols, 1962. More recently (and corrected from CCSL 32): BA 11.2, edited by Madeleine Moreau, with annotation and notes by Isabelle Bochet and Goulven Madec. Paris: Institut de Études Augustiniennes, 1997.
en. Ps.	*Enarrationes in Psalmos.* CCSL 38, 39, and 40, edited by E. Dekkers and J. Fraipont. Turnhout: Brepols, 1956.
ep.	*Epistulae.* CSEL vols.34, 44, 57, 58, edited by A. Goldbacher. Vienna: F. Tempsky; 1895–1923.
Gn. adu. Man.	*De Genesi aduersus Manicheos libri duo.* In CSEL 91, edited by D. Weber, 67–172. Vienna: Verlag der Österreichischen Akademie der Wissenschaften, 1998.
Gn. litt.	*De Genesi ad litteram libri duodecim.* In CSEL 28.1, edited by J. Zycha, 3–435. Prague/Vienna: F. Tempsky; Leipzig: G. Freytag, 1894.
Io. eu. tr.	*In Iohannis evangelium tractatus CXXIV.* CCSL 36, edited by Radbodus Willems, O.S.B. Turnhout: Brepols, 1954.
lib. arb.	*De libero arbitrio libri tres.* In *Il "De Libero Arbitrio" di S. Agostino: Studio introduttivo, testo, traduzione e commento*, edited by Franco De Capitani. Milano: Vita e pensiero, 1987.

mag.	*de magistro liber unus.* CCSL 29, edited by W. M. Green and K. D. Daur. Turnholti: Typographi Brepols, 1970.
mus.	*De musica libri sex.* CSEL 102, edited by Martin Jacobsson. Berlin: De Gruyter, 2017.
nupt. et conc.	*De nuptiis et concupiscentia ad Valerium libri duo.* In CSEL 42, edited by C. F. Vrba and J. Zycha, 211–319. Prague/Vienna: F. Tempsky; Leipzig: G. Freytag, 1902.
ord.	*De ordine libri duo.* In CCSL 29, edited by W. M. Green and K. D. Daur, 89–137. Turnhout: Brepols, 1970.
retr.	*Retractationes libri duo.* CCSL 57, edited by Almut Mutzenbecher. Turnhout: Brepols, 1984.
s.	*Sermones ad populum.* In *Discorsi*, Nuova Biblioteca Agostiniana 29, 30.1, 30.2, 31.1, 31.2, 32.1, 32.2, 33, 34. Rome: Citta Nuova Editrice, 1979–1989).
sol.	*Soliloquiorum libri duo.* In CSEL 89, edited by W. Hörmann, 3–98. Vienna: Verlag der Österreichischen Akademie der Wissenschaften, 1986.
trin.	*De Trinitate libri quindecim.* CCSL 50 and 50A, edited by W. J. Mountain and F. Glorie. Turnhout: Brepols, 1954. More recently, see *La Trinité (livres I–VII)*, BA 15 edited and translated by M. Mellet, O.P. and Th. Camelot, O.P., with an introduction by E. Hendrikx, O.E.S.A. Paris: Desclée de Brouwer, 1955 (repr. by Institut d'Études Augustiniennes with additions and corrections, 1997). See also *La Trinité (livres VIII–XV)*, BA 16 edited and translated by edited and translated by P. Agaësse, S.J. and notes in collaboration with J. Moingt, S.J. [Paris]: Desclée de Brouwer, 1955 (repr. by Institut d'Études Augustiniennes with additions and corrections, 1997).
uirg.	*De sancta uirginitate liber unus.* In CSEL 41, edited by J. Zychi, 235–302. Prague/Vienna: F. Tempsky; Leipzig: G. Freytag, 1900.
util. cred.	*De utilitate credendi liber unus.* In CSEL 25.1, edited by J. Zycha, 3–48. Prague/Vienna: F. Tempsky; Leipzig: G. Freytag, 1891.

1

The Structure and Intention of Augustine's *De Trinitate*

Augustine often commented on the "extreme difficulty" of his work *On the Trinity* (*trin.*), repeatedly remarking that it would be comprehensible only "to few."[1] This may explain why, while there is a surfeit of modern discussions which draw upon material from the *trin.*, there are virtually no modern treatments of the work as a whole.[2] Perhaps this is because, of all of Augustine's works, the *trin.* appears to us to be the most moorless, an intractable mass of speculation floating oddly aloof from foundation in any particular social context. Peter Brown, commenting on the *trin.* in his biography of Augustine, warns us that we are wrong if we do not think that Augustine was capable of writing a book out of purely speculative motivation.[3]

But perhaps this too is merely a polite way of suspecting that the work is essentially irrelevant, and indeed Brown immediately drops the work from further consideration, and others have followed suit. In this chapter, I would like to take an exploratory first step toward removing the stigma of pure speculation from this work by suggesting a location for it within a circle of discourse peculiar to Augustine's intellectual milieu, and I would like to propose that the key to such an enterprise will lie in a consideration of the *structure* of the work as a whole.

Despite Augustine's insistence, in the letter affixed by his design to the beginning of every copy of the work, that "the subsequent books are linked to the preceding ones by a continuous development of the argument,"[4] a standard interpretation of the unity of the work divides

Visioning Augustine, First Edition. John C. Cavadini.
© 2019 John Wiley & Sons Ltd. Published 2019 by John Wiley & Sons Ltd.

it in half, something like this: A first "half" (usually construed as books 1–7 but sometimes given as 1–4 or 1–8) presents the teaching on the Trinity, which constitutes the Catholic "faith," while the remaining "half" of the treatise presents an attempt to "understand," through the use of reason, the faith so presented.[5] Apart from the fact that Augustine does not divide the treatise this way, but rather conceives of the whole work as an attempt to bring the reader to understanding,[6] on this interpretation of the structure, there remain in the work masses of material, both large and small, which are not accounted for. The long discussions of redemption in books 4 and 13, the discussion of contemplation in book 1 and in the prologues to books 1–5, the treatment of original sin and human renewal in book 14, as well as the sheer extent of the discussion of the theophanies of Genesis and Exodus in books 2–3, are not easily fit into the standard plan. Those who adhere to it will probably find themselves lamenting, with McKenna (1963), that "the *De trinitate* of St. Augustine is not as systematically arranged as the medieval or modern studies of this dogma."[7] We would probably do well to remember that it actually is not a medieval or modern study of the dogma, if it is a "study" of a "dogma" at all, and is therefore most likely not structured by the understanding of "faith" and "reason" and their relation which may inform these later works.

Nevertheless, we may be forgiven for going astray since we are not among the "few" whom Augustine expected would understand the treatise. These "few" can however be glimpsed in numerous other places in Augustine's writings. Augustine often stops to address specialized remarks to them in the course of his homilies.[8] We first meet these "few" in the earliest pages of Augustine's first writings, as those accomplished in or invited to the study of "philosophy." They would include the dedicatees of the early writings – for example, Augustine's patron Romanianus, and the Christian Platonist Manlius Theodorus.[9] These people, some of whom can be glimpsed by name in the Letters,[10] would know (or, in Augustine's view, be capable of knowing) that "knowledge" or "understanding" of that which is uncreated and eternal consists in a sort of intellectual "seeing" or "vision" of it,[11] one which involves a mode of thinking completely free of images or of any mental construct applicable to the creature,[12] much as Augustine himself had learned from his first reading of Plotinus.[13] The "few" would also realize (or at least be expected to be able to grasp) that the mind could be "exercised"[14] in this image-free thought through a process of step-by-step ("gradatim") "ascent" from the consideration of physical things, to that of finite spiritual things, to the eventual vision of things eternal. Such an "ascent" would also represent a turning inward as one passes from bodily things to the things of the soul and mind.[15] In short, the "few" whom Augustine expected might understand his treatise would be those familiar with a standard Plotinian and especially Porphyrian characterization of the "return" of the soul to contemplation or *noesis*.[16]

Clearly, the *trin.* is predicated upon such a notion of understanding. The guided tour of the human mind which we receive in books 9–14 is nothing less than an attempt at a directed "ascent" (with several detours) from the consideration of that which is created to the contemplation – the Plotinian *noesis* – of the Creator. These books are, in effect, an extended exercise[17] of the mind in the "non-corporeal" mode of thinking with which the Trinity will ultimately be grasped. Perhaps, as a unit, they could therefore be regarded as one of the finest examples of what could be called Neoplatonic anagogy[18] that remains from the antique world. The question now becomes, what is it doing here in Augustine's *trin.*?

We can answer this question in part by remembering that the quest for the Neoplatonically conceived direct vision of God is not a new theme in the work of Augustine, and appears with particular strength in the early philosophical dialogues, which Augustine wrote shortly after his conversion. These works are characterized by a frankly Neoplatonic agenda aiming at the contemplation of a Plotinian divine triad.[19] Augustine lavishes praise upon both Plato and Plotinus;[20] employs Cicero's *Hortensius* as his main instrument of the philosophical conversion of the youth attached to him;[21] and there is everywhere breathed an (almost insufferable) optimism regarding the capacity of "philosophy" to induct those converted to it into the vision of God's eternal light.[22] The only function which the Incarnation seems to have in this system is as an authoritative injunction to a faith in the ability of philosophy to lead one back to God – a faith which will serve to purify our minds so that the philosophical ascent may be successfully completed.[23]

Du Roy (1966) has characterized this early relation between faith and reason as one in which the philosophical agenda remains definitive, essentially unaffected by a faith which serves only as a sort of extrinsic adjunct helpful to the process but not even, in every case, necessary.[24] However, it is more difficult to agree when he (and others echoing him)[25] go on to remark that this relation remains character- istic of Augustine's work for the rest of his life, with minor variation.[26] In the first place, such a way of thinking ignores Augustine's pointed remarks, both in the *conf.* and in the *retr.*, about his earlier works in general, as well as the more specific observation made about each of the earlier works in the various chapters of the *retr.*[27] But what this view fails to take seriously above all is the *trin.*, and here we can begin to see the deleterious effect of regarding this work as separable into two "halves," essentially extrinsic to each other, one belonging in a general way to "faith" and one to "reason."

I would suggest, instead, that the *trin.* uses the Neoplatonic soteri- ology of ascent only to impress it into the service of a thoroughgoing critique of its claim to raise the inductee to the contemplation of God, a critique which, more generally, becomes a declaration of the futility of any attempt to come to any saving knowledge of God apart from Christ.

In books 5–7, Augustine attacks the "Arians,"[28] as well as what he conceives to be an inadequate orthodox response to the Arian posi- tion. This discussion serves to point the reader to an awareness of the absolute uniqueness of the being of God and hence the necessity of a new sort of thinking which rises beyond images or categories appro- priate only to creaturely life.[29] The language developed in book 5 for speaking about the Trinitarian relations is a way of constructing a vocabulary which will preserve rather than reduce (as the "Arians" do) the absolute uniqueness of the *esse* of God. And in book 7, with the failure to discover any positive content for the term *persona*,[30] we are forcefully pushed as it were to the brink of language itself, per- suaded, finally, that any closer apprehension of the divine essence will have to be without words and without any mental pictures whatso- ever. We are persuaded, in other words, of the necessity of the ascent, upon which, in book 8, we immediately embark.

There are actually two consecutive attempts to tread the way of the ascent in the *trin.*, one coincident with book 8, and the other devel- oped off and on in the sequence of books 9–14.[31] But the most strik- ing point about both attempts is that they fail. Neither one of them delivers us to the contemplation of the Trinity which we have been expecting all along. Of course, there is nothing new in attempts at

Plotinian ascents ending in failure. We can all recall that Porphyry reports that he completed the ascent only once, and that even Plotinus was not many times more successful.[32] But there *is* something new in structuring a work so that the whole is predicated upon a *deliberate* failure, especially when the work has already persuaded us that the ascent is necessary. The failure of the first attempt is recorded in language very similar to Augustine's account of his own first encounter with the divine "light" in book 7 of the *conf.*[33] What Augustine discovered there when he finally succeeded in making the ascent was not the secure contemplation of God, but rather the *distance* that existed between himself and God.[34] And we, reading book 8 of the *trin.*, also find from the very experience that we are too "weak" to keep the "eye of our minds fixed" on the splendor we glimpse.

We should not be surprised to reach this point of failure, for Augustine had announced it as his intention from the opening chapters of book 1 (chapters which were among the last to be written,[35] and which therefore have some claim to reflecting Augustine's final view of the work). Pointing out how difficult it is to "see" and "fully know" the substance of God,[36] and that faith is necessary if we are to "see the ineffable ineffably,"[37] Augustine goes on to state that his treatise will serve to point out precisely this. His reasoned explanation of how the "Trinity is the one, only, and true God"[38] will function to show all who inquire, from their own "actual experience,"

> *both* that the highest good, which is perceived only by minds which are wholly purified, exists, *and* that they themselves are unable to see or to comprehend it … because the weak eye of the human mind cannot be fixed on a light so dazzling, unless it has been nourished and become stronger by the justice of faith.[39]

This is not a promise to deliver the reader to contemplation, but simply a promise to show us, by our own experience, that what we seek to contemplate does exist, but that we are too weak to actually contemplate it.[40] And the rest of book 1, in the process of laying out exegetical rules for Trinitarian disputation,[41] develops into a discussion of contemplation as something which will be achieved only eschatologically, when Christ delivers the kingdom – that is, that body in whom he now reigns by faith – to God the Father.[42] Right from the outset, therefore, the ultimate context of the endeavor upon which we have embarked has been laid out as one which is eschatological.[43] *Noesis*, Plotinianly conceived, has receded to the limiting point of the eschaton, and, if it remains the goal, is only so eschatologically.

Even here, however, Augustine is to some extent echoing Porphyry, who also held that, for most persons, *noesis* would be postponed until after death.[44] But for Augustine, the difference between the two positions is made clear as we proceed upon the second, extended attempt, in books 9–14, to slowly ascend to contemplation through a consideration of our own created minds. This attempt ends in an even more spectacular failure in book 14, where we discover that the image of God which we bear in our minds has become radically disfigured through sin.[45] And thus, when the results are reviewed in book 15, and we attempt to rise to the direct consideration of the Creator, we find that we cannot.[46] Or, more precisely, we find that we have been contemplating an image which is more notable for its lack of similarity than for its similarity, even apart from the disfigurement caused by sin.[47] What we have discovered by making the ascent, by learning to think non-corporeally, is the painful awareness of our own *distance* from God, and that our coming to contemplation will be an onerous lifetime project of seeking, if it is possible at all.

But we have also discovered that to continue the purely introspective Neoplatonic ascent is to continue a process which has not only failed but which *cannot but fail*, for the more we persist in contemplating a disfigured image as though it were not disfigured, as though it were, so to speak, an accurate image of God, the more we persist in furthering the disfigurement. For Augustine, it is this second failure, impossible to avoid, which is meant to definitively break open the absolutely introspective character of the soteriology of ascent. For what is necessary now is not so much an uninterrupted consideration of the image but a "renewal" of the image. And this consists not in the static regard of an essentially unchanging intellect or in the eschatological cleansing of that image from extrinsically accrued bodily taint at death, but in the genuine "growth" of that image itself in, as Augustine puts it, a "gradual," "day by day" "progress," one which is accomplished "holding fast to the faith of the Mediator."

This faith, for Augustine, is what enables us to break the impasse of the introspective soteriology of ascent, and Augustine has already prepared us for this realization. The discussion of the economy of redemption in books 2–4[48] serves to make the point that if we can see God in this life, it is only, like Moses, the "backparts" of God ("posteriora," Ex. 33:11–23) which we see, namely the flesh of Christ in which he was crucified.[49] And in book 13, in more direct preparation for the failure of book 14, Augustine's lengthy discussion fixes our regard even more firmly outward, on the blood of Christ. He asks, "What is the meaning of *justified by his blood*? What power is there in this blood that believers are justified by it?"[50] Faith in Christ, Augustine insists, means clinging to his blood as the price paid for our redemption, and subsisting on the confidence in the love of God which it reveals. "For what," Augustine asks, "was so necessary for raising our hopes and for liberating the minds of mortals … than to show how highly God esteemed us and how much God loved us?"[51] Our minds are liberated by this faith because, in faith, the awareness of the absolute distance separating God and ourselves – an awareness which we necessarily come to on our ascent to contemplation – becomes a coincident awareness of the love of God which crossed that distance. And the greater and more painfully aware we are of the distance, the more we become aware of the love of God. Thus, we are freed from the necessity of what Augustine regards as stop-gap, self-generated, and self-defeating philosophical measures which serve to remove the painful awareness of distance by in effect denying it rather than actually bridging it.[52]

But what it is important to note here is not simply that we have a new "way" for completing an ascent which remains definitively Neoplatonic in its goal, but that the goal – *noesis* itself – has acquired a new character. Our contemplative regard is pushed outward, from the consideration of a static metaphysical self essentially disconnected from the uncomfortable realm of the bodily and historically contingent – that realm which defines our ontological distance from God – to that very realm itself and to the blood, irreducibly contingent and irreducibly historical, which for Augustine became its central node. "Faith" is thus revealed not merely as a propaedeutic to vision, but as a redirecting of the noetic regard to a decidedly un-noetic realm, and "understanding" becomes the position of the self that is constituted by a growth wholly defined in that realm – it becomes, that is, a "seeking." We come to learn then, by book 15, why the Psalmist could say, "Seek his face evermore" (Ps. 104.4):

If therefore, He who is sought can be found, why was it said, *Seek his face evermore?* Or is He perhaps still to be sought even when He is found? For so we ought to seek incomprehensible things, lest we should think that we have found nothing, when we find how incomprehensible is the thing which we are seeking ... Faith seeks; understanding finds; and therefore the prophet has said, *Unless you believe, you shall not understand.* And again the understanding still seeks Him whom it has found: ... for this reason, then, humans ought to attain understanding in order that we may seek God.[53]

Noesis itself has become, or at least has been replaced by, an "understanding" which is itself a seeking. In bringing us to this point, Augustine has discharged the intention first announced in the prologue to book 1, and he has created a work which is in effect a re-issuing of the earlier philosophical dialogues, but here radically redone, as a critique of the position that there is any accurate or saving knowledge of the Trinity apart from faith in Christ.[54]

And thus, the *trin.* is not in the first instance a purely "speculative" work inquiring into the mystery of the Trinity for the sake of systematizing Christian dogma, but finds its context rather in a polemical dialogue, visible in other, more familiar parts of the Augustinian corpus, against Neoplatonic views of salvation and also against (as Augustine sees it) overly Platonizing Christian views.[55] I agree with Zum Brunn (1988) when she notes in a related context that:

the problem that faces us ... appears to be that of the interpenetration of two spiritualities and of two cultures more than that of reason and Revelation, philosophy and faith.[56]

I would add, however, that, from Augustine's point of view, he is in the *trin.* arguing on behalf of one particular faith and spirituality against another,[57] and of the modification of the notion of "understanding" which that faith, as he sees it, entails.

Acknowledgments

Earlier versions of this chapter were presented at the Patristic, Medieval, and Renaissance Conference ("PMR," 1988) and the Annual Meeting of the North American Patristics Society ("NAPS,"

1990). An earlier version of this chapter was published as Cavadini, J. (1992) "The Structure and Intention of Augustine's De Trinitate." *Augustinian Studies* 23: 103–123. I would like to thank Kathryn Johnson, Robert Markus, Nicholas Lash, and J. J. O'Donnell, who all read earlier versions of this chapter and provided helpful comments. In addition, I would like to acknowledge helpful conversations with Celia Chazelle, Anthony Godzieba, and Robert Wilken, and with my colleagues David Burrell, Catherine LaCugna, and Blake Leyerle.

Notes

1 In *ep.* 169 (late 415), Augustine tells Evodius "… nec libros de trinitate, quos diu in manibus verso nondumque complevi, modo adtendere velim, quoniam nimis operosi sunt et a *paucis* eos intellegi posse arbitror" (*ep.* 169.1.1, p. 612.6–9). He thought of the *City of God* as a more pressing work, likely to be of benefit, by contrast, to many. Five years earlier, Augustine had written a reply to the monk Consentius (*ep.* 120.3.13), where he noted the "extreme difficulty" of the subject of the Trinity: "… volo, ut leges ea, quae ad istam quaestionem pertinentia iam multo conscripsimus, illa etiam, quae in manibus habemus et propter magnitudi- nem tam difficilis quaestionis nondum possumus explicare" (p. 715.18–21). Cf. also *ep.* 143.4 (ca. 412, to Marcellinus).

2 Still standard is Schmaus (1927), as well as Schindler (1965). La Bonnardière (1965) and Hendrikx (in his introduction to text at 9–14 of BA 15) provide the best chro- nology of the *trin.*, at which Augustine worked on and off for some 20 years (finished ca. 420), finally publishing it in a version less polished than originally planned – the unfinished work had previously been stolen and circulated in an unauthorized ver- sion, and Augustine did not want the final version to differ too drastically from what was already circulated (see *ep.* 174, the prologue to *trin.*). Since book 15 and the prologues to the earlier books were the last parts to be written, these have a special claim on our attention as representing Augustine's final understanding of the work as a whole. [See chapter 11 below for updated bibliography on *trin.*]

3 Brown (1967), 277.

4 *trin.* Prologue: "… praecedentibus [libros] consequentes inquisitione proficiente nectuntur" (lines 9–10). Translated by McKenna (1963).

5 Thus, for example, E. Hendrikx in his introduction to the BA edition and trans- lation (BA 15), divides the work into part I, "The Truth of the Church's Dogma Demonstrated from Scriptures," and part II, "The Explication and Deepening of the Dogma by Speculation," while the edition itself is divided into two volumes, books 1–7 corresponding to "*La mystère*," and books 8–15 to "*Les images*" (BA was edited and translated by P. Agaësse, S.J. and J. Moingt, S.J.). Even as recently

as 1986, Chadwick essentially repeats this standard conception of the work, which has authoritative defenders all the way back to Marrou (who keeps book 8 with the first seven books; see Marrou (1958), 315–27). Hill (1991), in the introduction to his new translation of the *trin.* (*WSA* I/5), notes that "the *De Trinitate* divides itself fairly obviously into two parts, Books I–VII … and Books VIII–XV" (21). Hill, however, modifies this by describing a chiastic structure (26–27) and pointing to the "dramatic" character of the *trin.* (18–19), linking books 9–14 with the economy of salvation (see 25–26, 258–263).

6   It is true that Augustine marks book 8 as a turning point in the work, both in the course of the text itself (8.P) and in the review given at 15.6.10 and at 15.3.5, and I do not wish to underestimate these markers. But the standard interpretation tends to over-interpret them, holding the two "halves" apart to the point where their relation becomes almost purely extrinsic, as though the two "halves" could almost be separate works (or at least separate volumes), and thus the "understanding" of what one "believes" becomes a moment formally separable from faith itself (as perhaps in some later scholastic treatments of "faith seeking understanding"). Surely one of the reasons these two halves are placed together – one of the reasons for Augustine's special insistence on the "continuous development of the argument" – is precisely to qualify any claims, philosophical or otherwise, that what one knows in faith and what one knows by understanding are different, or that what one learns by philosophical intro-spection is different and over and above what one learns from exegesis (see n. 42). In book 8, we are informed that we are now proceeding "modo interiore," but this does not mean that we have not been operating on the basis of "reason" before this; actually, it implies a continuity of process, only in a different "style." In the summary of the treatise given in book 15, book 8 is marked as that book where the Trinity began "to dawn on us," but this once again can signify the term of a process, not a new process.

7   McKenna (1963), xii.

8   As, for example, in the *Tractates on John*, a project that Augustine was working on concurrently with the *trin.* See, for example, *Io. eu. tr.* 1.1.13–17. For other passages, and on the distinction between the *animales* and *spiritales*, see Teske (1984).

9   At *Acad.* 2.1, Romanianus is invited to join the "few" (2.1.1.14) for whom philosophy will bear fruit in the knowledge of the truth (2.3.9.56–58). In the *beata u.*, the "few" ("pauci," 1.1.6) are those who make it to the "port of phi-losophy" (1.1.1), some of whom go on to arrive at the happy life, where, Augustine presumes, Manlius Theodorus has already arrived (1.5.118–19; cf. *ord.* 1.11.31.18–23).

10   A full-scale study of this issue will have to await another article, but we can surely include Evodius among correspondents from the period during the composition of the *trin.* In *ep.* 169 (see n. 2), Augustine discusses with Evodius

all of the issues which, from his point of view, will limit the appeal of the *trin.* to only a "few," and he fully expects Evodius to understand the discussions in the *trin.* when it is finally published. In *ep.* 162, Augustine identifies the issues which Evodius has repeatedly raised (in *ep.* 158, 160, and 161) as those which will be treated in the *trin.* and the *Gn. litt.* (*ep.* 162.2, p. 512.18–513.3). In *ep.* 159.2 (p. 499.17–18), Augustine refers Evodius to *Gn. litt.* 12, a highly sophisticated discussion of visions and the seeing of God such as only the "few" would understand. The list of correspondents would also include the lady Paulina, who had asked Augustine about how God is seen. Augustine's answer is a small treatise (*ep.* 147), denoted "On the Vision of God" at *retr.* 2.67, where Augustine also notes that its subject is "truly most difficult." If anything, it is treated more thoroughly than the corresponding treatment given for Evodius in *ep.* 162. Chapters 3–4 and 41–44 are typical of the exhortation to vision and spiritual ascent, which are reserved for the "few" and are reminiscent of many passages in the *trin.* Our list must also include Dardanus, praetorian prefect of Gaul and recipient of *ep.* 187, the treatise "On the Presence of God" (*retr.* 2.75). Prompted by Dardanus' request, and prefaced by a compliment on Dardanus' powers of reflection (a compliment which Augustine only rarely gives out, *ep.* 187.1.2, p. 83.4–5), it is a complex treatment of issues related to how to think about the non-corporeal omnipresence of God who is "everywhere wholly present" (see n. 56 for further treatment). A preliminary list would also have to include Paulinus of Nola, as well as Marcellinus, frequent correspondent and the dedicatee of the *ciu.*, and Marcellinus' friend Volusianus, who deftly raises explicitly philosophical questions for discussion by Augustine (see *ep.* 135 and 136), and whom Augustine answers in the complex *ep.* 137. The monk Consentius (of *ep.* 119 and 120) may also be included, although his understanding is not accorded the same esteem that Augustine cedes to those already mentioned. Among Augustine's correspondents before the period of the composition of the *trin.* (and not already mentioned here), we can recognize Nebridius (*ep.* 3–14; note especially *ep.* 11, an early letter on the Trinity), Zenobius (*ep.* 2, to whom the *ord.* is dedicated), Romanianus (*ep.* 15; cf. Paulinus and Therasia's letter to him at *ep.* 32), and perhaps Hermogenianus (to whom Augustine has submitted the *Acad.* for correction or comment, *ep.* 1).

11   For example, in the *beata u.*, Augustine explains that this is what he learned from Ambrose and Manlius Theodorus (1.4.91–94), and, in the *ord.*, Augustine explains that a "few" healthy intellects "behold" the invisible, spiritual world: "Esse autem alium mundum ab istis oculis remotissimum, quem paucorum sanorum intellectus intuetur" (*ord.* 1.11.32.44–46). By the time of *ep.* 169 to Evodius, what is "discerned" by the "few" (*ep.* 169.1.2, p. 612.17) is much more specific, namely the "ineffabilem trinitatis unitatem, sicut discernitur in animo nostro memoria, intellectus, voluntas" (*ep.* 169.1.2, p. 612.13–15). The parallels with the subject of books 9 and 10 of the *trin.* are obvious. Further, it is clear

from Evodius' own letter (*ep.* 158.6) that he is himself in the habit of thinking about just these issues, including the incorporeal oneness of memory, understanding, and will (p. 492.3–7).

12 See, for example, his instructions to Paulina at *ep.* 147.43; the long instruction to Consentius in *ep.* 120.2.9–12 (followed by the recommendation to read the *trin.* when it is finished, 120.3.13, p. 715.18–21); and that to Volusianus at *ep.* 137.2.4–8 (in the *trin.*, cf., e.g. 1.1.1, 5.1.1–2, 10.10.16).

13 In the *conf.*, as a result of reading the "Platonic books" (*conf.* 7.9.13.5–6), Augustine can say, "Numquid nihil est veritas, quoniam neque per finita neque per infinita locorum spatia diffusa est?" (*conf.* 7.10.16.22–23). The *beata u.* (1.4.99) specifies Plotinus as the source (following Green's text, which defends the reading "Plotinus" as opposed to "Plato").

14 See Marrou's classic treatment of this theme (1958, 298–327), and also BA 16, 612–614 ("note complémentaire," 30). For a parallel idea in Plotinus, see Trouillard (1955), 163–165 ("Sciences et dialectique purificatrices"). On the ascent in general, see also Van Fleteren (1974), 29–72.

15 Note, for example, the expression at *trin.* 12.8.13.1, "Ascendentibus itaque introrsus quibusdam gradibus …," cf. *trin.* 14.3.5.29–30, where "ab inferioribus ad superiora ascendentes" is parallel to "ab exterioribus ad interiora ingredientes."

16 On *noesis* in Plotinus and Porphyry, see Smith (1974), esp. 20–39. The philosophical "few" of Augustine's early dialogues are the same "few" to whom Porphyry thought high philosophical vision would be limited. See, for example, Augustine's citation of him at *ciu.* 10.29 (= Bidez fragment 10, in Bidez (1964), p. 37, lines 12–13): "'ad Deum per virtutem intellegentiae pervenire paucis' dicis esse concessum." On Porphyry and Augustine, see TeSelle (1974), 113–147.

17 With reference to the preceding six books: "Volentes in rebus quae factae sunt ad cognoscendum eum a quo factae sunt exercere lectorem iam pervenimus ad eius imaginem quod est homo in eo quo ceteris animalibus antecellit, id est ratione vel intellegentia …" (*trin.* 15.1.1.1–4; see also 15.6.10.55–58, cited in n. 46).

18 On the word "anagogy," see Zum Brunn (1988), 4. She takes the expression over from du Roy (1966), who explains his usage at 170, n. 6.

19 See du Roy (1966), 147–148. Note, for example, at *ord.* 2.9.26, what makes the "few" the "few" is that they can contemplate Intellect and the First Principle (= Nous and the One): those eager to learn ("studiosi," line 1) will in fact eventually learn "quid [sit] intellectus, in quo universa sunt – vel ipsa potius universa – et quid praeter universa universorum principium. Ad quam cognitionem in hac vita pervenire *pauci*, ultra quam vero etiam post hanc vitam nemo progredi potest" (lines 17–20). See also *ord.* 2.5.16.2–3, 47–50: "philosophia rationem promittit et vix paucissima; liberat … Germana philosophia est, quam ut doceat, quod sit omnium rerum principium sine principio quantusque in eo maneat intellectus quidve inde in nostram salutem sine ulla degeneratione manaverit …"

20 For example, *Acad.* 3.18.41.41–46: "... os illud Platonis, quod in philosophia pur-
    gatissimum est et lucidissimum, dimotis nubibus erroris emicuit maxime in
    Plotino, qui Platonicus philosophus ita eius similis iudicatus est, ut simul eos vixisse,
    tantum autem interest temporis, ut in hoc ille revixisse putandus sit" (cf. also *Acad.*
    3.17.38.42, which refers approvingly to "Platonica illa velut sacrosancta decreta").
    Augustine retracts this praise at *retr.* 1.1.4.99–102: "Laus quoque ipsa qua Platonem
    vel Platonicos sive Academicos philosophos tantum extuli, quantum impios hom-
    ines non oportuit, non inmerito mihi displicuit, praesertim contra quorum errores
    magnos defendenda est christiana doctrina." This sentence could sum up the *trin.*
    as itself a kind of *retractatio* of the earlier dialogues (see n. 55).
21 For example, the whole agenda of the *beata u.* derives from the *Hortensius*, the
    beginning ("Beatos nos esse volumus," see *trin.* 13.4.7.32–35) of which is cited
    as the announcement of the argument of the *beata u.* (2.10.85; note how promi-
    nent the *Hortensius* is in Augustine's account of his conversion just previously, at
    beata u. 1.10.85). See also *Acad.* 1.1.4.97–98, which shows that Augustine is still
    using Cicero's *Hortensius* as a kind of textbook, useful for helping people begin
    their study of philosophy.
22 As, for example, at *Acad.* 1.3.77–80.
23 On Augustine's early view of the role of the Incarnation, see O'Connell (1968),
    265–278. In du Roy (1966), see pp. 109–148, where he notes "Les dialogues de
    Cassiciacum nous confirment aussi que, dès sa première théologie, il a tire les
    conséquences de l'ordre des mystères chrétiens qui fut celui de sa découverte:
    la Trinité peut être connue avant même l'Incarnation, et sa connaissance,
    quoique confuse et orgueilleuse, se trouve déjà chez les philosophes païens.
    L'autorité ou la foi n'est là que pour nous purifier de la convoitise des sens et
    de l'orgueil de l'esprit" (148).
24 See, for example, du Roy (1966), 125, commenting on *ord.* 5.16, 157.16–20.
25 For example, Zum Brunn (1988), 93, and 95, n. 8.
26 There is a particularly damning judgment on 105: "Si le mode suprême de con-
    naissance a pu être atteint en quelque mesure par les philosophes païens sans la
    foi, si donc l'illumination suprême n'est transformée intrinsèquement par la foi,
    si c'est seulement le degré et la stabilité qui diffèrent, alors le Dieu révélé, le
    Dieu Trinité, peut être connu en dehors de l'économie de la révélation ... On
    conçoit que, la foi ne modifiant radicalement (ni explicitement, ni consciem-
    ment du moins) le mouvement propre de *l'intellectus* ..." The "anteriority" of
    knowledge of the Trinity to knowledge of the Incarnation is a "fundamental
    articulation" of Augustinian theology (97), and as such it constitutes Augustine
    as a kind of crypto-gnostic (see especially 419). In Augustine, the relation
    between faith and understanding always remains "extrinsic" (456).
27 In the *conf.*, Augustine notes of his literary activity at Cassiciacum, "Ibi quid
    egerim in litteris iam quidem servientibus tibi, sed adhuc superbiae scholam
    tamquam in pausatione anhelantibus testantur libri disputati cum praesentibus

et cum ipso ne solo coram te ..." (*conf.* 9.4.1.4–1). One need only peruse the early chapters of the *retr.* to provide specification for this observation. Many of the comments are directed against excessive praise of philosophers or of philosophy itself.

28 Eunomius is mentioned at *trin.* 15.20.38.1–2, but it is not clear that the "Arians" refuted in books 5–7 (*trin.* 5.3.4.3; 6.1.1.8; 6.9.10.11; cf. 2.15.25.15) are Eunomians. On the identity of these "Arians," see Barnes (1993).

29 See especially *trin.* 5.1.1.1–6, 39–46, and note the specification of this in terms of the 10 categories (given at *trin.* 5.7.8), some of which apply only metaphorically to God (*trin.* 5.8.9), and the rest of which, except for the category of substance (and, at *trin.* 1.5.10, even this is suspect, so that God, and God alone, should rather be called "essentia"), must be applied only in an accommodated sense, since there is no accident in God (*trin.* 5.4–5). In particular, there are no accidental, but only eternal, relations (*trin.* 5.5.6).

30 *trin.* 7.4.7.1–5; 7.4.9.117–120.

31 This is clear from the summary that Augustine gives at *trin.* 15.6.10. Book 8 attempted to "raise" ("erigere," *trin.* 15.6.10.34) our minds to the unchangeable nature which is not our mind, but this failed because we could not keep the eye of our mind fixed firmly on the brilliance of its ineffable light (*trin.* 15.6.10.46–48), and thus we turned in books 9–14 (*trin.* 15.6.10.54) to a consideration of the image, in order that, with Romans 1:20 – Augustine's favorite biblical description of the ascent – we might understand the invisible things of God through those which are made.

32 See Porphyry's *Life of Plotinus*, in Armstrong (1966), 23.

33 In *trin.* 15.6.10.34–40, Augustine points out that in the eighth book "erigere temptavimus mentis intentionem ad intellegendam illam praestantissimam immutabilemque naturam quod nostra mens non est. Quam tamen sic intuebamur ut nec longe a nobis esset et supra nos esset, non loco sed ipsa sui venerabili mirabilique praestantia ita ut apud nos esse suo praesenti lumine videretur. In qua tamen nobis adhuc nulla trinitas apparebat quia non ad eam quaerendam in fulgore illo firmam mentis aciem tenebamus" (cf. *trin.* 15.6.10.46–48; and see also 8.2.3.28–40). These passages may be usefully compared to *conf.* 7.17.23.27–32 and similar passages.

34 Of course, *conf.* 7.10.16.17 ("et inveni longe me esse a te in regione dissimilitudinis") comes to mind, but see also, for example, *conf.* 11.9.11.4–15.

35 See La Bonnardière (1965), 176.

36 *trin.* 1.1.3.69–71.

37 *trin.* 1.1.3.72–75.

38 *trin.* 1.2.4.3.

39 "... suscipiemus ... reddere rationem, quod trinitas; sit unus et solus et verus deus ... ut non quasi nostris excusationibus inludantur sed reipsa experiantur et esse illud summum bonum quod purgatissimis mentibus cernitur, et a se

propterea cerni comprehendique non posse quia mentis humanae acies invalida in tam excellenti luce non figitur nisi *per iustitiam fidei* (Rom. 4:13) nutrita vegetetur" (1.2.4.1–2, 3, 6–11).

40   Augustine goes on to give a hint about those for whom this service will be accomplished: "… si voluerit et adiuverit deus, istis garrulis ratiocinatoribus, elatioribus quam capacioribus atque ideo morbo periculosiore laborantibus, sic fortasse serviemus ut inveniant aliquid unde dubitari non possint, et ob hoc in eo quod invenire nequiverint, de suis mentibus potius quam de ipsa veritate vel de nostris disputationibus conquerantur. Atque ita si quid eis erga deum vel amoris est vel timoris, ad initium fidei et ordinem redeant …" (*trin.* 1.2.4.13– 20). Can we begin to put faces on "these chattering reasoners," for whom Augustine says he will render this service? They are certainly a part of the "discerning few" in *ep.* 169 to Evodius (169.1.2), those in particular about whom Augustine complains later in the letter: "nonnulli a corporibus incorporea discernentes, cum sibi ex hoc magni videntur et inrident *stultitiam praedicationis* (1 Cor. 1:21), qua salvi fiunt credentes, ab unica via longe exerrent, quae ad vitam aeternam sola perducit" (*ep.* 169.1.4, p. 614.10–13). It is these whom the *trin.* promises to "return" to the "initium fidei." Perhaps one may think, in this connection, of Manlius Theodorus, to whom Augustine dedicated the *beata u.* but later regretted the dedication (or, at least, the praise with which it was given – see *retr.* 1.2). Did Augustine come to regard him as overly Platonizing? Courcelle (1950) describes Manlius Theodorus as Augustine's "maître" after Ambrose, and explains Augustine's later severity toward Theodorus as follows: "la raison de cette sévérité tient à ce que, vers la date de rédaction des *Confessions*, Theodorus venait de reprendre une vie mondaine et quasi-païenne: Symmaque dans ses lettres, Claudien dans un panégyrique en vers, le félicitent d'avoir obtenu le consulat pour l'an 399 et de fournir aux Romains des jeux à grands spectacles" (154; see 153–56 on Theodorus in general). Such a Theodorus, Augustine might think, would need to be returned to the "initium fidei." One may also think of the relatively innocuous but obnoxious Dioscorus of *ep.* 117 and 118, for whom Augustine points out the errors of the philosophers, the "Platonists" included, in the context of the sort of discussion of God's incorporeality which he might have with a member of the "few" (in this case, a would-be member).

41   The best article on these rules is Pelikan (1987–1988). Pelikan points out quite rightly that the first, "exegetical," half of the *trin.* is often ignored by scholars despite its importance to Augustine. But if, as Pelikan points out (25), the "immediate source" for the *canonica regula* is Phil. 2:5–11, this implies that Trinitarian hermeneutics, or any attempt to "understand" Scriptural teaching on the Trinity, will consist in and arise from a sustained reflection on the mysteries of God's saving work in Christ. This is why the two "halves" are placed together: one's coming to understand the Trinity is not separable from reflection on the economy of salvation (*pace* Gunton (1990), esp. 48, italicized

passage), but is in fact coincident with such reflection. It is Scripture itself which, as Augustine points out at the very beginning of the treatise (*trin.* 1.1.2; cf. *ep.* 137 to Volusianus), mandates and engages us upon the ascent to understanding. The ascent *is* exegesis of the text, but it is an exegesis governed by *canonica regula* which forms the ascent, and thus the ascent itself occurs as a reflection upon the economy of salvation in which the Son of God "emptied himself." The point of placing the two "halves" together is that, when in book 8 we come to tread the path "modo interiore," we do not depart from reflection on the economy of salvation, but, on the contrary, we find its absolute priority demonstrated. The *Io. eu. tr.* would be another good example of the coincidence of exegesis and ascent.

42   1 Cor. 15:24; see, for example, *trin.* 1.18.17.80–95.

43   Note that the stages of this drama are marked by Scriptural citations which are introduced in book 1, and which serve, at crucial points in the narrative, as reprises of the eschatological themes laid out in book 1. These include Ps. 104:4 ("Seek His face evermore …"; *trin.* 1.3.5.5); 1 Jn. 3:2 ("We shall be like Him, since we shall see Him just as He is"; *trin.* 1.13.31.172); 1 Cor. 13:12 ("We see now in a glass darkly, but then face to face," *trin.* 1.8.16.63, cited 14 more times in book 1 alone, and then in every succeeding book except book 11); 2 Cor. 5:7 ("For we walk by faith, not by sight," *trin.* 1.8.17.114–115).

44   *ciu.* 10.29 = Bidez fr. 10 (in Bidez (1964), p37, 17–19): "nec ipse dubitas 'in hac vita hominem nullo modo ad perfectionem sapientiae pervenire …'"

45   Scripture teaches and "has pity upon" the deformed divine image ("deformitatem dignitatis eius miserans divina scriptura," *trin.* 14.4.6.13–14) which is the mind, and of which the reader is about to ascend to consideration (*trin.* 14.8.11.1–7). In fact, however, we were already at this point earlier: we *had* ascended to the consideration of this image in book 10, and were about to ascend to consideration of that immutable nature (God) of which the mind is an image ("Iamne igitur ascendendum est qualibuscumque intentionis viribus ad illam summam et altissimam essentiam cuius impar imago est humana mens sed tamen imago?" *trin.* 10.12.19.1–3; equivalent to the step about to be taken yet another time in book 15: see *trin.* 15.1.1; 15.4.6), when we were prevented from doing it because of the way in which the mind tends *not* actually to stay in self-awareness, as it would if it were truly philosophic and able to think incorporeally, but to picture itself in a "phantasy," as extended, etc. (*trin.* 10.5, 6, 7, 10). This inability is really a kind of failure of the ascent, and it causes the long detour of books 11–13, in which Augustine attempts to help the reader distinguish between the trinities of sense and the mind's knowledge of itself (*trin.* 10.12.19.6–12, 18–22; 14.6.9.55–61; 14.7.10.58–61). But this detour essentially comes back to the point of failure, as though we now learn that the mind's inability to be aware of itself was a more serious problem than first thought, and in fact reflects the deformity of the image of God itself, and thus of its radical

need for transformation by God's love. *Trin.* 14.14.20 and 16.22 describe the mind's inability to know and love itself as due to an undue attachment to and thus conformation to lust for things beneath it, and that it is our job to "turn away" from this disfigurement or conformation to the world (*trin.* 14.16.22.1–4) – but that this "reformation" (cf. Rom 12 :2) must be God's work (*trin.* 14.16.22.5–7); it does not occur in the one moment of conversion, but is a long course of healing (*trin.* 14.17.23.1–11) and of day-by-day progress and growth in clinging to the faith of the Mediator; and full vision will only come after death ("In quo provectu et accessu tenentem mediatoris fidem cum dies vitae huius ultimus quemque compererit, perducendus ad deum quem coluit et ab eo perficiendus …; in hac quippe imagine tunc perfecta erit dei similitudo quando dei perfecta erit visio," *trin.* 14.17.23.26–29, 31–32). Awareness of the need for reformation is the true fulfillment of the Delphic "Know Thyself" (*trin.* 10.9.12.4, 7, 16), and love of God and neighbor in faith (*trin.* 14.14.18.26–31) is the true delivery from misery to happiness, the true love of wisdom, or "philosophy" (*trin.* 14.1.2.32–38), which will, unbeknownst to Cicero, be the fulfillment of the exhortation in the *Hortensius* (*trin.* 14.19.26).

46   *trin.* 15.6.10.55–58: "Et ecce iam quantum necesse fuerat aut forte plus quam necesse fuerat exercitata in inferioribus intellegentia ad summam trinitatem quae deus est conspiciendam nos erigere volumus nec valemus"; cf. *trin.* 15.27.50.71–74, 89–91.

47   *trin.* 15.7.11–13 is an extended discussion of the unlikeness of God and God's image in us (cf. the parallel discussion in *ep.* 169.2.6, to Evodius, some 5 years earlier than book 15; note also the "ontological gap" mentioned by Van Fleteren (1987–1988), 224). Du Roy (1966) notices and comments upon the failures of ascent (of book 8 and book 15) and the discussions of the unlikeness of the image, but he can see them only as a "betrayal" of the "most profound aspirations" of Augustine's *intellectus fidei* (447), and he dissociates them from the overall anagogy of the *trin.*: "Le livre XV va consacrer cet échec de l'anagogie en s'installant résolument dans l'analogie et en faisant le bilan des livres VIII à XIV. Il commence donc par les résumer. Puis il invite à s'élever jusqu'à la Trinité divine. Mais ce n'est plus par une méthode anagogique, c'est par une attribution analogique des perfections créés au Créateur" (446). But Augustine, by reviewing the plan of the whole work, presents this moment as the culmination of the anagogy: it is the last "step," the one "above" (*trin.* 15.1.1.9) our nature, and it is our attempt to take this step which is analyzed. The language about "like" and "unlike"; "higher" and "lower"; and "better" and "best" (in this context, see especially *trin.* 15.4.6) is constitutive of the dissimilarities (e.g. eternal vs. temporal, immutable vs. changeable, spiritual vs. corporeal) which enable the ascent to proceed. The point is not that, at the end of anagogy, we come to "analogy," but rather that *the same logic which defines the ascent also defines its failure* – that is, that the spirituality of introspective ascent is inherently

self-defeating. The anagogical path itself becomes a demonstration of the need for transformation and grace (explained in *trin.* 15 at 15.8.14, immediately following the failure of the ascent and the discussion of the dissimilarity of the image). Du Roy's (1966) distinction between anagogy and analogy here seems without textual warrant, imported from another (Thomistic?) world of thought in order to preserve his contention that Augustine believes there is (natural?) knowledge of the Trinity available independent of faith. Thus, when the anagogy fails to raise us to understanding of the Trinity, the failure cannot be part of Augustine's own fundamental intentions – as a *critique* of the anagogical spirituality – but must instead be a "betrayal" of Augustine's intentions.

48   With prologues, which Augustine added later to ensure that we do not lose sight both of the request for vision which he is entertaining and of its limitations. Compare, for example, Books 2–4 of the *trin.* to *ep.* 137 to Volusianus, where the discussion of the theophanies and the Incarnation, in connection with a discussion on how we see God, is a response to a (Porphyrian?) critique that Christians localize God in a body.

49   "Non incongruenter ex persona domini nostri Iesu Christi praefiguratum solet intellegi ut posteriora eius accipiantur caro eius in qua de virgine natus est et mortuus et resurrexit … Facies autem eius illa dei forma … Illa est ergo species quae rapit omnem animam rationalem desiderio sui tanto ardentiorem quanto mundiorem et tanto mundiorem quanto ad spiritalia resurgentem, tanto autem ad spiritalia resurgentem quanto a carnalibus morientem. Sed *dum peregrinamur a domino et per fidem ambulamus non per speciem* (2 Cor. 5 :6–7), posteriora Christi, hoc est carnem, per ipsam fidem videre debemus…" (*trin.* 2.17.28.1–4, 6, 37–43). Aspiring to this contemplation means "building up" the neighbor in love (*trin.* 2.17.28.29–30).

50   *trin.* 13.11.15.1–3, "Sed quid est *iustificati in sanguine ipsius*? (Rom. 5 :9). Quae vis est huius sanguinis obsecro ut in eo iustificentur credentes?"

51   *trin.* 13.10.13.11–15: "Quid enim tam necessarium fuit ad erigendam spem nostram mentesque mortalium conditione ipsius mortalitatis abiectas ab immortalitatis desperatione liberandas quam ut demonstraretur nobis quanti nos penderet deus quantumque diligeret?"

52   In the *trin.*, see 4.15.20 (especially lines 1–3, 10–17: "Sunt autem quidam qui se putant ad contemplandum deum et inhaerendum deo virtute propria posse purgari, quos ipsa superbia maxime maculat … Hinc enim sibi purgationem isti virtute propria pollicentur quia nonnulli eorum potuerunt aciem mentis ultra omnem creaturam transmittere et lucem incommutabilis veritatis quantulacumque ex parte contingere, quod christianos multos [as opposed to the "few"] ex fide interim sola viventes nondum potuisse derident. Sed quid prodest superbienti et ob hoc erubescenti lignum conscendere [the only "ascent" which works] de longinquo prospicere patriam transmarinam?" Also see *trin.* 13.19.24.32–55 ("sine mediatore, id est sine homine Christo

philasophati sunt," lines 40–41; cf. 14.19.26.64–68, where books 4 and 13 are mentioned).

53   "Si ergo quaesitus inveniri potest, cur dictum est *Quaerite faciem eius semper* (Ps. 104:4)? An et inventus forte quaerendus est? Sic enim sunt incomprehensibilia requirenda ne se existimet nihil invenisse qui quam sit incomprehensibile quod quaerebat potuerit invenire…. Fides quaerit, intellectus invenit; propter quod ait propheta: *Nisi credideritis, non intellegetis* (Isa. 7:9). Et rursus intellectus eum quem invenit adhuc quaerit… Ad hoc ergo debet esse homo intellegens ut requirat deum" (*trin.* 15.2.2.13–17, 27–29, 31–32).

54   Augustine directs the reader of the *retr.* specifically to the *trin.* for a correction of views expressed in the earlier dialogue literature (the *sol.*, at *retr.* 1.4.4; cf. the comments on the *an. quant.*, *retr.* 1.7.2). The *trin.* is the only work mentioned by name as actually correcting earlier books (of those written up to the time of his priesthood). Also, Augustine returns to his earliest practice of using Cicero's *Hortensius* to set his own agenda. The opening gambit of the *Hortensius* sets the agenda of book 13 in much the same way it set the agenda for the *beata u.* (see n. 22), as though Augustine were almost rewriting or reissuing that treatise but from a new perspective. For if it is true that *beate vivere omnes homines velle* (*trin.* 13.4.7.24–25, 29–30, 35–36, 42–43, with the source actually cited at lines 33–34; 5.8.6, with long citation and attribution at 9–16; etc.), the question becomes what *is* the happy life? The ultimate conclusion is the same – contemplation of the Trinity ("Iam ergo in ipsis rebus aeternis, incorporalibus et immutabilibus in quarum perfecta contemplatione nobis beata quae non nisi aeterna est vita promittitur trinitatem quae deus est …." [*trin.* 15.4.6.1–4]; on the Trinitarian implication of the *beata u.*, which ends with a citation of the Ambrosian verse, "Fove precantes Trinitas," see du Roy (1966), 149–171). But unlike the *beata u.*, book 13 argues that inquiry into the happy life requires not simply an exhortation to philosophy but a discussion of a very unphilosophical topic, the blood of Christ, as the only liberation of human beings from "unhappiness" (*trin.* 13.10.13.2). Faith (*trin.* 13.20.25) is the beginning of the reformation of the image of God in charity (see 13.20.26.64–74, where the mind ["animus"], memory and will, is formed by faith in the blood of the mediator and by *the sort of life* [lines 71–71] which results). This sets the stage for the discussion of renewal in book 14, which continues to refer to the *Hortensius* and which ends by citing the end of the *Hortensius* (*trin.* 14.19.26.31–45), but qualifying its exhortation to philosophy: "Sed iste cursus qui constituitur in amore atque ivestigatione veritatis non sufficit miseris, id est omnibus cum ista sola ratione mortalibus sine fide mediatoris, quod in libris superioribus huius operis, maxime in quarto et tertio decimo quantum potui demonstrare curavi" (*trin.* 14.19.26.64–68). One could think of books 13 and 14 – a discussion whose beginning and end coincides with the beginning and end of the textbook Augustine used at Cassiciacum – as a revision of that textbook and of the works which drew their inspiration from its use.

55 In many cases, what the "few" of the letters and the homilies from the period of the composition of the *trin.* finally learn is the impossibility of seeing God apart from faith and the works of charity. In the *Io. eu. tr.*, the distinction between the few and the many, the milk-fed and those capable of solid food, tends to be sublated by the mere fact that Augustine addresses the same homilies to both, and also by Augustine's tendency to collapse both into an inclusive "we" (see, e.g. *Io. eu. tr.* 21.1; 22.1), none of whom can be saved apart from faith in the Incarnation and Passion (*Io. eu. tr.* 2.3–4). What purifies the eye is not introspection but the works of mercy; love of neighbor is the way in which God may be seen (*Io. eu. tr.* 17.8, 18.11). In the letter to Dardanus "On the Presence of God" (417), there is a progressive erosion of the idea of the philosophical few. God's metaphysical presence is "everywhere whole" ("ubique totus"), and awareness of it as such would be restricted to the few who can think "incorporeally" (see, e.g. *ep.* 187.1.2, p. 83.4–5; 187.4.11, p. 90.2–15; 187.6.18, p. 96.4–5; note the implications for Trinitarian speculation carefully laid out at *ep.* 187.4.15). But, under the increasing exigencies of the polemic against Pelagius (see *retr.* 2.75), this presence is, in the course of the letter, distinguished from God's "indwelling" by grace (see, e.g. *ep.* 187.5.16, p. 93.18–19; p. 94.6–7: "Verum illud est multo mirabilis, quod, cum deus ubique sit totus, non tamen in omnibus habitat… unde fatendum est ubique esse deum per divinitatis praesentiam sed non ubique per habitationis gratiam"; cf. *ep.* 187.5.17, p. 94.19–20 and 187.13.58, p. 116.4–8). But if the philosophical few and those in whom God dwells by grace are not coincident groups (see *ep.* 187.9.29), this hugely qualifies any efforts to know God through philosophical introspection and greatly relativizes claims to know God from God's (mere) metaphysical presence. Finally, and this is the most exhaustive qualification, it is only Christ in whom *the fullness of Godhead dwells bodily* (Col. 2:9, *ep.* 187.13.39, p. 116.9–10), and this is a grace different from and greater than that of any of the saints "quantalibet sapientia et sanctitate praestantibus" (*ep.* 13.40, p. 117.16) – that is, no matter how exclusive a group you choose to select, no matter what the criterion. The *few* have shrunk down to *One*, and it is only by being joined to his Body that anyone has any claim on God's indwelling presence. This means that when we think of God's presence, we are, as usual, not to think of masses and extension (*ep.* 187.13.41), but now the substance of our vision, its content, and the direction of our gaze is outward, at the unity and charity of the Body of Christ ("Deus caritas est, cum vero eius habitationem cogitas, unitatem cogita congregationemque sanctorum …" [*ep.* 187.13.41, p. 118.9–11]), and our knowledge of God, while not a matter of images or extension (c. 11, c. 40), is our growth in charity (*ep.* 187.13.40). Paulina, too, discovers that seeing God will mean ascending from corporeal images, but that this ascent is accomplished not by introspection but in the renewal of the image of God in acts of charity (*ep.* 147.43; Augustine makes sure that the

passage he cites from Ambrose is not understood as meaning that we have any knowledge now apart from faith [*ep.* 147.35] – whether or not Ambrose did mean that is another, and very interesting, question). One could think of the beginning of this process of sublating the "few" as extending back to Augustine's inclusion of his mother – a most unphilosophical figure – in the philosophical discussions of Cassiciacum (see especially *ord.* 1.11.31–33, where Augustine includes Monica as one of the few in whom "philosophy" is advanced even to the point of the fearlessness of death, while at the same time he has to explain to her what the word means).

56   Zum Brunn (1988), 116.
57   See, for example, *trin.* 13.20.25.

References

Armstrong, A. H., trans. (1966) *Plotinus vol. 1: Porphyry on the Life of Plotinus and the Order of His Books [and] Enneads I. 1–9*. Loeb Classical Library 440. Cambridge, MA: Harvard University Press.

Barnes, Michel R. (1993) "The Identity of the Arians in Book Five and the Genre of Augustine's *De trinitate.*" *Journal of Theological Studies* 44: 185–195.

Bidez, Joseph (1964) *Vie de Porphyre, le philosophe néoplatonicien*. Hildesheim: Georg Olms.

Brown, Peter (1967) *Augustine of Hippo*. Berkeley, CA: University of California Press.

Chadwick, Henry (1986) *Augustine*. Oxford: Oxford University Press.

Courcelle, Pierre (1950) *Recherches sur les Confessions de Saint Augustin*. Paris: E. de Boccard.

du Roy, Olivier (1966) *L'Intelligence de la Foi en la Trinité selon Saint Augustin*. Paris: Etudes Augustiniennes.

Gunton, Colin (1990) "Augustine, the Trinity, and the Theological Crisis of the West." *The Scottish Journal of Theology* 43: 33–58.

Hill, Edmund, O. P., trans. (1991) *The Trinity, WSA I/5*. Brooklyn, NY: New City Press.

La Bonnardière, Anne-Marie (1965) *Recherches de chronologie augustinienne*. Paris: Etudes Augustiniennes.

Marrou, Henri Irénée (1958) *Saint Augustin et la fin de la culture antique*, 4th ed. Paris: E. de Boccard.

McKenna, Stephen, CSS.R., trans. (1963). *The Trinity, FC 45*. Washington, DC: The Catholic University of America Press.

O'Connell, R. J. (1968) *St. Augustine's Early Theory of Man*. Cambridge, MA: Belknap Press of Harvard University Press.

Pelikan, Jaroslav (1987–1988) "*Canonica Regula:* The Trinitarian Hermeneutics of Augustine." *Proceedings of the PMR* 12(13): 17–29.

Schindler, Alfred (1965) *Wort und Analogie in Augustins Trinitätslehre*. Tübingen: Mohr.

Schmaus, Michael (1927) *Die psychologische Trinitätslehre des heiligen Augustinus*. Münster: Aschendorff.

Smith, Andrew (1974) *Porphyry's Place in the Neoplatonic Tradition*. The Hague: Martinus Nijhoff.

TeSelle, Eugene (1974) "Porphyry and Augustine." *Augustinian Studies* 5: 113–147.

Teske, R. J. (1984) "Spirituals and Spiritual Interpretation in Augustine." *Augustinian Studies* 15: 65–81.

Trouillard, Jean (1955) *La purification plotinienne*. Paris: Presses Universitaires de France.

Van Fleteren, Frederick E. (1974) "Augustine's Ascent of the Soul: A Reconsideration." *Augustinian Studies* 5: 29–72.

Van Fleteren, Frederick E. (1987–1988) "Thematic Reflections on the *De Trinitate*." *Proceedings of the PMR* 12(13): 221–227.

Zum Brunn, Emilie (1988) *St. Augustine: Being and Nothingness*. New York, NY: Paragon House.

2

The Sweetness of the Word

Salvation and Rhetoric in Augustine's *De doctrina christiana*

In book 2 of *De doctrina christiana* (*doctr. chr.*), Augustine discusses briefly the "precepts" of eloquence. He classifies eloquence with the sciences "not of human institution but rather discovered with the logic of things."[1] To us, the rules of rhetoric may seem to be anything but natural, but Augustine points out that, if speech is to be persuasive, it must adapt itself to the contours of human understanding and motivation, and these are givens:

> It was not instituted by human beings that an expression of charity should win over a listener … or that the variety of discourse should keep listeners attentive without annoyance …. That which moves minds to long for or to avoid something is not invented but discovered.[2]

In a way, the study of rhetoric is the study of human motivations, or at least of the motivating of human beings.[3]

It is precisely as such that Augustine talks about the theory of "rhetorical art"[4] in book 4. The primary aim of the *Scripturarum tractator*[5] *et doctor* is not only to teach what he has learned but also to present it in such a way that it will "move minds."[6] "Healthful teaching"[7] is of no avail if it has no power to delight those to whom it is presented. It is not enough simply to speak the truth; in fact, if one's teaching is "wise" or "healthful," it is all the more crucial that it be eloquent.[8] Augustine is quick to point out that his remarks will not

---

Visioning Augustine, First Edition. John C. Cavadini.
© 2019 John Wiley & Sons Ltd. Published 2019 by John Wiley & Sons Ltd.

teach the precepts of eloquence themselves: he recommends that persons be trained in them at the appropriate time, or else read eloquent literature and teach themselves thereby.[9] What we have in book 4 is less a theory of rhetoric per se than a theory of conversion. The art of rhetoric is useful not so much in its particular rules but precisely because it embodies a science of human motivation and therefore helps us to learn what will make the truth not only true but *moving*. The fact that it is true is not, normally, enough.[10]

In particular, if the truth is to be moving, it must be presented *suaviter* – sweetly – that is, in such a way that it will delight the listener. Eloquence is the art of speaking sweetly:

> For one who speaks eloquently speaks sweetly; one who speaks wisely, speaks healthfully; ... But what is better than a sweetness with the power of healing, or a power of healing that is sweet? The more eagerly the sweetness is desired, the more readily the power of healing (*salubritas*) avails.[11]

Scripture itself is characterized by such an eloquence;[12] the role of the Christian *tractator* and *doctor* is to make its sweetness, its power to move to conversion, available to others. Thus will Augustine, slightly later, present Ambrose – the "sweetness of his speaking" caught Augustine and made him finally appreciate the "delights" of God's "law."[13]

"Sweetness" of discourse can be cultivated improperly as an end in itself,[14] but "if the just rather than the wicked" are to be *willingly* heard (*libenter audiantur*), they must speak *suaviter* – "persuasively," that is, "sweetly."[15] And although Augustine, in his interpretation of Ciceronian theory, associates the effect of "sweetness" more narrowly with the "moderate" style of speaking (as opposed to the simple and grand style),[16] no speech can finally move anyone if it is not in some way "sweet," if it does not in some way "delight."[17] The effect of the grand style, used with adequate "sweetness," is dramatic. The orator is to expect, not applause, but tears. The audience shows the effect "rather through their groans, sometimes even though tears, and finally through a change in their way of life."[18] This sounds familiar – it is in fact an apt description of the state to which Augustine is reduced at his final conversion as he describes it in *Confessions* 8.

What has the student of the art of speaking finally learned?

If he wants to delight or to persuade the person to whom he speaks, he will not do it simply by speaking in any way at all; whether he does it depends upon the way in which he speaks.[19]

This, presumably, applies to God as well. If conversion is a matter of persuasion, then if God is to convert anyone, God too must speak persuasively. In this way, book 4 of *doctr. chr.*, precisely because it is not a treatise on rhetoric per se but on (in effect) the dynamics of conversion, provides a kind of commentary on, or key to, the interpretation of the rest of the work.[20] For when we hear that we are distant from God, Neoplatonic wanderers, as it were, from our homeland (*patria*), and when we hear that what this means is that we are "tangled up in perverse sweetness"[21] and that our way back to God will not be a "road from one place to another but a road of the feelings,"[22] we cannot doubt that we have thus been aptly described as subjects ripe for the persuasive power of an eloquent speaking that will disentangle us from perverse sweetness and will delight us with that "sweetness which actually would make us happy."[23] When we hear that our plight is that we "enjoy" things which we should not,[24] and that we need to learn to place our "delight" in something which presently does not delight us,[25] and that we are to learn to "refer" all our present delights to that final goal,[26] who can fail to see that what we need is not simply to be told the truth, but to be told it in a way that will delight us? Who cannot see that, just as the sweetness of the moderate style is to be used not as a pleasure in itself but to refer us to the final end of conversion,[27] so too we are in the position of needing to be persuaded to transfer willingly our affections' goal elsewhere? We are in need not simply of a teacher but of a persuasive speaker, a delightful speaker.

And so (citing 1 Cor. 1:21 twice in the same chapter) "it pleased God, by the foolishness of preaching, to save them that believe."[28] The Wisdom of God comes to us not from place to place but by appearing in mortal flesh.[29] She who is the goal has become the way, but this way consists of "unblocking" our affections: like the rhetor, God's Word speaks not only wisely (and indeed is Wisdom herself), but movingly, and, in some sense, sweetly – this is the "foolishness of preaching." The Word made flesh is God's Wisdom made not simply visible but persuasive; it is God's eloquence:

Indeed, the resurrection of our Lord from the dead (and his ascension into heaven), once believed, has supported our faith with a great hope.

For it shows very clearly how freely it was that he laid down his life for us, since he had the power to take it up again. How great a trust with which the hope of believers consoled, as they consider that such a man suffered so greatly for people who were not yet believers! When he is awaited as the judge from heaven of the living and the dead, the thought strikes great fear into the indifferent, so that they are converted to diligence and prefer to long for him in doing good than to hear him in doing evil.[30]

From the perspective of book 4, we easily recognize here the effects of grand eloquence. Jesus' laying down of his life as the revelation of God's compassion "unblocks" our affections or feelings, disentangling them from false and truncated enjoyments:

Moreover, since we are on a road and it is not a road from one place to another but a road of the feelings, which was blocked by the bad will of our past sins as if by a thorny hedge, what more generous and compassionate thing could he do – he who willed to lay down himself as a means for our return – than to forgive all the sins of those converted, and to tear away the firmly fixed prohibitions against our return by being crucified for us?[31]

Christ's work is not finally to teach us something – knowledge is not enough – in fact, it "puffeth up" (1 Cor. 8:1).[32] Christ's accomplishment is to rework our affections, that is, to create in us a new character, described, again with 1 Corinthians (13:8, 13), as "faith, hope, and charity." One who achieves this character does not need the Scriptures except to teach,[33] and, in fact, has become, by this very fact, eloquent,[34] a mirror of God's eloquence. In book 1 of *doctr. chr.*, Augustine has presented an interpretation of 1 Corinthians by offering an analysis of God's work in Christ with a paradigm that is unmistakably rhetorical.[35]

   This is a fundamental shift – or at least the articulation of a fundamental shift – in Augustine's understanding of the work of Christ and of salvation. We might think of his earlier paradigm as philosophical. As is well known, the language of "return to the fatherland" is Neoplatonic and is familiar from Augustine's earlier treatises. The language of referring our enjoyment of things to enjoyment of God is drawn from the vocabulary of the Neoplatonic ascent to contemplation. One ascends, through consideration of corporeal things, to contemplation of the incorporeal. But because we have become entrapped in things corporeal, because of the influence of the body,[36] our ascent is impeded, something *doctr.* holds in common with other works such as *beata u.*, *Acad.*, *ord.*, etc., and even *lib. arb.*

But in the earlier works, what we need to complete this ascent is philosophy. In a well-known passage from the *Acad.* directed to his patron Romanianus, Augustine describes his conversion precisely as a conversion to "philosophy":

> ... a soreness of the chest compelled me to give up the bombastic profession [i.e., rhetoric] and to flee to the bosom of philosophy. And now, in the leisure which we have always desired, it sustains and comforts me .... It teaches – and rightly so – that we ought to have no concern for anything that can be discerned by mortal eyes, or reached by any of the senses, but rather that all such things are to be disregarded. It promises to give a lucid demonstration of the most true and distinct God, and even now it deigns to furnish a glimpse of him, as it were, through transparent clouds.[37]

Augustine notes how he is presently attempting to convert Romanianus to philosophy (from Manichaeism),[38] hoping in the example of Romanianus's son Licentius and other young charges who are now living the philosophic life with Augustine.[39] This life involves a program of study in the liberal arts, which exercise the mind to purify it of its carnal attachments and prepare it for the interior ascent and incorporeal vision.[40] The liberal arts are studied so that philosophy may take hold, and in this vein Augustine undertakes the writing of a kind of encyclopedia of the liberal arts, of which the *mus.* is the sole surviving artifact.[41]

In this scheme (overgeneralized here, but adequate for our purposes), the function of Christ, the Word made flesh, is simply to admonish us to interiority, that is, to philosophy.[42] Because our minds are fixed on visible things, Wisdom herself becomes visible, but only to admonish us authoritatively to recognize our essential identity and destiny as spiritual, and to invite us to philosophy and to a study of the liberal arts that will prepare us for philosophy. If Christ gives us faith, hope, and love, it is faith, hope, and love that we will eventually come to sight, that is, we will make the ascent, even if, because we are "little ones" who cannot understand philosophy, it is postponed to the afterlife.[43] What did the reading of the Apostle Paul reveal to Augustine as he relates it in the *Acad.*? Philosophy.[44] But the Christ of these earlier works, from the point of view of *doctr. chr.*, is naive – he is an orator who attempts merely to teach, thinking that knowledge and understanding of the truth alone will suffice, not understanding that teaching in and of itself cannot persuade; not understanding, finally, the well-springs of human motivation. He would certainly not qualify as a professional rhetor.

Doctr. chr. presents a cohesive rethinking of Augustine's earlier philosophical synthesis of Christian doctrine. What we have instead is what we might think of as a rhetorical synthesis. But by this I do not mean that the philosophical Christ of the earlier works has simply learned to be less naive – more suave, as it were, more streetwise – and to give admonitions to the inner life which are more rhetorically compelling. Augustine, in fact, seems already to have tried this in *lib arb*. In book 2 of that work, Augustine had described our plight thus:

> O Wisdom, most sweet light of the purified mind! … Those who love what you make in place of you yourself are like people who, when they hear a wise and eloquent speaker, listen too eagerly to the sweetness of the voice and the arrangements of carefully placed syllables, and so lose the principle matter, the meaning of the speaker, of which the words are only signs.[45]

Here, Augustine draws on the vocabulary of rhetorical theory to help us understand our problem. But what we need here is to be somehow unlocked from our attachment to the signs of Wisdom, that is, her creatures, so that we can see their meaning – in other words, what we need to be shown is that creation is merely like an eloquent speech.

And in book 3 of *lib. arb.*, Christ is presented, in perhaps one of the only really moving (if brief) passages in this most philosophical of works, as one who does not merely teach, but who acts in such a way that our attention is diverted from the sweetness of the speech. Augustine presents Christ as a model of humility: "While the devil showed himself a model of pride, the Lord should show himself, through whom we are promised eternal life, a model of humility." But then he modulates into something more:

> Thus the blood of Christ having been offered for us after unutterable
> (*ineffabiles*) distress and pain, we ought to follow our Savior with such
> charity, and be so enraptured by his brightness (*claritate*), that no lower
> object may detach us from so superior a sight (*a conspectu superiore*).[46]

Christ's "ineffable" Passions moves us better than the "speech" of
lower things, but this only serves to remove us from the realm of
speech, the realm of the finite and contingent, and to return us to the
contemplation of the highest unchangeable Wisdom,[47] to the invisible
things within – that is, to the bosom of philosophy. And yet, in the
hint that it is in the Passion in which we see the splendor of eternal
Wisdom, in the hint that it is the Passion which is the content of the
conspectus to which we arrive, there is signaled a change, even if the
final reference is ultimately philosophical.

In *doctr. chr.*, the balance is shifted, and the change consummated.
Our plight is depicted in terms drawn from the vocabulary of the
Neoplatonic ascent of the soul. But that language is refigured,
recontextualized, as soon as the saving eloquence of God – Christ – is
presented not only as the way of our ascent but as the goal as well.
Interpreting Jn. 14:6, "I am the Way and the Truth and the Life,"
Augustine notes that the Word made flesh means to say, "you are to
come through me, to arrive at me, and to remain in me," because,
arriving at Christ, we arrive also at the Father (Jn. 14:10). Augustine
glosses his own comment by saying that it is not Christ's intention,
having become our way, to hold us on the way,[48] but this does not
mean that we leave the humanity of Christ behind, as though it were
separable from him. Rather, we simply do not absolutize it as though
it were not a way, that is, as though it were not God's moving eloquence
but simply just another "thing" to be attached to. It means seeing
Christ's humanity as speech, but only *in* the speech do we see the
meaning; we do not depart from the realm of speech, from the realm
of the temporal. God's eloquence gives everything else a voice, invests
the world of temporal things with significance, but only by keeping
our attention fixed on God's eloquence can anything else speak. We
"remain in Christ." We are "freed" from temporal things, that is, from
clinging to them as though they were our end, but our attention does
not leave the temporal realm; instead, it becomes, for the first time for
us, a way: we can "use" it.

The content of that "use" is not, however, philosophical intro-spection. This use is our traveling of the "way of affections," but that way has been, and is, formed for us by the sweet eloquence of God, Christ. Christ becomes the content of our affections – he is our way of affections; we do not depart from his continuing formation of them in faith and in hope, and in the charity which they yield.[49] Our "use" of *res* is the very charity which the divine eloquence forms in us, the love of God and neighbor – but, in particular, the love of neighbor. For God's moving eloquence consists in God's having become our neighbor out of compassion,[50] and this moves us to love of, instead of "enjoyment" of, the neighbor. The refusal to rest in the neighbor, to "enjoy" him or her as though they were our personal ends, constitutes "enjoyment" of God and proper enjoyment of the neighbor: "The highest reward is that we enjoy [God] and that all of us who enjoy him may enjoy one another in him."[51]

This means that we cease to take part in the social project of constructing the neighbors as our personal ends, as subjects to be dominated.[52] It means that we do not escape the realm of the neighbor, the realm of the temporal, the historical, the contingent, to make an inward ascent to the enjoyment of the eternal. Our enjoyment of God is not the result of philosophy or inward ascents, but an enjoyment whose content and substance are continual acts of charity performed towards whatever neighbor chance or circumstance sends us.[53] This is the via that God's eloquence forms in us. "Scripture teaches nothing but charity."[54]

We encounter in *doctr. chr.* a significant advance over the paradigm presented in *lib. arb.* In the *lib. arb.*, created things are in and of them-selves speech, speech so beautiful that we become captivated by its sweetness. But in *doctr. chr.*, the sweetness which captivates us and holds us to created things is much more sinister; it is not anything resident in the things themselves but a "perverse sweetness" that we invent and invest them with. It is an artificial sweetness, furthermore, which is culturally constructed. In book 2, in passages which sound (without actually being) Tertullianesque, we learn how permeable culture is to idolatry,[55] described as the construction of the universe as though it were a language which we invented,[56] the rendering of creation into a set of "imaginary signs," and then worshiping it as though it were the Creator.[57] But what we are worshiping is a construct of our own sign systems. In effect, we use culture, the realm of signs and signification, to construct ourselves as the creators, and this is the perverse sweetness which "delights"[58] us – it is our own pride, and we are worshipping ourselves. Even those arts and sciences which are not directly idolatrous are nevertheless infected because we use them in the service of pride – they "puff up."[59]

As for philosophy, it has a use, but its utility is exactly the same as any other useful thing. If it has a usefulness, that usefulness is constructed by Christ and not separable from him. It has no independent, useful value to which Christ admonishes us.[60] We may take the gold of the Egyptians,[61] but only through the Pasch which is the blood of Christ:

> Thus one will feel that, although he has fled rich from Egypt, he cannot be saved unless he has observed the Pasch. "For Christ our pasch is sacrificed" (1 Cor. 5:7), and the sacrifice of Christ emphasizes for us nothing more than that which he said as if to those whom he saw laboring under pharaoh: "Come to me ... for my yoke is sweet and my burden light" (Mt. 11:28–30). To whom is it thus light except to those ... whom knowledge does not puff up but charity edifies (1 Cor. 8:1)?[62]

We do not leave our new way of affections, that is, charity, the work of God's eloquence within us, when we engage in philosophy. Our attention does not leave the realm of eloquence, the temporal and the historical, where Christ's blood was poured out. By our clinging to faith in these, even philosophy can be referred to the love of God.

And, as for the liberal arts, Augustine notes:

> ... It seems to me that studious and intelligent youths who fear God and seek the blessed life might be helpfully admonished that they should not pursue those studies (*doctrinas*) which are taught outside the Church of Christ as though they might lead to the blessed life.[63]

This is a direct unsaying of the premise of *mus.* and the encyclopedia of which it was to be a part.[64]

We can think, in the last analysis, of *doctr. chr.* as a revisioning of the projected encyclopedia, as that project which in effect replaced the encyclopedia, rendering it obsolete[65] – for the earlier conception of an encyclopedia of the liberal arts was predicated upon a conception of our predicament as one of being trapped by the sweetness of created (and especially corporeal) things, and the belief that the best of culture – liberal arts and philosophy – had value because they could detach us from these sweetnesses. The view of *doctr. chr.* is different. *Doctr. chr.* recognizes that there is no culturally unmediated sweetness inhering directly in things – that, in fact, we construct the sweetnesses which trap us in things, that these sweetnesses are really a delight in pride, and that these delights are *culturally* constructed. Into this situation, knowing well how to move us, the sweet Wisdom of God speaks persuasively with her blood, disentangling us from the web of sweetnesses that is our own construction, and forming our affections instead by her charity. Charity, as it were, deconstructs[66] those sweetnesses, dismantling them in the ultimate sign (*signum*), the sign of the cross.[67] There is no question of a philosophical escape from temporal things into the eternal. As long as we live, we never leave the realm of sign and signification, of eloquence and the word, to arrive at an inner world apart from them. In the sign of the cross is our breadth, length, and height.[68] But this means also that *doctr. chr.* is not an attempt to establish a "Christian culture."[69] What finally renders any cultural artifact "useful" is the sign of the cross, the "foolishness of God ... the foolishness of preaching," which disassembles the sweetnesses formed by perverse sign systems, and which turns everything else into a sign – in effect a sacrament – of God's Wisdom.[70] We never leave the temporal because, in Christ, the temporal becomes sacramentalized; it becomes our enjoyment of God.

Acknowledgments

An earlier version of this chapter was published by University of Notre Dame Press as Cavadini, J. C. (1995) "The Sweetness of the Word: Salvation and Rhetoric in Augustine's *De doctrina christiana*." In *De doctrina Christiana: A Classic of Western Culture*, edited by Duane W. H Arnold and Pamela Bright, 164–181. Notre Dame: University of Notre Dame Press. Reproduced with permission.

Notes

1   *doctr. chr.* 2.35.53.3–4: "neque ab hominibus instituta sed in rerum ratione com-
perta" (spoken with immediate reference to dialectics but characterizing the
whole class of sciences, consideration of which began in 2.27). Rhetoric, the
"praecepta uberioris disputationis, quae iam eloquentia nominatur" (*doctr. chr.*
2.36.54.1–2), is clearly in this class. All references to the *doctr. chr.* are to the
edition of Daur and Martin, by book, chapter, section, and line(s).

2   *doctr. chr.* 2.36.54.5–13: "Nam neque hoc ab hominibus institutum est, ut caritatis
expressio conciliet auditorem … aut varietas … sine fastidio teneat intentos; et
… quae … ad expetendum fugiendumve animos movent, et inventae potius
quod ita se habeant, quam ut ita se haberent institutae." This view is recalled and
implied in what Augustine has to say at 4.4.6.13–15: "Ibi obsecrationes et incre-
pationes, concitationes et coercitiones, et quaecumque alia valent ad commovendos animos, sunt necessaria."

3   Compare Cicero's view, as at *De oratore* 1.12.53, where the best orator will have
thoroughly considered "naturas hominum, vimque omnem humanitatis,
causasque eas quibus mentes aut incitantur, aut reflectuntur" (cf. 1.15.68–69). No
speaker will be able to move anyone without having studied "rerum omnium
naturam, mores hominum atque rationes" (1.51.219; cf. 1.51.223–52.224). All
references to *De oratore* are to the edition of Sutton (1942).

4   *doctr. chr.* 4.2.3.1–2ff.: "Nam cum per artem rhetoricam et vera suadeantur et
falsa." Although written later, Augustine's comments here clearly echo those at
2.36.54. In both places, Augustine stresses the value-neutral character of rhetoric
as a natural act, and thus its usefulness for arguing truth as well as falsehood.

5   For a study of this word and its cognates (*tracto-tractatio*) in the *doctr. chr.* as a way of
learning how to understand the aim and character of the work, see Press (1980)
(with an exhaustive survey of the literature). Press argues that "the *whole* work
concerns the "treatment" of scriptures and the whole work [not just book 4]
therefore falls within the rhetorical tradition" (118), books 1–3 being concerned
with discovery (*inventio*) of what is to be understood, and book 4 with the manner
of setting forth (*modus proferendi*) what has been understood. The emphasis on
inventio is a return to a conception of the rhetoric characteristic of ancient theories (here, Aristotle, and then Cicero), but Augustine's insistence that what is
invented is *quae intellegenda sunt*, that is, "the proper meaning of a text or a group
of texts" (120), and that (further) there is, in fact, a correct interpretation to be
discovered, shifts the whole focus and concern of ancient rhetoric: "The aim of
this rhetoric, therefore, is to discover the truth in texts, the articles of the Christian
faith, and to teach it to others. Thus rhetoric is reborn as an important social
force" (121). Marrou (1958), however, pointed out long ago the tendency of
ancient culture to base itself upon the deep knowledge and explication of a privi-
leged text. Of the *doctr. chr.*, Marrou says, "Le double problème posé à l'intellectuel

chrétien est celui-là même que grammairiens et rhéteurs s'étaient depuis tant de siècles attachés à résoudre" (403, cf. 409; Brown [1967], 263, echoes Marrou).

6   *doctr. chr.* 4.4.6.15: "ad commovendos animos," echoing 2.36.54.11, "animos movent."

7   For example, at *doctr. chr.* 4.5.8.40ff.: "Qui enim eloquenter dicunt, suaviter; qui sapienter, salubriter audiuntur …. Sicut autem saepe sumenda sunt et amara salubria, ita semper vitanda est perniciosa dulcedo. Sed salubri suavitate, vel suavi salubritate quid melius? Quanto enim magis illic appetitur suavitas, tanto facilius salubritas prodest." The "health" metaphors are echoes of the discussion of God's economy of healing in book 1 (see e.g., 1.12; 1.14).

8   "Nam cum per artem rhetoricam et vera suadeantur et falsa, quis audeat dicere, adversus mendacium in defensoribus suis inermem debere consistere veritatem, ut videlicet illi, qui res falsas persuadere conantur, noverint auditorem vel benevolum, vel intentum vel, docilem prooemio facere; isti autem non noverint? … illi animos audientium in errorem moventes impellentesque dicendo terreant, contristent, exhilarent, exhortentur ardenter; isti pro veritate lenti frigidique dormitent?" (*doctr. chr.* 4.2.3.1–6, 10–13).

9   See *doctr. chr.* 4.1.2; 4.3.4. Brown (1967) observes that Augustine did not envision the collapse of the pagan schools of rhetoric. For Marrou (1958), Augustine's profoundest innovation was to separate "eloquence" from "rhetoric," thinking of the rules and culture of rhetoric as useful but not indispensable: "Il faut mesurer la hardiesse d'une telle affirmation. Poser cela, n'était rien moins que rompre avec une tradition huit fois séculaire, s'opposer à ce que, pour les hommes de sons temps, paraissant l'essential de la culture. Séparer l'éloquence de la rhétorique, concevoir toute une formation de l'orateur qui délibérément ignorera ces recettes, cet art sur lequel depuis des siècles tant d'attention a été concentrée, c'était là vraiment innover" (516–517 – echoed in part by Brown [1967], 267, who, however, thinks that Augustine was apt to underestimate the degree of sophistication and training that had gone into the construction of his "simplicity" of style). *Doctr. chr.* 4.1.2 may be usefully compared to the answer given by Augustine to Dioscorus in 410–411 (beginning and end of the letter), and also to *doctr. chr.* 2.28.42, which refers to history as useful even if learned "praeter Ecclesiam puerili eruditione" (cf. *doctr. chr.* 2.39.58, also envisaging a course of study outside of the Church, "doctrinas quas praeter Ecclesiam Christi exercentur," which Augustine expects a student to have followed).

10   One could think of this as the fundamental premise of the whole rhetorical project. It does not imply a very flattering view of human nature. The rhetorical paradigm for conversion, if it may be so called, is stated well by Cicero at *De oratore* 2.42.178–179: "Plura enim multo homines iudicant odio aut amore aut cupiditate aut iracundia aut dolore aut laetitia aut spe aut timore aut errore aut aliqua permotione mentis, quam veritate aut praescripto aut iuris norma aliqua aut iudicii formula aut legibus."

11 See n. 7.

12 *doctr. chr.* 4.6.9; 4.7.21; cf. *conf.* 3.5.9; 6.5.8.

13 *conf.* 5.13.23.19 and 11.2.4.43–44 (cf. 3.19). Note that this is not the way Augustine presents the effect of Ambrose's preaching in his earlier works, where he is customarily presented only as teaching that God is incorporeal, and as helping Augustine to see that the Scriptures are in agreement with such a doctrine (i.e. from the point of view of rhetorical theory, that they are *merely* true): see *beata u.* 1.4; *util. cred.* 8.20. On the notion of the "congruous" ("effective" or "persuasive") vocation, the call to conversion which is effective because it is given in a way that is congruent to a person's place and character, see Burns (1980), especially 37–51.

14 *doctr. chr.* 4.14.30; cf. 4.28.61. These are clear echoes of a theme prevalent in book 2 as announced, for example, at 2.13.20.29–33: "eo sunt infirmiores [homines], quo doctiores videri volunt, non rerum scientia qua aedificamur, sed signorum qua non inflari omnino difficile est, cum et ipsa rerum scientia saepe cervicem erigat" (1 Cor. 8:1); see also 4.28.61.6–10, with further reliance on 1 Cor.: "In ipso etiam sermone malit rebus placere quam verbis nec existimet dici melius, nisi quod dicitur verius, nec doctor verbis serviat, sed verba doctori. Hoc est enim, quod ait Apostolus: 'Non in sapientia verbi, ne evacuetur crux Christi'" (1 Cor. 1:17). Compare this passage with the exhortation in *cat. rud.* 9.13.8–11 (*c.* 400) to the rhetor who would be a Christian: "discant non contemnere quos cognoverint morum vitia quam verborum amplius devitare; et cordi casto linguam exercitatam nec conferre audeant quam etiam praeferre consueverant."

15 *doctr. chr.* 4.14.30.18–19.

16 See *doctr. chr.* 4.17.34.

17 *doctr. chr.* 4.26.56.4–16. Augustine explains that anyone using any one of the styles must nevertheless aim for the effects associated with each of the three. On the need for the grand style to be "sweet" as well, see 4.26.58.

18 *doctr. chr.* 4.24.53.4–5 (translated in Robertson [1958]): "Grande autem genus plerumque pondere suo voces premit, sed lacrimas exprimit .... quid in eis [hominibus] fecerit sapientis granditas dictionis, non clamore potius quam gemitu, aliquando etiam lacrimis, postremo vitae mutatione monstrasse." This effect is described as *conversion* in the example Augustine gives of the Mauretanians: "Moxque sermone finito ad agendas deo gratias corda atque ora converti" (lines 20–21).

19 *doctr. chr.* 4.12.27.11–13: "Quod si etiam delectare vult eum, cui dicit, aut flectere, non quocumque modo dixerit, faciet, sed interest, quomodo dicat, ut faciat."

20 The fourth book and the final sections of the third were added by Augustine as he reexamined the work during the writing of the *retr.* (in 427; see *retr.* 1.30.1). The fourth book thus clearly gives clues to how Augustine understood the

work upon his rereading of it in 427, and, in any interpretation of the work in its final form, this must be decisive. However, Augustine's thinking on the nature and place of rhetoric does not develop significantly between the earlier books and the last, as the connections between books 1 and 2 given earlier (especially in notes 2, 4, 6, 7, and 14) demonstrate. In a letter of 395 (*ep.* 29, to Alypius), Augustine describes his own preaching in terms very similar to how he talks about preaching in general in *doctr. chr.* 4. In particular, his description of how he reduced the congregation to weeping is much like the similar description at *doctr. chr.* 4.24.53.

21 *doctr. chr.* 1.4.4.12–13: "perversa suavitate implicate alienaremur a patria, cuius suavitas faceret beatos."

22 *doctr. chr.* 1.17.16.1–2: "nec via ista locorum est, sed affectuum."

23 *doctr. chr.* 1.4.4.13.

24 *doctr. chr.* 1.3.3.7–8: We are those who "eis quibus utendum est frui voluerimus." On the precise, and sometimes shifting, nuances attached to *uti* and *frui* in the *doctr. chr.*, see the excellent study by O'Donovan (1982).

25 To "enjoy" is to "use with delight" ("vicinissime dicitur frui, cum delectatione uti," *doctr. chr.* 1.33.37.21); what we should enjoy is the Trinity (1.5.5); for us, that means transferring our delight from the vehicles of the journey to the goal (1.4.4).

26 For example, at *doctr. chr.* 1.22.21.37–42: "Quisquis ergo recte diligit proximum, hoc cum eo debet agere, ut etiam ipse toto corde, tota anima, tota mente diligat Deum. Sic enim eum diligens tamquam se ipsum, totam dilectionem sui et illius refert in illam dilectionem dei, quae nullum a se rivulum duci extra patitur, cuius derivatione minuatur." Cf. 1.33.37.21–24: "Cum enim adest, quod diligitur, etiam delectationem secum necesse est gerat, per quam si transieris eamque ad illud ubi permanendum est, retuleris; uteris ea, et abusive, non proprie diceris frui."

27 See *doctr. chr.* 4.26.57.

28 *doctr. chr.* 1.12.11.3–6; 12.14–15.

29 *doctr. chr.* 1.12.12.1–2.

30 *doctr. chr.* 1.15.14.1–9: "Iam vero credita domini a mortuis resurrectio et in caelum ascensio magna spe fulcit nostram fidem. Multum enim ostendit quam voluntarie pro nobis animam posuerit, qui eam sic habuit in potestatem resumere. Quanta ergo se fiducia spes credentium consolatur considerans, quantus quanta pro nondum credentibus passus sit? Cum vero iudex vivorum atque mortuorum exspectatur e caelo, magnum timorem incutit neglegentibus, ut se ad diligentiam convertant eumque magis bene agendo desiderent, quam male agendo formident."

31 *doctr. chr.* 1.17.16.1–7: "Porro quoniam in via sumus nec via ista locorum est sed affectuum, quam intercludebat quasi saepta quaedam spinosa praeteritorum malitia peccatorum, quid liberalius et misericordius facere potuit, qui se ipsum

nobis qua rediremus, substernere voluit, nisi ut omnia donaret peccata conversis, et graviter fixa interdicta reditus nostri pro nobis crucifixus evelleret?"

32 See, for example, *doctr. chr.* 2.41.62.3–4; 42.63.15; 13.20.31–32; etc.

33 *doctr. chr.* 1.39.43.1–3: "Homo itaque fide et spe et charitate subnixus eaque inconcusse retinens non indiget Scripturis nisi ad alios instruendos."

34 This character is itself "instructio" (*doctr. chr.* 1.39.43.7); it is itself a "copia dicendi" (4.29.61.35; cf. 4.27.59.1–2: "Habet autem ut oboedienter audiamus, quantacumque granditate dictionis maius pondus vita dicentis").

35 We may remember that Cicero says that the perfect orator would have to be God/a god (*Orator* 5.19, cf. *De oratore* 1.46.202). Also, note Augustine's description of the work of "the Son of God" at *conf.* 13.15.18.47–48: "Attendit per retia carnis et blanditus est et inflammavit, et currimus post odorem eius." This sounds very much like the orator who has spoken in the right mixture of the moderate and grand styles, and Augustine in this passage has just finished speaking of Scripture's eloquence: "Non novi, domine, non novi alia tam casta eloquia, quae sic mihi persuaderent confessionem et lenirent cervicem meam iugo tuo et invitarent colere te gratis" (*conf.* 13.15.17.21–23).

36 In many of the early works, there is evident a strong Platonic disgust with bodily things, simply because they are bodily: one is converted to God *from* the "uncleanness of the body and its stains" (*ord.* 1.8.23 – the context is Augustine's partial defense, against Monica, of Licentius's singing, in the latrine, Psalm 79:8, "O God of Hosts, convert us"). In the *sol.*, Reason (at 1.14.24) demands that Augustine forsake things of the senses and the sticky lime of bodily things (cf. *retr.* 4.3.37–42).

37 *Acad.* 1.1.3.71–73, 75–81 (trans. Kavanagh [1948]): "me pectoris dolor ventosam professionem abicere et in philosophiae gremium confugere coegisset. Ipsa me nunc in otio, quod vehementer optavimus, nutrit ac fovet ....Ipsa enim docet et vere docet nihil omnino colendum esse totumque contemni oportere, quicquid mortalibus oculis cernitur, quicquid ullus sensus attingit. Ipsa verissimum et secretissimum deum perspicue se demonstraturam promittit et iam iamque quasi per lucidas nubes ostentare dignatur."

38 The whole of *ord.* 1.1 is an extended exhortation to Romanianus, as is 2.1–2 (at 2.2.3.1, Augustine entreats Romanianus, "Ergo adgredere mecum philosophiam"); cf. 1.9.25.51–52.

39 *Acad.* 1.1.4; 1.9.25.53–55. Note that it was a reading of Cicero's *Hortensius* that accomplished the conversion – this is apparently part of Augustine's curriculum (1.1.4.97–98).

40 For the best account of this "Reductio Artium ad Philosophiam," see Marrou (1958), 277–327. Note that the paradigm for conversion here is different from the rhetorical passage given in *doctr. chr.* (and *De oratore*). The paradigm in the earlier works is more philosophical and Platonic, not only because the *terminus ad quem* of conversion is, by and large, the "port of philosophy" (*beata u.* 1.1.1–2),

but because it proceeds on the assumption that the truth, once glimpsed, in and of itself is enough to persuade. Education in the liberal arts provides the gradual strengthening necessary to bear the dazzling brilliance of the vision of truth. This is illustrated at *sol.* 1.13.23, which concludes: "Nam ordine quodam ad eam [sapientiam] pervenire bonae disciplinae officium est," where "ordine," in the extensive metaphor preceding, was compared to a process of introducing someone's eyes to the light of the sun in stages. At another point in the *sol.*, training in the liberal arts is unmistakably conflated with a process of Platonic reminiscence: "Tales sunt qui bene disciplinis liberalibus eruditi; siquidem illas sine dubio in se oblivione obrutas eruunt discendo, et quodammodo refodiunt; nec tamen contenti sunt, nec se tenent donec totam faciem veritatis, cuius quidam in illis ortibus splendor iam subrutilat, latissime atque plenissime intueantur" (2.20.35; cf. *retr.* 4.4). In the earlier dialogues, one can take the figure of Licentius as an illustration of this paradigm of conversion. In the *Acad.*, Augustine tells Romanianus that Licentius is applying himself to philosophy, but that Augustine is restraining him so that he may first acquire strength from education ("ut discipulis necessariis prius excultus vigentior et firmior insurgat," 2.3.8). In the *ord.*, Augustine exults in the progress of his student, saying (1.6.16.20–22, 23–25): "ego me ipsum non caperem gaudio, quod videbam adulescentem, carissimi amici filium ... cuius studium vel in mediocres litteras desperaveram, quasi respecta possesione sua toto impetu in mediam venire philosophiam." Licentius himself, singing Psalm 79:8, "O God *convert* us ...," goes on to report, "alia, longe alia nescio quid mihi nunc luce resplendit. Pulchrior est philosophia, fateor, quam Thisbe, quam Pyramus, quam illa Venus et Cupido talesque omnimodi amores. – Et cum suspirio gratias Christo agebat" (1.8.21.4–8). He is pictured as unable to find words to express his experience, and as finally speaking ecstatically and oracularly, especially in 1.7.18, where he declaims, breathing heavily ("ingemescens difficultate verborum," lines 17–18), the Neoplatonic doctrine of order, and in 1.7.19, where Trygetius is amazed, "ammirans et horrens subito condiscipuli et familiaris sui afflatum nova inspiratione sermonem" (1.7.19.38–40). Augustine tells Licentius that he has not chanted the prayer for conversion in vain (1.8.23.27–29), and Licentius, recounting his experience, answers, "Nonne hoc est vere in deum convertit?" (1.8.23.33–34; a conversion *to* God *from* the uncleanness of the body, lines 40–41). Augustine agrees but tells Licentius that he must return "to order," that is, to his education, for the face of God is the vision of truth, and the process of conversion a matter of lifting oneself up to it by virtue and temperance, and training in the liberal arts (1.8.23–24.50): "Nam eruditio disciplinarum liberalium modesta sane atque succincta et alacriores et perseverantiores et comptiores exhibet amatores amplectendae veritati, ut et ardentius appetant et constantius insequantur et inhaereant postremo dulcius, quae vocatur, Licenti, beata vita" (1.8.24.50–54).

41 On the *mus.*, see Ubaldo Pizzani and Guido Milanese (1990). The plan for the encyclopedia into which it was to fit, along with the rationale for the encyclopedia, is given in the *retr.*, where the *mus.* is mentioned as the only surviving treatise from the abandoned project. Note especially the rationale: "Per idem tempus, quo Mediolani fui baptismum percepturus, etiam disciplinarum libros conatus sum scribere, interrogans eos qui mecum erant atque ab huiusmodi studiis non abhorrebant, per corporalia cupiens ad incorporalia quibusdam quasi passibus certis vel pervenire vel ducere" (1.6.40–44; cf. *mus.* 6.2). In the corpus of Augustine's writings closest to the period of composition of the *mus.*, the plan of study represented by the encyclopedia, together with the theory of this *paedeia*, is most fully elaborated in the *ord.* The system of the liberal arts is laid out in 2.11–19, with their *terminus ad quem* in philosophy (2.18.47) and the ascent to the vision of God which philosophy accomplishes (2.18.48–19.51, note especially section 51). Cf. *ord.* 1.1.3.50–55 to 1.2.3. On the encyclopedia, see Marrou (1958), 211–235, 570–579; Pizzani and Milanese (1990), 14–39.

42 For a good account of Augustine's early theory of Christ, see R. J. O'Connell (1968), 265–278. At *ord.* 2.9.27.38–41, divine authority in the incarnation admonishes us not to be limited to the senses, but to ascend to the intellect. Thus, those who live by authority alone and not the liberal arts cannot be said to be happy while in this life (2.9.26; rejected at *retr.* 1.3.2), even where that authority is divine, because that authority only functions to recall us to philosophical interiority. When Alypius voices the paradox that someone who has believed does not necessarily behave accordingly, something which requires divine assistance (2.10.28), Augustine immediately dismisses this nonphilosophical gloominess, noting among other things that both our capacity to change and the ways in which people have changed are often underestimated (2.10.29). And, in the passage from *ord.* cited in n. 40, 1.8.21.8, Licentius thanks Christ – for leading him to *philosophy*.

43 Faith is in lieu of, and inferior to, instruction in the liberal arts at *ord.* 2.5.15.34–41. The incarnation is mentioned at 2.5.16, and the clemency it shows, but there is no mention of the Passion. At *ord.* 2.8.25, faith, hope, and love seem totally submerged in, and defined by, a morass of commonplace aspirations familiar even to the casual reader of Cicero. The only question remaining to be discussed is educational – "quomodo studiosi erudiri debeant, qui sicut dictum est vivere instituerunt" (2.9.26.1–2). At *sol.* 1.6.12, faith, hope, and love are precisely faith, hope, and love in the prospect of enlightenment or vision! *Acad.* 2.3.9 contains an encomium on what philosophy is able to do; what one must *believe* is that philosophy is indeed able to do it. For a qualification of Augustine's development on this matter, see Chapter 11 in this book, titled "Trinity and Apologetics in the Theology of St. Augustine."

44 *Acad.* 2.2.5–6, especially 2.2.5.63–6.69.

45 *lib. arb.* 2.16.43: "O suavissima lux purgatae mentis sapientia! ... Similes autem sunt, qui ea. quae facis pro te amant, hominibus, qui, cum audiunt aliquem facundum sapientem, dum nimis suavitatem vocis eius et structuras syllabarum apte locatarum avide audiunt, amittunt sententiarum principatum cuius illa verba tamquam signa sonuerunt."

46 *lib. arb.* 3.25.76: "ut praerogato nobis Christi sanguine post labores miseriasque ineffabiles tanta caritate liberatori nostro adhaereamus et tanta eius in eum claritate rapiamur ut nulla nos visa ex inferioribus a conspectu superiore detorqueant."

47 *lib. arb.* 3.25.76: "Ut autem in contemplatione summae sapientiae – quae utique animus non est, nam est incommutabilis –, etiam se ipsum qui est commutabilis animus intueatur et sibi ipse quodam modo veniat in mentem."

48 *doctr. chr.* 1.34.38.21–27.

49 For, among other things, if we fall from faith, we will fall from charity (*doctr. chr.* 1.37.41.9–10).

50 *doctr. chr.* 1.30.33.52–56.

51 *doctr. chr.* 1.32.35.17–19.

52 The failure to refer enjoyment of the neighbor to God is a false self-love which amounts to a prideful domination of the neighbor (*doctr. chr.* 1.23.23). On self-love in Augustine, see O'Donovan (1980).

53 "Neighbor" is taken quite literally, as anyone who happens to be "near" us, including enemies. See *doctr. chr.* 1.30.31.

54 *doctr. chr.* 3.10.15, 12.18, 15.23; 1.36.40, etc.

55 Note (as with Tertullian) how identical culture is with idolatry. Augustine "secularizes" history (see Markus [1989], especially chapter 7) and culture (Brown [1967], 266). However, I would add that, for Augustine, this is a kind of formal *analysis* of culture, a statement about what culture *essentially* is, not a phenomenology, or a description of what culture has actually *become*. This would be analogous in a way to his analysis of human nature in terms of what it essentially is by creation and the way it has been wounded by sin. For culture, this means its vulnerability to idolatry, the way in which it tends to be constructed by pride rather than by charity. One could found a "culture" on the basis of biblical imagery (Brown [1967], 263), and this may be in some sense a "Christian" culture, but it is not necessarily a "converted" culture – it, too, would be susceptible to the glacial drift towards idolatry (this is reflected in Augustine's discussion, at *doctr. chr.* 1.37.41, of how interpreters can become attached to their own interpretations simply because the interpretations are their own, even if wrong, and this is a fall from charity). For Augustine, persons are converted, not "cultures." It may be better to say that culture is, in this way, de-reified or even de-mythologized, rather than simply secularized. Thus, one would preserve the balance which the *doctr. chr.* attempts to articulate – an ability to engage in the pursuits and fruits of the (essentially good) cultural

enterprise – but with a healthy fear and distrust of the actual and ever-present tendency towards, and thus implication in, idolatry. But this is to carry us into the subject for another essay altogether.

56 See, for example, *doctr. chr.* 2.21.32.22–25, 29–31, where Augustine discusses how we have affixed names to months and stars, which had always existed as God created them before they received these names: "Pro quintili enim et sextili mensibus Iulium atque Augustum vocamus de honoribus hominum Iulii Caesaris et Augusti Caesaris nuncupatos, ut facile, qui voluerit, intellegat etiam illa sidera prius sine his nominibus caelo vagata esse .... Sed quodlibet vocentur ab hominibus, sunt tamen sidera, quae deus instituit et ordinavit ut voluit." The universe itself becomes part of a sign system independent of its creation, and while this is not evil, it makes the universe miscible with the world of sign and signification, and we rarely resist the temptation to integrate it even further, to the point where the distinction between creation and culture is obscured: all the astrology and related idolatry in chapters 20–24 is predicated on this "naming" of the universe, the ("presumptuous," sec. 34) construction of the universe as a sign system of our making – in effect, the substitution of ourselves for the Creator.

57 See, for example, *doctr. chr.* 2.18, 20.

58 This is true not only of the linguistic reconstruction of the cosmos, which "placuit humana vanitate" (*doctr. chr.* 2.21.32.27), but also of how even legitimate, non-superstitious sciences become the stuff of pride. We "delight" in being able to "boast" of our wisdom: the general case has already been discussed (2.13.20.29–33, see n. 14), but, in particular, with regard to the science of numbers, at 2.38.57.14–24: "Quae tamen omnia quisquis ita dilexerit, ut iactare se inter imperitos velit et non potius quaerere unde sint vera, quae tantummodo vera esse persenserit, et unde quaedam non solum vera, sed etiam incommutabilia, quae incommutabilia esse comprehenderit, ac sic a specie corporum usque ad humanam mentem perveniens, cum et ipsam mutabilem invenerit, quod nunc docta, nunc indocta sit, constituta tamen inter incommutabilem supra se veritatem et mutabilia infra se cetera, ad unius dei laudem atque dilectionem cuncta convertere, a quo cuncta esse cognoscit, doctus videri potest, esse autem sapiens nullo modo." One delights in *seeming to be learned* by denying to God what is God's – a form of self-idolatry.

59 Clearest with regard to philosophy, *doctr. chr.* 2.40–42, but always as a specific instance of 2.13.20.

60 This can be forcefully realized by comparing the way the *doctr. chr.* simply lists philosophy at the end of a catalogue of helpful sciences, to Augustine's tearful expressions of rejoicing at his pupil Licentius's progress at *ord.* 1.6.16 and 1.8.22–24 (cited in n. 40). It is inconceivable that, from the perspective of the *doctr. chr.*, Augustine could extol philosophy as "our true and serene dwelling place" (*ord.* 1.2.9). How antique this sounds to the reader of the *doctr. chr.*,

where philosophy is in effect relativized to a position with the rest of the valuable sciences!

61   *doctr. chr.* 2.40.60–61.

62   *doctr. chr.* 2.41.62.4–13, translated by Robertson (1958).

63   *doctr. chr.* 2.39.58 (preceded by 38.57, cited in n. 58) explains why the ascent from number does not work – the more we know, the stronger the temptation to "boast" (translated by Robertson [1958]).

64   This is the unsaying of many passages from the *ord.* as well, including some cited in n. 40 (*ord.* 1.8.50–54) and n. 42 (*ord.* 2.9.26), as well as the opening lines of the *beata u.* These passages are unsaid also in Augustine's remarks on the *mus.* in the *retr.* (1.11.1–11). The remark that those who have the power to see the "invisible things" of God (Rom. 1:21) but have no faith in Christ will perish *with all their wisdom* is an echo of the *doctr. chr.*

65   Aligning himself in a general way with the position of Marrou (1958), Brown (1967) notes that the *doctr. chr.* "is one of the most original works that Augustine ever wrote …. It is no small thing to be able to transcend one's own education …. In Cassiciacum, surrounded by young aristocrats, feeling a little out of place among the polished Christians of Milan, Augustine had not dreamt that he could transcend this education: it might be subordinated to a quest for Wisdom; but it remained intact, massive and irremovable as the foothills of the Himalayas" (264). I agree. And yet, in a certain sense, the *doctr. chr.* represents a return to Augustine's own education. Marrou (1958) begins to point this out when he contrasts the methods of the *ord.* and the *doctr. chr.* as philosophic versus literary (409). But more importantly, the plight of humankind and the work of God with respect to human beings are understood according to a rhetorical, not a philosophical, paradigm. What Brown refers to as "The Lost Future" could be seen differently, in a way, as a return to himself, as a recovery of the voice he had so carefully learned to polish before his discovery of the *Hortensius*, albeit in a new key.

66   Charity "aedificat" (*doctr. chr.* 2.41.62.3–4; 1 Cor. 8:1), it "builds," but from the ground up; we become "rooted and founded" (line 19; Eph. 3:17) in charity when the pride formatting cultural achievements is deflated, as it were, "purged" by the blood of the Lamb (the purgative power of which is symbolized by the hyssop with which it is applied in Ex. 12:22): "est etiam in ysopo vis purgatoria ne inflante scientia [1 Cor. 8:1] de divitiis ab Aegypto ablatis superbe aliquid pulmo tumidus anhelet" (lines 20–32). "Founded" and "built" by charity, one resists other principles of construction – knowledge can no longer "puff up" ("fundatum et radicatum et aedificatum in charitate, quam scientia inflare non possit," *doctr. chr.* 2.42.63.14–16).

67   *doctr. chr.* 2.41.62.25–27: "Quo signo crucis, omnis actio christiana describitur, bene operari in Christo, et ei perseveranter inhaerere, sperare caelestia, sacramenta non profanare."

68 Eph. 3:17–18; *doctr. chr.* 2.41.62.18–19.
69 For a different view of the *doctr. chr.*, see Kevane (1991) – for example, 1018 and
1025, where Kevane assumes complete continuity between the point of view
of the *doctr. chr.* and that of the *mus.* and the *Libri disciplinarum* (the encyclopedia): "Augustine is showing how to accomplish a new approach in teaching all
the arts and sciences of human culture. This points forward to the Christian
West, for it is nothing else than a structuring of a new kind of education, quali-
tatively different from that of the secularized Schools of Rhetoric of the
Classical civilization. This is the reason why he embarked upon his project of
the *Libri disciplinarum* in his earlier period of the philosophical dialogues, and
this is the reason for his purgation of the curricular sciences and disciplines in
Book Two of the *de doctrina christiana*. It is the concept of *Si rite pertractentur* in
Vatican I" (1025). On this view, it is hard to imagine, however, why Augustine
not only left the *Libri disciplinarum* unfinished, but even was careless enough to
lose all that he had completed (treatise on grammar and the prefaces to the
other books) apart from the *mus.* (which itself may have only been preserved
because someone asked for it, *ep.* 101).
70 On this point, see Williams (1989) and Jordan (1980). On the theory of signs in
general in Augustine, see Markus (1957), and Jackson (1969).

References

Brown, Peter (1967) *Augustine of Hippo*. Berkeley, CA: University of California Press.

Burns, J. Patout (1980) *The Development of Augustine's Doctrine of Operative Grace*. Paris:
Institut d'Études augustiniennes.

Jackson, B. Darrell (1969) "The Theory of Signs in St. Augustine's *De doctrina
christiana*." *Revue des études augustiniennes* 15: 9–49.

Jordan, Mark D. (1980) "Words and Word: Incarnation and Signification in Augustine's
De doctrina christiana." *Augustinian Studies* 11: 177–196.

Kavanagh, Denis J., O.S.A., trans. (1948) *Writings of St. Augustine, FC 1* New York,
NY: Cima Pub. Co.

Kevane, Eugene (1991) "Augustine's *De doctrina christiana* in World Historical
Perspective." *Augustiana* 41: 1011–1031.

Markus, R. A. (1957) "St. Augustine on Signs." *Phronesis* 2: 60–83.

Markus, Robert (1989) *Saeculum: History and Society in the Theology of St. Augustine*.
Cambridge: Cambridge University Press.

Marrou, Henri Irénée (1958) *Saint Augustin et la fin de la culture antique*. 4th ed. Paris:
E. de Boccard.

O'Connell, R. J. (1968) *St. Augustine's Early Theory of Man*. Cambridge, MA: Belknap
Press of Harvard University Press.

O'Donovan, Oliver (1980) *The Problem of Self-Love in St. Augustine.* New Haven, CT: Yale University Press.

O'Donovan, Oliver (1982) "*Usus* and *Fruitio* in Augustine's *De doctrina christiana* I." *Journal of Theological Studies.* 33: 361–397.

Pizzani, Ubaldo and Guido Milanese, commentators. (1990) *"De Musica" di Agostino d'Ippona.* Palermo.

Press, Gerald A. (1980) "The Subject and Structure of *De doctrina christiana*." *Augustinian Studies* 11: 99–124.

Robertson, D.W., Jr., trans. (1958) *On Christian Doctrine.* Indianapolis and New York: Bobbs-Merrill.

Sutton, E.W., B.C.L., M.A., trans. (1942) *Cicero: De Oratore*, 2 vols, completed, with an introduction, by H. Rackham. Cambridge, MA: Harvard University Press.

Williams, Rowan (1989) "Language, Reality, and Desire in Augustine's *De Doctrina*." *Journal of Literature and Theology* 3: 138–150.

3

The Quest for Truth in Augustine's *De Trinitate*

Augustine of Hippo's *De Trinitate* (*trin.*) is, as he himself remarked, a difficult work,[1] and its difficulty seems only to have increased over time. It is largely out of favor at present. First, because it seems to commentators so hopelessly speculative that it has appeared impossible to locate within any social or polemical context that might somehow mitigate its difficulty by affording some sense of what was at stake in its composition in the first place.[2] Second, from a theological perspective, the *trin.* is now held responsible for having hopelessly interiorized the Christian doctrine of God, for having restricted awareness of God to awareness of the enigma of God's interior image within the individual mind, and thus for having set the doctrine of God adrift from any meaningful understanding of human community. If God is visible first and foremost to the individual soul in an introspective moment of Neoplatonic ascent, then the attention of the individual seeking God seems irretrievably propelled away from the human community as locus of the economy of God's self-revelation. The individual is left almost as a self-sufficient, or self-constituting, subject,[3] the "alone seeking the alone," to quote a Plotinian tag.

Visioning Augustine, First Edition. John C. Cavadini.
© 2019 John Wiley & Sons Ltd. Published 2019 by John Wiley & Sons Ltd.

The Work in Its Context

Elsewhere, I have suggested that the *trin.* was actually meant to argue against such an interiorized view of the individual's relation to God,[4] but here I would like to experiment with a different strategy of con-textualization, focusing on the presence of motifs of education and the liberal arts. The *trin.* is not, of course, a treatise on education or the arts; yet, especially in its second half, there are multiple references to themes related to education – as well as discussions of how and why one learns;[5] of the "appetite for inquiry;"[6] of the distinction between knowledge and "wisdom"[7] and the place of philosophy;[8] of the function of letters and signs; of the "disciplines" and "doctrina"[9] in general – all along with a wealth of illustrations explicitly appealing to knowledge of the arts.[10] From the viewpoint of Augustine's own cor-pus, there is even more reason to experiment with reading the treatise from this perspective, for many of the distinctive themes of Augustine's early educational dialogues are present here, as though the *trin.* were in some sense their reissue or restamping.

The deliberate and repeated invocation of the reader as a partner in a quest for tracking down truth is reminiscent in tone if not in form of the dialogue genre of the Cassiciacum literature. Book 13 takes up issues from *beata u.* and *Acad.*;[11] in both books 13 and 14, Cicero's *Hortensius*[12] makes an appearance (after a long absence in Augustine's writings). There is even a short soliloquy,[13] and the "interior teacher" himself makes a cameo appearance, although, like all of these ghosts of Augustine past, in a transformed and distinctively anti-Pelagian way.[14] What would an interpretation of the *trin.* look like that emphasized these aspects without reducing the work to them?

One could say initially that we find what we might expect from Augustine's reworking of educational themes in the *doctr. chr.*[15] The process of "seeking" or "tracking down truth"[16] is not in the first instance an appeal to the disciplines or to the moral or speculative truths of the philosophers; it coincides with the investigation and explication of Scripture, complete with rules of interpretation com-ing not from grammar or rhetorical criticism but from Scripture itself and the rule of faith.[17] From this perspective, the *trin.* is not a study of a dogma comparable to medieval or modern treatises "De Deo trino"[18] – in fact, nothing seems less comparable to the spirit of this work, undogmatic, open-ended, and experimental as it constantly proclaims itself to be.[19] Rather, it is self-consciously an example of the deployment of a new kind of "teaching" or *doctrina* in which "seeing truth" is coincident with understanding the scriptural text, and all the arts and philosophy itself are drawn into that enterprise.[20] They can be used by, but do not define, this *doctrina*, and in fact are often qualified in the process.[21]

The Human as Image of the Triune God

I would argue further, however, that Augustine's positioning of the cultural disciplines in this manner is not limited to his explicit observations on the arts, but is carried over directly into his trinitarian theology, where it is replicated, and given a kind of theoretical underpinning, in his analysis of the human person as an image of the triune God. For, as Augustine presents it, the *imago Dei* is, among other things, specifically an image of word production. The mind is an image of God precisely in its capacity to beget a "word" wholly consubstantial and equal to itself. Augustine is careful to remark, however, in several places that he is speaking of an "inner word" (*intimum verbum*) which precedes all individual words or even thoughts in any language, including Latin or even Greek.[22] It is a word which precedes all signs and sign systems,[23] and therefore all the arts and disciplines, all cultural reality as we might put it. In other words, the individual's status as *imago Dei* is not dependent upon what we might think of as a particular cultural identity. It is an eternally valid precultural reality focused on a capacity for self-awareness and self-expression which is productive of culture – of signs and sign systems – but not reducible to any particular cultural expression.

Augustine points out, as well he might, that this is an exceedingly difficult idea to grasp, and that is why, after he first brought it up in book 9 and analyzed it further in book 10, he had chosen to exercise the reader in a series of considerations about the workings of sensation and sense-related thought where the "word" which the mind begets is temporally distinct from the knowledge it expresses.[24] But these trinities of sensation and perception, of knowledge based on sensation and of discursive thought, are all analyses of our involvement in the world of body and time, and thus of sign and signification, of language and culture. They are not merely heuristic exercises in any simple way, but, in fact, if read backwards from book 15's final analyses of the *verbum* before language, they represent the movement from the mind's inner word of self-awareness as image of God, to the ways in which the mind's prelinguistic self-expression is actualized in the world of sign and signification – that is, of culture.

Inner Word to Outer Word

To put it this way is to overstate the case somewhat, for none of these trinities, either alone or together, provide an account of the actual mechanism by which the mind produces particular signs, moving from the inner word to specific outer words and gestures. Augustine is not interested in this precise mechanism – he takes it for granted, and there is a certain legitimate arbitrariness attached to it: Augustine will not say which language is better, Latin or Greek.[25] Still, if even the "outer" trinities do not take us over the boundary between the prelinguistic inner word and its particular expression in exterior sign, they take us right to it, and in fact they characterize all voluntary bodily action precisely as the incarnation of an inner word,[26] as expressive, as a kind of language, though not necessarily Latin or Greek. For, despite his depiction of the *imago Dei* as antecedent to cultural specification, Augustine is acutely aware of the culturally specified character of all human experience.[27] He describes the beauty of the "discipline (*doctrina*) that contains all knowledge of all signs," because, without any means of communication, human society would in effect cease to exist as such. It would be "worse than any kind of solitude if people could not exchange their thoughts in conversation (*colloquendo*)." Awareness of the "lovely and beautiful form," "the ideal of learning" (*speciem doctrinae*), prompts the urge to cultivate the arts of communication and the disciplines based on them (*trin.* 10.1.2). Embodied subjects are necessarily involved in the "utilization of changeable and bodily things without which this life cannot be lived" (*trin.* 12.13.21) – nor can we come to know, much less "love" and "enjoy" (*perfruendi*) (*trin.* 9.6.11, see 9.8.13; 10.9.12), the neighbor, "unless bodily signs are given," whether these are gestures (*trin.* 15.10.19), or spoken or written words.[28]

Augustine's trinitarian analysis of the origin of these signs in a prelinguistic inner "word" does not permit us to know whether any given sign is a particularly effective means of communication.

However, to cast our participation in the bodily and temporal as expressive of an inner "word" is, in a way, precisely to identify our experience of the bodily and the temporal as what we now would call the "cultural." If we read backwards, we go from the inner word of book 15 – the mind aware of itself becomes aware of God and the divine form of justice (8.9.13; 9.6.11; 14.15.21) – to the inner words conceived in the outer trinities of books 13, 12, and 11 – that is, to the subject poised for action. The question is not how well the particular signs generated communicate, but how well our cultures reflect or even image that eternal form of justice.[29] How truthful are they?

The Production of Culture

And so, one could think of the whole "boxed set" of trinities, described in books 9–15, not simply as analyses of human consciousness, but also as a kind of phenomenology of culture production, an account of the necessary movement from the mind's precultural self-expression in an inner *verbum* antecedent to language, to the expression of the *verbum* in the particularities of sign and signification. One might even suggest, in a particularly experimental moment, that Augustine transforms the Plotinian account of the fall of mind into bodies into an account of the way in which the embodied mind, although always transcendent with respect to any particular cultural form, descends as it were into specification in expression – and hence identity – in particular signs and sign systems. This is no longer a "fall" in a pejorative sense; it is simply an account of how human beings, who are inescapably social beings, are able to "enjoy" the fellowship which social living implies.

Still, this descent into cultural specification of the mind's prelinguistic self-expression can go awry and become a full-fledged fall.[30] Yet, it is not, as Augustine presents it, the descent into cultural specification which is itself the problem. The problem occurs, rather, on the level of the inner *verbum* and, in particular, the will. The role of the third member of the internal trinity is crucial, for, as Augustine presents it, the inner word is "conceived either in covetousness or charity," and is born "when on thinking it over we like it either for sinning or for doing good" (9.8.13; 15.11.20, 23). It is only "loved knowledge" (9.10.15) that constitutes an inner "word" which is then capable of signification. The sign systems we create are no better than the love in which they were ultimately begotten, and the soul which is dominated by pride, analyzed in the *trin.* as a disordered love of power over justice,[31] will inevitably produce cultures which instantiate or express this preference of power over justice.

Worse still, to the extent that this preference is instantiated in cultural systems, the options for sign and signification of the inner word become radically delimited. The inner word, as presignificatory, has a kind of vulnerability to deformation when even the gestures, not to mention the words, in which it is forced to express itself, are contextualized by sign systems which have encoded in them the preference for power over justice. Those described in book 2 of *doctr. chr.* and recalled in book 4 of *trin.* as superstitious or demonic are completely corrupted.[32] Others, the arts and disciplines of learning, retain their ability to raise their practitioners to philosophical contemplation of eternal truths. "For example, the sheer arithmetic of a beautiful piece of music" can lead one to the "sight" of "intelligible and incorporeal ideas (*rationes*)," however fleeting (12.14.23), and literature can assist the reader in discovering the truth that illuminates the mind (14.7.9). But these disciplines, the mastery of which is a "beautiful" thing (10.1.2) granting access to truth, can just as easily "puff up" (1 Cor. 8:1).[33] That is because, in Augustine's trinitarian analysis of the matter, one can never simply reproduce one's knowledge in an unmediated fashion. It has to be "spoken," even interiorly, that is, in the inner *verbum*, itself begotten in a particular act of the will, in a particular kind of love or intention. There is no knowledge which is not in some sense "intentional."[34] The intention or love is part of the "word" in which the knowledge is begotten and communicated, so that a preference for the creature over the Creator, for "correctness of words over the truth of things" (14.11.14, describing the use of words in "secular literature"), is easily encoded into the discipline itself. One learns to value correctness of form over truth at the same time as one learns letters.[35]

The Ascent to Philosophy and God's Descent

Not only the liberal disciplines but philosophy itself is infected, as the case of Cicero shows (14.19.26). Philosophy cannot make good on its own promises, because, even when successful, its achievements are

formatted by the glacial drift of a culture in which the very attainment of contemplation has become an occasion for complicity in
pride (4.15.20; see 15.24.44 with reference to philosophies of mind).
The very vision of God's eternal things is seized as a personal accomplishment, available to an educated few, who then "affect to be above
other souls which are given over to their senses" (12.9.14). One may
be able, with the aid of the liberal arts, to ascend to philosophy and
learn to contemplate God's image, but it is an image distorted by
pride as one's attention is riveted, finally, on only one thing – the
power, or at least the prestige, of being oneself "wise."[36] As Augustine
points out, the image ceases to function as an image[37] – it loses its
power to refer one to God – and so do all the cultural artifacts, signs
and sign systems, disciplines, and *doctrina* leading up to it, the whole
boxed set of trinities of word production and their cultural products.
None of them present words adequate to image God or serve as signs
pointing to God.

That is why God, the very divine Word, "became flesh," which for
Augustine in the *trin.* means that God's very Word chose to make a
descent into the world of embodied signification. Augustine is careful
to talk about the Incarnation as a process parallel to our own production of (descent into) signs and signification:

> Thus in a certain fashion our [inner] word becomes a bodily sound by
> assuming that in which it is manifested to the senses of human beings,
> just as the Word of God became flesh by assuming that in which it too
> could be manifested to human sense.[38]

That is why, as Augustine explains further, it is specifically the Word,
not the Father or the Holy Spirit, that became flesh, because precisely
as flesh the Word becomes the "Good Teacher" (*magister bonus*) whose
divine "*doctrina*" will (using Pauline language) "transform" our own
inner word by enabling it to be conformed to his "example."[39]
Augustine characterizes this *doctrina* of the "Good Teacher" specifically as persuasive, appealing to the will by presenting to it a moving
sign of God's love, capable of detaching it from its addiction to power
and returning it to justice in the exercise of charity.[40]

Note here that our inner trinity is not healed by a contemplative
escape from the world of sign and signification, but rather by conformation to the divine *paideia* over a lifetime of loving attention to and

imitation of the example of the Good Teacher.[41] Gone for the most part is the interior teacher of the *mag.*; he has been replaced by one who justified us by his blood (Rom. 5:9).[42] This is not, in the first place, an exhortation to look within but to look without, for paradoxically that is how the inner image becomes healed and transformed. We never outgrow the divine *paideia* until the image is perfected in eternity. God's entry into the realm of sign and signification does not mean that *we* leave it behind – nor does it necessarily mean that God has provided a specific blueprint for a Christian society – but rather that, in our use of cultural forms (at least those not classified as hopelessly demonic), they become more and more transparent to the justice that the divine *doctrina* is teaching us to love, themselves ever more able to participate in imaging God. The whole boxed set of trinities, which I have characterized as Augustine's phenomenology of culture production, becomes a phenomenology of cultural *transformation*. The transcendence of the inner word over culture is now recognized not in any immunity from culture but specifically as its ability to work transformatively within it – a capacity for cultural self-critique formed by the tutelage of the divine *doctrina*.

Thus, in the *trin.*, we have a theology which is, strictly speaking, neither apophatic nor kataphatic, but specifically trinitarian in its call neither to renounce language nor to accept its limitations as received, but to present the image of God ever more clearly in a transformed and transforming begetting of words.

Acknowledgments

An earlier version of this chapter was published by SAGE publications as Cavadini, J. (1997) "The Quest for Truth in Augustine's *De Trinitate*." *Theological Studies* 58 (3): 429–440. doi:https://doi.org/10.1177/004056399705800302.

Notes

1   "Libris de trinitate ... nimis operosi sunt et a paucis eos intellegi posse arbitrer," *ep.* 169.1.1, CSEL 44:612.6–9. For citations from the *trin.*, I use Hill (1991), by far the best English translation. Latin citations, except where otherwise indicated,

are from CCSL 50 and 50A. Orthography and punctuation have been adjusted. I thank Kathryn Johnson, Jim Buckley, Nancy Cavadini, Lawrence Cunningham, Robert Markus, Jean Porter, Michael Signer, and Jim Turner for their assistance. I acknowledge especially my debt to my late colleague Catherine LaCugna, from whom I learned the importance of thinking in a trinitarian way.

2   Brown (1967) locates his biography of Augustine "along the side of a mountain-face: … above the plains of Augustine's routine duties as a bishop, and far below the heights of his speculations on the Trinity" (277); though Brown does not intend to dismiss Augustine's "speculative masterpiece," subsequent scholarship has tended to neglect it.

3   "Augustine's quest for the Trinity within the soul, the inner Trinity, risks reducing the Trinity to theological irrelevance, for it becomes difficult to ask in what way the doctrine of the Trinity may in other ways throw light on the human condition ….The outcome is another, theologically legitimated, version of the tendency to individualism…." (Gunton 1991a, 49); see also the expanded version of this critique in Gunton (1991b), 42–48. For more on this topic, see Chapter 7.

4   Cavadini (1992), reprinted in the current volume.

5   The discussion at *trin*. 8.4.6, on how we can love something we do not know, becomes by *trin*. 9.12.18 an explicit discussion of inquiry and learning, continuing well into book 10 (*trin*. 10.1.1–2.4, at 10.1.1, explicitly recalls the question from *trin*. 8.4.6, "no one can love a thing that is quite unknown"). Certainly, many of the created "trinities" that Augustine analyzes are themselves analyses of *learning*; see, for example, his characterization of the trinities of sensation and sense knowledge: "All these things [learned from the senses], produce a kind of trinity when they are learnt, consisting of the look which was knowable even before it was known, and of the learner's awareness joined to this, which begins to be when the thing is learnt, and the will as third element which joins the two together" (*trin*. 14.8.11). This passage tends to qualify all the preceding discussion of sensation and sense-acquired knowledge as an analysis of a kind of learning. And the whole discussion of the "inner word," from its very first suggestion, is a discussion of the begetting of knowledge (see esp. *trin*. 9.7.12, 9.12.18).

6   There is an especially noteworthy treatment of the "appetitus inveniendi" at *trin*. 9.12.18.

7   *trin*. 12.14.23; 13.1.2; 13.19.24.

8   *trin*. 13.19.24; 14.1.2; 14.19.26; 4.15.20–18.24; etc.

9   The term *doctrina* in the *trin*., as in Augustine's usage generally, means more than the word "doctrine" in English can possibly express, including in its most general sense the act of teaching and learning considered as one (as at *trin*. 10.1.2, "speciem doctrinae," which could just as easily be translated as "learning" or "teaching"); in the second place, simply the act of teaching or communicating (see n. 40, and 14.8.11), and thirdly with reference to a particular *kind* of teaching, a "discipline" (as at *trin*. 9.12.18, 10.1.1 repeatedly, 10.1.2; the "doctrina" *contains*

the knowledge, so here the discipline itself is not equated with the content; 10.5.7; 15.9.16, which uses *doctrina* and *disciplina* almost as synonyms). It can also refer to the results of teaching and learning, from the point of the learner (one's "learning," as at 10.11.17 *bis*), or more abstractly, as the content taught, "teaching" or "a teaching" (*trin.* 1.13.31, "sana doctrina"; 14.1.2). More often than not, more than one overtone is present, as in the oft-cited Jn. 7:16, *Mea doctrina non est mea* (*trin.* 1.12–13; 2.2–3; 15.27.48) or at *trin.* 15.11.20, 15.9.15, and some of the passages already cited. On the meaning of "doctrina" in the *doctr. chr.*, see Mario Naldini's comments in Hill (1996), 11–12, and Hill's own comments (ibid., 95–97).

10 See the brief discussions of such topics as "inventio" ("discovery," or the "research" stage of rhetoric, *trin.* 10.7.10); grammar (*trin.* 9.10.15; 10.5.7; see 14.11.14, which appeals to the usage of Virgil as authoritative; 14.14.18); the connection between education and character (*trin.* 10.11.17); history (*trin.* 12.14.22; 14.8.11; 14.10.13); how the mind is trained in the disciplines (*trin.* 12.14.23); Plato's theory of learning by reminiscence (*trin.* 12.15.24); a man learned in many disciplines (*trin.* 14.5.8–6.8); the function of literature (*trin.* 14.6.9–7.9); and the uses of Cicero's *Hortensius* (n. 12).

11 The titles, of course, of Augustine's two earliest works; see *trin.* 13.3.6 for the introduction of the theme, programmatic for book 13, that all people desire happiness, explicitly phrased in terms of the "happy life" (*beata vita*) at *trin.* 13.4.7. This also provides a link to Augustine's antiskeptical agenda: that all people want to be happy is a universal truth that even "Cicero the Academic" cannot doubt (see *trin.* 15.12.21; 10.10.14; 10.1.3).

12 Augustine's reference to the *Hortensius* recalls his earlier use of it as a school text at Cassiciacum, when he was prompting students to the study of philosophy (*Acad.* 1.4, reflecting Augustine's autobiographic comments at *beata u.* 4; compare with the exhortation to philosophy and inquiry cited by Augustine from the *Hortensius* at *trin.* 14.19.26), and as a starting point for raising the issue of the happy life (*trin.* 13.4.7–5.8; see *beata u.* 10; *trin.* 14.9.12).

13 *trin.* 15.27.50, where Augustine addresses his own soul (*anima*). The word is suggested by Hill (1991), 434.

14 At *trin.* 14.15.21, once we receive the Lord's Spirit, we are taught by an inner "teaching" or "instruction" that we cannot rise from sin except by the action of grace.

15 For this reworking, see Cavadini (1995), reprinted as Chapter 2 of this volume, and the literature cited there.

16 Augustine writes "carried away with the love of tracking down the truth" (*trin.* 1.5.8), echoing Cicero's exhortation to inquiry, which Augustine cites at *trin.* 14.19.26 and summed up as "this course, set in the love of and inquiry into truth." In what follows, Augustine, having accepted Cicero's terms, qualifies his acceptance: for mortals, this course cannot succeed by reason alone, without faith in the Mediator. One can think of the *trin.* as a whole as a demonstration of that claim, a deployment of the *doctrina* which bases itself on that claim.

17 Note the collocation of "the discovery of truth" and "the interpretation of Scripture" (*trin.* 2.P.1). Augustine has just finished explaining that those who "seek God and strive for an understanding of the Trinity" will have to negotiate the difficulties and complexities of Scripture. He argues (*trin.* 2.1.2–3, echoing 1.6.12) that Scripture itself, as exposited by previous Catholic interpreters, provides a "rule" (*canonica regula*) to assist the interpreter to understand correctly passages about Jesus (based on Phil. 2:6–7), and that it provides an additional rule to supplement the first one (based on passages such as John 5:26); see Pelikan (1987–1988) and Cavadini (1992, reprinted as Chapter 1 of this volume), 118 n. 42. Augustine mentions the "rule of faith" at *trin.* 15.27.49 and again at 15.28.51, where it is presented as a summary of what we read in Scripture ("litteris veritatis").

18 As, for example, English translators (before Hill [1991]) had characterized it. McKenna (1963) groups it with "medieval [and] modern studies of this dogma" (xii); Haddan (1887) call it the "most weighty" of Augustine's "doctrinal treatises" (iii).

19 Augustine disclaims authoritative status for the work, saying he will learn by writing ("So I have undertaken this work ... not so much to discuss with authority what I have already learned, as to learn by discussing it with modest piety," *trin.* 1.5.8), and proclaiming his willingness to inquire and to learn ("Nor will I, for my part, wherever I stick fast be loath to seek, nor wherever I go wrong be ashamed to learn," *trin.* 1.2.4). He asks the reader to recall him from error if necessary as he and the reader set out together on a joint venture of inquiry, emphasizing his willingness to accept correction, posthumously if necessary (*trin.* 1.3.5). Augustine continues to be insistent about the active involvement of the reader and his own openness to correction (*trin.* 2.P.1; 3.P.2), warning the reader not to value his work above Scripture or Catholic faith, keenly aware both of his liability to error (*trin.* 4.P.1) and of the way in which all knowledge of God is hardly a final result, but itself the occasion for further inquiry (see *trin.* 9.1.1; 15.2.2).

20 As recommended at *doctr. chr.* 2.40.60. It is Scripture itself which engages us on the ascent to the vision of eternal things, accommodating itself to our present "sickly" power of seeing (*trin.* 1.2), while on the other hand presenting difficulties sufficient to recommend God's grace to us (*trin.* 2.P.1).

21 For example, the discussion of how the categories of predication apply or do not apply to God, on the evidence of scriptural usage (*trin.* 5.8.9); also, the disruption of the absolute contrast between accidental and substantial predicates to include the category of non-accidental eternal relations on the basis of scriptural teaching (*trin.* 5.5.6).

22 *trin.* 14.7.10. See also *trin.* 15.10.19: "If anyone can understand how a word (*verbum*) can be, not only before it is spoken aloud but even before the images of its sounds are turned over in thought – this is the word that belongs to no language, that is, to none of what are called the languages of the nations, of

which ours is Latin; if anyone, I say, can understand this, he can already see through this mirror and in this enigma some likeness of that Word of which it is said, *In the beginning was the Word* ... [Jn. 1:1]." Later in the same section, "It is the thought (*cogitatio*) formed from the thing we know that is the word which we utter in the heart (*verbum* ... *quod in corde dicimus*), a word that is neither Greek nor Latin nor any other language." As a "thought," however, it is still prelinguistic: "if you wish to arrive at some kind of likeness of the Word of God ... do not look at that word of ours which sounds in the ears, neither when it is uttered vocally nor when it is thought of silently, for the words of all spoken languages are thought of silently ..." (*trin.* 15.11.20). This inner word, before all thought of sound, is a kind of seeing of what is known and thus its image: "a word before any sound, before any thought of sound. For it is then that the word is most like the thing known and most its image, because the seeing (*visio*) which is thought springs direct from the seeing which is knowledge, and it is a word of no language, a true word from a true thing, having nothing from itself, but everything from that knowledge from which it is born" (*trin.* 15.12.22). See also 15.14.24–15.25; 15.21.40; 15.27.50; 14.10.13; 9.7.12–11.16, and esp. 9.12.18. It was in listening to a talk by David Dawson that my attention was drawn back to the inner word of *trin.* 15, and I have benefitted from his excellent and suggestive comments, now published as Dawson (1995).

23 "[T]he word which is neither uttered in sound nor thought of in the likeness of sound which necessarily belongs to some language, but which precedes all the signs (*signa*) that signify it and is begotten of the knowledge (*scientia*) abiding in the consciousness (*animo*), when this knowledge is uttered inwardly (*intus dicitur*) just exactly as it is" (*trin.* 15.11.20). Gunton (1991b), 44, cites this passage but ignores Augustine's crucial contextualization of it in his sign theory, aided by Burnaby's (1955) translation which translates "signa" as "tokens" (147). Augustine's distinctions, between the presignified and the signified, are evidence unobserved and unaccounted for by Gunton, who sees a distinction only between the "abstract" and the "concrete" or "material," distinctions which Augustine's categories seem to override (the inner word is not "abstract," but knowledge "intended" in some very concrete act of the will, and the "material" is itself an abstract, never entering human experience unmediated by culture).

24 Explained at *trin.* 14.7.10, the "inner word that is not part of any people's language," that is, the "thought formed" as the "offspring" of memory, is easier to observe in cases "where something crops up in time and where parent precedes offspring by an interval of time." These cases include all the "trinities" in Books 11, 12 and 13 (as Augustine explains at length at *trin.* 14.1.3, 14.3.5, 14.7.10, 14.8.11, 14.10.13), embracing all dealings with "sensible things" and "knowledge of human affairs" (14.7.10), and thus including all under the domain of "word production."

25 He normally respects the customs of speech in individual languages as valid; see, for example, the advice on translations at *doctr. chr.* 2.13.19.

26 "Nobody voluntarily does anything that he has not previously uttered as a word in his heart" (*trin.* 9.7.12); "so there are no human works which are not first uttered in the heart .... [W]e cannot have a work which is not preceded by a word" (*trin.* 15.11.20).

27 At least since the *doctr. chr.*, where not even illiterate eremitic ascetics are permitted a culturally unmediated understanding of Scripture, since all of them heard it read in a particular language which they had to learn at some point (*doctr. chr.*, preface 4–5), and since even the signs divinely given in the Bible are of the "conventional" type and were presented through human beings (*doctr. chr.* 2.2.3).

28 Augustine remarks further that there is no one so indifferent to the good of cultural life that "when they hear an unknown word they do not want to know what it means, and do not ask if they can," and presents an extensive discussion on this (*trin.* 10.1.2).

29 Strictly speaking, it is inappropriate to talk about as "imaging" God anything but the innermost trinity of the mind's memory, understanding, and love of itself remembering, understanding, and loving God, but Augustine himself warrants our extension of this language of imaging, if not of "image," from the innermost trinity to the "outer" trinities, and even to the "outer actions" which they produce (*trin.* 11.5.8). The implication is that the more reformed or transformed our innermost image, the less our actions will be "conformed to this age" (Rom. 12:2), and the more they will image God for others.

30 Described, in particular, in book 12; see esp. 12.8.13–11.16.

31 "Just as the devil in his pride brought proud-thinking man down to death ... so he holds him in subjection by his swollen self-esteem and his determined preference for power over justice" (*trin.* 4.10.13). Since the devil's pride makes him a "lover of power and deserter and opponent of justice" (*trin.* 13.13.17), and since human beings, in their studied devotion to power and their neglect of justice, have imitated him, God wills in Christ to conquer the devil not by power but by justice, a work of God's humility (*trin.* 13.14.18; cf. 15.19.34; 15.25.44).

32 The demons appeal to our preference for power over justice by flaunting the immortality and prodigies of their "airy" bodies over our weakness, and thus establish themselves as false "mediators" in superstitious rites (*trin.* 4.11.14–12.15; 4.13.18–14.19) and in false sciences such as soothsaying and divining (*trin.* 4.16.21–17.22, see 14.1.3; see also *doctr. chr.* 2.20.30–24.37). At *trin.* 12.9.14 and 12.11.16, the fall is analyzed as originating from the soul's inordinate love of its own power (*potestas*).

33 *trin.* 12.11.16, 12.14.21; see *trin.* 4.P.I. Note that, at *trin.* 12.11.16, it is the soul's attachment to power that leads it to the point where knowledge "puffs up." The theme is familiar from *doctr. chr.* 2.41.62; 2.42.63; etc.

34 The "intentional" character of signification, based on the involvement of the will, has been brought out well by Dawson (1995); as well as in Markus (1996), especially the sub-section "Augustine on Magic," 138–139.

35 See the "wine of error" drunk in with the exquisite and precious vessels of beautiful words (*conf.* 1.26). To put it another way, the usefulness and importance of the doctrine of the inner word is that it enables Augustine to show how human beings cannot simply transmit pure knowledge independent of value judgments. Knowledge cannot simply be read off the mind and replicated in the exterior world of sign. But the problem in the communication and signification of knowledge is not primarily the difficulty of representing what is "inner" in what is "outer" (a problem more characteristically emphasized by the earlier Augustine), but rather the difficulty that knowledge cannot be represented at all until it is "spoken" within, "conceived" by a love which binds it to the understanding as a word "begotten." And because the image of God within is distorted by original sin, by a primal preference for power over justice, our sign systems will inevitably be marked by and inevitably transmit this preference encoded into them, and so fail in their own way to "image" God effectively.

36 *trin.* 4.17.23, recalling *doctr. chr.* 2.18.28, and *conf.* 7.20.26. The philosophers have been able to ascend beyond creatures to a vision of the "light of unchangeable truth," but this very success only increases their pride because they seize their success as due to their own "power" or "virtue" (*virtute propria;* 4.15.20).

37 *trin.* 15.23.44–24.44. It is interesting to note that the soul, as the image of God, is a "mirror" which is also an "enigma," an obscure mirror (see 1 Cor. 13:12). Augustine indicates that "enigma" is a trope under the category of allegory, so that "every enigma is an allegory." Since, as Augustine points out, allegories can be things as well as texts (like the two sons of Abraham), the soul as image is thus the most fundamental or primary "allegory" we have (certainly after the fall but even before the fall, since, in its finiteness, it can only inadequately represent its eternal archetype (*trin.* 15.11.21–16.26). As in the case of the two sons of Abraham, so in any "enigma" or "obscure allegory," we need to be told that it *is* an allegory. It is the rule of faith which provides the interpretive key to this "allegory," and thus permits us to read this "text" (in the broadest sense of the word) as it should be read (see *trin.* 15.27.49; also 15.23.44–24.44, where, without faith, one doesn't know [that] the mind is an image; in a way then, it is the rule of faith which tells us we are not exhaustively identified by, or restricted to, whatever identity a given culture might assign us, but are each of us, properly "interpreted," the image of God).

38 *trin.* 15.11.20. This is a frequent theme in Augustine's preaching: see, for example, *s.* 28.5; 119.7; 288.4; 187.3; 223A.2; and esp. 225.3.

39 "And the reason why it was not God the Father, not the Holy Spirit, not the trinity itself, but only the Son who is the Word of God that became flesh (although it was the trinity that accomplished this) is that we might live rightly by our word following and imitating his example; that is, by our having no falsehood either in the contemplation or in the operation of our word .... To achieve it we are instructed by the Good Teacher in Christian faith and godly doctrine (*doctrina*), in order that we might be *transformed into the same image from glory to glory* [2 Cor. 3:13]" (*trin.* 15.11.20; compare the reference to transformation in the first line of *trin.* 15.11.21). *Doctrina* here refers not in the first instance to the content of the teaching (i.e., "Christian faith"), but to the act of communicating or teaching it. The same usage is found at *trin.* 13.2.5, where faith "comes by hearing" (Rom. 10:17, prominent in *doctr. chr.* 4 on preaching), impressed from one single (act or manner of) teaching on the hearts of all believers. It is appropriate that the Son and not the Father or Holy Spirit become incarnate because, precisely, as unique and eternal Word, he already is the Father's *doctrina* (*trin.* 1.12.27), "for the Father's teaching (*doctrina*) is the Father's Word, who is his only Son" (cf. 2.2.4). The Father's *doctrina* incarnate becomes the Good Teacher (Mt. 19:16; Mk. 10:17; Lk. 18:18).

40 Augustine notes, for example, that when we think of Jesus, it is not relevant that we do not picture his face exactly as it was. Just as in languages and other exterior signs of inner words, in the Incarnation, the particular sign is not as important as the love in which the inner word, represented by the sign, was begotten. It is the "love of God for us" that the Incarnation "demonstrates" or is a sign of. This is the "medicine" which heals the pride of our hearts (*trin.* 8.5.7), persuading us of what we need persuading of most, God's love for us (*trin.* 4.1.2). The Word of God made flesh "persuades" us not to despair over our mortality by demonstrating the "great value" God places on us (*trin.* 13.10.13); on Christ Incarnate as not merely God's Word but God's rhetoric or persuasive eloquence, see Cavadini (1995), 166 (reprinted in this volume, in pp. 28-29).

41 Using language taken from Rom. 12:2, the "reformation" of the image in a lifelong process of healing initiated and sustained by grace is described at *trin.* 14.16.22–19.25; see *trin.* 14.17.23, especially for the metaphors of healing. It is a "renewal" (*renovatio*) which does not occur "in a single moment of conversion," but in a life of "progress little by little," of "daily advances" in the "'recognition of God' [Col. 3:10], that is, in 'justice and holiness of truth' [Eph. 4:24]" (*trin.* 14.17.23).

42 The theme of *trin.* 13.11.15–16.21. The philosophers who "philosophized without the mediator" lacked precisely something to consider in the exterior realm, and so set up false mediators to help them obtain the heights they had fleetingly glimpsed (*trin.* 13.19.24).

References

Brown, Peter (1967) *Augustine of Hippo*. Berkeley, CA: University of California Press.

Burnaby, John, trans. (1955) *Augustine: Later Works*. Philadelphia, PA: Westminster Press.

Cavadini, John C. (1992) "The Structure and Intention of Augustine's *De trinitate*." *Augustinian Studies* 23: 103–123.

Cavadini, John C. (1995) "The Sweetness of the Word: Salvation and Rhetoric in Augustine's *De doctrina Christiana*." In *De doctrina Christiana: A Classic of Western Culture*, edited by Duane W. H. Arnold and Pamela Bright, 164–181. Notre Dame: University of Notre Dame.

Dawson, David (1995) "Sign Theory, Allegorical Reading, and the Motions of the Soul in *De doctrina Christiana*." In *De doctrina Christiana: A Classic of Western Culture*, edited by Duane W. H. Arnold and Pamela Bright, 217–243. Notre Dame: University of Notre Dame Press.

Gunton, Colin E. (1991a) "Trinity, Ontology and Anthropology." In *Persons, Divine and Human*, edited by Christoph Schwöbel and Colin E. Gunton, 47–61. Edinburgh: T. & T. Clark.

Gunton, Colin E. (1991b) *The Promise of Trinitarian Theology*. Edinburgh: T. & T. Clark.

Haddan, Arthur W., B. D, trans. (1887) *On the Trinity*, revised and annotated, together with an introductory essay by the Rev. Professor W. G. T. Shedd, D.D. Nicene and Post-Nicene Fathers ser. 1, vol. 3. Buffalo, NY: Christian Literature Publishing Co.

Hill, Edmund, O.P., trans. (1991) *The Trinity, WSA I/5*. Brooklyn, NY: New City Press.

Hill, Edmund, O. P., trans. (1996) *Teaching Christianity, WSA I/11*. New York: New City Press.

Markus, Robert A. (1996) *Signs and Meanings: World and Text in Ancient Christianity*. Liverpool: Liverpool University.

McKenna, Stephen, CSS.R, trans. (1963) *The Trinity, FC 45*. Washington, DC: The Catholic University of America Press.

Pelikan, Jaroslav (1987–1988) "*Canonica Regula:* The Trinitarian Hermeneutics of Augustine." *Proceedings of the PMR* 12 (13): 17–29.

4

Augustine's Book of Shadows

Introduction

What is book 2 of Augustine's *Confessions* (*conf.*) about? As with many things in the *conf.*, it depends on how you look at it. The *conf.* is one of those texts whose beauties emerge gradually to the person willing to read and reread over time, to one who is willing, too, to see its various facets from different perspectives. Sometimes, if you are looking in just the right direction, one facet glimmers out and seems to illuminate all of the others, and it is a source of further enjoyment and understanding to share these discoveries with others.

Book 2 contains, among other things, Augustine's depiction of his being carried away by the currents of youthful libido, some reminiscences of his father and mother, and the long, seemingly overscrupulous examination of conscience on the theft of pears he committed as a youth with a gang of other boys. Book 2 is therefore one of the more "infamous" books in the eyes of the interpreters of Augustine, not so much for the content itself, but for the proportion, or lack thereof, that the book seems to exhibit between its content and the rhetoric used to describe it. This is the book most likely to be cited for evidence of Augustine's propensity to overstatement, adducing, for example, his extravagance in obsession over an adolescent prank,[1] or his habit of indulging the luxurious language of sexual excess without, it is suspected, very much of actual excess to show for

---

Visioning Augustine, First Edition. John C. Cavadini.
© 2019 John Wiley & Sons Ltd. Published 2019 by John Wiley & Sons Ltd.

it.[2] He seems to say as much himself.[3] Book 2 is also, therefore, one of the prime loci for commentators who would deflate the rhetoric into the plainer terms of a more commonplace narrative readily seen, by the trained observer, to underlie the overstatement. For example, Augustine reserves some of his choicest words of filial contempt for his father to this book, while he treats Monica at one point as a virtual oracle, and this has proved irresistible to those looking for indications of the oedipal narrative as the underlying story.[4] The melodramatic language of overflowing and of uncontrolled flux seems to others to mask little more than the narrowly male narrative of loss of control over seminal emissions.[5] Perhaps, on the other hand, the prominence of the allusions to the Catiline conspiracy shows that the underlying story is one of social transgression, of acting against the established social order in turning to sexual excess instead of marriage.[6]

Another, more promising way of looking at book 2 comes from scholars who would see in it the narrative of Augustine's fall into "concupiscence of the flesh," the first of the three sins given in a catalogue at 1 Jn. 2:14 (the others being "concupiscence of the eyes," and *ambitio saeculi*, the vain ambition of the world).[7] Book 2 begins the pattern of Augustine's declension through each of these three sins, one per book through book 4, followed by a chiasmus of healing in books 6–8 in reverse order. The narrative of the fall in Gen. 2, mediated to the text through the allusive story of the theft of pears, stands as the master narrative of the fall into sexual concupiscence. Surely this reading of book 2 as the story of Augustine's fall into concupiscence of the flesh is correct, and yet this reading is far from rendering the rhetoric of Augustine invulnerable to the narrative-narrowing strategies mentioned earlier, especially if concupiscence of the flesh is taken as a kind of absolute. For one thing, as already noted, it still seems extravagantly overstated. Concupiscence of the flesh, if it stands on its own terms, seems unable to sustain the claims of the great magnitude of iniquity with which the lavish rhetoric of this book is weighted. If concupiscence of the flesh qua concupiscence of the flesh is the main reference of book 2's lament, such that it is the literal referent of all the narratives in the book (including the theft of pears as a kind of parable for the fall into concupiscence of the flesh, and even the Genesis narrative of the fall as mainly a story of the fall into this sin), then the text is still vulnerable to the strategies of reduction mentioned earlier, because the interpreter will always want to know what is at the bottom of the seemingly exaggerated (both to antique and to modern ears) worry over the universal experience of adolescent turbulence.[8]

The Empty Self[9]

A different tactic would be to try to find the story that, rather than being the one "underlying" the rhetoric, would be instead one larger than the rhetoric, as it were, something to which it can only point, but not in the end fully describe. After all, as a trained rhetor, Augustine had a good sense of how to match style with audience and subject.[10] Along these lines, let us begin our search with an image, programmatically and strategically placed in the very last words of the book, the image of the self reduced to a *regio egestatis*, a land of want or lack, a land of famine or of emptiness. Perhaps it is the saddest confession in the whole work: "I had made of myself a land of empty lack."[11] Book 2 is pervaded not only by fulsome rhetoric, but by sadness, the sadness of someone who has "emptied himself" not in the way Christ did, but in the sense of evacuating oneself of oneself in exchange for precisely nothing, of simply canceling the gift of selfhood in favor of nothing.[12] It is the sadness, or even pity,[13] of someone who has haplessly, if culpably, paid out his whole self to purchase nothing, and now has no leverage to get it back. The book is suffused with the sadness of the Prodigal at the moment he came to realize the extent and folly of his waste of his inheritance and his father's love,[14] and, in Augustine's case, the waste of his own precious self and of the love that had given it to him in the first place.

This sadness is therefore present in the text as evoked by an act of memory. Book 2 begins with the words *Recordari colo*, "I want to call to mind," and so sets its sadness in a particular rhetorical structure, not as the memory of how he felt as he was experiencing lust, but of the memory of that time from the perspective of the one who realized finally what was happening and was accepted back in love. It is the sadness of narration created in the memory of someone who had squandered the joy of having a self, having learned to love emptiness instead, and contrasted with the joy of receiving oneself back only "late,"[15] and only as a complete gift out of the "ruin" or "want" he had made of it. It is the act of memory, pervading the narrative with a

sadness that was not present at the time itself, that forms the poles of
the rhetoric of this book, charging it with emotion and generating all
of the striking rhetorical paradoxes of the book: "There was a time ...
when I was afire to take my fill of hell" (*conf.* 2.1.1, *exarsi enim aliquando
satiari inferior*); "I was in love with my own ruin" (*conf.* 2.4.9, *amavi
perire*). The rhetorical paradoxes arising out of the sadness of memory
give expression to the larger rhetorical or narrative problem of book
2. It is, in a way, a major rhetorical problem of the whole of the *conf.*,
namely, how do you give an account of something for which there is
no accounting? Putting together the first and last phrases of the book
demonstrates the problem: "I would like to call to mind" (*conf.* 2.1.1)
how "I made myself into an empty land of want" (*conf.* 2.10.18). But
how can you construct a narrative of the passage into incoherence,
something the very essence of which is irrational, so that to try to
account for it would be, in effect, to push it past its own inherent
unintelligibility, to make it accessible to thought and reflection? The
rhetorical paradoxes say it all: How can I account for my burning
desire for the hellish? For my love of my own perishing? Apart from
the paradoxes that evoke the problem, any attempt to reduce what
they represent to narrative logic will have caused the incoherence to
be lost in the coherence of the narrative. The narrative will have been
narrowed to a "logical" account.

Why does Augustine tell his story? Not so much for God, but for
fellow members of the human race, "So that I and whoever reads this
might think together about how deep is that depth from which we cry
to you."[16] It is the description or evocation of that depth, the depth
from which the psalmist cries, that Augustine hopes to accomplish
with his narration. But here is the narrative problem, once again. In
order to render that depth, he has to collect himself from it: "recalling
my most wicked ways (*recolens vias meas nequissimas*) and thinking over
the past with bitterness ... I will try now to give a coherent account
of my disintegrated self (*conligens me a dispersione*), for when I turned
away from you ... and pursued a multitude of things, I went to pieces"
(*dum ab imo te aversus in multa evanui, conf.* 2.1.1). The *conligens* here cannot refer to his actual reconstitution from dispersal, since that was
God's doing and has already happened. Rather, the participle is parallel
to *recolens*, so the "collecting" is to be done in the recalling, the remembering, the narrating: it is the narrative problem of "collecting" a self
which has "disappeared" or "evaporated" (*evanui*) into incoherence.

How can one remember or "re-cultivate" where there is only a void of dissipation, a wasteland, in a sense no subject to have a memory of, a scorched earth rendered sterile? The memory of such a depth of der-eliction is the sadness or, as it is put more strongly in this passage, the "bitterness" (*amaritudo*) that pervades this book.

The key to Augustine's resolution of this problem is to see how, in book 2 the fall into concupiscence of the flesh is, surely, to be taken literally, but not merely literally. Augustine's "unquiet adolescence" (*conf.* 2.3.6) becomes the interpretation or presence of the "unquiet heart" (*conf.* 1.1.1), the heart that has not rested in God but promiscuously tried to rest everywhere else instead. Augustine's illicit love affairs are described in a way that presents a veritable feast of restless motion: "I was tossed to and fro, I poured myself out, was made to flow away in all directions and boiled off" (*conf.* 2.2.2; my translation). The result of this restless motion is expressed later in terms that keep with the metaphor of flowing and boiling: *evanui*, "I evaporated [into the nothingness of dispersion]."[17] Augustine's for-nications are, though real fornications, precisely, as such, figures of the underlying evaporation and dispersal of the self. As literal fornications, they are themselves representations, they are *res* ("things, realities") that are *signa* ("signs"), to use the language of the contemporaneous book 2 of *doctr. chr.* The very indeterminate character of the references to the sexual sins, far from serving a purpose of empty "titillation,"[18] serves to keep the language open rather than closed. It keeps the sin described open enough to mediate a sense of the spiritual state it reflects, the state of the wasting away of the self with all its beauty (*contabuit species mea*) in the pursuit of "shadowy loves." Here, the very phrase *umbrosis amoribus* ("shadowy loves," *conf.* 2.1.1; my translation) is just determinate enough to refer to furtive physical trysts, but indeterminate enough to make those trysts themselves stand for the deeper, darker loves, the sterile seed of which they are but the useless fruit.[19] As Augustine explains:

> A soul that turns away from you therefore lapses into fornication when it seeks apart from you what it can never find in pure and limpid form except by returning to you.[20]

Fornication itself is a kind of figure here for abandoning God, who is pictured as a Lover in whose embraces we find ourselves and can take

joy in ourselves as God's.[21] Augustine in this sentence gives us the
literary key to the book, effortlessly, since this use of the word *fornicatio*
is common in his oeuvre.[22] The *umbra*, "shadows," of the "shadowy
loves" are identified here, too: "Behold! Here is that servant who,
fleeing from his Lord, went to hide in the shadows!"[23] – unmistakably
a reference to Adam, who fled from the Lord after his sin (Gen. 3:8,
10). But the only shadows Adam could find was the darkness of his sin
itself, that pride (*superbia*) barely named in the narrative,[24] but evoked
as the "shadowy similitude of omnipotence," the nowhere and nothing of perverse independence from God that is the only refuge of
the dissipated, disfigured self, lost in its bitterness: *O monstrum vitae
et mortis profunditas!* ("What a parody of life in death's deep!"; *conf.*
2.6.14; my translation). More than any other in the *conf.*, book 2 is the
Book of Shadows, of insubstantiality, of emptiness, of want.

The Pear Tree: Empty Companionship

This mention of the servant who fled from his Lord occurs in the
middle of Augustine's recounting of his theft of pears with a gang of
other youths,[25] and its presence there is enough to tie the story
conclusively to the narrative of the fall in Gen. 3, if the parallels of
forbidden fruit and the plucking of it were not already enough. What
is the function of this evocation of the biblical narrative? It is nothing
less than the solution of the narrative problem of book 2. It is this
narrative, in itself opaque in its declaration of a mystery, that renders
all the other narratives of evil transparent, and makes them windows
to a deeper narrative, the one of the fall of Adam and Eve. Its opacity
is the fruitful opacity characteristic of all authoritative biblical narratives for Augustine. The Bible in its simplicity, as Augustine will
explain later, blunts the pride of the would-be interpreter and his or
her easy assumptions that the divine letters will carry no more than
the rhetorical products of the schools would. Scripture is a thing
"veiled in mysteries," opaque to the proud whose sight cannot penetrate its interior parts or inner meaning, while for the humble these
very narratives, as it were, grow up with them.[26] In book 2, therefore,
the allusion to the Genesis narrative of the fall does anything but
return the narrative to the level of literal fornication (as though the
story of the fall were simply itself a story of a fall into *concupiscentia*

carnis ["concupiscence of the flesh"]). Instead, the presence of the Genesis narrative in the tale of the theft of pears, and so in the surrounding story of Augustine's fall into *concupiscentia carnis*, serves to make these other narratives a conduit into the master narrative, which itself remains opaque, irreducibly veiled with mystery. All the other narratives become windows onto this mystery, partake of its irreducibility in the very process of becoming transparent to it. Augustine's physical fornication, as an image (and instance) of the fornication of the soul dissipating itself into the embrace of everything and anything besides its true, divine Lover, becomes a symbol of the irreducibly mysterious evil of fleeing from the Creator to hide in a self independent of the Creator, a self that evaporates in that very fleeing.

The story of the pear theft, linked as it is to the story in Genesis, is an especially clear instance of a narrative window onto the primal scene of the fall narrative, a particularly powerful evocation of the mystery at the heart of the fall narrative. Augustine will go on later to exegete the fall narrative without the aid of a parable drawn from his own life. In *City of God*, book 14, he tells the story of how Adam and Eve's sin, though merely the plucking of a fruit, was so heinous because there was no possible particular motivation for it. They had absolutely everything they wanted there – food, comfort, companionship, even sex if they had desired it – nor was there anything in Eden to provoke fear. Their sin was therefore a fully deliberate act of pride.[27] And, although Augustine only elaborates on this text in this way years after the writing of the *conf.*, the pear tree story is meant to serve in the same way as this more discursive later exegesis. Augustine's rhetoric builds up the significance of the story of the pear theft precisely by emphasizing the trivial and motiveless character of the theft itself. The rhetorical minimization of the deed itself is a way of telling us that the story points beyond its own letter, almost erasing the letter of the story itself in favor of the Genesis narrative of the fall. That is another way of saying that it serves as a commentary or an exegesis of the Genesis narrative.

So, for example, as Augustine tries to analyze his motivation for the theft, he finds nothing in particular that could have motivated him. As with Adam and Eve in the garden, he was under no compulsion of need, but lived in the midst of abundance, at least as far as pears were concerned:

> I was under no compulsion of need .... I already had plenty of what I
> stole, and of much better quality too, and I had no desire to enjoy it
> when I resolved to steal it .... We took enormous quantities, not to
> feast on ourselves but perhaps to throw to the pigs .... We derived
> pleasure from the deed simply because it was forbidden (*conf.* 2.4.9).

Augustine's rhetoric drives relentlessly toward the conclusion that
there was no reason for him to have committed this act, as he goes
over the kinds of specific motivations that usually prompt one to sin
(*conf.* 2.5.10): "Even Catiline did not love his criminal acts for their
own sake, but only the advantages he had in view when committing
them" (*conf.* 2.6.12). Here, we have come right to the deep, or, in this
case, more emphatically, "the depths of the abyss" (*conf.* 2.4.9), from
which we cry to God:

> Look upon my heart, O God, look upon this heart of mine, on which
> you took pity in its abysmal depths (*in imo abyssi*). Enable my heart to
> tell you now what it was seeking in this action which made me bad for
> no reason, in which there was no motive for my malice except malice
> (*conf.* 2.4.9).

This malice is irreducible to any further account, or accounting for it:

> The malice was loathsome, and I loved it. I was in love with my own
> ruin, in love with decay: not with the thing for which I was falling into
> decay but with decay itself (*conf.* 2.4.9).

How to explain this without explaining it away? It must be linked to
the biblical narrative, which presents this mystery (of loving one's own
decay) in an authoritative fashion and so ratifies its opacity, its irreducibility to any further narrative except as an exegesis of the Genesis
text. The story of the pear tree, as a kind of window onto the biblical
scene, must be taken finally as just such an exegesis. There is simply no
accounting for such an irrational act except insofar as it can serve to
illustrate the biblical narrative.[28]

Augustine peers closer and closer at his sin in an examination that,
as already indicated, has seemed obsessive for such a trivial incident,
but it is just its triviality that Augustine belabors:

What did I love in you, O my theft, what did I love in you, the nocturnal crime of my sixteenth year? There was nothing beautiful about you, for you were nothing but a theft. Are you really anything at all, for me to be speaking to you like this? (*conf.* 2.6.12).

Augustine reiterates that he did not want the pears themselves:

I had plenty of better ones, and I plucked them only for the sake of stealing, for once picked I threw them away. I feasted on the sin, nothing else, and that I relished and enjoyed (*conf.* 2.6.12).

He remarks that his theft did not even have the "sham, shadowy beauty with which even vice allures us" (*conf.* 2.6.12), and he gives examples of these (*conf. 2.6.13*). Augustine's relentless rhetorical examination makes the story of the sin efface its own "letter." The sin is rhetorically constructed into a direct window, unobstructed by the particularities of wants and desires, onto the essence of sin itself. But since there is, in fact, no essence to sin, it cannot be represented except by referral to the authoritative narrative that preserves the original sin in all its mysterious and irreducible emptiness. Not even the story of Catiline, oddly enough, can stand in as an adequate account of evil in its "essence," for Catiline was, after all, seeking money and power (*conf.* 2.5.11). The story of the Catiline conspiracy may rank in Roman imagination as an archetypal tale of evil, but for Augustine the obvious and finally pedestrian nature of Catiline's motivation precludes one from seeing past it to a more profound, staggeringly abysmal depth. It must yield to the biblical account as the archetypal narrative of evil.

After considering all of the alternatives, Augustine comes to the short section, *conf.* 2.6.14, from which we have already taken many passages, and which is in a way the key to the whole of book 2. Here, the governing themes of fornication – of turning away from God in the quest for a self-subsistent existence without God, the consequent lapse into the insubstantiality of shadow and death, and allusion to the Genesis text – all come together. Every soul that commits fornication, turning away from its Creator and Lover to set itself up against him and apart from him, thereby tries to replace God – that is, "perversely imitates" God. But such a soul only achieves a "crippled liberty," which, if it has any agency at all, has it only in shadows, in darkness, furtively, like a thief. It is the liberty of a "prisoner" (*conf.* 2.6.14). Augustine's theft is an image of Adam's fleeing the Lord because it demythologizes the attempt to replace the Omnipotent. Far from looking like something glorious, something terrifically evil like Catiline, or like a grandiose mythical rebellion such as that of Zeus against Kronos, the best image of pure or archetypal evil is something so unpoetic as an adolescent prank carried out in the dark whose uttermost success resulted "at best" (*vel, conf.* 2.4.9) in a few more satisfied pigs. At the bottom, evil is unglamorous and irrational, the seeking out and enjoying of a radical constriction of the self, leaving the warmth of a lover's close embrace for the insubstantiality of a shadow. Why? "How like that servant of yours who fled from his Lord and hid in the shadows!" (*conf.* 2.6.14). Here, Augustine brings us rhetorically to the edge of the abyss out of which we cry to God in a passage we have already quoted once: *O putredo, O monstrum vitae et mortis profunditas!* "What rottenness! What a misshapen life! Rather a hideous pit of death!" (*conf.* 2.6.14). And he got us here through a literary exegesis of the narrative in Genesis that presents the irreducible mystery of someone who did what was wrong simply because it was wrong.

In its poignant statement of gratitude to God, the next section (*conf.* 2.7.15) serves to evoke this abyss in a different way, more explicitly from the perspective of having been rescued from it. Augustine asks God what he could repay God for being able to recall all of these things without fear.[29] "Without fear" because God forgave the sins and so there is no penalty, but also perhaps because he can call these things to mind without fear that he is slipping back into the abyss. He is clinging to God in the very confession of God's mercy and grace, which not only forgave him his past sins, but gave him the power to refrain from the sins he did not commit: "For what deed is there I could not do, I who loved a gratuitous, unprofitable crime?"[30] To remember the crime is to remember the abyss of the self which loved a crime without reason. To look on that abyss without fear is to have freedom in clinging to God in the act of confession: *ut amem te,* "let me love you," Augustine had told God at the outset. In this love, there is no fear of the fornication of the soul, the fornication of even the physically chaste soul, which would ascribe its bodily chastity to itself, and not to God, so that it might "love God less."[31] Such a soul, though physically chaste, is at the edge of the abyss, desperately trying to love

God less as it ascribes more to its own power. We are all this close to the abyss, perhaps *especially* in our chastity; and yet, in acknowledging this closeness and God's mercy in keeping us from falling in, we have, in this very vulnerability and dependence (even though it may seem like insubstantiality), the solid freedom of God's creatures when they cling to him in love. It is in this paragraph, it seems, where the confession of God's mercy is at once a memory of the joy of being rescued in the nick of time (*O tardum gaudium meum!* "O my joy, how long I took to find you!" *conf.* 2.2.2), and a self-awareness of how we all still hover at the verge of self-destruction. This is made the most poignant moment in book 2 by the fact that this self-destruction is the irrational love of death instead of a Lover's embrace, in the awareness that we have absolutely nothing to repay God for all of this love and mercy, no leverage over God whatsoever, not even our virtues.

The book ends, though, with a return to the recollection of the theft of pears. Augustine reemphasizes that he received no benefit, no "fruit" literally or metaphorically, no "enjoyment" or "gratification" from his theft, but only more unhappiness.[32] Yet, as Augustine goes on to point out, he (like Adam)[33] would not have done it alone. This final pass over the inscrutable does resolve the love involved, irrational as it may have been, one degree of magnitude further. Augustine says he loved the *consortium*, the fellowship of those with whom he committed the sin. Augustine loved nothing but the crime, but would not have loved doing it alone, but only in the company of others. The pleasure was in the crime committed with others who were sinning at the same time: "it [my pleasure] must have been in the crime as committed in the company of others who shared the sin."[34] But what kind of love or emotion is this?[35] Why would it not have been thrilling to steal alone, but only together?[36] The only thing one cannot have alone is praise, and there is no worthy "similitude of omnipotence" unless there is praise: "When someone says, 'Let's go! Let's do it!' I feel shamed not to be shameless."[37] The little band of thieves is a kind of mutual admiration society,[38] praising each other for doing something that they did just because it was forbidden, for breaking the law just to break it. Pride is not something that can be enjoyed alone, for there must be others to praise you, even if present only by the social conventions that make something praiseworthy or prestigious, such as the orthographic and rhetorical conventions that mark praiseworthy speech.[39] Augustine's little band of young thieves becomes an image of the sinful fellowship of Adam and Eve, as well as an analytical image of the society depicted in book 1, a society bound together by conventions of speech that enable one to be praised without being virtuous, where it is easy to seem larger than life simply by one's pronunciation.

In fact, this passage, describing a fellowship or friendship based upon mutual admiration in breaking God's law, is tied to other passages in this book and book 1. For example, Augustine notes that he was ashamed to follow the counsel of his mother, a woman, to be at least somewhat chaste. By contrast, he was part of a group of friends who boasted about their excesses, glorying in them and expecting to receive praise for their stories:

> When I heard other youths of my own age bragging about their immoralities I was ashamed to be less depraved than they. The more disgraceful their deeds, the more credit they claimed; and so I too became as lustful for the plaudits as for the lechery itself.[40]

He goes on to remark, in a passage already noted (in note 3), that he even made up vices so that he would not be caught without something about which to boast. Augustine is following the example of his teachers, who, he reports in book 1, would be embarrassed to commit a barbarism while narrating some blameless deed they committed, but would happily seek praise by narrating licentious deeds in perfect Latin.[41]

Lust is something that is against the Creator's law, but licensed by human custom:"The frenzy of lust imposed its rule on me ... licensed by disgraceful human custom, but illicit before your laws."[42] To put it another way, lust is something forbidden that one can brag about. The deeds committed in lust are praiseworthy, but only to a fellowship bent on breaking the laws of the Creator. Not to try to curtail the lust of one's offspring is to participate in the underlying fellowship that sanctions lust in the first place. This is the position of both of Augustine's parents: "Yet none of my family made any attempt to avert my ruin by arranging a marriage for me; their only concern was that I should learn to excel in rhetoric and persuasive speech."[43] In their own desire to have their offspring become the most persuasive, and thus the most prestigious, speaker possible, they don't take care that he be married. It would thwart his career. Augustine's father is particularly guilty. His overweening ambition (*animositas, conf.* 2.3.5) to get his son an education at all costs is praised by everyone, but he did not care that Augustine be chaste. He cared only that he got an education so that he might be skilled in speaking, *disertus*, and yet, by these very actions, his father was actually seeing to it that he became a void, an empty place, *desertus*, far from the cultivating (*cultura*) of God. Augustine's father sees to it that he becomes a member in good standing of the fellowship of the world, the *consortium* of those sinning together and praising each other for it. He is the author, in a way, of his son's emptiness. Augustine's father is a symbol of the culture at large and its lust to propagate its own sterility.[44] The parable of the Prodigal Son, as it is evoked in book 2, has the effect not only of indicating the distance that Augustine travels away from God, but of indicating the distance between his own physical father and that of the father in the parable. Augustine's father is completely unsuited for that role. The "bitterness" of remembering that is infused into this book of the *conf.* is in part bitterness at the shocking distance between the father of the parable and Augustine's own father, who not only did not rescue his own son from emptiness, but positively cultivated it in him.

Conclusion

Where in the *conf.* is book 2, as it were, completed? The spell it casts of sadness and bitterness is dissipated only slowly in the text, persisting unabated until book 5, when Augustine finally meets someone else he is willing to refer to, even if briefly, as "fatherly," namely Ambrose.[45] As "father" to Augustine, Ambrose is the symbol of the exegetical culture of humility, which he propagates in Augustine. Later, amid tears, Augustine is comforted by the figure of Continence in book 8, and in joy he interprets Ps. 4 in book 9. But there is still plenty of sadness to go around in book 9, as we read of the deaths of his friends, his son, and his mother, and the same is lingeringly true for book 10 as we listen to Augustine's struggles with temptations. His lament about the lateness of God as Joy to him is the most direct echo of book 2 in the latter part of the *conf.* It is not until the final book that the story of book 2 comes to a close and its sadness is finally dissipated. It is there that Augustine gives the praise of confession as he unfolds the narrative in Genesis, and uses the story of creation from nothing as a figure for God's re-creation of the self from the nothingness of sin.[46] It is only with book 13 that, in a sense, we complete our reflection, with Augustine, on the "depths out of which we cry" to God, for it is there that we recognize those depths as the primal nothingness out of which we came by God's gratuitous act. But having read book 2, we can also recognize this nothingness better, as the nothingness to which, by our own inscrutable choice, we had burned to return. When we recognize how far we had retreated into this nothingness, and the gratuitous love by which God re-created us, we are in a renewed position to see the goodness of the original creation, which came equally gratuitously from God's love. Against the Manichees, we can, from the perspective of a narrative of redemption, see creation in its beauty for the first time, unencumbered by pride or bitterness, and so understand both ourselves as God's creation, and the narrative of Genesis, which declares that truth. We can offer the "sacrifice of praise" in which all bitterness and sadness has been forgotten in the joy of the fecundity of love, enriching all the earth with fruits of charity and vision, as we enjoy fellowship (*consortium*) in witness to God's goodness, the culture of true praise. The story of book 2 is completed only when the narrative from Genesis, present in book 2 only by allusion, in shadow and figure, can be spoken explicitly, in the heartfelt voice of joyful praise that is confession.[47]

Acknowledgments

An earlier version of this chapter was published by Westminster John Knox Press as Cavadini, J. C. (2003) "Augustine's Book of Shadows." In *A Reader's Companion to Augustine's Confessions*, edited by Kim Paffenroth and Robert P. Kennedy, 25–34. Westminster: John Knox Press. Reproduced with permission.

Notes

1 In a letter to a friend, Nietzsche (see 1975, 3.3.34) singled out Augustine's comments on his theft of the pears and his expression of grief for his childhood friend (*conf.* 4.7.11). He is a kind of forerunner of the twentieth-century critiques we will mention. At one point, he exclaims in exasperation, "Oh these ancient rhetoricians! How false! How outlandish!" – and Nietzsche goes on to criticize Augustine's high-flown rhetoric and "psychological falsity." These passages are cited in O'Donnell (1992), 2:227.

2   For example, see Brown (1967), 39. See also the comment of O'Donnell (1992), 2:104: "There is little here that is so unusual: adolescent sexual profligacy of a sort that seemed inconceivable to some of our pious ancestors, but that is less so today and was certainly far less so in antiquity."

3   When the time came to brag about them, he seemed to find his libidinous behavior not quite up to standards: "… and when I had no indecent acts to admit that could put me on a level with these abandoned youths, I pretended to obscenities I had not committed, lest I might be thought less courageous for being more innocent, and be accounted cheaper for being more chaste" (*conf.* 2.3.7), translated by Boulding (1997). Unless otherwise noted, all translations are Boulding's.

4   For example, Kligerman (1990), Bakan (1990), and Dittes (1990), as well as the interesting critique by Burrell (1990) – all four to be found in Capps and Dittes (1990).

5   For one example, see Miles (1992b), 98.

6   Courcelle (1971) gave this the most prominence of anyone, without necessarily drawing the conclusions about marriage.

7   Crosson (1989), and O'Donnell (1992), 1:xxxv–xxxvi, 2:127.

8   This seems to be the implication of O'Donnell's (1992) mention of the fall passage (2:126–127: "The parallel to the fruit of the tree of good and evil in the Garden dominates …. The result for Adam and Eve was that their eyes were opened '*ad invicem concupiscendum*' [citing *Gen. litt.* (*On the Literal Interpretation of Genesis*) 11.31.40]"). But O'Donnell is right to point out that the belaboring of the incident is not out of an exaggerated sense of guilt on Augustine's part (2127).

9   For further development of this theme, see Chapter 7.

10   Nowhere insisted upon more strongly perhaps than in his *doctr. chr.*, though not until book 4, which was written much later than the *conf.* A more nearly contemporaneous statement of the principle would be in *cat. rud.*, 1.15.23, 1.8.12–9.13, written some 5 years after *conf.*

11   "Factus sum mihi regio egestatis," *conf.* 2.10.18, my translation.

12   Compare the closing of book 1, with its image of the beautiful little boy who is totally God's gift, and on the other hand the emptiness left by the time we get to book 2. Moving from one image to another, we can gauge the depth of the sadness on which the rhetoric of book 2 flows.

13   The evocations of the mercy of God in retrospect lend to the prose the invitation to show mercy or have pity on the hapless subject of the narrative, upon whom God is taking mercy even in his seeming silence, and in Augustine's ignorance of it (see *conf.* 2.3.7).

14   On the theme of the Prodigal Son (Lk. 15:11–32) in the *conf.*, see Ferrari (1977). See also O'Donnell (1992), 2:95–98. As with all scriptural texts except for the Psalms, this passage is present by allusion only in book 2: in the image

of the young man exiled from his father's house (2.2.4), the reference to the pigs (2.4.9), and the closing image of the land of want. Augustine had introduced this parable explicitly at *conf.* 1.18.28, so these echoes refer back not only to the parable itself but to Augustine's preparation for them in book 1.

15   We do not have to wait for book 10 for this pole of memory to appear: here it is in book 2, which first sets out the narrative poles of the rhetoric. "O my joy, how long I took to find you!" (*O tardum gaudium meum!*), the narrator laments at 2.2.2 (literally, "O my late Joy"; cf. 10.27.38, *sero te amavi*, "late have I loved you!").

16   *conf.* 2.3.5, echoing Ps. 129:1, my translation ("ut videlicet ego et quisquis haec legit cogitemus de quam profundo clamandum sit ad te").

17   *conf.* 2.1.1, my translation.

18   Cf. Miles (1992b), 50. The vagueness has even led to speculation that Augustine's youthful lust was homosexual in orientation: Smith (1980), 34–36.

19   Note the language of sterility that pervades the book (see, e.g., also at 2.3.5 the image of Augustine's self as a desert or wasteland, and the final image of the empty land of want). Cf. O'Donnell (1992), 2:111, on the phrase "sterilia semina" ("sterile seeds") in 2.2.2.

20   *conf.* 2.6.14: "ita fornicatur anima, cum avertitur abs te et quaerit extra te ea. quae pura et liquida non invenit, nisi cum redit ad te."

21   *conf.* 2.2.3, "amplexus."

22   In the *conf.* itself, we should note at least that it has already occurred in book 1, in a context where there is no question of literal fornication (1.13.21). See O'Donnell's (1992) comment (2:78). See my article on pride in Fitzgerald et al. (1999), 679–684. Note the connection between *libido* and the wanderings of the prodigal at 1.18.28, exhibiting the same connection between lust in its sexual sense and wandering from God. As an example of what happens when the rhetoric denouncing fornication is taken too literally and then applied directly to sexual ethics, here is a comment by Cahill (2001): "Margaret Miles even describes Augustine as a sex addict, although it is difficult to weigh his level of actual compulsiveness against his overwhelming revulsion in the face of sexual drives and reactions, especially in view of the fact that they represented to him a shameful lack of control" (188, citing Miles 1992a, 134). Both the ascription of sexual addiction and the qualification of it in terms of revulsion take Augustine's rhetoric as referring to the literal sin alone. In the case of the charge of sexual addiction, this assumes that the rhetoric matches the literal reality; in the case of "overwhelming revulsion," this assumes that the rhetoric is meant to refer to literal events that either did not happen or are grossly exaggerated (by revulsion).

23   *conf.* 2.6.14: "ecce est ille servus fugiens dominum suum et consecutus umbram." Cf. Job 7:2, a text Augustine connected to Gen. 3:8 elsewhere: see O'Donnell (1992), 2:139. The "Ecce est" tells us that somehow this servant, Adam, is present

in this, the narrative of Augustine that the reader is reading or to which the listener is listening.

24 Clearly mentioned ("the punishment for my soul's pride," *poena superbiae animae meae*) in 2.2.2, where the phrase "abased by my pride," *superba deiectione*, also connects pride with the ejection from God's face, which is an allusion to Gen. 3:8, 10. The infrequency with which this sin, underlying all other sin, is named is related to the way in which Augustine wants to depict the essence, or really the anti-essence, of sin as precisely shadowy, precisely *not* a substance. If there is a trinity of sin taken from 1 Jn. 2:14, each of these "personae" are con-non-substantial in the underlying non-essence of sin, pride, if I may speak so archly. On words used for pride in the *conf.* in the sense meant here, see O'Donnell (1992), 2:170.

25 The story, with Augustine's reflections on the incident, takes up chapters 4–9 (2.4.9–9.17). See Ferrari (1970).

26 Cf. *conf.* 3.5.9: Scripture is "something veiled in mystery" ("rem velatam myteriis") such that it is "not accessible to the scrutiny of the proud." For this reason, Augustine could not appreciate it: "My swollen pride recoiled from its style and my intelligence failed to penetrate its inner meaning" ("tumor enim meus refugiebat modum eius et acies mea non penetrabat interiora eius").

27 *ciu.*, 14.12, written ca. 418. (For the date, see Brown [1967], 284.)

28 Any account that would give a reason for it has to deny the story, has to say he really *was* after something, and it's *this*. The link to the biblical account precludes these reductionisms in favor of exegesis of that account.

29 "How can I repay the Lord for my ability to recall these things without fear?" (*Quid retribuam domino quod recolit haec memoria mea et anima mea non meruit inde?*) *conf.* 2.7.15; cf. Ps. 116:12.

30 "Quid enim non facere potui, qui etiam gratuitum facinus amavi?" (*conf.* 2.7.15), here disagreeing with Boulding's translation of "wanton" for *gratuitum*, for it is precisely the gratuitous character of his sin that he has been emphasizing all along, not its unruliness (which is present but as a feature derivative from its primary character as irrational).

31 "Quis est hominum qui suam cogitans infirmitatem audet viribus suis tribuere castitatem atque innocentiam suam, ut minus amet te, quasi minus ei necessaria fuerit misericordia tua, qua donas peccata conversis ad te?" (*conf.* 2.7.15), disagreeing again here with the translation of Maria Boulding, which seems to miss the parallelism of purpose between the *ut* of the opening *ut amem*, and this *ut*. The parallelism highlights the perversity of wanting to do something *in order to* love God less.

32 "What fruit did I ever reap … from that theft in which I found nothing to love except the theft itself, wretch that I was? It was nothing, and by the very act of committing it I became more wretched still" (*quem fructum habui miser in illo furto in quo ipsum furtum amavi, nihil aliud, cum et ipsum esset nihil et eo ipso ego miserior*), *conf.* 2.8.16.

33 See *ciu.* 14.12.

34 "ea [voluptas mibi] erat in ipso facinore quam faciebat consortium simul peccantium" (*conf.* 2.8.16).

35 *conf.* 2.9.17, and who understands sins anyway, he adds rhetorically, "delicta quis intellegit?" – echoing Ps. 18:13 and using it to state the rhetorical problem of the book.

36 *conf.* 2.9.17: "The theft gave us a thrill, and we laughed to think we were out-witting people who had no idea what we were doing, and would angrily stop us if they knew. Why could I not have derived the same pleasure from doing it alone?" (*risus erat quasi titillato corde, quod fallebamus eos qui haec a nobis fieri non putabant et vehementer nolebant. Cur ergo eo me defectabat quo id non faciebam solus?*)

37 *conf.* 2.9.17: "Cum dicitur, 'eamus, faciamus,' et pudet non esse impudentem."

38 As such, it is an image in miniature, not to mention parody, of the society described in book 1, bound together in a lust for praise (apart from the praise of God), where the social bonds, located in this shared desire for praise, are collectively "fornication" (1.13.21). This is the "friendship of the world" (*amicitia enim mundi huius fornicatio est abs te*), and the *consortium* of teenage thieves, their *nimis inimica amicitia*, is an image of it meant to deglamorize the quest for praise and prestige so pointedly described in book 1.

39 *conf.* 1.13.22, 1.18.29.

40 *conf.* 2.3.7: "inter coaetaneos meos puderet me minoris dedecoris, quoniam audiebam eos iactantes flagitia sua et tanto gloriantes magis, quanto magis turpes essent, et libebat facere non solum libidine facti verum etiam laudis."

41 See, for example, *conf.* 1.18.28.

42 *conf.* 2.2.3: "accepit in me sceptrum vesania libidinis, licentiosae per dedecus humanum, inlicitae autem per leges tuas."

43 *conf.* 2.2.3: "Non fuit cura meorum ruentem excipere me matrimonio, sed cura fuit tantum ut discerem sermonem facere quam optimum et persuadere dictione."

44 Augustine's *concupiscentia carnis* could be tied to the praise of the Creator by letting it wash up on the shores of the marriage bed (*conf.* 2.2.3), where it would be turned to the "use" of procreating children. This "use" is part of the work of the Creator and Redeemer, because lust as such is not formative but dissipative. Yet, the Creator "forms the offspring of our mortality" through it, and so, through marriage, lust tends toward form (see Cavadini [2005], reprinted in this volume). But, in this text, this possibility recedes into the withering power of the rhetoric that Augustine generates to describe the spilling out of the self that lust both is and stands for. Lust is the most intimate symbol or sacrament of the fall, the one that brings it closest to our persons, and so the one that gives rise to the saddest cases of illusion and self-deception – as Dante shows as he por-trays himself fainting at Francesca's story, the only sinner's story that causes such a reaction in the *Inferno*.

45 *conf.* 5.13.23: "this man of God welcomed me with a fatherly kindness" (*suscepit me paterne ille homo dei*).

46 For Augustine on creation out of nothing, see Cavadini (2018).

47 I would like to thank Nancy Cavadini, Larry Cunningham, Cyril O'Regan, and Jean Porter for reading this chapter and offering advice and assistance.

References

Bakan, David (1990) "Augustine's *Confessions:* The Unentailed Self." In *The Hunger of the Heart: Reflections on the Confessions of Augustine*, ed. Donald Capps and James Dittes, 109–105. West Lafayette: Society for the Scientific Study of Religion.

Boulding, Maria, O.S.B., trans. (1997) *Confessions. WSA I/1*, edited by John E. Rotelle, Hyde Park, NY: New City Press.

Brown, Peter (1967) *Augustine of Hippo*. Berkeley, CA: University of California Press.

Burrell, David (1990) "Reading the *Confessions* of Augustine: The Case of Oedipal Analyses." In *The Hunger of the Heart: Reflections on the Confessions of Augustine*, ed. Donald Capps and James Dittes, 133–142. West Lafayette: Society for the Scientific Study of Religion.

Cahill, Lisa Sowle (2001) "Sex, Marriage, and Family in Christian Tradition." In *Sexuality, Marriage, and Family: Readings in the Catholic Tradition*, edited by Paulinus Ikechukwu Odozor, C.S.Sp., 183–215. Notre Dame: University of Notre Dame Press.

Capps, Donald and James E. Dittes, eds. (1990) *The Hunger of the Heart: Reflections on the Confessions of Augustine*. West Lafayette, IN: Society for the Scientific Study of Religion.

Cavadini, John C. (2005) "Feeling Right: Augustine on the Passions and Sexual Desire." *Augustinian Studies* 36: 195–217.

Cavadini, John C. (2018) "*Creatio ex nihilo* in the Thought of Saint Augustine." In *Creation Ex nihilo: Origins, Development, and Contemporary Challenges*, edited by Gary A. Anderson and Markus Bockmuehl, 151–171. Notre Dame, IN: University of Notre Dame Press.

Courcelle, Pierre (1971) "Le jeune Augustin, second Catalina." *Revue des Études anciennes* 73: 141–150.

Crosson, Frederick (1989) "Structure and Meaning in St. Augustine's *Confessions.*" *Proceedings of the American Catholic Philosophical Association* 63: 84–97. Reprinted in *The Augustinian Tradition*, edited by Gareth B. Matthews, 27–38. Berkeley and Los Angeles: University of California Press, 1990.

Dittes, James E. (1990) "Continuities Between the Life and Thought of Augustine." In *The Hunger of the Heart: Reflections on the Confessions of Augustine*, ed. Donald Capps and James Dittes, 117–131. West Lafayette: Society for the Scientific Study of Religion.

Ferrari, Leo C. (1970) "The Pear-Theft in Augustine's *Confessions.*" *Revue des études augustiniennes* 16: 233–242.

Ferrari, Leo C. (1977) "The Theme of the Prodigal Son in Augustine's *Confessions.*" *Recherches Augustiniennes* 12: 105–118.

Fitzgerald, Allan D., John Cavadni, Marianne Djuth, James O'Donnell, and Frederick Van Fleteren, eds. (1999) *Augustine through the Ages: An Encyclopedia.* Grand Rapids, MI: Eerdmans.

Kligerman, Charles (1990) "A Psychoanalytic Study of the Confessions of St. Augustine." In *The Hunger of the Heart: Reflections on the Confessions of Augustine,* ed. Donald Capps and James Dittes, 95–109. West Lafayette: Society for the Scientific Study of Religion.

Miles, Margaret (1992a) "The Erotic Text: Augustine's Confessions." *Continuum* 2: 132–149.

Miles, Margaret (1992b) *Desire and Delight: A New Reading of Augustine's Confessions.* New York, NY: Crossroad.

Nietzsche, Friedrich (1975) *Nietzsche Briefwechsel: Kritische Gesamtausgabe.* Berlin and New York: Walter de Gruyter.

O'Donnell, J. J., trans. (1992) *Augustine: Confessions,* 3 vols. Oxford: Clarendon Press. [Volume 1 is a translation of the text. Volumes 2 and 3 are O'Donnell's extensive commentary.]

Smith, W. T. (1980) *Augustine: His Life and Thought.* Atlanta: John Knox Press.

5

Simplifying Augustine

[T]he very desire with which you want to understand is itself a prayer to God
(Augustine, *Sermon* 152.1).

Early in the year 800, Alcuin of York received a letter from two nuns, Gisela and Rotruda (daughter and sister of Charlemagne), asking him for an exposition of the Gospel of John. Styling Alcuin as their teacher, they explained that they had in mind something which would "lay open the venerable opinions of the holy Fathers." They had Augustine's expositions on the Gospel, but complained that these were, at points, "very obscure" and too stylistically complex.[1] Alcuin's *Commentary on John*, completed in response to their request and based on Augustine's *Tractates on the Gospel of John* (*Io. eu. tr.*), can thus be thought of as a simplified presentation of Augustine's tractates, which Alcuin largely follows both in content and sequence.[2] Alcuin's procedure for simplification is easily summarized: he quotes verbatim the passages he wants (without attribution), sometimes paraphrasing but generally omitting the rest, or else replacing it with easier material from Bede or Gregory the Great. Broadly speaking, we too might consider much of the omitted material to be difficult or esoteric, "philosophical," and Neoplatonic, concerning such topics as incorporeal substances, ascents to spiritual vision, and the character of God's eternal Word. This sort of material, very common in Augustine's text, is almost completely

Visioning Augustine, First Edition. John C. Cavadini.
© 2019 John Wiley & Sons Ltd. Published 2019 by John Wiley & Sons Ltd.

eliminated in Alcuin's. Indeed, such a huge proportion of the first 11 tractates is so preoccupied with philosophical issues that Alcuin, seemingly in desperation, omits them altogether and turns to other sources instead.[3]

How Alcuin "simplifies" Augustine raises the interesting question of what this material is doing in Augustine's text in the first place, since Augustine's tractates are themselves a series of homilies and thus, presumably, to some degree, accessible, or exoteric. These tractates are among the most carefully planned and retouched of Augustine's homilies. However, in their present form, they were meant more to be read than heard, though probably all of them, and at least the first 54 were originally preached. It is hard to believe that these philosophical themes were not originally present in some form, especially in the first few tractates.[4] Nor does it appear that such themes would, in themselves, have been any easier for most of Augustine's North African contemporaries to grasp than for Gisela and Rotruda.[5]

Thus arises the interesting question of the relation between the "esoteric" and the "exoteric" in Augustine's work itself. We have noted how Alcuin simplifies Augustine, and we will briefly examine in the following text how Caesarius of Arles simplified Augustine for his own congregation. The question here is how does *Augustine* simplify Augustine? Or is this even the correct question? More neutrally posed, what is the relation between Augustine's work in the more esoteric genres of commentary and treatise to that in the more exoteric genre of sermon and preaching?[6]

A note on terminology: I am not using the word "esoteric" in its more technical sense of "secret," as describing teachings that are intentionally veiled from the public at large and revealed only to a few worthy initiates. In this sense, the gnostics advocated esoteric teachings, sometimes with more "exoteric" versions designed expressly to entice potential insiders without actually revealing any hidden teachings.[7] Augustine did not have "esoteric" teachings or genres in this sense, but as a professional rhetor he had a keen sense of audience, and he made distinctions among his own works regarding their appropriateness for a particular audience, in some cases explicitly. For example, in *retr.*, he notes that he wrote *Psalmus contra partem Donati* specifically for the "most lowly mass of people," which he characterizes as "uneducated and unlearned."[8] It is surely appropriate to call this an "exoteric" work, precisely as something meant to be accessible to the "uneducated" as opposed to the educated, but not as an attempt to hide secret doctrines specifically reserved for elect initiates. Nevertheless, even this weaker sense of the contrast between "exoteric" and "esoteric" should not be underestimated, especially in late antiquity. The acquisition of a liberal education, of literary culture, could itself be likened to an initiation, or else to a process of transformation that, in the view of the educated, made them "as superior to the uneducated as they were to cattle."[9] An expensive literary education defined one as part of an elite. It was a mark of noble birth, and only very rarely an avenue of social advancement. As such, it was a "means of expressing social distance,"[10] and the cultural forms and practices associated with it are not inappropriately characterized as "esoteric."

To examine the question at hand, it is my intention to compare *De Trinitate* (*trin.*) with *Sermones ad populum* (*s.*). *Trin.* is arguably one of the most difficult or "esoteric" works Augustine ever wrote. He himself remarked repeatedly that he expected it to be understood only by "few";[11] presumably, this means a "few" among those who could read, already few enough in late antiquity.[12] The second half of *trin.* assumes familiarity with the liberal arts and presupposes skills in philosophical thinking, while books 5–7 require a facility with dialectic almost unique in the Augustinian corpus.[13]

On the other hand, the nearly 550 *Sermones ad populum*[14] verifiable as genuinely Augustinian are some of the most accessible or exoteric[15] works we have from Augustine, most of them neither written down nor dictated, but preached extemporaneously, recorded by notaries or others, and for the most part not significantly revised or retouched.[16] Augustine's audience varied with time and place, but generally included both educated and uneducated, literate and illiterate members,[17] and he developed a homiletic style that was intentionally simple, shorn of rhetorical intricacy, plain and vivid, specially created to reach just such a heterogeneous group.[18] Augustine's renunciation of the intricate, jeweled rhetorical style meant forgoing a traditional, identifying characteristic of the elite, so that such a rhetorical posturing was itself a kind of social statement.[19] Apart from the very early sermons from the period of Augustine's presbyterate, a reading of the *Sermones ad populum* betrays not the slightest hint that there ever was a "second sophistic."[20] Augustine has nothing to offer comparable to the funeral orations of Ambrose or the Eastern homilists.

"Faith Seeking Understanding"

Turning now to a comparison between *trin.* and the *Sermones*, perhaps the most salient feature is that Augustine does not "simplify" his own work by omitting particular topics of discussion, or at least not in any way easy to describe. Nearly all the topics taken up in *trin.* are well represented in the sermons, and some qualify as homiletic preoccupations. The theophanies in the Pentateuch, with special reference to the question of who appeared and how;[21] trinitarian relations;[22] rules for the interpretation of Scripture;[23] soteriology;[24] detailed anti-Arian polemic;[25] the human soul as trinitarian image of God;[26] discussions of love similar to that in book 8 of *trin.*;[27] and, above all, the question of "seeing" God, the character and quality of an incorporeal substance, and Neoplatonic "ascents" to contemplation[28] – each the subject of Alcuin's particular editorial censorship – are all taken into the *Sermones* with relish.[29]

In fact, there is a striking continuity in tone between *trin.* and the *Sermones ad populum.* It is true that, in the sermons, there are no passages of sustained dialectic, such as book 6 of *trin.*; there are no summaries of philosophical jargon, such as the review of Aristotle's categories in *trin.* 5.7.8. Nor is there any sustained argument based on Augustine's own jargon, such as the distinction between *scientia* and *sapientia* developed in book 12, or the lengthy discussion of substantial versus relational predicates from book 5. Extensive discussions of technical trinitarian terms, such as that of the word *persona*, do not figure largely in the sermons.[30] And there are very few citations of classical authors comparable to the sustained consideration of passages from Cicero extending over books 13 and 14 or the steady peppering of intertextual allusions to other authors there.[31] Nor is the concerted reference to the process of acquiring a liberal education[32] duplicated in the sermons. In short, what is missing from the sermons is any concerted appeal to the common culture of the educated elite, any sense that the discussion is among persons who know the repository of texts and skills that would characterize those educated in the liberal arts.

Yet, the two genres of work appear finally as variations on a common endeavor of inquiry, which Augustine explicitly structures as such, and, in particular, as "faith seeking understanding." It is certainly nothing new to use this phrase as a way of describing Augustinian theology, but a close reading of the homilies reveals that "faith seeking understanding" is as much a homiletic principle in Augustine as it is a theological principle. What emerges from a comparison of the homilies with *trin.* is not that Augustine is popularizing, or "exotericizing," the *results* of inquiry when he preaches, but that he recontextualizes inquiry itself for the people.[33] In his homilies, such inquiry is no longer the exclusive province of the liberally educated elites. And *trin.*, which explicitly styles itself as a defense of the "starting point of faith"[34] for those desiring understanding, becomes the theoretical justification of this recontextualization. If *trin.* succeeds, it succeeds only as a defense of a requirement before and beneath the sheer dint of educated expertise employed therein, detaching inquiry from any essential connection with that expertise and attaching it to the sort of seeking which faith in itself represents.[35]

In the first place, Augustine repeatedly and consistently styles his sermons as acts of inquiry, as instances of seeking understanding of Scripture.[36] Seeking for understanding, we are to look "in the books of the Lord" and knock on the Lord's door for understanding by praying.[37] Scripture, or the church in which Scripture is read, is styled as a "school," and those who come to hear Scripture read are "students of divine letters." They will know what the titles of the psalms mean;[38] those who have been "well educated" in the "school of Christ" will know that Jacob and Israel are the same person.[39] Biblical miracles are meant to enrich those who are in the school of Christ with understanding, not simply to strike them with wonder.[40] Among the hearers of *s.* 133 are both educated and uneducated people, but Augustine refers to both groups as those who have been "brought up in the church, educated in the Scriptures of the Lord." As for those who have not been schooled in the liberal arts, they are nevertheless not uneducated, since they have been raised "on the word of God."[41]

Further, Augustine always postures himself as essentially and primarily a listener to the Scriptures:

> Don't listen to me, but together with me. There's someone, you see, who says to us, 'Come, children, listen to me' (Ps. 34.11). And let's all come running, and stand there, and prick up our ears.[42]

Augustine notes explicitly that the preacher is above all a listener. It is Augustine's duty to speak, but "it's a futile preacher outwardly of

God's word, who isn't also inwardly a listener."[43] Augustine is very careful not to posture himself as the teacher in this school, but as a fellow inquirer, someone who is seeking for understanding just as much as other students in the school of Scripture:

> Your graces know that all of us have one teacher, and that under him we are fellow disciples, fellow pupils [*condiscipulos*]. And the fact that we bishops speak to you from a higher place does not make us your teachers; but it's the one who dwells in all of us that is the teacher of us all. He was talking to all of us just now in the Gospel, and saying to us what I am also saying to you; he says it, though about us, about both me and you: "If you remain in my word" – not mine, of course, not Augustine's, now speaking, but his, who was speaking just now from the Gospel.[44]

In another place, Augustine notes that:

> We bishops are called teachers [*doctores*], but in many matters we seek a teacher ourselves, and we certainly don't want to be regarded as masters [*magistros*]. That is dangerous, and forbidden by the Lord himself, who says 'Do not wish to be called masters; you have one master, the Christ' (Mt. 23:10). So the *magisterium* is dangerous, the state of disciple safe.[45]

Augustine expects to be judged, and not only by God but *by* his listeners; "You are listening as judges," he tells them.[46] He speaks from a higher place in church, but it is the hearers' office to pass judgment on what he says.[47] They too may consult the inner teacher: "inwardly, we are all hearers"; the inner teacher can prompt applause if the hearer is delighted with the truth spoken, or accusation: "'I would like to know if this guy who's speaking to me does all the things that he hears himself or says to others.'"[48]

> In this way, for whatever we say that is true (since everything true is from Truth) you will praise not us but him, and wherever being human we slip up, you will pray to the same him for us.[49]

Augustine rhetorically positions himself and his audience as embarked upon a joint venture of inquiry.[50] His choice of topic, therefore, was sometimes based on his listeners' interests. In *s.* 362, he focused on a particular verse because of his congregation's vocal reaction to it when read (362.1). He also shaped his expositions around questions which his fellow seekers had asked, or which he imagined them asking. "'Amen and Alleluia,' they say, 'we're going to say that forever and ever? Who will be able to endure it?'" (362.29). Augustine responds with an inquiry about the resurrected life in the hereafter "according to the Scriptures."[51]

When Augustine treats the scriptural passage read by the lector as a "problem" (*quaestio*) that challenges the inquiry and study of all its hearers, he is most effective rhetorically in posturing himself and his hearers as fellow seekers. Augustine sets out a passage of Scripture as presenting a dilemma, and says to his hearers that he will "seek with [them]" what it means. Another text presents a "problem which really must be solved."[52] Faced with Matt. 12:32, the passage about the sin against the Holy Spirit, Augustine notes: "It's a real problem that we are faced with, in this passage read just now from the Gospel" (*s.* 71.1). He draws out his exposition to heighten the sense of the difficulty of the problem and the desire for a solution, noting, after the resolution of some antecedent difficulties, that the passage is a "colossal problem," that "there is probably no greater problem to be found in all the holy Scriptures," and that he himself had avoided speaking about it, although not "seeking, asking, knocking" about it (71.7–8).[53] Passages such as this are specifically meant to prompt the reader or hearer to inquiry, for upon inquiry he or she may discover more than one "right meaning."[54] There is a real pleasure in the discovery of meaning in a text which had been obscure. In this sermon, Augustine heightens the sense of the problem so much and delays his answer so skillfully that he almost teases his hearers into seeking and appreciating that pleasure (71.13, 18). In another sermon on Jn. 7:2–10, where Jesus says he is not going up to the feast but then goes, Augustine poses the problem plainly in order to "engage [his hearers'] interest."[55] In another sermon, he speaks of the enthusiasm of the audience when he "sets some problems before [them] to be solved," and how it has prompted him to set even further inquiry before them.[56]

The sermons consistently present faith as the sine qua non for understanding,[57] but, even more importantly, they style the faith of the hearers as a posture of inquiry or seeking. Not everyone may understand at present, but the sermons direct everyone's faith, preacher as well as hearers, toward understanding. This occurs eschatologically, to be sure, but also in the present, in the time that the sermon is delivered and over the long term of attendance at the "school" of divine Scripture. Thus, faith is the basis for the joint venture of inquiry described earlier: "Let's be companions in believing. What am I saying? Let's be companions in seeking" (*s.* 53.13). Augustine remarks: "Faith is a step towards understanding"; faith is entitled to understanding.[58] For some, understanding may have to be postponed, but not necessarily for long, even for a difficult verse like Jn. 5:19, "The Son cannot do anything of himself, except what he sees the Father doing." Augustine proceeds immediately to an exhortation to understand, despite the presence of a large number of people whom he does not expect to understand immediately:

> God gave you eyes in your head, reason in your heart. Arouse the reason in your heart, get the inner inhabitant behind your inner eyes on his feet, let him take to his windows, let him inspect God's creation.[59]

Augustine is admonishing his hearers to a Neoplatonic ascent to interior or spiritual vision:

> Look at the facts, the things made, and seek the underlying factor, the maker. Observe what you see, and seek what you cannot see. Believe in the one whom you cannot see, on account of these things which you can (126.3).

It is the faith of the hearers that here is presented as an orientation, indeed almost an imperative, to make the ascent to spiritual vision, which alone can provide understanding of a difficult trinitarian verse like Jn. 5:19. If Augustine exhorts his hearers to faith, it is *so that* their minds might be capable of understanding, since the mind imbued with faith becomes capable of understanding (*intellectus capax*). Apart from eschatological vision, Augustine means "understanding" with regard to what he has just said – that is, the very words of his sermon.[60]

Since anyone can have faith, even those uneducated in the liberal arts, and since faith is an orientation to understanding, in the rhetoric of Augustine, faith could be said to "exotericize" the esoteric Neoplatonic quest for spiritual vision.[61] This is what permits Augustine to tackle Jn. 1:1 in a sermon. It is one of the most difficult passages of

Scripture – one which, in the *conf.*, he singles out as something the Neoplatonists had understood. It cannot be understood without some sort of ascent to spiritual vision, and, in a homily for Easter Sunday, preached to a packed house in Hippo, Augustine exhorts his hearers to "lift up [their] hearts, reject anything bodily from the imagination," and to "think of the Word as being everywhere whole and entire."[62] This is an undiluted teaching of Plotinus, the philosophical master, presented to the masses as something which they, and in particular those who have just been "enlightened" (120.3) by baptism, can understand. It is not that Plotinian doctrine has been simplified for the masses, but that inquiry, the quest for spiritual vision, has been recontextualized by faith. And thus, the rest of this brief homily is a kind of guided ascent to vision. In another Easter homily on the same text, Augustine admonishes, "If you understand, rejoice; if you don't understand, believe. Because the word of the prophet cannot be nullified, 'Unless you believe, you shall not understand' (Isa. 7.9)." The exhortation to faith is an exhortation to that which will permit understanding, to some degree even in the present (118.2). In another homily on the same text, Augustine exhorts his audience to the understanding of the Word of God conceived in strictly Platonic fashion as:

> ... a kind of form, a form that has not been formed, but is the form of all things that have been formed, an unchangeable form, that has neither fault nor failing, beyond time, beyond space, standing apart as at once the foundation for all things to stand on.[63]

Later in the homily (117.17), he describes the slow growth of understanding from faith, and the reason faith has this capacity to beget understanding. Faith is the indwelling of Christ, who is the loftiness of God made lowly, the indwelling of God's "instruction" (*praeceptio Dei*) begetting the charity that cleanses the inner vision. It is the incarnation that is God's teaching, which is, in a way, the exotericizing of teaching itself, and it dwells in our hearts through faith.

Finally, this means that Augustine's homiletic discussions of "mystery" are not exhortations to blind faith, but precisely the opposite. Faith is the healing of the eye of the mind and, as such, a capacity for understanding or "penetrating" mystery.[64] Having faith in Christ, whom we can see temporally, Augustine preaches, we come to

understand the divinity we cannot perceive, and not simply in the
eschaton, but even now, in the course of a sermon:

> How, then, are our eyes healed? Just as it's by faith that we perceive
> Christ passing by in his temporal activities, so we have to understand
> him stopping and standing still, as Christ in his unchanging eternity.
> The eye is healed, you see, when it understands Christ's divinity. Your
> graces must try to grasp this; pay attention to the sublime mystery
> (*grande sacramentum*) I am speaking of (*s.* 88.14).

On the other hand, the mysteries of faith are such that no one, no
matter how educated, can completely grasp them in this life; before
them, all, preacher and hearer, are "little ones to be educated."[65]
Speaking about Jn. 1:1–2, Augustine says, "Who can work it out? Who
can observe it, who contemplate it, who think fitting thoughts about
it? Nobody" (229E.4). In another homily on the same verse, he
remarks, "And I know, I'm telling you, that not even I who am speaking to you, not even I understand."[66] The continuing and permanent
need for faith in face of the mystery of the Trinity is the source of the
preacher's posturing of himself (and his rhetoric) as seeking, and as
doing so on essentially the same level as those to whom he speaks.[67]
And if Scripture is, for now, "the face of God" for us,[68] we are always
rendered seekers by the inexhaustible variety and depth of meaning
which presents that face to us.

Turning to *trin.* from the sermons, one finds the same rhetoric,
equally insistent, of a discourse shared between writer and reader as
co-seekers on a joint project of inquiry.[69] Augustine does not expect
simply to be believed, and expects to be corrected if he is wrong. He
gives readers the wherewithal to see for themselves, even if only in the
distorted "mirror" of their own souls, the long, drawn-out series of
Neoplatonic-like interior ascents of the second half of the treatise.
Trin., however, is not addressed simply to persons of faith, a point
Augustine makes after a lengthy citation of one of his own homilies[70]
(to my knowledge, the only time he cites one of his homilies in a treatise). The citation underscores the kinship between these two parts of
Augustine's oeuvre, but it also underscores the difference. *Trin.* has, as
at least part of its agenda, the defense of starting with faith if one is to
attain understanding. The tone in this treatise, suggesting dialogue, is
not necessarily predicated on shared faith, but on a shared educational

tradition, that of the liberal arts.[71] If the emphasis in the sermons is to propose faith as an orientation to understanding, as an inquiry, the emphasis in *trin.* is to demonstrate that inquiry can come to fruition only if founded on faith. Here, the rhetoric shapes the inquiry, or, more particularly, the dialogic rhetoric of philosophical inquiry is itself being employed as the dialectic of faith, enjoined to "seek God's face evermore" (Ps. 105:3).[72] The shared, conversational ascent to the vision of truth, in Augustine's dialogues the prerogative of the liberally educated, has been transformed in the sermons to become the dialectic of faith seeking understanding, available to all. *Trin.* can be imagined as the place where Augustine works out the theory behind the shift of the ancient, dialogic quest for wisdom to the exoteric provenance of the sermon.[73]

From Augustine to Caesarius

The effect of Augustine's work, presenting faith in his sermons as an orientation to understanding, can be underscored by a comparison with the sermons of Caesarius, the sixth-century bishop of Arles, and another "simplifier" of Augustine's work. Caesarius admired Augustine's plain style and imitated it.[74] In many cases, he took over parts of Augustine's sermons verbatim.[75] But he never takes over the rhetoric of "faith seeking understanding" (Isa. 7:9).[76] There is not, as far as I have been able to determine, a single reference to this verse.

Caesarius lays out at length the various figures and "mysteries" of Scripture in homily after homily, but it is almost as though he is merely reading a code which has long ago been cracked. In Caesarius, as in Alcuin, the results have, in principle, already been discovered by the Fathers. For him, the idea of preaching (or, in Alcuin's case, writing a commentary) is to convey the results in a simplified form, not to engage in a search together with the hearer or reader. Caesarius explicitly styles himself as presenting the results of the learned inquiry of the "holy fathers" in simplified form:

> If we wanted to make known to the ears of your charity an explanation (*eloquio*) of Sacred Scripture in the same order and language in which the holy fathers expressed it, the food of doctrine (*doctrinae*) could reach only a few scholarly souls (*paucos scolasticos*), while the remaining

crowd of people would remain hungry. For this reason, I humbly beg you that learned ears (*eruditae aures*) be content to hear with patience these simple words (*verba rustica*) …. Since inexperienced, simple souls cannot rise to the height of scholars, the learned (*eruditi*) should deign to bend down to their ignorance. What is said to simple souls can, indeed, be understood by the educated (*scolastici*), but what is preached to the learned cannot be grasped at all by the simple.[77]

This passage is the virtual unsaying of Augustine's most treasured homiletic principles. The faith of the simple is an absolute; it is not imagined or employed as an orientation to inquiry or study. If there is any need for the Christian people to seek, they do it only by asking questions "of the priests who reveal the secrets of Holy Scripture," like calves going after the udders of their mothers: "so also the Christian people should continually appeal to their priests, as the udders of holy church, by devout questions."[78] For Augustine, the "milk" for babes is prepared, not in the first place by Augustine the preacher, but by the Word Himself, in being made flesh in the Incarnation;[79] Augustine is perfectly ready to characterize himself as an infant, or *parvulus*, who is the recipient of the Word's milk.[80] On the other hand, there is a strict division of labor envisioned in Caesarius' analogy. There is no sense in which the preacher and hearers are embarked on a common inquiry. In his remake of Augustine's *s*. 8, Caesarius (*s*. 100) omits Augustine's approach to the sermon as "walking together on the way to [God's] truth" (8.1). And despite Caesarius' insistent recommendation that Christians read the Bible, or have it read to them, for 3 hours every day,[81] in none of his sermons is there a reference to the pleasure associated with the discovery of meaning in obscure texts. It goes almost without saying that hearers of Caesarius' preaching are never construed as people who might be in a position to judge the truth of what is said.

The "low" or "simple" rhetorical style, for which Caesarius argues so strongly in two key sermons (1 and 86), when divorced from the Augustinian rhetoric of "faith seeking understanding," becomes not a way of "exotericizing" inquiry but of distinguishing the hearers precisely *as* an exoteric, "simple" class, who have only to memorize the results of someone else's inquiry, conducted long ago and mediated by Caesarius. Caesarius implies that his hearers are children,[82] and he their father, as Augustine never does. In a way, what Caesarius has done is to "esotericize" the Fathers, and with them, the preachers who dole out "crumbs" from the loaves of Scripture.[83] Finally, if *trin.* has any relevance to the world of Caesarius' sermons, it is only as supplying the odd passage handy in the refutation of Arians.[84] Setting *trin.* next to the sermons of Caesarius only underscores the complementarity of Augustine's treatise with his own homiletic oeuvre. In a famous passage introducing his classic biography of Augustine, Peter Brown notes that he will steer a middle course along a cliff face, "above the plains of Augustine's routine duties as a bishop, and far below the heights of his speculations on the Trinity."[85] Perhaps, at least if preaching is one of the most salient elements of Augustine's routine pastoral duties, these two loci of Augustinian geography are not quite so far apart.

Acknowledgments

An earlier version of this chapter was published by Wm. B. Eerdmans Publishing Company as Cavadini, J. C. (2004) "Simplifying Augustine." In *Educating People of Faith: Exploring the History of Jewish and Christian Communities*, edited by John van Engen, 63–84. Grand Rapids: Wm. B. Eerdmans Publishing Company. Reprinted by permission of the publisher.

Notes

1 *Ep.* 196, in Societas Aperiendis Fontibus (1974), 324. All citations of Augustine's sermons are from the Nuova Biblioteca Agostiniana edition, which presents the best edition available for any given sermon. All translations are from Hill (1990–1997).
2 See Bullough (1983), and Contreni (1983).
3 For more on this topic, see John Cavadini, "Alcuin and Augustine on John," available online at http://icl.nd.edu.
4 The discussion, and the bibliography, is summarized by Rettig (1988).
5 On this point, see Teske (1984).
6 For an essay asking a similar question of Origen's work and specifically using the language of "esoteric" and "exoteric," see Junod (1994).
7 See, for example, Attridge (1986).
8 "Volens etiam causam Donatistarum ad ipsius humillimi vulgi et omnino imperitorum atque idiotarum notitiam pervenire …," *retr.* 1.20.1, CCSL 57, 61.1–2.

Augustine's style reflects this intention; not only is the "psalm" itself abecedarian, but its rhythm explicitly avoids classical meters which might force Augustine to use a word unfamiliar to the uneducated: "Ideo autem non aliquo carminis genere id fieri volui, ne me necessitas metrica ad aliqua verba quae vulgo minus sunt usitata conpelleret" (II.10–13). See also Augustine's comments about his *De agone Christiano*: "Liber de agone christiano fratribus in eloquio Latino ineruditis humili sermone conscriptus est ..." (*retr.* 2.3.1, CCSL 57, 91.2–3). *Cat. rud.* 1.8.12–1.9.13 shows Augustine giving instructions for adapting one's discourse to the educational level of the audience.

9   See Kaster (1988), 16–17. The quotation is from the grammarian Diomedes, cited by Kaster on 17.

10   Brown (1992), 39.

11   "... libros de trinitate ... nimis operosi sunt et a paucis eos intellegi posse arbitror" (*ep.* 169.1.1, CSEL 44, 612.6–9, ca. 415, to Evodius); cf. *ep.* 120.3.13, CSEL 34, 715.18–21, on the extreme difficulty of the subject of the Trinity as discussed in *De Trinitate* (hereafter *trin.*), then in progress.

12   See Kaster (1988), 35–48, based largely on the work of Duncan-Jones (1977). "We must imagine a state of very sparse literacy at best," Kaster writes (39), with the literate concentrated among the upper classes but found throughout the whole social pyramid. An even smaller proportion of the population would have been educated in liberal studies. Arguments for somewhat higher rates are advanced by Meyer (1989); lower estimates are defended by Harris (1989). Gamble (1995), 2–10, is a good summary. He assesses literacy, that is, "the ability to read, criticize, and interpret" Christian literature, at "not more than about 10 percent in any given setting" (5), although he argues that this does not mean only a small percentage of Christians knew Scripture, since they heard it read regularly (141).

13   *retr.* 1.5.1, CCSL 57, 16.

14   This is Augustine's own designation for them at *retr.* 2. Epilogus, CCSL 57, 143.5 (also see *ep* 234.2, when he refers to them as *tractatus populares, quos Graeci homelias vocabant*). On the signification of the word *sermo* and its relation to *populus* or *popularis* in the sense of something directed to the "people" assembled in church, see Mohrmann (1961), 2:71–72; also Pontet (1944) 51–52. See also Pontet on the connection between *sermo* and *tractatus*, and Mohrmann (1961), 2:63–72; Mandouze (1968), 599–615. On the number of authentic Augustinian sermons, see Verbraken (1976), 18, although this will have to be adjusted in light of the recent discoveries of about 26 more sermons (see Chadwick [1996]).

15   In book 4 of *De doctrina Christiana* (hereafter *doct. chr.*), contemporaneous with *retr.*, Augustine clearly marks out discourse addressed to the "people" as appropriately different from that found in books: "There are some things which with their full implications are not understood or are hardly understood, no matter

how eloquently they are spoken …. And these things should never, or only rarely on account of some necessity, be set before an audience of the people (*in populi audientiam*). However, in books – which, when they are understood, hold the readers to them in a certain way, and, when they are not understood, are not troublesome to those not wishing to read – and in conversations (*conlocutionibus*), the duty should not be neglected of bringing the truth which we have perceived, no matter how difficult it may be to comprehend (*quamvis ad intellegendum difficillima*) or how much labor may be involved, to the understanding of others, provided that the listener or disputant wishes to learn and has the capacity to do so (*nec mentis capacitas desit*), no matter how the material is presented" (4.9.23, CCSL 32, 132, trans. Robertson [1958]). That is, with a large crowd of listeners, some or many of whom may not have the "capacity" to understand intricate points, and none of whom can ask questions on the spot (cf. 4.10.25), some topics are inappropriate, not because they are secret, but because they will not be understood. This corresponds roughly to the distinction between "esoteric" and "exoteric" that I intend in this chapter.

16 Possidius, *Vita Augustini* 7.3; cf. *en. Ps.* 51.1; *ep.* 213.2. See Pellegrino's excellent general introduction to *The Works of St. Augustine*, pt. III, *Sermons* (Pellegrino [1990]), at 15–19. Also Mandouze (1968), 591–663, esp. 595–598. Oberhelman (1991) studies the prose rhythms across the genres in which Augustine wrote; he concludes: "Augustine's sermons were spontaneous creations that entered unplanned territory as the bishop extemporized" (89).

17 There has never been a thorough study of the audience of the homilies of Augustine. Van der Meer (1961) assumes a highly variegated audience but without much evidence (see "A Sunday in Hippo," 388–402, esp. 389, and "The Servant of the Word," pp. 412–452; cf. Brown [1967], 252). MacMullen (1989) assumes a homogeneous audience of the educated property-owning aristocracy (with their slaves) on the basis of equally slender evidence. His article devotes less than a page to Augustine (509); the article is seemingly a retraction of MacMullen (1966). Kaster's (1988) statement that Augustine's audience was "largely uneducated" (84) references only this earlier article of MacMullen, but MacMullen's later article rightly points out that we cannot necessarily take references to the "poor" or other classes in the congregation at face value, for the "poor" sometimes turn out to have substantial property. Pontet (1944), 55–61, provides a slightly fuller documentation for a mixed crowd of educated and uneducated, men and women, rich and poor, and analyzes in good detail the differences in audience based on the place Augustine is preaching (72–91); see also Becker (1977). Olivar (1991), 761–770, adds no new evidence on this point. Pellegrino's (1990) discussion (84–93) is a good basis for further inquiry, although the worries of MacMullen need to be considered more fully. What seems beyond doubt, however, is that the congregation to which Augustine preached was usually a mixture of the educated and uneducated, though in

varying proportions, and that Augustine was explicitly concerned to address both: see, for example, *s.* 131.9; 241.5 (most of Augustine's audience knows the *Aeneid* from the theater, not from having read it); 247.1; 264.4; 299 M.3; 277.13; 313B.3; etc. Cf. 352.4, which distinguishes between the *veloces* and the *tardos* among the listeners and directs the exposition to the latter. By contrast, *s.* 52 may be directed only at the literate (see 52.10), and, at *s.* 150.3, Augustine remarks that, since he is preaching in Carthage, he can expect some of the congregation to know the difference between Stoic and Epicurean, although some will not. This concern to appeal to a heterogeneous audience including the uneducated captures the sense of "exoteric" as I am applying it to the sermons; cf. Junod's (1994) characterization of Origen's struggle to appeal to a similarly "heterogeneous" audience (80). Note: hereafter, *s.* will refer to both *Sermo* and *Sermones*.

18 Augustine himself provides the theory for a style that emphasizes clarity over ornamentation (*doct. chr.* 4.8.22), and editors since Erasmus have commented on it (see the preface to his Basel edition of Augustine's *Opera*, 1529, cited by van der Meer [1961], 417). For an evocation of Augustine's preaching style in English, see van der Meer, 412–452; Brown (1967), 244–258. Auerbach (1965), 1–66, "Sermo Humilis" is fundamental in the treatment of this topic. Auksi (1995), 110–126, summarizes and provides basic bibliography; see also Pellegrino (1990), 111–131. Banniard (1992) describes the style and its connection to a mixed audience of literate and illiterate, and documents the connections to Augustine's theory in *doct. chr.* 4 and *cat. rud.* (65–104). Mohrmann's work on Augustine's style is foundational. She shows that Augustine's use of puns in his sermons is more indebted to Plautus and the popular speech he reflects than to Cicero and the rhetoric of the schools (see Mohrmann [1932], reprinted in Mohrmann [1961], 1:323–349). She shows how Augustine invented a new style, based on popular speech and the Bible, which he used to modify the eloquence taught by the schools of rhetoric (Mohrmann [1947], reprinted in Mohrmann [1961], 1:351–370), and demonstrates how this style is especially characteristic of his sermons: "Augustin a consciemment créé un style homilétique qui devait répondre aux besoins de la prédication populaire .... La langue de la prédication augustinienne n'est. pas le latin vulgaire de son époque, c'est. plutôt une forme très stylisée du latin tel. qu'il se parlait dans un milieu cultivé, mais qui était, dans sa simplicité, facile à comprendre, même par l'homme du peuple. Sans descendre au niveau du peuple, il parle une langue qui lui reste accessible" (Mohrmann [1954], reprinted at Mohrmann [1961], 1:391–402, quotation from 96, partly reversing the earlier 1931 judgment of Ferdinand Lot [reprinted in Lot (1968)], fully refuted by Banniard [1992], 98–101). Mohrmann also shows that this lively, direct style was not a feature of Augustine's earliest sermons, but developed as Augustine learned to speak directly to his hearers (Mohrmann [1958], reprinted at Mohrmann [1961], 2:246–275); this study also

calls attention to the predominance of rhyme as a feature of the popular style of the sermons). See also Mohrmann (1957), reprinted as a whole at Mohrmann (1961), 2:277–323. Mohrmann's emphasis on the Bible as a formative influence in the style of Augustine's preaching is corroborated by the work of Uthemann (1996).

19 "The style was … a subtle form of episcopal discipline. Implicitly discounting the distinctions and prestige of the traditional literary culture … his style … was another continuing form of self-restraint"; "his language … a unifying force, moving downward to instruct the simple, reaching upward to set the *docti* an example" (Kaster [1988], 84). Klingshirn (1994) points out the struggle that Caesarius of Arles, admirer and imitator of Augustine's style, had in persuading aristocratic bishops to give up the ornamented style, a traditional mark of prestige and status, in favor of plain speech: see 81–82, 146–151. Spence (1988) also comments that Augustine's rhetorical practice involved a shift in the relationship between audience and orator: "Instead of insisting on the absolute power and verity of language and reason, the Christian persuader must remain part of the audience even while assuming temporarily what is objectively the role of teacher. There is consequently a reorganization of the hierarchy implicit in classical rhetoric, for no matter how much the Christian teacher or preacher is like the classical orator, he is also like the Ciceronian audience. Such power as the classical orator has over his audience – a power possible only if a distance exists between them – is thus denied …. The shift in pragmatics is thus a shift in underlying assumptions: the Christian orator must persuade laterally, not from on high, and all that he says is subject to a higher authority" (76).

20 See Mohrmann (1961), 1:396.

21 See, for example, two homilies on the burning bush: 6 (esp. 6.2, with its discussion of the manner in which God appeared – through an angel, not in his unchangeable essence) and 7 (esp. 7.3–7, with discussion of which person of the Trinity appeared to Moses and later to Abraham); cf. *trin.* 2.19–22; 3.22–27; and *s.* 23.14.

22 For example, *s.* 71.18 (an "improvement" on *trin.*? – see Hill's [1990–1997] comments on *s.* 71, in *WSA* III/3, 271, n. 1); *s.* 25–27 (cf. *trin.* 1.7, 25; 2.3 on the inseparability of the works of the Trinity, also the subject of *s.* 135); *s.* 28–33 on the Holy Spirit (cf. material in *trin.* 15.27–49); *s.* 103–104 (cf. *trin.* 5.11, etc.); *s.* 117.7 (cf. *trin.* 1.1 on not applying characteristics of creatures to God); *s.* 118; *s.* 126.11 (cf. *trin.* 12.6); *s.* 127.4–5; *s.* 195.1; *s.* 196.1; *s.* 212; *s.* 213.7; *s.* 214.5–6, 10; *s.* 215.3–4, 8 (a series of homilies on the creed); *s.* 229G; and *s.* 288.5 (cf. in both cases *trin.* 1.17); etc.

23 *s.* 89.4; 341.10–12 (cf. *trin.* 1.14; 2.2–3; note also that *s.* 186.2–3 uses Phil. 2:6–7 as a rule for interpreting Jn. 14:28 and 10:30, etc., without actually calling it a rule, as also at *s.* 229G.3 and other places).

24 Most extended treatment at *s.* 80.

25   *s.* 7.4; 117.6–16; 126.7–9; 139.3; 229G.4–5; 244.3–4; 341; etc.

26   Esp. at *s.* 52, but this seems directed at a more educated audience (see 52.10).

27   *s.* 21.5; 23.13; 34.4–5; cf. 90.10, where growth in love is the renewal of the image of God.

28   One theme especially worth noting in this regard is the ubiquity of the comparison between God's Word and our words. Ascent from consideration of our own words, both exterior and especially interior, to God's Word is a pivotal theme in *trin.* (see, e.g. 9.12–15; 14.10; 15.19–20, 22–25, 50): see *s.* 28.4–5; 119.7; 120; 179.6; 187; 223A; 225.3; 288.3–4; etc. On seeing God in general, see esp. 68–69; 179.6; 362.3–4. Excellent, fully explicit ascent, very reminiscent of *conf.* 10, at *s.* 293.5 and 52.7; see also 43.3; 68.6; 369.2.

29   The presence of Augustine's favorite theological themes in his sermons is frequently noted: "One could briefly describe the essential character of the content of his sermons by saying that they contain the sum of his profoundest spiritual knowledge and experience adapted to the pattern of everyday practical life …. That which he had stated in his great works in packed and highly articulated form he gave bit by bit in his sermon, never giving too much at once, but giving what he did give without adulteration" (van der Meer [1961], 433–434; cf. Pellegrino [1990], 56–70; and Rondet [1971], 81–105, 241–257). Mohrmann (1961) comments, "C'est. un fait remarquable que ce prédicateur qui s'efforce de parler une langue simple et compréhensible, qui fait des concessions à ses auditeurs en ce qui concerne la forme extérieure de sa prédication, ne leur relâche rien quand il s'agit de la doctrine. La prédication augustinienne revêt un caractère nettement théologique et spéculatif. Il donne dans ses sermons la plénitude de ses connaissances théologiques et de ses expériences spirituelles" (1:402). See also Mülhlenberg (1994), who points out that "Augustin bringt für sein Predigen die ganze Theologie mit" (17). However, the question I have posed is not simply whether Augustine incorporates theology into his sermons, but more precisely *how*. How does he adapt his theology for a mixed audience of educated and uneducated, literate and illiterate people? Mülhlenberg's conclusion is that Augustine's theology is present in his sermons as that which serves to bind together his biblical citations, a kind of "coordinate system" both governing and explaining the extent of his citations (19) – an excellent conclusion, although, to my mind, the result is more than a "lay dogmatic" ("Laiendogmatik," 19), the summary results of Augustine's inquiries, but rather a new context for inquiry itself.

30   There are a few exceptions, for example, the discussion of "consubstantial" at *s.* 139.2–3.

31   See, for example, citations of Ennius (*trin.* 13.6), Terrence (*trin.* 13.10), and Virgil (*trin.* 14.14, 18; 15.25). One exception is Augustine's defense of the *Christiana tempora* against charges that they have been the destruction of the empire: *s.* 81.9, where Augustine cites both Virgil and Sallust against claims that "Christian

times" have resulted in the fall of Rome; but here, he is careful to explain what "penates" means and to retell the story of the fall of Troy. Also, in the same context, *s*. 105.10.

32 As at *trin.* 9.15, 18; 10.1–4, 7; 12.23; 14.9, 11; etc.; in fact, many of the "trinities" that image God in the senses and mind are actually analyses of *learning*.

33 "Exotericizing," while awkward enough, is better than "popularizing," both because "popularizing" implies watering down, and also because of what Momigliano (1972) called "the Christian abolition of the internal frontiers between the learned and the vulgar," noting that "Christian intellectuals succeeded where pagan intellectuals had failed for centuries, both in transmitting their theories to the masses and in sharing the beliefs of the masses" (17), continuing, "However divided they were, the Christians were not divided culturally in the upper and lower strata …. Indeed I do not know of any ecclesiastical historian who condemns a Christian practice simply as being vulgar" (19). As such, strictly speaking, there were no "popular" beliefs – that is, beliefs discredited because they were characteristic of the masses. A comment such as this, however, begs for clarification, since distinctions between the educated and uneducated certainly persisted. I am suggesting that, instead of focusing on the communication of "theories," that is, the *results* of inquiry to the "masses," although that surely must be considered, there is the additional focus of recontextualizing the process of inquiry itself, making the homilies of Augustine, in some sense, themselves an educational venue. Brown (1992) comments that "Fourth-century Christianity, in fact, was far from being a 'popular' movement," and that this image of it is a function of Christian self-representation on the part of highly cultivated, educated bishops whose very education (*paideia*, passim) continued to mark them as members of the elite (75–76). However, to the extent that inquiry itself is recontextualized in Augustine's rhetoric as something available to all people of faith, it is not only represented as such, but, actually, in the delivery of the homilies, "exotericized," thus vindicating to some extent Momigliano's (1972) insight. On this topic, see also Brox (1972), Carpenter (1963), and Frend (1972).

34 *trin.* 1.4; see Cavadini (1992), 107, reprinted as Chapter 1 of this volume. See also Cavadini (1997), reprinted as Chapter 3 of this volume.

35 It is faith, not the liberal arts, which purifies the heart for the happy life of understanding (*trin.* 13.25), a reversal of Augustine's position in the Cassiciacum Dialogues – see Cavadini (1995), 167–168, and nn. 40–43 (reprinted as Chapter 2 of this volume) – although I believe that, in that discussion, I underestimated the role that faith, hope, and love played even in the dialogues, especially *sol.*

36 *s.* 32.7. The idea is not only to hear Augustine's "discussions" (*tractatus*), but to understand the Scripture which Augustine's treatment is meant to clarify: "… non solum ad audiendos tractatus nostros, sed etiam ad intellegendas ipsas

Scripturas, de quibus vobis ista tractamus."At 36.1, it is not only Augustine who will investigate the text in the hopes of understanding it, but the audience as well: "Sancta Scriptura quae modo in auribus vestris lecta est admonuit nos ... quaerere vobiscum et pertractare quid sit et quid sibi velit quod lectum est ...."

37   "Et ubi quaeras? Ubi, nisi in dominicis libris" (*s.* 105.3).

38   Augustine singles out those who pay attention and come frequently as those "Qui rudes non sunt in Scripturis divinis, qui amant frequentare istam scholam, qui non oderunt magistrum sicut pueri desperati, et intentam aurem praebent in ecclesia lectoribus atque exceptorium cordis sui in fluentia Scripturae divinae patefaciunt ..." (32.2), but the sermon is explicitly addressed to those who are not regulars, not "usitata intentis et studiosis litterarum divinarum" as well. These latter will need to be told the story of David and Goliath before it can be expounded (32.2).

39   "... in schola Christi cruditi estis" (*s.* 122.3). At 74.1, Augustine admonishes his hearers not to come to school unprepared. Because the words of Scripture often have meanings distinct from their "worldly" usage, a lack of preparation could lead his hearers to misunderstand Scripture: "Debemus enim non frustra intrare scholam, sed nosse in qua significatione Scripturarum verba teneamus; ne cum aliquid de Scripturis sonuerit, quod in alio saeculari usu intellegi solet, aberret auditor ...." In 399, Augustine talks about "what is to be learned (*discatur*) here," that is, in church, and goes on to compare the process of learning that goes on when the Scriptures are read and expounded to secular education (399.11–12): Christ is the teacher, his school (*schola*) is on earth, his school is his body, and the Head is teaching the members (399.15); his house is a house of "discipline" because it is a house of learning, as *disciplina* comes from *discendo* (399.1).

40   "With regard to miracles, some saw them and also understood them, and of such sort should we be who are in the school of Christ" (*tales nos in schola Christi esse debemus*) (*s.* 98.3).

41   "Videte, fratres mei, distinguite nutriti in Ecclesia, eruditi in Scripturis dominicis, non rudes, non rustici, non idiotae. Sunt enim inter vos docti ct eruditi viri et quibuscumque litteris non mediocriter instructi: et qui illas litteras quae liberales vocantur, non didicistis, plus est quod in sermone Dei nutriti estis" (*s.* 133–4).

42   "Audite non a me, sed mecum simul. Ait enim nobis quidam: *Venite, filii, audite me.* Et concurramus, et stemus, et aures arrigamus, et corde intellegamus Patrem qui dixit: *Venite, filii, audite me*" (*s.* 108.6). Cf. 60.6, "I have spoken, and you have listened – or rather he has spoken and we have all listened together" (*Nos diximus et vos audistis, immo ille [Christus] dixit et simul audivimus*).

43   "Intus auditor" (*s.* 179.1).

44   *s.* 134.1; cf. 23.2; 16A.1.

45   *s.* 23.1. Note that, at 213.11 (a sermon for handing the creed over to the catechumens), Augustine tells the catechumens not to be afraid if in 8 days they

have not memorized the creed perfectly, for "we [clergy?] are your fathers, we aren't carrying the canes and switches of schoolteachers (*grammaticorum*)." In other words, unlike the *grammaticus*, he is not concerned with exact wording, but with the faith underlying it: "Si quis in verbo erraverit, in fide non erret" (cf. *en. Ps.* 138.20, where he explains he would rather offend the *grammatici* than speak in a way the people cannot understand).

46   "Iudices auditis" (*s.* 52.8).

47   "... adiuvet [Dominus] nos misericordia et gratia sua me loquentem, vos iudicantes. Quamquam enim propter commoditatem depromendae vocis altiore loco stare videamur, tamen in ipso altiore loco vos iudicatis, et nos iudicamur" (*s.* 23.1).

48   "Intus autem ... omnes auditores sumus" (stated twice in *s.* 179.7); "Vellem scire, si iste qui mihi loquitur, omnia facit quae vel ipse audit, vel ceteris elicit" (179.10; note 355 and 356 as defenses against just such a question, and note at 180.10 Augustine's admission that he still swears ["For all that, I'm not telling you that I don't swear. I mean, if I do say that, I'm lying"]).

49   "... ut in eo quod verum dicimus – quoniam omne verum a veritate est – non nos, sed ipsum laudetis; ubi autem sicut homines offendimus, eumdem ipsum pro nobis oretis" (*s.* 23.2).

50   Perhaps best summed up at 379.4: "Try and understand, my brothers and sisters, recall the saving mystery, have a hunger for the Word of God, grasp what I am proclaiming (*praedicamus*), and let us together find joy in the truth."

51   "... secundum Scripturas quaereremus, qualis in resurrectione futura sit vita iustorum" (362.1). On the way in which Augustine's sermons respond to concerns of the people, see Rebillard (1994).

52   "Oritur quaestio profecto solvenda" and "videtis certe profunditatem quaestionis" (*s.* 99.4), followed by "Iam nunc quia ut potuimus, quaestionem profundam in tantilla temporis brevitate solvimus; aut si nondum solvimus debitores, ut dixi, teneamur" (99.7). Cf. 52.6–8.

53   Cf. 362.1, where the subject for discussion is called a *questio*.

54   See n. 69.

55   "But let me tell you briefly where the problem (*quaestionis*) lies in this reading (*lectio*), and then, when your interest is engaged by the problem we have been set (*facti intenti per propositam quaestionem*), pray that I may be enabled to solve it" (*s.* 133.1).

56   "Cum quaedam solvenda proponerem, studium vestrum me fecit et aliud poponere, quod forte non quaereretis" (*s.* 352.4). At other places, he comments on the pleasure of discovery in a way reminiscent of *doctr. chr.* On the figurative meaning of the bodily death of Moses: "O mira mysteria! Hoc certe expositum et intellectum, quanto dulcius quam manna?" (352.5), and again later, "Non ad fraudem, sed ad iucunditatem clausa erant. Neque enim tam dulciter caperentur, si prompta vilescerent." The obscurity of passages is a source of "fun" for the

inquirer. At 71.11, Augustine points out that we are nourished by the clear passages in Scripture, and exercised by the obscure or difficult ones, which serve to save us from boredom ("pascimur apertis, exercemur obscuris; illic fames pellitur, hic fastidium"); cf. 8.18 on the pleasure generated by the successful search for the meaning of a text. See *doctr. chr.* 2.6.7–8.

57   *s.* 43, an exegesis of Isa. 7:9, glossed with Mk. 9:24, "Help my unbelief," is one of the best expositions of this principle, especially because, like *trin.* (or at least, like Augustine in a letter referring its reader to *trin.* [*ep.* 120.3, CSEL 34, 707.2–5]), it concedes that some measure of understanding must come before faith.

58   "Fides enim gradus est intellegendi; intellectus autem meritum fidei" (*s.* 126.1).

59   *s.* 126.8, where he addresses both groups, apologizing if what he says appears to be a waste of time to those who will not immediately understand, yet going on to give the explanation which the text (Jn. 5:19) as he sees it demands. There is no hiding of "esoteric" material here.

60   "In his enim quae supra diximus hortantes ad fidem, ut animus imbutus fide sit intellectus capax, ea. quae dicta sunt, festiva, laeta, facilia, sonuerunt, exhilaraverunt mentes vestras, secuti estis, intellixistis quae dixi" (126.8). Augustine's exhortation to faith is a stimulus to understanding. The same progression is evident in *s.* 127: "'I've never seen this', you will say, 'someone begetting, and the one he has begotten always with him ....'You're quite right; I've never seen this, because it belongs to *what the eye has not seen* .... It is to be believed, and cultivated. When it is believed, it is cultivated; when cultivated, it grows; when it grows, it is grasped" (*Credatur, et colatur; cum creditur, colitur; cum colitur, crescitur; cum crescitur, capitur* [I have modified Hill's translation]). Faith here *is* the cultivation of understanding, and it bears at least partial fruit (or at least could bear partial fruit) now, in the course of this sermon. For the theme of "faith seeking understanding" in the sermons, see Pontet (1944), 113–115.

61   Note that the issue of rhetorical posturing does not mean that this is *merely* a rhetorical device, that it is *mere* rhetoric. Brown (1992) has shown that, by representing reality in a certain way, it *made* reality – the rhetors evoked a set of classical expectations for deportment that was, as he puts it, the "only effective constitution" that the empire ever knew (59). And Gleason (1995), in somewhat the same vein, has recently shown how the eunuch Favorinus "made" himself a man by his rhetorical practice.

62   *s.* 120.2; cf. 52.15. On the Easter homilies of Augustine, see Poque (1966): 9–153; see esp. at 119: "... parmi les *Sermones ad populum*, la prédication de la Pâque est certainement celle qui met l'orateur en présence de son public le moins cultivé, non le petit noyau des fidèles assidus mais le peuple accouru en raison de la solennité, avec au premier rang, adultes et enfants, les derniers catéchisés" (cf. Pontet [1944], p. 61). This makes the similarity of theme between *s.* 120, preached in Hippo on Easter, and *s.* 52, preached in Carthage to what is perhaps a more select audience, very significant.

63   The text shows the power of Augustine's preaching, "simple" though its style may be: "Est enim forma quaedam, forma non formata, sed forma omnium formatorum: forma incommutabilis, sine lapsu, sine defectu, sine tempore, sine loco, superans omnia, existens omnibus et fundamentum quoddam in quo sint, et fastigium sub quo sint" (117.3, compare to *trin.* 5.1–2, and even to the prologue of the *conf.*). Note also *s.* 53 as explicitly taking the faith of a "carnal" believer – one who interprets Isa. 66:1 and 40:12 to mean that God has a body – and leading that faith, through a course of reasoning, to understanding.

64   "Videamus ergo, et adhuc quantum possumus conemur penetrare mysterium" (*s.* 352.4).

65   "Erudiendos nos parvulos," *s.* 88.14; cf. 117.16, where Augustine styles himself as a *parvulus* along with the audience, "lacte parvuli nutriremur"; cf. 127.5, where it is the milk of faith that nourishes "us *infantes*" until the solid food of sight.

66   "Et ego scio, inquam, qui tecum loquor; nec ego comprehendo" (*s.* 225.3). Augustine goes on to point out that thinking about these things stretches our capacity to understand, but that even the enlarged capacity which results will not enable us to understand completely: "cogitatio facit nos extendi, extensio dilatat nos, dilatatio nos capaces facit. Nec facti capaces totum comprehendere poterimus."

67   Ultimately, the mystery of the Trinity and its unfathomableness is, for Augustine, not simply the mystery of a divine nature, a divine puzzle to try our wits, but the mystery of God's love as displayed in the economy of salvation, that is, the mystery of the incarnation, "this stupendous gift of God" (*s.* 215.3), before which all our intellects are humbled and all our speech insufficient, itself definitive of God's greatness (see the whole of 215.3).

68   "Ergo pro facie Dei, tibi pone interim Scripturam Dei" (*s.* 22.7). Not only does this mean that the same passage can have different, legitimate interpretations, but that it is impossible to codify figurative or allegorical meanings of *res* because these meanings shift and are determined by context (32.6). Yet, some meanings are consistent enough so that those who come to the *schola* of Scripture regularly can learn them, and understand even before Augustine speaks, for example, that the "valiant woman" of Prov. 31:10 is the church (37.1). This inexhaustibility of figurative meanings keeps those who already understand something seeking more: "Ne forte et ibi aliqua figura expressa sit, et innuerit intellegenti, et ad inquirendum commoverit et provocaverit animum." The text can have an indefinite quality, open to the discovery of more than one true meaning, and that invites and even impels continuing inquiry; see, for example, 71.10, regarding the blasphemy against the Holy Spirit, the nature of which is left indeterminate in the text, as Augustine points out: "Exercere quippe nos voluit [Dominus] difficultate quaestionis …. Quaeri, inquam, voluit …. Quia ergo nec universaliter nec particulariter enuntiata

sententia est … sed indefinite …. Id exprimere noluerit, ut petendo, quaerendo, pulsando, si quid recti intellectus acceperimus, non viliter habeamus." The passage implies that more than one right meaning may be found (on this, see *doctr. chr.* 3.27.38, with regard to possible multiplicity of figurative meanings, and *Gn. litt.* 1.20–21 on the fruitful difficulty of establishing even the correct literal interpretation of many passages).

69 See, for example, *trin.* 1.5; 2.1; 3.2; 5.1. In a more general way, Auerbach (1965) comments on the stylistic connection between the sermons and a treatise such as *trin.*: "[T]he *sermo humilis* … has other features besides vulgarisms and the like; one is its implication of direct human contact between you and me, a note that was lacking in the sublime style of Roman antiquity; another is its power to express human brotherhood, an immediate bond between men: all of us here and now …. My primary purpose in quoting the passage from the *trin.* was to show precisely that this style also pervaded the most speculative and least popular writing" (56–57). Banniard (1992), 83 and 94, also comments on the presence of such a style in the treatises, precisely, in part, as an appeal to the illiterate, who could not read but certainly could be read to.

70 *Io. eu. tr.* 99.8–9, at *trin.* 15.48.

71 The sermons, too, with their stylized give-and-take, where the audience sometimes speaks out but more often is presented as giving voice to questions, can themselves be imagined as a reincarnation or recasting of the dialogue form that Augustine tried out early on and then abandoned. This feature of the sermons as in some sense "dialogic" is commented on frequently. Mandouze (1968) entitles his chapter on the sermons "Dialogues avec la foule" (591), insists on the "real" character of the dialogue with the audience (641–642), and also compares them to the *sol.* (663). Note too the characterization of Augustine's rhetoric in Spence (1988), 82, as one that allows "an increase in the participation and power of the audience" (cf. 72, where "the audience, who, at least theoretically, had no voice, now has, at least in part, the voice of the orator, since the orator is always part of the audience"). See also Poque (1966): 121–123, on the relation between Augustine's style and the technique of diatribe; and Barry (1924), 149–151. More recently, Vessey (1993) has commented on the "conference"-style mode of exegesis developed by Augustine in the *conf.*, although I would argue for more continuity between the *Sermones ad populum* and the theory behind them in *doctr. chr.* 4 on the one hand, and *conf.* 11–13 on the other, than what the contrast on 209 implies (but see n. 15, where *doctr. chr.* does distinguish between a sermon and an actual conversation; yet, the same would apply to *conf.* 11–13, itself part of a book and not an actual conversation).

72 *trin.* 15.1. I have argued elsewhere that *trin.*, complete with its dialogic tone of a shared endeavor of seeking, is a kind of avatar or transmogrification of the early dialogues (see Cavadini [1992], reprinted as Chapter 1 of this volume).

73 It may well be that one of the most abstruse parts of *trin.* – the teaching on the "inner word" – is a teaching that very closely links it with the sermons, and it

may be an example of a teaching that went from the sermons to the treatise, rather than the other way around (see n. 28 for some examples).

74   On Caesarius' style and its relation to Augustine's, see Klingshirn (1994), 148–151.

75   See the discussion of Delage (1971) at SC 175:101–110.

76   Note in particular Caesarius' long *s.* 12 on faith. The absence of any reference to "seeking understanding" or any hint that faith is even related to understanding is glaring for a reader used to Augustine. See also *s.* 82.1, where Caesarius describes those who believe in the Trinity as "carnal" and "spiritual," which in Augustine generally leads to a description of some who can "see" or "understand" while some, the carnal, cannot, although they will come to understand by believing. For Caesarius, "carnal" merely means those who do not avoid sins and vices that the "spiritual" do in fact avoid.

77   *s.* 86.1, translated in Mueller (1964), 24–25. The source for this passage is probably Augustine, but not a sermon; see *Gn. adu. Man.* 1.1.1, cited by Banniard (1992), 83.

78   *s.* 4.4. Earlier in this section, the comparison had been slightly different: the priests were instructed to gather flowers from Holy Scripture and so offer spiritual milk to them, feeding the Christian people with their two udders, the Old and New Testaments, just as cows eat grasses and leaves and feed their calves with the milk prepared from them.

79   Although Augustine is perfectly ready to describe the preacher's task as offering, more generically, "nourishment" (*alimentum, s.* 8.1; etc.).

80   See *s.* 229E.4. Also at Augustine *s.* 10.8, the church, schismatic communions included, offers the milk (compare Caesarius' *s.* 123 to Augustine's *s.* 10, both on the story of Solomon's judgment over the two women claiming the same baby).

81   *s.* 6–8. The reading of Scripture is to replace long meals leading to drunkenness, especially in winter.

82   *s.* 6.1, remarking on how glad he is to see the people, "Quis enim pater est, qui filios suos, et praecipue fideles et bonos, non frequenter videre desideret?" (SC 175, edited by Delage [1971], 320).

83   *s.* 93.1, said, however, with a note of self-deprecation, as though he should be able to dole out more; and, in general, one must finally not underestimate Caesarius' achievements as a preacher. He could raise and answer, based on his readings in the Fathers, awkward objections to the faith (such as "why did God force the Canaanites out of their land" [*s.* 114.1–2, against the Manichees], or if the devil is bound, "why is he so powerful?" [121.6]) in a way that listeners could easily grasp and repeat. He consistently presented biblical figures as exemplars of virtue (such as the series on the patriarch Joseph [90–93]); hammered away unceasingly at the typological connections between the two Testaments; preached a program of Scripture reading, almsgiving, and chastity, which was easily summed up (at 6.8, Caesarius calls upon his congregation to

try to remember parts of what he had said so that, in conversation later, they could piece together the whole program); and inveighed against pagan religious practices and practices he considered holdovers from paganism; etc. Perhaps Caesarius' congregations were less well educated than Augustine's, but it is hard to tell, especially since Caesarius worked very hard to remove from his homilies all place and time references, so that they could be easily preached anywhere at anytime by anyone (see Delage [1971] in SC 175: 67–69). He certainly indicates the presence of both where any reference is made (such as at *s*. 86, cited earlier in text). It is true that he "uniformly gave preference to the least well-educated members of the audience" (Klingshirn [1994], 149), while Augustine did not observe this preference and sometimes warns that the unlearned may not be able to follow certain points; and yet, there is also a cost to Caesarius' practice. In Augustine's practice, the faith of all present, learned and unlearned, becomes styled as an orientation to inquiry in which all are *condiscipulos*; whereas, in Caesarius' case, no one's faith is styled that way, faith becomes not the doorway to understanding but a kind of closure to it, and the conceptual possibilities for any theory of *condiscipuli* seem obliterated. One might be able to compare this to the "dumbing down" of preaching and political rhetoric sometimes noted as a characteristic of our own time.

84　As, perhaps, at *s*. 212–213, but even here, the Augustinian teaching is mediated through Faustus of Riez.

85　Brown (1967), 9.

References

Attridge, Harold W. (1986) "The 'Gospel of Truth' as an Exoteric Text." In *Nag Hammadi, Gnosticism, and Early Christianity*, edited by Charles W. Hedrick and Robert Hodgson, Jr., 239–255. Peabody, MA: Hendrickson.

Auerbach, Erich (1965) *Literary Language and Its Public in Late Latin Antiquity and in the Middle Ages*. Ralph Manheim, trans. London: Routledge and Kegan Paul.

Auksi, Peter (1995) *Christian Plain Style: The Evolution of a Spiritual Ideal*. Montreal and Kingston: McGill-Queen's University Press.

Banniard, Michael (1992) *Viva Voce: Communication écrite et communication orale du IVe au IXe siècle en Occident latin*. Paris: Institut des Etudes Augustiniennes.

Barry, M. Inviolata (1924) *St. Augustine the Orator: A Study of the Rhetorical Qualities of St. Augustine's "Sermones ad populum."*. Washington, DC: Catholic University of America Press.

Becker, Aimé (1977) *L'appel des beatitudes*. Paris: Editions Saint-Paul.

Brown, Peter (1967) *Augustine of Hippo*. Berkeley, CA: University of California Press.

Brown, Peter (1992) *Power and Persuasion in Late Antiquity: Toward a Christian Empire*. Madison, WI: University of Wisconsin Press.

Brox, Norbert (1972) "Der Einfache Glaube und die Theologie: Zur altkirchlichen Geschichte eines Dauerproblems." *Kairos* 14: 161–187.

Bullough, Donald A. (1983) "Alcuin and the Kingdom of Heaven." In *Carolingian Essays*, edited by Uta-Renate Blumenthal, 1–69. Washington, DC: Catholic University of America Press.

Carpenter, H. J. (1963) "Popular Christianity and the Theologians in the Early Centuries." *Journal of Theological Studies*. 14: 294–310.

Cavadini, John C. (1992) "The Structure and Intention of Augustine's *De trinitate.*" *Augustinian Studies* 23: 103–123.

Cavadini, John C. (1995) "The Sweetness of the Word: Salvation and Rhetoric in Augustine's *De doctrina Christiana.*" In *De doctrina Christiana: A Classic of Western Culture*, edited by Duane W. H. Arnold and Pamela Bright, 164–181. Notre Dame: University of Notre Dame.

Cavadini, John C. (1997) "The Quest for Truth in Augustine's *De Trinitate.*" *Theological Studies* 58: 429–440.

Chadwick, Henry (1996) "New Sermons of St. Augustine." *Journal of Theological Studies*, 47: 69–91.

Contreni, John J. (1983) "Carolingian Biblical Studies." In *Carolingian Essays*, edited by Uta-Renate Blumenthal, 71–98. Washington, DC: Catholic University of America Press.

Delage, Marie-José, ed. (1971) *Caesarius. Sermons au peuple. Sources chrétiennes [SC] 175*. Paris: Les Éditions du Cerf.

Duncan-Jones, R. P. (1977) "Age-Rounding, Illiteracy, and Social Differentiation in the Roman Empire." *Chiron* 7: 33–353.

Societas Aperiendis Fontibus, ed. (1974) *Monumenta Germaniae Historica, Epistolarum tomus IV (Karolini aevi II)*, reviewed by Ernestus Duemmler. Berlin: Weidmann.

Frend, W. H. C. (1972) "Popular Religion and Christological Controversy in the Fifth Century." In *Popular Belief and Practice*, edited by G. J. Cuming and Derek Baker, 19–29. Cambridge: Cambridge University Press.

Gamble, Harry Y. (1995) *Books and Readers in the Early Church*. New Haven, CT: Yale University Press.

Gleason, Maude (1995) *Making Men: Sophists and Self-Presentation in Ancient Rome*. Princeton, NJ: Princeton University Press.

Harris, William V. (1989) *Ancient Literacy*. Cambridge: Harvard University Press.

Hill, Edmund, O.P., trans. (1990–1997) *Sermons, WSA III/1–11*. New York, NY: New City Press.

Junod, Eric (1994) "Wodurch unterscheiden sich die Homilien des Origenes von seinen Kommentaren." In *Predigt in der alten Kirche*, edited by E. Muhlenberg and J. van Oort, 50–81. Kampen: Kok Pharos.

Kaster, Robert A. (1988) *Guardians of Language: The Grammarian and Society in Late Antiquity*. Berkeley, CA: University of California Press.

Klingshirn, William (1994) *Caesarius of Arles: The Making of a Christian Community in Late Antique Gaul*. Cambridge: Cambridge University Press.

Lot, Ferdinand (1968) "A quelle époque a-t-on cessé de parler Latin?" In *Recueil des travaux historiques de Ferdinand Lot. 3*, vols. 1: 415–477. Geneva: Librairie Droz.

MacMullen, Ramsay (1966) "A Note on *Sermo Humilis.*" *Journal of Theological Studies* 17: 108–112.

MacMullen, Ramsay (1989) "The Preacher's Audience (A.D. 350–400)." *Journal of Theological Studies* 40: 503–511.

Mandouze, André (1968) *Saint Augustine: L'Aventure de la raison et de la grâce*. Paris: Études Augustiniennes.

Meyer, Elizabeth Ann (1989) "Literacy, Literate Practice, and the Law in the Roman Empire, A.D. 100–600." PhD diss., Yale University.

Mohrmann, Christine (1932) "Das Wortspiel in den Augustinischen sermones." *Mnemosyne* 3: 33–61. Reprinted in Mohrmann (1961), 1:323–349

Mohrmann, Christine (1947) "Augustinus en de Eloquentia." In *Christendom en Oudheid*, edited by J. Fruytier, 26–46. Eindhoven: Vrijdag. Translated by Mary Hedlund as "Augustine and the 'Eloquentia,'" and reprinted in Mohrmann (1961): 1:351–370.

Mohrmann, Christine (1954) "Augustin Prédicateur." *La Maison Dieu* 39: 83–96. Reprinted in Mohrmann (1961), 1:391–402.

Mohrmann, Christine (1957) "Considerazioni sulle 'Confessioni' di Sant'Agostino." *Convivium* 25: 257–267; and 27 (1959): 1–12, 129–39. Reprinted as a whole in Mohrmann (1961), 2:277–323.

Mohrmann, Christine (1958) "Saint Augustin Ecrivain." *Recherches Augustiniennes* 1: 43–66. Reprinted in Mohrmann (1961), 2:246–275.

Mohrmann, Christine (1961) *Etudes sur le Latin des Chrétiens*, vols. 4. Rome: Edizioni di Storia e Letteratura.

Momigliano, Arnaldo (1972) "Popular Religious Beliefs and the Late Roman Historians." In *Popular Belief and Practice*, edited by G. J. Cuming and Derek Baker, 1–18. Cambridge: Cambridge University Press.

Mueller, Sister Mary Magdeleine, O. S. F., trans. (1964) *Caesarius. Sermons vol. II (81–186), [FC 47.]* Washington, DC: The Catholic University of America Press.

Mülhlenberg, Ekkehard (1994) "Augustins Predigen." In *Predigt in der alten Kirche*, edited by E. Muhlenberg and J. van Oort, 9–24. Kampen: Kok Pharos.

Oberhelman, Stephen M. (1991) *Rhetoric and Homiletics in Fourth-Century Christian Literature*. Atlanta: Scholars Press.

Olivar, Alexandre (1991) *La Predicación Cristiana Antigua*. Barcelona: Editorial Herder.

Pellegrino, Michele Cardinal (1990) "General Introduction." In *Sermons, (1–19) on the Old Testament, WSA III/1*, 13–137. Brooklyn, NY: New City Press

Pontet, Maurice (1944) *L'Exégèse de S. Augustin Prédicateur*. Paris: Aubier.

Poque, Suzanne (1966) "Introduction." In eadem, trans., *Augustin d'Hippone: Sermons pour la pâque*, 9–153. Sources chrétiennes 116. Paris: Les Éditions du Cerf.

Rebillard, Eric (1994) "Contexte local et prédication: Augustin et le détresse des mourants." In *Cristianesimo e specificità regionali nel Mediterraneo Latino (sec. IV–VI), Studia Ephemerides Augustinianum 46*, 179–187. Rome: Institutum Patristicum Augustinianum.

Rettig, John W., trans (1988) *Tractates on the Gospel of John, FC 78*. Washington, DC: The Catholic University of America Press.

Robertson, D. W. Jr., trans. (1958) *On Christian Doctrine*. Indianapolis and New York: Bobbs-Merrill.

Rondet, H. (1971) "La théologie de S. Augustin prédicateur." *Bulletin de Litterature Ecclesiastique* 72 (81–105): 241–57.

Spence, Sarah (1988) *Rhetorics of Reason and Desire*. Ithaca, NY: Cornell University Press.

Teske, R. J. (1984) "Spirituals and Spiritual Interpretation in Augustine." *Augustinian Studies* 15: 65–81.

Uthemann, Karl-Heinz (1996) "Bemerkungen zu Augustins Auffassung der Predigt." *Augustinianum* 36: 147–181.

van der Meer, Frederick (1961) *Augustine the Bishop*, Brian Battershaw and G. R. Lamb, trans. New York, NY: Harper and Row.

Verbraken, Pierre-Patrick (1976) *Études critiques sur les sermons authentiques de Saint Augustin*. Steenbrugis: Martinus Nijhoff.

Vessey, Mark (1993) "Conference and Confession: Literary Pragmatics in Augustine's 'Apologia contra Hieronymum'." *Journal of Early Christian Studies* 1: 175–213.

6

Feeling Right
Augustine on the Passions and Sexual Desire

There are so many fine studies on Augustine and the passions, and particularly on Augustine and sexuality, that it seems a shame to add one more. Peter Brown (1988), Elizabeth Clark (1986a), David Hunter (1994), Richard Sorabji (2000), and, most recently, Mathijs Lamberigts (2000),[1] among others, have demonstrated the complexity of Augustine's thought on this issue. It is, certainly, the complexity of Augustine's thought which emerges from these fine studies. Peter Brown so eloquently situates the discussion away from "the body," per se, and firmly toward "society," such that physical existence as such is no longer regarded, as it was with more ancient ascetic theorists, as the "aboriginal catastrophe" of human life. Rather, it was part of God's original intention that human beings live together in embodied existence, reproducing by means of sexual intercourse in marriage. Even Adam's sin, as Clark (1986a) has emphasized, was due to his reluctance to abandon Eve, his only companion, once she had ventured past the boundaries of God's commandments.[2] Peter Brown (1988) reminds us that, for Augustine, the fundamental human catastrophe is not embodiedness, but rather a catastrophe of the will, a "dislocation of the human person," an "abiding, unhealed fissure in the soul" stemming from Adam's Fall, a distortion of the soul itself in which the soul "lost all ability to summon up all of itself, in an undivided act of will." Sexual desire, in this "austerely psychological" theory, was taken from

Visioning Augustine, First Edition. John C. Cavadini.
© 2019 John Wiley & Sons Ltd. Published 2019 by John Wiley & Sons Ltd.

the realm of physiology and complexified beyond a mere biological impulse, the *calor genitalis* favored as the theory of choice of Julian of Eclanum, Augustine's younger rival. *Concupiscentia carnis* is desire disintegrated against will and against itself, not simply an innocent impulse, like hunger, though more difficult to use in moderation.[3] Paradoxically, such a seemingly pessimistic view of sex yielded an ethic of marriage at once more tolerant and more affirming than that of many of the older ascetical theorists such as Jerome and even Ambrose, as David Hunter (1999) has shown us.[4]

If this further small study has any use at all, it will be because it will have forwarded the complexifying movement already well underway in earlier studies. Even in its complexified form, Augustine's view of sexual desire has not found many takers among his modern commentators. Cassian's implicit rebuttal has seemed persuasive to many.[5] No matter what benefit accrued to theories of sexuality from Augustine's complexifying of them, most commentators would agree with Brown's (1988) observation that "Augustine never found a way ... of articulating the possibility that sexual pleasure might, in itself, enrich the relations between husband and wife."[6] Lamberigts (2000) agrees when he says that "our present day positive sentiments with regard to sexuality"[7] would certainly prompt us to see the justice in many of the criticisms which have been lodged against Augustine in this matter. It is hard not to see the truth in these claims.

Nevertheless, it is here that it may be possible to complexify the matter even further, because our views of Augustine on the subject of sexuality are even more closely tied to our contemporary feelings on the issue than on most other subjects in Augustinian studies. I think I would have to ask this question on behalf of Augustine: precisely toward what aspect in "sexuality" do we have "positive sentiments" today? As both Brown (1988) and Lamberigts (2000) corroborate, Augustine had very positive sentiments toward sexuality, but not toward what he called "lust" in its specifically sexual sense. If we answer that it is with regard to sexual pleasure in marriage that we now have a more positive attitude, Augustine could still very well ask us what precisely we mean by "sexual pleasure." Perhaps not all of our contemporaries have "positive" sentiments with regard to sexuality or to the place of pleasure in intercourse. With regard to "intercourse in a man-made world" (read, "fallen" world from Augustine's perspective), Dworkin (1987) notes:

The experience of fucking changes people, so that they are often lost to each other and slowly they are lost to human hope. The pain of having been exposed, so naked, leads to hiding, self-protection, building barricades, emotional and physical alienation or violent retaliation against anyone who gets too close.[8]

With regard to pleasure:

Because a woman's capacity to feel sexual pleasure is developed within the narrow confines of male sexual dominance, internally there is no separate being ….There is only the flesh-and-blood reality of being a sensate being whose body experiences sexual intensity, sexual pleasure, and sexual identity in being possessed: in being owned and fucked.[9]

The corresponding male version of sexual pleasure is, in this scheme, scarcely distinct from the pleasures of domination, of hatred, and, even in its tenderest moments, of the threat of violence.[10] Dworkin agrees that our contemporary view of sexuality is positive, but she criticizes this view as unreflective and shallow:

In Amerika [*sic*], there is the nearly universal conviction – or so it appears – that sex (fucking) is good and that liking it is right: morally right; a sign of human health; nearly a standard for citizenship. Even those who believe in original sin and have a theology of hellfire and damnation express the Amerikan creed, an optimism that glows in the dark: sex is good, healthy, wholesome, pleasant, fun; we like it, we enjoy it, we want it, we are cheerful about it; it is as simple as we are, the citizens of this strange country with no memory and no mind.[11]

Some of us may be tempted to say, as Brown (1988) said of Augustine's view, that this is "a drastically limited vision of a complex phenomenon,"[12] and undoubtedly it would be true to some extent as it would be in Augustine's case as well. Nevertheless, in some ways, Dworkin's radical hermeneutic of suspicion *vis-à-vis* our own culture gets closer to the approach that Augustine takes than the rest of us do, content as we are to isolate "sexual pleasure" as though it were an unimpeachably fixed quantity innocent of political dynamics, far from being contoured or warped by ideologies of power and domination.

The first step in complexifying our view of Augustine's vision of sexual desire is to notice its context in Augustine's view of emotion and passion in general, and for this we can turn to book 14 of the *City of God* (*ciu.*). Augustine is suspicious not only of lust in the sexual sense but of all of the passions, and not only of the passions themselves but of the very idea of "passion" as though it offered a complete description of the range of human emotions, or as though "emotion" were equivalent to "passion." Augustine is very careful about his use of language in book 14, though his translators do not often reflect his precision. "Passions," if one chooses to use that term, are always bad, while "emotions" can be either bad or good. Augustine, in the midst of refuting both Manichees and Platonists (who are a milder version of the Manichaen position as Augustine sees it), points out that tendencies to sin do not come from the body, certainly not from the body as originally constituted, and not even primarily from the mortal bodies we have inherited from Adam, but from the soul itself.[13] In fact, Augustine wants to say that tendencies to sin do not even come from the emotions as such, though they are normally blamed. Tendencies to sin – in fact, "all defects in human character"[14] – are comprised by the four passions: desire, joy, fear, and grief.[15] But it is crucial to notice that the emotions corresponding to these words do not have to be "passions" to be emotions. Passions are pathologized versions of these emotions, such that they are experienced as "disturbances" (*perturbationes*), to use Cicero's expression for what Augustine says are called by the Greeks as "passions" (*passiones*). The hallmark of a "passion" or "disturbance" is that it is a movement of the soul, an "emotion," contrary to reason or "irrational." Animals may have strong movements of the soul, but they do not have passions, because they do not have reason. Passions have a life seemingly independent of ourselves as reasoning beings. As such they are disturbances, they are like "storms and tempests," properly compared to a sea in a storm,[16] and so they seem to come from somewhere else other than the rational mind, which they disturb, which can be said to "suffer" them as passions – and hence the Manichaean and Platonist temptation to theorize that they do in fact come from somewhere else, to wit, the body.

Augustine deconstructs the Platonist position by refusing to accept the implied identification of passion with emotion. He does not use the word "passion" or the word "disturbance" to carry on his discussion of the emotions, but rather the word "motus," which we could translate simply as "motions [of the soul]" or "emotions," or sometimes the word "affectus," which we can translate as "affect" or "feeling," or sometimes there is no noun at all, but a passive verb such as "movetur."[17] These emotions – desire, joy, fear, and grief – are neither right nor wrong in themselves; they are not *as emotions* tendencies to sin:

> What makes the difference is what kind of will a person has. If the will is perverse, the person will have perverse emotions, but if the will is right, not only will the emotions be blameless, but even praiseworthy.[18]

Augustine goes on to comment that the emotions are shot through with will, that in fact they are nothing but "voluntates," "wills" in the sense of "acts of will."[19] Augustine is suspicious of claims of any independent volition coming from a source other than the soul or self. "Passions" too are acts of the will, though they are acts of the will as corrupted and warped by the primal sin of *superbia* or pride, so warped that they seem to represent a will different from our own.

"Pride" in the *ciu.* is the original sin, the sin of an illusory elevation of the self over God, a will to be independent of God as though one were one's own "principium" or foundation of being. In book 14, it is described in terms which lend themselves to an analysis of the emotions as they are formatted by a prideful will. The prideful will is itself characterized as an "appetite," specifically, an appetite for a perverse exaltation, a being pleased with oneself more than one is pleased with God.[20] The prideful are the "self-pleasers" (*sibi placentes*),[21] those who are pleased with themselves in the sense that they came to enjoy themselves as their own "first principle."[22] Since this, however, is contrary to reality, a "lie"[23] (since one is not one's own first principle), living with oneself as one's primary pleasure means living an affective life that cannot give an account of itself, except as a dissimulation. One loves as though one were the sovereign ground and origin of one's own good, and since that is a lie, one is somehow loving a situation in which one's own sovereignty is precisely what one loses. The "self-pleasers" are "given over to themselves" (e.g. last section of 14.24), and the moment of self-pleasing, of pleasure in one's own power or ability independent of God, is a moment of turbulence of emotions and desires, a disintegration of the life of willing and loving in which the emotions can seem to oppose and even win out over the will. This disintegration is itself not simply a consequence of an act of the will but an act of the will itself which persists as a "punishment," because it is a defect that cannot be reversed on its own. The passions are "bad fruit," but bad fruit of a "bad tree" (14.13; see Mt. 7:18), namely, the self in the false state of loving itself[24] as though it were its own end, but having more love and desire than it can possibly bestow on itself because the self is not as great as the Good which corresponds to the depth of its willing. Being too pleased with oneself (cum *sibi nimis placet*, 14.13) means feeling the depth of one's own emotion as though it came from somewhere else, not oneself, for such a degree of frankly and desperately needy desire would be its own verification that one was not self-sufficient, the ground of one's own being. Thus, to conflate "emotion" or "affect" with "passion" is a kind of ideology of this original lie, the lie that one commits oneself to in pride, and we might say that the hermeneutic of suspicion is one which does not accept the "passions" at face value, that is, as somehow an external agency instead of what they are, emotions of one's own formatted by one's own will into an alienated structure of feeling. Augustine's hermeneutic of suspicion will not accept the passions as an exhaustive catalogue of human emotional life.

As already noted, for Augustine, if the will is right, that is, fixed in love of God, in charity, then the emotions will be right, and if the will is wrong, that is, fixed in love of self over love of God, then the emotions will be wrong (see also 14.7). They will be "sicknesses,"[25] pathologized versions of feelings which would otherwise be commendable. On what grounds does Augustine refuse to accept the "passions" as an exhaustive description of human affective life? On the grounds of revelation. He appeals to the usage of Scripture, showing from it all kinds of desiring, fearing, grieving, and joy which are commendable, such as Apostle Paul's desire to depart and be with Christ or his instruction to work out our salvation in fear and trembling, or the Psalmist's joy in the Lord.[26]

But it is primarily the example of Christ as recorded in the Gospels that serves for Augustine to decouple "passion" and "emotion" or "feeling" most forcefully. Jesus, according to the Gospel narratives, had feelings or emotions, and these were real, not feigned, because Jesus, being truly human, had a real human body and a real human mind (*animus*).[27] Augustine emphasizes that these were real feelings or emotions but distinguishes them from "sicknesses," from "vicious feelings, the passions" (14.9). He observes that "the Lord himself, having condescended to live a human life *in the form of a servant* [Phil. 2:7] but having nothing whatsoever of sin, showed these feelings in situations where in his judgment they ought to be shown. Nor is it the case that in him, who had a true human body and a true human soul, human feeling (*humanus affectus*) was false .... Rather, he took up these emotions in his soul, in keeping with his unwavering providential intention, when he willed to, just as he was made a human being when he so willed" (14.9).

We are inclined, I think, to react to this passage and others like it thinking that, if he *willed* to have or take up these feelings, they can't be real feelings. But the point is that, just as Christ's will to take up human life *in forma servi* is a function of charity and humility, so too are Christ's feelings. All of them are a function of the same perfectly free love that motivated the providential design of the Incarnation. If we were not so used to equating "emotion" with "passion," if our imaginations were not so enfeebled by the pride that sickens them, we would realize that Christ's human emotions, as a function of the charity and compassion of God, are felt more deeply than our own because they are perfectly willed, perfectly *his* acts, not in any way alienated from himself, perfectly integrated acts of the self in love and humility. God in his divine nature does not "feel" anything (a frequent assertion of Augustine),[28] but God declares solidarity with us by having real human emotions in Christ, by deigning "to be moved" and truly moved, truly grieved (for example) at the sight of human suffering or truly (not metaphorically) angered at obduracy. That God would "feel" with us in Christ is a mark of God's love and humility, and so Jesus's emotions are functions of, windows into, the love and humility, and so the compassion, of God. His emotions, one might say, are the truest, most real emotions possible. Christ in his human nature has no need to fake or to dissemble in any way. We are the ones who refuse to experience our own "being moved" as co-terminus with our own willing, that is, as in some way an act of our own will. We choose instead to experience the "being moved" as though it were the result of another agency outside of ourselves, moving us. We thus experience our emotions therefore as "passions." Thus it is our emotions, if any, that have an element of (almost theatrical) falseness about them, an element of the primal lie, the primal commitment to dissimulation which is *superbia*.

I would like to move from here back to a consideration of the subject of sexual desire, or more precisely what Augustine calls "lust" in its specifically sexual sense.[29] Like the emotions of Christ but in a different way, this lust was always, for Augustine, among other things, specifically a problem of the imagination. I would like to treat it specifically as such in this chapter. Augustine often complains that his discussion of the matter is hemmed in by lust itself because even a learned discussion of sex might arouse lust or shame in the writer or in the reader. It is important to keep in mind that lust, for Augustine, is precisely not "spontaneous sexual desire" in our modern sense[30] of a free and innocent natural urge, but a desire which cannot be assessed apart from the other commitments of the will with which it is co-terminus, and which, for Augustine, it seems to represent most fully. It is a desire which is supremely unfree, which, when present, is felt as a kind of "goading" (14.23), and which, when absent, cannot be called up at will (14.16). It gives rise to a pleasure which is "unsurpassed among physical pleasures" and which involves the almost complete obliteration of the mind's powers of discernment (14.16, *acies*). Lust is the expectation of and desire for that pleasure (14.15). It is for Augustine the parade example of a "sick" movement of the soul, one so alienated by pride into a seemingly independent agency that it is powerful enough, simply as an emotion, to move the sexual parts of the body without any intervening decision of the will (in other cases, the will may be swayed by the emotion, e.g. of anger, but the emotion itself does not move the body directly, 14.19). This causes shame because, paradoxically, it belies the mythos of self-sufficiency to which pride is committed.[31] It is the sole external indicator or sign that the claim to self-sufficiency, to sovereignty, is a lie. It gives rise to hiding, and the immodesty of the Cynics, for Augustine, only serves as the exception which proves the rule.[32]

It is because lust is both so forceful and so elusive that it constitutes a limit to discussion and indeed to signification in general. This is true especially of discussions of sex. The problem is particularly evident when one tries to think not about sex as it is but about what sex might have been like without lust. To us, it hardly seems imaginable, partly because it seems to us, used to conflating "passion" with "feeling" or "emotion," that Augustine is asking us to imagine sex without feeling or emotion. But if it is accepted that lust is a pathologized desire, trying to imagine sex without lust is not the same thing as trying to imagine sex without feeling, even intense feeling. And yet, it almost amounts to the same thing because lust has such a firm grip on the emotional life of the fallen that it is hard to imagine or to speak beyond it.

First of all, Augustine takes it from Scripture that intercourse in Paradise would have occurred without lust, because the telltale sign of lust, shame, shows up in Paradise only after the Fall (14.21), even though there is now no "example" to work from to describe what it might have been like without lust.[33] Even to try to imagine sex before lust or to speak of it means using words and expressions which now arouse lust, even if obscenities are avoided. The only referent we have for these signifiers involves lust; they signify lust for us.[34] That is why Augustine turns at first to non-sexual examples of unusual control of the body by will. Augustine's main point in giving these examples is to emphasize that the current scope of our conscious will need not be a limit on our imagination. They are simple mind experiments meant to emphasize that parts of the body which seem only under somatic control, such as the ability to perspire or to regurgitate or to break wind, can come under the control of the will (14.24). These examples show that it is not beyond imagining that the sex organs, which are now moved directly by a feeling rather than by the will in response to a feeling, could possibly come under the command of the will. The examples are not meant to say anything about whether any feeling or emotion would be involved or not, but simply to be a first attempt at thinking or imagining past lust with examples that could not possibly arouse lust.

But then we come to ground zero, the primal scene, as it were, sex in paradise. Augustine continues to warn the reader that lust puts a boundary on his discussion and his eloquence, such that, though he is doing his best to imagine or conjecture what sex might have been like, "shame impedes speech" because no one has ever had experience of sex committed *tranquillo arbitrio*, that is, with a will undisturbed by passion. Instead, the very mention of the subject only serves to bring to mind "the turbulent lust which in fact we experience" (14.26). Augustine recalls the bliss of paradise. It is not without feeling, but it is without passion, and it is altogether without fear or sadness since there was nothing to occasion such emotions. "Real joy poured forth perpetually from God, towards whom there blazed forth *charity from a pure heart and a good conscience and a faith unfeigned* [1 Tim. 1.5]. Between the spouses there was a faithful partnership based on an honest love."[35] Perhaps part of Augustine's point is that, under the dominion of lust, such an honest and open partnership is just as hard to imagine as what comes next. "In the circumstances of such human happiness," Augustine says, "let us not imagine that it was impossible for the seed of children to be sown without the sickness of lust."[36] Instead, what we should imagine is at least the following:

> [W]ithout feeling the goading of seductive and burning agitation, the husband would have come to rest on his wife's bosom in tranquility of mind and without any corruption of her body's integrity.[37]

This latter point Augustine explains by suggesting that, perhaps when the relevant parts of the body were not driven by turbulent heat but by a capability of acting freely, the male seed could be introduced into the wife's womb without damage to her genitals.[38] Augustine opines that by whatever passage menstrual flow can issue without such damage, so could the seed be introduced.

Some contemporary readers might be inclined to read this and think, "No thanks, that doesn't sound like it's even interesting, never mind fun!" Other readers may and have wondered if this really *is* intercourse, if there really is any penetration at all. Could there really be any penetration if somehow it could be accomplished without loss of virginity? But, in a way, that is Augustine's whole point: once lust has been taken out of the picture, the picture looks blank to us, because all the signifiers used to describe the scene are, for us, laden with lust. To take lust out of the scene means to take signifiers out altogether. In any event, to put this description of sex in paradise into perspective, one might look at another description of sex in the *ciu.*, this time from book 6. Here, Augustine's main purpose is to criticize pagan religion and, in particular, to show that the "civil theology" of the commonwealth's rites and rituals is no different from the "fabulous theology" of the myths and theaters which the learned would eschew even as they embrace the former. An example of the former – civil theology – is the ritual and belief that accompany the bride and groom on their wedding night. In subjecting it to ridicule, Augustine at the same time also paints a picture of what might happen on a typical wedding night. It is a compelling passage whose power derives from its narrative, so I quote here at length:

> The god Jugatinus is brought in when a man and a woman are "yoked" in marriage. So far, so good. But the bride has to be escorted home, so

the god Domiducus is also employed to "lead her home." To install her
in the house, the god Domitius sees to her "going home." The goddess
Manturna is called in as well, to see that she will "remain" with her
husband. What else is needed? Have some pity on human modesty! Let
the sexual desire of flesh and blood achieve the rest once the proper
privacy has been secured. Why crowd the bedroom with a throng of
deities, when even the wedding attendants retire? And what is the
purpose of so crowding it? That the thought of the presence of the
gods should make the couple more concerned to preserve decency?
Not at all. It is rather to ensure that with their cooperation there shall
be no difficulty in ravishing the virginity of a girl who feels the weakness of her sex and is terrified by the strangeness of her situation. For
here are the goddess Virginensis, and Father Subigus, and Mother
Prema and the goddess Pertunda, as well as Venus and Priapus. What
does all this mean? If the husband finds the job altogether too much
for him and needs divine assistance, would not one god or one goddess
be enough? Why wouldn't Venus alone be up to it? She is, they say, so
named because "not without violence" (*vi non sine*) can a woman be
robbed of her virginity. If there is any modesty among human beings
(there seems to be none among the gods!), I feel sure that the belief in
the presence of so many divinities of both sexes to urge on the business
in hand would so embarrass the couple as to quench the enthusiasm of
the one and stiffen the reluctance of the other! And surely if the goddess Virginensis is among those present to see to the untying of the
virgin girdle, and Subigus, to see that the bride is subdued to her husband, and Prema, to make sure that, when subdued, she is pressed tight
to keep her from moving – if they are there, then what is the function
of the goddess Pertunda? She should blush for shame and take herself
off! Let the bridegroom have something to do for himself! It would be
most improper for anyone but the husband to do what her name
implies.[39]

To Augustine's readers, this may have been commonplace knowledge, but to us this lawful wedded intercourse sounds much more
like rape, with its talk of subduing, pressing, and penetrating someone
who is reluctant and fearful. Perhaps sex in paradise as Augustine
describes it may not seem like much to us, but perhaps it would have
sounded great to the young wife of this narrative,[40] maybe something
in fact beyond the imagination. Augustine seems to have in mind at
very least something more gentle, something in fact so completely

free of violence that it would not injure the woman in the least, even the first time.

To return for a moment to Andrea Dworkin (1987), she too, though perhaps even more pessimistic about intercourse in a man's world than Augustine is about intercourse in a fallen world, essays a few modest experiments of the imagination that try to reach beyond the current reality of intercourse, namely, as she sees it, entry, occupation, and colonization/collaboration, as well as the construction of pleasure for both sexes accordingly. She quotes with approval a suggestion by Shere Hite, namely, that there might be:

> … an intercourse in which "thrusting would not be considered as necessary as it now is … [There might be] more a mutual lying together in pleasure, penis-in-vagina, vagina-covering-penis, with female orgasm providing much of the stimulation necessary for male orgasm …"

However, after citing this suggestion, Dworkin notes it only as an example of an improbable vision of "a humane sensuality based in equality" that seems inexplicably to persist in the aspirations of women, "deep humane dreams that repudiate the rapist as the final arbiter of reality." They are the stuff of "resistance," but, like Augustine's description of sex in paradise, they are a huge stretch of the imagination, and in the stretching, as in Augustine's scenario, you end up with a picture that may not look much like intercourse to many readers. Or, to put it more bluntly, these visions "do not amount to much in real life with real men."[41]

Another thing worth noticing about the passage from book 6 is that, in this passage, lust is exposed not as something merely "personal" and "private" but something which is, in effect, a cultural project. The rape of the newly married wife is something all of the deities of the civil religion urge forward, and so there is carried forward in the lust at work in that rape all the force of the cultural reality of the Empire, which in the *ciu.* is a kind of image or even sacramental representation of the "city of this earth," the collectivity of those dominated by love of self over love of God. The *libido dominandi*, the lust for domination which is the hallmark of the city of this earth in its pride, could never brook a situation in which, as Augustine imagines in Paradise, the man and the woman existed in a perfectly joyful fellowship of noble, transparent love with no dissimulation. Such a thing, which would bear witness to the glory of God the Creator and the status of male and female as God's beloved creatures, could never be allowed to exist in the face of the claims of the Empire to define fully on its own terms the meaning of human life in all its aspects. This will have to be the very first thing to go if the world is to be safe for empires. Pride cannot grant that one will be moved in one's deepest self, *as* one's deepest self, by the beauty of someone else *qua* someone else, but rather by one's own capacity for sovereignty on its own terms. Lust ensures that the procreation of children will also be the procreation of the ideals that underlie the Empire, if "ideals" is the proper word for a humanity enfeebled in its ability to imagine any relationship that is not based upon complacency in the pursuit of power – on "self-pleasing" in some way. Original sin is perpetuated by lust because, to the lustful, there is no other reality imaginable, and all selves are defined socially within that reality. Procreation becomes the same as propagation of imperial values.[42] We can say that, for Augustine, the personal is very much the political.

To fault Augustine in this context for not realizing that "sexual pleasure" can enrich a couple's relationship, or to assess Augustine's views against our own more "positive" view, may be, with all due respect, to beg a question: for Augustine, the question would not be whether sexual pleasure can enrich a couple's relationship, but whether there is any sexual pleasure possible without a taint of violence or complacency ("self-pleasing") in it. The question would be, what are we taking pleasure from? Pleasure, as Augustine is at pains to point out, is an affair of the soul, not the body. The pleasure that satisfies lust, *qua* lust, is not the enjoyment, physical or otherwise, of the awesome beauty of another person as the creation of God. It could not be, because lust is based on pride, while pleasure in someone else's being – a being that is a gift of God – is rather pleasure in humility. For example, can we say that any act of sexual delight is completely free from smugness, from self-admiration, from the slightest hint of "self-pleasing" in the mastery of the "skill sets" of popular magazines, in the thought that one is an accomplished, or at least halfway-decent, lover? Violence includes the admiration of power or ability *as* power or ability (as Augustine reminds us at the end of book 14).[43]

So, where does that leave us? If lust cannot be redeemed, as (for Augustine) it cannot be,[44] where are we? Can we speak meaningfully, if lust is a disease, of its healing? Can lust be replaced as we are healed of it, such that, even if we can never engage in sex without it, it does not fully define the experience any longer? Can we learn to take pleasure apart from lust? These questions bring us to the threshold of the imagination, as we have seen, and that truly is where Augustine leaves us. We can have these realities in imagination.

This, however, is more concrete than it may sound – for the content and determinant of the imagination, when it comes to questions of the emotions, is Christ, as we have already seen. Christ offers to us the reality of an emotional life which is fully free of the dissembling that is at the heart of "passion," and so calls to us beyond that dissembling to deeper feeling, to self-possession.

As a fallen being, my emotions are passions; they threaten to overwhelm me, seemingly, from a source outside myself; they are not my own very self's needing something outside myself badly. But as such they are themselves a temptation even to those aspiring to virtue because one may think that the way out is to conquer and eliminate emotion itself through the exercise of power (*virtus*).

That, at least, is the claim the Stoics make for the ideal state of *apatheia*. The Stoics are present in the *ciu.* in a way as the enantiomer of Christ, the mirror image of Christ's emotional life only formatted according to pride instead of love. Augustine ponders what *apatheia* might involve. Strictly speaking, does it mean the absence of passions, namely, "feelings which arise contrary to reason and disturb the mind," "sick" movements of the soul? "If so," Augustine comments, "it is clearly a good and desirable state; but it does not belong to this present life" (14.9, translated by Bettenson [1972]) because none of us are without sin. "But," he continues, "if *apatheia* is the name of a state in which the mind cannot be touched by any feeling whatsoever, who would not judge such insensitivity to be the worst of all vices?" (14.9).[45] In this sense, *apatheia* is the worst, or at least the most translucent, form of pride, one which leaves behind one's very *humanitas* in a height of "self-pleasing" so great that it precludes compassion (14.9, but also see 19.4).

If Augustine reserves some of his sharpest words in the *ciu.* for the Stoics, it is because they appear in the *ciu.* not really "as themselves," as they say in movie credits, but in a way as the exact analogue, in the world of pride, to Christ. They substitute perfect self-control for what Christ can offer, which we have characterized as self-possession, and so the Stoics serve as a kind of a clamp on the imagination, a dead end which blocks the imagination even more firmly than lust did, because they present the prospect not of a healed humanity but of the complete renunciation of humanity. At least lust, because of the potential for shame, left a doorway to repentance.[46]

This is a problem because Christ is not something abstract for Augustine; in fact, we, that is, the baptized, *are* Christ, and so Stoicism limits our imagination about ourselves.[47] To understand this, we must leave behind the text of the *ciu.* and find some links to Augustine's *Enarrationes in Psalmos.*

Though most are very difficult to date, one theme that is constant throughout the *en. Ps.* is that the speaker of the Psalms is Christ, and that some of the things he says apply directly to himself as Head, and some apply to us as members, but all, Head and members, are one person, the speaker of the Psalms. This means the speaker of the psalms is *us* insofar as we are members of the one Body of Christ. What is relevant to our discussion here is that much of what the Psalmist talks about are his emotions, his desires, his longings, his rejoicings, etc.[48]

For example, in the second sermon on Psalm 30, Augustine comments on the title of the psalm, which, as he reads it, is "A Psalm for David, an ecstasy." Augustine comments that one possible reason for "ecstasy," that is, for being outside oneself, is fear. But whose fear? "Christ's, certainly."[49] But this is problematic, especially since "even if he had been human only, not God, he could have been more joyful at the prospect of future resurrection than fearful because he was about to die, couldn't he?" Behind this criticism is the criticism coming from philosophic quarters that Jesus does not appear to play the role of the sage very well, since he is more afraid at the approach of his death than Socrates, etc. Augustine comments further:

> But in fact he who deigned to assume the *form of a servant,* and within that form to clothe us with himself (*in ea nos vestire se*), he who did not disdain to take us up into himself, did not disdain either to transfigure us into himself (*non est dedignatus transfigurare nos in se*) and to speak in our words, so that we in our turn might speak in his words. This is the wonderful exchange (*mira commutatio*), the divine business deal, the transaction effected in this world by the heavenly dealer (*divina sunt peracta commercia, mutatio rerum celebrata in hoc mundo a negotiatore caelesti*). He came to receive insults and give honors, he came to drain the cup

of suffering and give salvation, he came to undergo death and give life. Facing death, then, because of what he had from us, he was afraid, not in himself but in us. When he said that his soul was sorrowful [*tristem*] unto death [see Mt. 26:38], we all unquestionably said it with him. Without him, we are nothing, but in him we too are Christ. Why? Because the whole Christ consists of Head and Body.

Christ has real fear, but, echoing a theme familiar from the *ciu.*,[50] his fear is a function of the Incarnation, of his having declared his solidarity with our life. He feels *our* fear, he feels our fear *with* us, and so in that feeling of fear there is, equally and precisely to the same extent as the fear is accepted and felt, compassion. Christ's feeling of our fear is his compassion. Christ feels fear truly but that very feeling is an act of solidarity and love for us. That also means, however, that as we use Christ's words, *My soul is sorrowful unto death*, we, as members of his Body, are being transfigured into Christ's way of feeling. We speak in faith and in hope, at the threshold of the imagination, our fear integrated into love of God and love of neighbor. Without being able to describe the state, we can use Christ's words as though they were ours. Later, when Augustine comes to the verse *Into your hands I commend my spirit* (Ps. 30:6; cf. Lk. 23:46), he comments that Christ said this verse on the Cross, as well as Ps. 21:2, *My God, my God why have you forsaken me?* The latter applies more properly to his Body, and so uttering it in fear and desperation, he "transfigures" this cry. Now, uttering this cry, though we be forsaken as ever, we utter it in the words of Christ, and that means in the solidarity of love in which he uttered it. Our cry of desolation is, at the very same time, at least in faith and hope, a feeling of love.

In another passage, Augustine comments on Ps. 93:15, *All who have justice are right of heart*. The "right of heart" are those, Augustine observes, "who want what God wants." How can those of us with twisted wills, however, want what God wants?" Augustine asks. We can in Christ, *as* Christ, as Christ's members who exist in one person with the Head.

He prefigured certain weak persons in himself, in his own body; and because he felt compassion for them he cried out in the name of these weak members, *Father, if it is possible, let this cup pass from me.* He revealed the human will that was in him, but if he had continued to insist on that will, he would have seemed to display perversity of heart. If you recognize that he has had compassion on you, and is setting you free in himself, imitate the next prayer he made: *Yet not what I will, but what you will be done* (Mt. 26:39; *en.* 93.19).

The "right of heart" are those whose heart is contoured to Christ's as Christ's member. Even Paul, Augustine notes, managed to be joyful in the face of death (citing 2 Tim. 4:7–8 later in *en. Ps.* 93.19). But Christ is saddened, saying *My soul is sorrowful to the point of death* (Mt. 26:38). Was he really sad?

> Certainly he was sad, but he voluntarily accepted sadness (*voluntate suscipiens tristitiam*) just as he had voluntarily accepted flesh; and just as freely as he took on real flesh, so he freely took on real sadness (*sic voluntate tristitiam veram*). He chose to manifest it in himself for your sake.

Christ's taking on sadness is, once again, an act of solidarity in love with us. This means though that our sadness is also his, and so is in some way transfigured by his, formed according to "justice" and so rightness of heart. Christ the Creator is not changed into a creature in the Incarnation, but takes up a creature "who needs to be changed" and becomes with us "one human being" to the point where, again, he can cry out "My God, my God, why have you forsaken me?"

> Let no one then, on hearing these words, maintain, "This [particular Psalm text] is not said by Christ," or, on the other hand, "I am not speaking in this text." Rather let each of us who know ourselves to be within Christ's Body acknowledge both truths, that "Christ speaks here," and that "I speak here." Say nothing apart from him, as he says nothing apart from you.[51]

Even then, in our sadness, as a member of Christ's body, we feel sadness as transfigured by the compassion of Christ, suffused by the compassion of Christ, regardless of the fact, or even necessarily because of the fact, that it is still real sadness. In our sadness, we "feel" the depth of the compassion of Christ, and we have his words to speak so that the love in which they are spoken will be ours.[52] We are, in a way, an ongoing experiment in imagination as we accept in faith, hope, and love whatever sadnesses come our way, and also, as Augustine points out in other expositions, whatever joys.

It is not irrelevant to this chapter to point out that the unity of the Head and Body is often expressed by Augustine as the unity of the Bridegroom and Bride, "two in one flesh, two in one voice."[53] Whatever else this metaphor might mean, incorporated as the "Bride" of Christ, The Body in its members may still feel lust, but in the struggle to imagine something else, to be formed in our desires according to Christ's love, we discover that what the passions kept us most from imagining was the love of God, the unfathomable compassion of God in Christ. Not being able to imagine emotion without passion – the emotions of Christ – means not being able to imagine God's love. That is the fundamental barrier set up by lust and all of the other passions, and setting the heart right in justice means beginning, just beginning, to imagine that love actively, in our own feelings, and so to learn new pleasures we had not imagined before.[54]

Afterword

In response to questions put to me at the conference at which the text from this chapter was read, and in fairness to both Andrea Dworkin and Augustine, I would like it to be clear that I have compared them because I find their points of convergence interesting and illuminating. There are some ways in which Dworkin is more "Augustinian" than many liberal and conservative defenders or critics of Augustine. I take this partly from her own fleeting use of texts from book 14 of the *City of God* (Dworkin [1987], 151–152), which I take as a cue that there is more Augustine at work in the book than meets the eye. I think this use of Augustine prompts us to see in Augustine more than we might have guessed was there because, like Augustine, she asks us to look at ourselves and the investments we have, hidden or explicit, in the matter in question. On the other hand, she parts company with him. In part, this is caused by her use of a faulty translation of the passage from book 14 describing sex in Paradise:

> [A] man and his wife could play their active and passive roles in the drama of conception without the lecherous promptings of lust, with perfect serenity of soul and with no sense of disintegration between

body and soul (Dworkin [1987], 151, citing Augustine, *City of God*, translated by Walsh et al. [1958], 318).

It is a supreme irony, given what Augustine has to say about speech and lust-induced shame, that the "active and passive role" language is sheer circumlocution, invented by the translators to avoid Augustine's more direct description, which apparently was too strong for them. Dworkin (1987) assumes that Augustine is saying that "*Nature*, however, is the same in Eden and outside it: a man and his wife; active and passive roles in intercourse; a natural intercourse, even in Eden, of the fucker and the fucked" (152). Augustine is trying to get at something farther beyond the imagination than this.

Yet, mistranslations aside, the two do part ways. For Dworkin, it is a genuine question whether evil (male domination) is not simply something that thematizes intercourse as we know it, but that it in fact arises from intercourse itself as a purely structural matter:

> By definition, as the God who does not exist made her, [a woman] is intended to have a lesser privacy, a lesser integrity of the body, a lesser sense of self, since her body can be physically occupied and in the occupation taken over. By definition, as the God who does not exist made her, this lesser privacy, this lesser integrity, this lesser self, establishes her lesser significance: not just in the world of social policy but in the world of bare, true, real existence. She is defined by how she is made, that hole, which is synonymous with entry; and intercourse, the act fundamental to existence, has consequences to her being that may be intrinsic, not socially imposed (Dworkin [1987], 123).

This is tantamount to saying that human nature is evil, and that human beings cannot reproduce without in each case reproducing evil no matter how one engages in intercourse. In this sense, human nature is not evil because fallen, but evil because it is human.

If for Dworkin this is a genuinely possible reading of human beings, Augustine cannot agree, and might call such a view Manichaean (he was also subject to the charge of Manichaeism from Julian). Augustine does not believe that the hierarchies of domination caused by the Fall can be reversed without undoing human nature itself, but he does believe they can be substantially mitigated by love, and by a love which does not have as its source one's own "virtus" or power. It is a love for which we can take no credit, and so cannot use to "fuck" someone else. Surely, we are justified if we view this rhetoric with a good degree of skepticism as we see Augustine allowing the coercion of schismatics and also slaves and other members of his household out of love (e.g. *ciu.* 19.16).Yet, just as we need not allow Dworkin's most extreme rhetoric to stand for her entire position in its complexity – in which case, there would be no way out of the hierarchies of domination since only the most technically advanced cultures, and only an elite within them, would be able to reproduce apart from these hierarchies – so we can allow Augustine to invite us to imagine the possibilities of a world where these structures are not and cannot be entirely replaced, but can be substantially mitigated in the *societas* whose bonds of empathy are progressively located in, conformed to, the unreserved solidarity which God in his humility declared with us in Christ.[55]

Acknowledgments

An earlier version of this chapter was published as Cavadini, J. (2005) "Feeling Right." *Augustinian Studies* 36:195–217.

Notes

1 Lamberigts (2000) offers a critical and comprehensive overview of the literature. See also Sorabji (2000).
2 Clark (1986a).
3 Passages quoted are from Brown (1988), 404–418.
4 Hunter (1994). See also "General Introduction" in Hunter (1999), as well as his introductions to the particular works.
5 For a very sympathetic treatment of Cassian on this matter, see Brown (1988), 420–422.
6 Brown (1988), 402.
7 Lamberigts (2000), 188.
8 Dworkin (1987), 21.
9 Ibid., 67.
10 For example, "[T]he hatred of women is a source of sexual pleasure for men in its own right. Intercourse appears to be the expression of that contempt in pure form, in the form of a sexed hierarchy; it requires no passion or heart because it is power without invention articulating the arrogance of those who do the

fucking. Intercourse is the pure, sterile, formal expression of men's contempt for women" (Dworkin [1987], 138).

11   Ibid., 47.

12   Brown (1988), 422.

13   *ciu.* 14.5, and also 14.3, where Augustine criticizes Virgil for the same fault. Latin citations of the *ciu.* are from CCSL 47–48, edited by Dombart and Kalb.

14   Ibid. 14.5, "ut … sint morbi cupiditatum et timorum et laetitiae sive tristitiae; quibus quattuor vel perturbationibus, ut Cicero appellat, vel passionibus, ut plerique verbum e verbo Graeco exprimunt, omnis humanorum morum vitiositas continetur" (CCSL 48, 420).

15   *Cupiditas, laetitia, timor, tristitia* as enumerated in *ciu.* 14.3, 5: "quattuor animi perturbationes, cupiditatem timorem, laetitiam tristitiam, quasi origines omnium peccatorum atque vitiorum," referring to Virgil (14.3, CCSL 48, 417). Augustine makes the point, however, that this labelling is fluid (see 14.8), and he himself does not stick to a fixed terminology. In 14.6, he uses "metus" instead of "timor" (CCSL 48, 421, line 7). Alternative terminology is also given in 14.3: "afficitur anima ut cupiat metuat, laetetur aegrescat"; "metuunt cupiuntque, dolent gaudentque," speaking of the citizens of the holy City of God and so in a good sense (14.9, but also echoing Virgil, *Aeneid* 6.733, cited at 14.8 as an example of their use to refer to passions).

16   See *ciu.* 8.17.

17   "Motus" is exemplified in the passage directly under discussion, *ciu.* 14.6, quoted in the next note. At ibid. 14.9, the two words are used side by side as synonyms, "Hi motus, hi affectus" (CCSL 48, 427 line 59), or as noun and verb, "his moventur affectibus" (CCSL 48, 426, line 33), speaking of citizens of the City of God. In two parallel discussions where Augustine is making the same point, namely, that the character of the emotions is determined by the will or love underlying them, he uses "motus" in one (*ciu.* 14.6, at CCSL 48, 421, line 2) and "affectiones" in the other (*ciu.* 48, 426, line 8) to refer to the four classical passions or disturbances in a neutral way (cf. ibid. 14.9, "omnes affectus istos vita recta rectos habet, perversa perversos," CCSL 48, 429, lines 141–142).

18   "Interest autem qualis sit voluntas hominis, quia si perversa est, perversos habebit hos motus; si autem recta est, non solum inculpabiles, verum etiam laudabiles erunt" (*ciu.* 14.6, CCSL 48.421).

19   "Voluntas est quippe in omnibus; immo omnes nihil aliud quam voluntates sunt" (ibid.).

20   "*Initium* enim *omnis peccati superbia est* [Wis. 10:13]. Quid est autem superbia nisi perversae celsitudinis appetitus? Perversa enim est celsitudo deserto eo, cui debet animus inhaerere, principio sibi quodam modo fieri atque esse principium. Hoc fit cum sibi nimis placet. Sibi vero ita placet, cum ab illo bono inmutabile deficit quod ei magis placere debuit quam ipse sibi. Spontaneus est autem iste defectus" (*ciu.* 14.13, CCSL 48, 434).

21 *ciu.* 14.13 (CCSL 48, 435, line 31, after 2 Pet. 2:10).

22 See later in *ciu.* 14.13, where Augustine explains that Adam and Eve would not have transgressed God's commandment if they had not already lapsed into being more pleased with themselves than with God, thus electing to exist as though they were their own first principle, needing to obey no other: "Manifesto ergo apertoque peccato, ubi factum est quod Deus fieri prohibuerat, diabolus hominem non cepisset, nisi iam ille sibi ipsi placere coepisset. Hinc enim et delectavit quod dictum est: *Eritis sicut dii* [Gen. 3:5]. Quod melius esse possent summo veroque principio cohaerendo per oboedientiam, non suum sibi existendo principium per superbiam" (CCSL 48, 435).

23 See, for example, 14.3, where the human choice to live *secundum se ipsum*, "according to one's own self," instead of according to God, is, Augustine says, what Paul means when he condemns living according to the "flesh" (it is not a condemnation of the body). This choice makes human beings like the devil, who chooses to live according to his own self, and in this choice "did not adhere to the truth" (*in veritate non stetit*, Jn. 8:44). "Mendacium," lying or falsehood, begins with him, as does sin. Those who are not living "according to God," that is, those living according to the "flesh," in Pauline terms, or "according to Man in himself" are living "according to a [the?] Lie" (*secundum mendacium*, 14.3–4, CCSL 48, 417–418, lines 54–64, 1–17). This echoes an earlier discussion at *ciu.* 11.13, where the pride of the devil is represented as a primal "joy" in and commitment to counterfeiting something which really does not exist, an "unreality," a fiction or mythos, a lie, namely, a world in which his power is a private possession, independent of God: "ab initio suae conditionis in veritate non steterit et ideo numquam beatus cum sanctis angelis fuerit, suo recusans esse subditus creatori et sua per superbiam velut privata potestate *laetatus*, ac per hoc falsus et fallax, quia nec quisquam potestatem Omnipotentis evadit, et qui per piam subiectionem noluit tenere quod vere est, adfectat per superbam elationem simulare quod non est" (CCSL 48, 334, my emphasis). Strictly speaking, "joy," insofar as it is a disturbance or passion, that is, an emotion formatted by pride, when humans feel it, is a dim echo of the primal joy of the devil in falsehood, joy in the lie of "self-pleasing."

24 On this theme, see also Chapter 7, "The Darkest Enigma: Reconsidering the Self in Augustine's Thought."

25 For example, "morbi," *ciu.* 14.5 (CCSL 48, 420, line 17); and, "Civitas … impiorum … his affectibus pravis tamquam morbis … quatitur," *ciu.* 14.9 (CCSL 48, 429, lines 153–154).

26 *ciu.* 14.7, alluding to Phil. 1:23 ("Concupiscit apostolus dissolvi et esse cum Christo"), citing Ps. 32:11 (*Laetamini in Domino et exultate iusti*) and Phil. 2:12 (Cum *timore et tremore vestram ipsorum salutem operamini*), among other passages. Augustine does not find corresponding usage for "tristitia," but suggests that there are equivalent words, and later, in 14.8, cites 2 Cor. 7:8–11 as an example

of feeling grief in a godly way: "contristati fuerint secundum Deum," speaking of the Corinthian Christians.

27 Jesus was grieved with anger by the hardness of heart of some of his listeners ("the Jews"); he cried at Lazarus's death, his soul was grieved as his Passion drew near, he rejoiced that his listeners might believe, and he desired to eat the Passover with his disciples, etc. (*ciu.* 14.9).

28 *ciu.* 15.29 offers a glimpse of the views that Augustine expands upon more fully in many other places.

29 "Cum igitur sint multarum libidines rerum, tamen, cum libido dicitur neque cuius rei libido sit additur, non fere adsolet animo occurrere nisi illa qua, obscenae partes corporis excitantur" (*ciu.* 14.16, CCSL 48, 438). Augustine gives a small catalogue of these lusts just before this passage, at 14.15. Note that none of the uses of "libido" offered are positive: lust for revenge, lust for having money, lust for winning no matter what the price, lust for bragging, and lust for domination (*libido dominandi*). These lusts are all related as the desires which lead to the "works of the flesh" (Gal. 5:19, etc.), arising from the original commitment to self-pleasing.

30 *Pace* Pagels (1988), 112.

31 In a sense, it is an instance of punishment by truth; the truth of the matter will always come out, and thus God cannot be thwarted, not because God exerts any special force to keep from being thwarted, but because the truth cannot ultimately be hidden.

32 The fact that Diogenes' supposed public intercourse is considered so outrageous by everyone else is an indication of what people truly feel about intercourse in public. And, Augustine drily remarks, it is not even clear if Diogenes could have actually achieved intercourse in public, thus insinuating that, in this situation, he was impotent and there was only the pretense of intercourse *sub pallio*, "under the [philosophers'] cloak" (*ciu.* 14.20, CCSL 48, 442).

33 "nunc non est quo demonstretur exemplo," *ciu.* 14.23, CCSL 48, 445, lines 14–15. Even the act of imagining such a thing is itself an act of faith, faith in the goodness of creation revealed by Scripture: Augustine objects to those who suppose that experience is a sufficient catalogue of reality, whose "unfaithfulness" relies for argument on "its opinion on the facts of our experience" rather than "faith in things outside our experience," *non de fide rerum inexpertarum, sed de sensu expertarum argumentantem* (ibid. 48, 446, lines 70–71; cf. ibid. 14.26, "Neque enim quia experientia probari non potest, ideo credendum non est," speaking of one possible characteristic of sex in Paradise, CCSL 48, 449, lines 22–23).

34 *ciu.* 14.23, CCSL 48, 446, where Augustine notes that the shame occasioned by lust acts as a barrier to speech (*sermo*), which cannot be as free (*liber*) in discussing these matters. Also, at ibid. 14.26, Augustine emphasizes that lust impedes the imagination when these matters are spoken of: "nunc, cum ista

commemorantur, sensibus occurrit humanis nisi experientia libidinis turbidae, non coniectura placidae voluntatis." Rhetorical eloquence (*eloquentia*) cannot help, for it would only make matters worse; "modesty" (*verecundia*) must put a check on it (CCSL 48, 449–450, lines 32–44).

35   "Gaudium verum perpetuabatur ex Deo, in quem flagrabat *caritas de corde puro et conscientia bona et fide non ficta* [1 Tim. 1:5], atque inter se coniugum fida ex honesto amore societas" (*ciu.* 14.26, CCSL 48,449). The translation of *honesto amore* follows Levine (1966) and Dyson (1998). Bettenson's (1972) "based on love and mutual respect" may be a stretch.

36   "In tanta ... felicitate hominum absit ut suspicemur non potuisse prolem seri sine libidinis morbo, sed eo voluntatis nutu moverentur membra illa quo cetera," *ciu.* 14.26, CCSL 48, 449.

37   "sine ardoris inlecebroso stimulo cum tranquillitate animi et corporis nulla corruptione integritatis infunderetur gremio maritus uxoris" (ibid.); following the lead of Bettenson (1972), 591, and Levine (1966), 397, who cite a parallel with *Aeneid* 8.406, Dyson (1998) translates, "the man would have poured his seed into his wife's womb," but this has the difficulty of supplying an unspecified implied subject ("his seed").

38   "quando illas corporis partes non ageret turbidus calor sed spontanea potestas, sicut opus esset, adhiberet, ita tunc potuisse utero coniugis salva integritate feminei genitalis virile semen inmitti, sicut nunc potest eadem integritate salva ex utero virginis fluxus qua hoc potest eici" (ibid.). Oddly enough, Dworkin (1987) brings up the same association of intercourse with mutilation: "The wounding [involved in male and female genital mutilation] is literal; yet it is also psychologically true – in sex, the act itself is often wounding – scarring, hurting, a jagged edge of pain and grief. Certainly this is true often for women ... with the penis doing the cutting" (193–194).

39   *ciu.* 6.9, in the translation of Bettenson (1972), 245–246, with some modifications.

40   The same might go for Sophie Tolstoy, as Dworkin (1987) depicts her, esp. at 19–20.

41   Dworkin (1987), 128–129. See also 171–172 for another suggestion (this time from Victoria Woodhull, the first publisher of the *Communist Manifesto* in the United States, as well as the first woman stockbroker on Wall Street). She suggests that to equalize the inherent imbalance in intercourse stemming from the man's capacity to enter and "own" the woman in a way the woman cannot, women ought to have absolute control over intercourse, so as to balance out the physical dominance inherent in the structure of the act.

42   In the *ciu.*, the insistent connection made in anti-Pelagian works, between the passing on of original sin and lust as the agent of its passing, is not much evident, though this connection is operating in works written at the same time as books 13–14. The contention that the lust inevitably involved even in married

intercourse is what perpetuates original sin seems the worst mixture of physical-
ism and psycho-somatic mysticism to most people, and, at certain points, Augustine
does seem to descend this far (see Clark, "Vitiated Seeds and Holy Vessels:
Augustine's Manichaean Past," in Clark [1986b], 291–249). But the doctrine has
overtones much richer. Human nature is not simply physical and individual, but
irreducibly social. The human being is to be distinguished in the *ciu.* not only from
the natures of animals who have solitary habits, but even from gregarious, flocking
animals. Human beings are "kin" by virtue of their origin from one common
ancestor, something not true of any other being according to Scripture (12.22).
Solidarity, the "feeling of kinship," is part of human nature, not some separate
good (as in the case of the gregarious animals, who simply like congregating).
Thus, what falls in Adam and Eve is that original solidarity. But that solidarity is
part of our nature, since human beings are "social by nature but discordant by
perversion" (*nihil enim est quam hoc genus tam discordiosum vitio, tam sociale natura*,
12.28). Augustine thus relativizes the disjunction between "social propagation" of
original sin (e.g. by bad education) and "natural propagation" (by biological reproduction), because the nature includes and is defined by the social. It is the original
solidarity which falls, and which is reproduced in a vitiated state of discord, the
solidarity, or anti-solidarity, of pride, a communion (if that is the right word) of
"self-pleasers." It is lust which generates this corrupted fellowship, which *wills* it,
and in that very willing achieves its end. Human beings brought into existence as
a result of this willing are, apart from their own individual choices, already a part
of this fellowship. Nor can this vitiated solidarity heal itself. For one thing, this is
always a characteristic of a "weakened" or "vitiated state," its loss of the power to
fix itself. For another, the supreme characteristic of the fellowship of self-pleasers,
the "city of this earth," is its complacency, its lack of self-perspective which could
prompt change. Lust is the taking of pleasure in refusal to change, blocking the
pleasure of self-critique in humility from even emerging, especially in sex.

43   Book 14.28 returns the reader to a consideration of the two cities, and in the
first explicitly political discussion of the second half of the treatise. The earthly
city, fixed in the primal self-pleasing of the devil (mentioned in 14.27), glories
in itself instead of in God, fixated in admiration of its own excellence – "virtus" – as visible most clearly in the powerful who are the agents of domination
but who are really dominated by the "lust for domination." The "wise men"
(*sapientes*) of the earthly city, far from lending any perspective on this ecology
of self-pleasing by referring the *virtus* and glory of the earthly city to God, and
themselves equally "under the dominion of pride" (*dominante sibi superbia*), are
pleased with their own wisdom and promote the worship of gods who will not
question it, creatures instead of the Creator. By concluding his treatment of lust
with this overview of the two cities, Augustine makes it clear that lust does not
stand alone as a personal, individual obsession, but in fact only makes sense as
part of a larger ecosystem of power and complacency.

44 Augustine believes that marriage can bring good out of the evil of lust, but it does not make lust good. Only God can bring good out of evil, so the fact that marriage can do this is a mark of its own great goodness in the Creator's original design. See *nupt. et conc.* 1.8; see also Cavadini (2017).

45 Fear and grief were not present in paradise, though at least fear might be present in some form in the final blessed life – the point being that these emotions do not arise in situations where there is stability and bliss, but they do and must arise in our present life, no matter how virtuous it is, because we do not have assurance of perseverance or the full vision of God, nor do we know this for any of our friends.

46 And, in this sense, to use the happy phrasing of Patout Burns, it is the "sacramental sin" – although it is more proper to say that the sacramental part is imparted not by lust itself but by the commandment of God, which allows one self-knowledge in the face of sin. See "Augustine on the Origin and Progress of Evil," in The Ethics of St. Augustine, edited by William S. Babcock, (Atlanta: Scholars Press, 1991), p. 83.

47 On the Stoics and the passions, see Nussbaum (1994), esp. 316–401. It is interesting that Nussbaum, who does not treat Augustine in this book, seems to reflect some of Augustine's judgments on the Stoics. Their ideal of extirpation of the passions (broadly speaking) leads one "to solid self-absorption" (401). "The bold Stoic attempt to purify social life of all its ills, rigorously carried through, ends by removing, as well, its finite humanity, its risk-taking loyalty, its passionate love" (510). See also, O'Daly (1999), 155; and Sorabji (2000).

48 See the excellent "General Introduction" of Fiedrowicz (2000), 13–66, esp. 40–43. Translations of the *Ennarationes in Psalmos* (*en. Ps.*) are by Boulding (2000), with some modifications.

49 *en. Ps.* 2 of psalm 30, sec. 3, text at CCSL 38, 191–193 (edited by Dekkers and Fraipont).

50 This *enarratio* was a sermon preached to the people, perhaps in the summer of 411 (Boulding [2000] in *WSA* III/15, 321, n. 1).

51 *en. Ps.* 85.1; CCSL 39, 1176–1177.

52 In an earlier article (Cavadini [1997], reprinted as Chapter 3 of this volume), I tried to show how Augustine's trinitarian model of communication implies that there is no neutral speech, no speech that is simply conveying information, but rather that all speech conveys the spirit or love in which it was begotten. This can help us understand why Augustine would find some speech ineluctably lustful, and Christ's speech, on the other hand, as carrying the love in which it is spoken, and so potentially healing when we speak it.

53 For example, *en. Ps.* 2 of Psalm 30, sec. 4.

54 Augustine gives examples of some of these transformations at *en. Ps.* 84.15. In general, it means being moved from taking delight in iniquity to taking delight in justice, and in particular from enjoying theft to enjoying giving to those in

need; from delighting in shows to delighting in prayer; from enjoying lewd songs to enjoying hymns instead, among other nearly unimaginable shifts (CCSL 39, 1174–1175, lines 19–31). The newfound pleasure is, and always will be, at its most global, Christ. That is the point of calling him the Bridegroom. Insofar as we are joined in the charity of the Church, conformed to Christ's humble love in our dealings with each other, we are enjoying Christ, who is not so much the spouse of any individual Christian but of the Church. We enjoy the Bridegroom's love when we live in the mutual charity of his Body and so take pleasure in justice. Unlike Ambrose, who is more concerned with the relation of the individual soul to Christ as bride and bridegroom, Augustine generally avoids this individualist strand of Song of Songs interpretation in favor of a more sacramental view, where the Church, if one could put it this way, is the sacrament of delight in Christ. (For more on this issue, see Cavadini (2011), reprinted as Chapter 9 of this volume.) Lust is replaced not by a stasis but by the transfiguration into Christ, the becoming of one flesh with him, the transformation of all our feelings into intense joy and pleasure in the Humility of God, which we feel not abstractly but in whatever situation we deal with our neighbor justly. (In the *ciu.* note 13.21, where Paradise, though given a literal interpretation, is allegorized to refer to the Church, following the Song of Songs. In the middle of this Paradise grows the Tree of Life, Christ. The unity of charity which is the Church is Paradise, a place in the imagination where lust can be replaced by pleasure in justice appropriate for each particular situation and activity. Note that this passage in 13.21 is followed by a description of a transformation of affections described in terms of psalm recitations.)

55 I would like to thank Jim Wetzel for his kind response and helpful comments, as well as Nancy Cavadini, Kathryn Johnson, Cyril O'Regan, Jean Porter, and Robin Darling Young, who kindly read an earlier draft and offered helpful comments.

References

Bettenson, Henry, trans. (1972) *Concerning the City of God against the Pagans.* Harmondsworth, Middlesex: Penguin Books (repr. 1987, 2003).

Boulding, Maria, O.S.B., trans. (2000) *Exposion the Psalms 1–31, WSA III/15.* Hyde Park, NY: New City Press.

Brown, Peter (1988) *The Body and Society: Men, Women, and Sexual Renunciation in Early Christianity.* New York, NY: Columbia University Press.

Cavadini, John C. (1997) "The Quest for Truth in Augustine's *De Trinitate.*" *Theological Studies* 58: 429–440.

Cavadini, John C. (2011) "Eucharistic Exegesis in Augustine's Confessions." *Augustinian Studies* 41: 87–108.

Cavadini, John C. (2017) "Reconsidering Augustine on Marriage and Concupiscence," *Augustinian Studies* 48 (1–2): 183–199.

Clark, Elizabeth (1986a) "Adam's Only Companion: Augustine and the Early christian Debate on Marriage." *Recherches Augustiniennes* 22: 139–162.

Clark, Elizabeth (1986b) *Ascetic Piety and Women's Faith: Essays on Late Ancient Christianity*. Lewiston/Queenston: Edwin Mellon.

Dworkin, Andrea (1987) *Intercourse*. New York, NY: The Free Press.

Dyson, R. W., trans. (1998) *The City of God Against the Pagans*, Cambridge: Cambridge University Press (repr. 2007).

Fiedrowicz, Michael (2000) "General introduction." In *Augustine, Expositions of the Psalms 1–31, WSA III/15*, edited by John Rotelle, O.S.A., 13–66. Hyde Park, NY: New City Press.

Hunter, David. G. (1994) "Augustinian Pessimism? A New Look at Augustine's Teaching on Sex, Marriage and Celibacy." *Augustinian Studies* 25: 153–177.

Hunter, David G., trans. (1999) *Marriage and Virginity, WSA I/9*, 193–216. Hyde Park, NY: New City Press.

Lamberigts, Mathijs (2000) "A Critical Evaluation of Critiques of Augustine's View of Sexuality." In *Augustine and His Critics*, edited by Robert Dodaro and George Lawless, 176–197. London and New York, NY: Routledge.

Levine, Philip., trans. (1966) *The City of God Against the Pagans, Vol. IV (books 12–15)*, Loeb Classical Library 414. Cambridge, MA: Harvard University Press (rep. 2006).

Nussbaum, Martha (1994) *The Therapy of Desire*. Princeton, NJ: Princeton University Press.

O'Daly, Gerard (1999) *Augustine's City of God: A Reader's Guide*. Oxford: Clarendon Press.

Pagels, Elaine (1988) *Adam, Eve and the Serpent*. New York, NY: Random House.

Sorabji, Richard (2000) *Emotion and Peace of Mind: From Stoic Agitation to Christian Temptation*. Oxford and New York, NY: Oxford University Press.

Walsh, Gerald G., Demetrius B. Zema, Grace Monahan, O.S.U., and Daniel Honan (1958) *Augustine, City of God, Abridged*. Garden City, NY: Doubleday & Company.

7

The Darkest Enigma
Reconsidering the Self in Augustine's Thought

Those who frequent the pages of learned literature on Augustine will know that almost nothing is more easily encountered there – unless it is reflections on Augustine and sex – than reflections on Augustine and "the self,"[1] so firmly is it entrenched in our contemporary understanding of Augustine that one of his most characteristic accomplishments was his pioneering exploration of something called the "self." So easily does this idea find an agreeable and inconspicuous familiarity in our own expectations of Augustine that we may actually forget that Augustine does not treat this topic at all, and that the English phrase "the self" has no equivalent in Latin. In other words, the claim that Augustine thinks of, talks about, has theories of, or discovers something called "the self" seems so *self*-evident that it recedes from view precisely as a claim in need of argument. Precisely as a claim, it almost vanishes from sight, conveniently for us, perhaps, because once one becomes used to talking about Augustine and "the self," and once one forgets that Augustine does not actually talk about the thing we moderns call, and we post-moderns used to call, "the self," then it is so much easier for us to argue for retrospective connections between Augustine and any modern theory of "the self" because most of the work is already done simply in the selection, use, and repetition of the phrase, "the self." Augustine is then understood primarily in the context of how he ends up, or does not end up, in Descartes or Locke or

Visioning Augustine, First Edition. John C. Cavadini.
© 2019 John Wiley & Sons Ltd. Published 2019 by John Wiley & Sons Ltd.

others, disconnected from his own concerns in their own proper fullness – so much so that a contemporary reader can now discover, for example, that the main subject of Augustine's treatise on the Trinity, that is, on God, is actually "the self."[2] Use of the phrase "the self" in interpretations of Augustine can carry freight, intended or unintended, that should not receive such easy passage into Augustine's world and texts.

Part of this is the fault of English language translations, which often supply the word "self" where the Latin has an entirely different word. For example, Augustine does use language about the "interior homo," and this is sometimes carried into English as the "inner self" instead of the "inner man" or "inner human being": "But what am I loving when I love you? … a light, voice, fragrance, food and embrace for my inmost self."[3] In this famous passage, the English phrase "inmost self" is the translation of "interioris hominis mei," and translating it this way actually hides the doctrine of the inner human being, present with all five inner senses intact, and not just inner vision. The translation "inmost self" makes it easier to picture the "interior homo" as simply an interior place or space, when it is obviously something full bodied enough, in the metaphor, to have at least metaphorical sex. Nor is this misleading English translation simply a matter of supplying an inclusive language translation; translators of Origen have no trouble having him talk about the "interior man" or "inner human being" with all five spiritual senses.[4] Augustine is *expected* to talk about a thing, an inner reality, called the "self."

To make matters worse, the English language has reflexive pronouns, such as "myself," "yourself," and "oneself," that sound like possessive pronouns plus the noun "self." "Then toward myself I turned, and asked myself, 'Who are you?'" can sound like there is a thing called "self," which is "mine," and towards which I am turning, when in Latin all we have are forms of the first person reflexive pronoun.[5] Sometimes the temptation actually to split the English reflexive pronoun into its component parts is seemingly unbearable: "Magna vis est memoriae … et hoc animus est, et hoc ego ipse sum" translated by Boulding (1997) as "What a great faculty memory is …! It is the mind, and this is nothing other than my very self," separating the "my" and the "self" of the English word "myself" by the word "very," and making it sound like Augustine's memory is a thing called his "self," when all we have in the Latin is the intensive "ipse."[6] Since Augustine does depict memory with the use of spatial metaphors, it makes it easy to imagine "the self" that Augustine is (supposedly) talking about as more – or less – than what Augustine has in mind, as essentially an interior space or a place, for example.[7]

All of these tendencies sometimes create a very powerful synergy of illusion. Continuing the passage from book 10 where Augustine turns towards himself to ask himself who he is, he answers:

> "A man." See, here are the body and soul that make up myself, the one outward and the other within …. My inner self recognized [heaven and earth] through the service of the outer. I, who was my inmost self, I, who was mind, knew them through the senses of the body.[8]

This passage makes it sound like there is a thing inside Augustine called the "self" which is his, when all we have is "homo interior," translated as "my inner self," and "ego interior" in parallel to "homo interior," translated as "my inmost self."[9] Reading the English, it is hard not to conclude that Augustine has a doctrine of "the self," in this case an inner or innermost self, when there is actually no abstract noun corresponding to the English word at all. One could just as easily translate, "See, in me there are my body and my soul, one exterior and one interior. I, the inner human being, I, as mind, through the senses of my body, recognized [heaven and earth]."[10]

Such language in the English Augustine can aid and abet theories that rely on or advocate the idea of "the self" in Augustine. Some of Augustine's imagery in the *Confessions* (*conf.*), for instance, seems to allow us to find and to depict the "inmost self" that is mentioned in these translations, and to picture it variously as a stable, interior reality, always ready to be glimpsed by the purified inner vision, much like the image Plotinus presents of a gold statue which has been dirtied by bodily lusts – these simply need to be removed for the true self to resolve itself before our inner eyes. Or, we can picture this inner reality, "the self," as a kind of stable, private space, above which God stably hovers as an immaterial light, or at least as a stable, interior reality, always ready to be glimpsed by the purified inner vision. This private, inner reality is almost ready-made, so the story will go, for modern philosophers to perform the final minor adjustment necessary for the genesis of the modern idea of the self as a disembodied, thinking monad, accessible to self-consciousness but essentially isolated from all other, and similar, "selves."

But the imagery of self-awareness in Augustine is not limited to the imagery of stable space or stable substance (and these are, after all, only images) invoked in such a description of "the self" in Augustine, not even in the *conf.*, and certainly not in the sermons and in other Augustinian literature. In fact, the closer one examines the imagery which Augustine uses to express the content of self-awareness, the more one becomes convinced that he does not use it to describe a stable reality called "the self" that becomes more and more clearly visible as one's interior vision becomes purer, but rather something that defies reification. The content of self-awareness, for those truly self-aware, is much more disturbing and mysterious, more exciting and hopeful, and more treacherous and riskier. Someone who is self-aware is aware not of "a self" but of a struggle, a brokenness, a gift, a process of healing, a resistance to healing, an emptiness, a reference that impels one not to concentrate on oneself, in the end, but on that to which one's self-awareness propels one, to God. Someone who is properly self-aware is aware of a transformation, a re-configuring, a re-creation of an identity from nothing, of a becoming better, and not of a stable entity that endures as a private inner space or object.

The images that Augustine uses for the content of self-awareness all defy the attempt to reify this content in the form of a "self" which persists essentially unchanged throughout interior observation. They are all essentially images trying to describe self-awareness as precisely *not* the awareness of a stable, statue-like entity which may need cleaning or some touch-up polishing,[11] but rather the awareness of a subject in transformation, undergoing transformation, being transformed, re-created; of subjectivity that − to the extent that it is truly self-aware − is *resisting* a premature foreclosure of identity and yielding to a process that will be complete only eschatologically, and only as a gift partly received and mostly hoped for, and not in the first place an accomplishment. If one is aware of anything else, it is false self-awareness; one is fooling oneself; one is holding on to "the self" as essentially stable, an accomplished set of competencies and excellences, philosophical and otherwise, an illusion of self-sufficiency, the product of its own devising and doomed to eternal incoherence. The "interior homo" is just as incomplete as the "exterior homo," and just as needy − its senses in need of just as much correction and re-orientation as that of the exterior human. That is why "interior homo" is such a useful metaphor − because it defies reduction to a pure metaphysical entity to which the accidents of history and body are essentially irrelevant. The interior "self," if you want to use that language, is no less opaque than the "exterior."

The "interior human" is a metaphor for the intelligent soul or "animus," as we can see from the *conf.* passage earlier, a metaphor for the mind, meant to complexify, not simplify. The higher part of the *animus*, the *mens* or mind, strictly speaking, is also complexified in Augustine with the aid of Scriptural imagery, incipiently in *Confessions* and magisterially in the *De Trinitate* (*trin.*), where Augustine refers to it as the "image" of God familiar to readers of the book of Genesis. However, to become aware of one's mind as an "image" of God, and so to be truly and properly self-aware, is not to become aware of a stable, self-contained entity with the self-verifying status of "image," but to become aware of a relationship to God in which one's self-consciousness, thought, and way of loving – one's whole way of relating and expressing oneself, one's "mind" – is being renovated and transformed. One is aware, in Augustine's expression, of a "renewal" of the image, disfigured by sin. Here is a description of what one is aware of when one is aware of oneself as "image" of God:

> [T]he one who is being renewed (*renovator*) in the recognition of God and in justice and holiness of truth by making progress day by day, is transferring his love from temporal things to eternal, from visible to intelligible, from carnal to spiritual things; he is industriously applying himself to checking and lessening his greed for the one sort and binding himself with charity to the other. But his success in this depends on divine assistance; it is after all God who declares, *Without me you can do nothing* (Jn. 5:5). When the last day of his life overtakes someone who has kept faith in the mediator, making steady progress of this sort, he will be received by the holy angels to be led into the presence of the God he has worshiped to be perfected by him and so to get his body back again at the end of the world, not for punishment but for glory. For only when it comes to the perfect vision of God will this image bear God's perfect likeness.[12]

One is aware of a process and progress over which one does not have full control and of an identity that is not fully specifiable by any accomplishment of self-awareness in this life, but rather liable at any moment to premature foreclosure by wrongheaded attempts at self-awareness. This self-awareness is only genuine when it is primarily

"in agnitione Dei," in the recognition or acknowledgment or awareness of God.

The "awareness" of God that is required is not an awareness that
is confined to, or even primarily defined by, interior vision. To see
how this is true, we must look a little more closely at Augustine's use
of the image of "image" in *trin. We see now through a mirror in an
enigma, but then it will be face to face* (1 Cor. 13:12) is one of Augustine's
favorite Scripture passages to express the relationship of the mind as
"image" to that which it images. To the extent that we can, we see
God now in a mirror, that is, in an image, "which we ourselves
are."[13] So far, so good, but this image is not a clear image. Paul characterizes it as an "enigma," which, Augustine comments, is a form of
allegory: "An enigma, to put it briefly, is an obscure allegory,"[14]
Augustine says, and then he illustrates what he means by quoting a
text from Scripture, Prov. 30:15, which in the *Vetus Latina* was about
as obscure an allegory as you can get: "The Bloodsucker had three
daughters," as Hill (1991) translates.[15] Like the person encountering
Prov. 30:15 for the first time, the person who is properly self-aware
is aware of obscurity, darkness, a crabbed striving for representation,
something crying out for interpretation, something more like a
cryptograph than a space or statue.

What does one need to interpret this allegorical text? "An allegory
is nothing but a trope in which one thing is understood from
another."[16] The first thing one needs is to know its referent. Augustine
had once spelled out what one needs to interpret allegory in the *De
doctrina christiana* (*doctr. chr.*); in *trin.*, he gives the shorthand version:
one needs the "rule of faith."[17] The rule of faith enables one to see an
allegory as an allegory in the first place, and in this case, the rule of
faith lets us know that the soul is precisely a representation, an image.[18]
The rule of faith tells us what God, who is the referent, is like,[19] and
also contains everything else we need to make sense of this allegory,
all the "res" that Augustine discusses in *doctr. chr.* book 1. We need to
know about sin, or we will not know why the allegory is so obscure.
The rule of faith enjoins us to "follow the Lamb, *who takes away the sin
of the world*" (Rev. 14:4; Jn. 1:29).[20] We need to know, in faith, the *caritas* that is the ultimate referent of Scripture, that is the key to resolving
all unclear passages, and that is likewise the key to the allegory that is
the soul, for God, which the soul represents as image, is Love (a point
amply made in book 8 of the *trin.*). Ascent to awareness of God and

oneself is more like exegesis than simple observation. What is called "ascent of the soul" and exegesis of Scripture are tied together in this image of the soul as an allegory. Either allegory (Scriptural, or the soul) has meaning only in reference to the whole story from Scripture, summarized in the rule of faith, of the Love revealed in the Incarnation, which puts justice ahead of power, which emptied itself for us, whose blood freed us from the blandishments of the devil.[21]

The person who, like the Platonist philosophers of book 7 of *conf.* or book 4 of *trin.*, has mastered the art of introspective ascent, has cultivated intellectual vision, and is aware of God, as Augustine analyzes it, from a great distance, as people who see the goal to which they are tending but not the Way to get there[22] – such a person does not experience the mind or soul as *image*, as drawing its significance from the Scriptural story, as pointing to or representing God's love, but they rather invert the reference. God is afar, on the long side of a great gulf that signifies the potential accomplishment or achievement of the spiritually skilled, prideful mind. The soul aware of itself in this way is *an inverted image* because its remembering, understanding, and loving are so formed that it knows, understands, and loves *God*, in effect, as the image, and *itself* as the reality. God is reduced to a credential in the résumé of the wise man, redounding to his glory precisely as "wise."[23] Knowing the goal but rejecting the Way means a complete denial of oneself as signifier and of one's own ultimate referent, the love of God in Christ. That love is both Way and Goal. If the phrase "the self" has any warrant for use in Augustine, it would be for this prideful soul which has reified itself as the ultimate *res* for which even God has become a signifier. If "the self" corresponds to anything in Augustine, it is this reified structure of pride, an attractive illusion, but ultimately a self-contradiction, doomed to eternal incoherence.

The answer to "righting" this image, to re-forming it away from its inversion and towards its proper status as reference, is not more introspection, but attention to the outward things that help mediate re-formation in the love of God in Christ. Have you ever seen a dog, whimpering and begging for scraps from the table? That is what we are like, or should be like, Augustine sometimes tells his congregation. We are the dog in the parable.[24] Augustine tells us we have to get in touch with our inner dog. Looking at a hungry dog as proposed in a Scriptural image is looking at ourselves. To cast aside the image as though it were fully replaceable by philosophical language is to reject the purifying love of God, the highest *res*, which the Scriptural image ultimately represents. We are too proud to picture ourselves whining like a dog for something we want desperately, and so we reject formation in and by God's love in favor of complacency, the illusory, static self-sufficiency of pride. Commenting on the Psalm text *Blessed is everyone who understands about the needy and poor man* (Ps. 40:2, Vulgate), Augustine notes:

> Keep in mind all the poor, needy, hungry and thirsty people, travelers far from home, the ill-clad, the sick, the prisoners. Try to understand about a poor person of this sort, because if you do, you will understand about him who said, *I was hungry, I was thirsty, naked, a stranger, sick and in prison*. (Mt. 25:35–36)[25]

If we do not keep in mind the external, literal poor, we reject as irrelevant the Scriptural images of Christ's identification with the poor as a synecdoche for his loving identification with the whole human condition, and so we reject the only riches – Christ's love – that can possibly transform our neediness.[26] Attention to the real poor, the literal, external poor, in our minds is an authentic and necessary locus of the purifying love of Christ. Only by noticing and "keeping in mind" the actual poor do we begin to understand the love of Christ in which we are transformed and enriched.

Trying, in effect, to peer behind the economy of images offered by Scripture, to resolve the economy of image as essentially incidental and instrumental, as a mere step on the way to realization of "the self" which the Platonists see without the economy of images, is to reject God's love. To try to go beyond the images in Scripture to a system or structure of spiritual endeavor, in this case, "ascent," which becomes absolute, which can be fully translated into non-Scriptural images, and into which the images of Scripture are then fit, is precisely to construct "the self" as a reified interior object to which everything else, even God, ultimately, refers. It is to construct the self as the signified, and not a signifier.

Referring to actual or potential readers of his *conf.*, Augustine notes that, "None of these have laid their ears to my heart, though it is only there that I am whoever I am."[27] The heart! Perhaps this is at last the stable entity, "the self," which we need only to look within to discover. Instead, heart language, though used to describe one's most intimate identity by Augustine, is the last place one should look to find something stable, settled, and solitary. Instead, to know one's own heart is to be aware, as the *conf.* famously reminds us, of a great restlessness.[28] The heart is the subject of an ongoing formation in the purifying love of the one who says, "I am gentle and humble of heart,"[29] the humble, Incarnate Word. Augustine describes this ongoing formation as the virtue of continence, directed to the mouth and speech of the heart:

> ... it is not enough to keep the exterior mouth of the body under control, to ensure that nothing harmful escapes from it in speech. There is also the internal mouth of the heart ....There are many things that we do not say outwardly with our lips, but which we shout out in our heart ... and if anything bad has its origin there, even if the tongue stays still, it soils the soul.[30]

The speech of the heart has to be re-formed according to the speech of God, which we can see not by looking within at our own hearts but only by looking out at the Incarnate Word as depicted in Scripture. For example, Augustine does not advise consecrated virgins to spend their time gazing within, at a thing called "the self" which can be found by interior vision, but instead he says:

> Gaze with the mind's eyes on the wounds of the crucified one, the marks in the flesh of the risen one, the blood of the dying one, the price paid for the faithful, the transaction completed by the redeemer.[31]

There is no gazing beyond this economy of wound, stigma, blood, and redemption, to something to which this economy refers, because this economy is the revelation of God's love, which it simultaneously presents and effects, the Way that is also the Goal. This love is the ultimate referent of Scripture and of ourselves, that which gives any of us, strictly speaking, any significance. Trying to gaze beneath or beyond the economy of wound and blood is making Christ's wounds and blood ultimately signifiers of oneself, of one's own greatness in being able to transcend and leave behind the love of God. Gazing at the wounds of Christ is gazing at the fullness of charity, and charity, Augustine says, *disturbs* inwardness. Commenting on verse 9 of Psalm 54, *Lo, I fled away, and stayed in the desert*, he observes:

What *desert*? Do you mean, perhaps, the inner place of your own soul, where no other human being gains entry, where no one is with you, where there is only yourself and God? ... Perhaps the speaker sought refuge in his own soul ... and there found some measure of solitude where he could rest. Yet charity disturbs him there. He is alone in his soul, but not alone as far as charity is concerned.[32]

In this life, the *desert* of inwardness is always going to be disturbed by charity, because, in this life, one invariably has enemies, who, like the wind and the waves in the Gospel story (Mt. 14), cause a storm in one's heart because one is inclined to hate these enemies instead of loving them. In this situation, Augustine says:

... there is no hope for you except to shout, *Lord, I'm, sinking!* (Mt. 14:30). May he who walks fearlessly upon the waves stretch out a hand to you, and lift you up in your terror, and grant you safety and stability in himself. May he speak to you interiorly and bid you, "Keep your eyes on me and on what I endured."[33]

The heart that is being formed in the charity of Christ is disturbed from a solipsistic inwardness by that very charity, which keeps it restless, keeps it looking for the Christ who will still the turbulence, keeps it mindful of Christ's sufferings:

Your heart is very likely to be turbulent if you have forgotten about him in whom your faith rests; you will find your troubles unendurable if you do not keep in mind what Christ suffered for you. If you do not keep Christ in mind, it is as though for you he is asleep. Awaken Christ and remember your faith. He sleeps in you when you forget his sufferings; he is awake in you when you are mindful of his sufferings. When you contemplate with all your heart what he endured for you ... your experience of suffering likens you in some degree to your king.[34]

There is no question here of leaving behind the wounds, the blood, and the death of Christ in order to find some inward entity that they represent which has any reality independent of this representation. "The central part of a human being, we might say, is the heart," Augustine comments, and, he continues, "Christ dwells in our hearts through faith."[35] When we try to find a stable "self," hoping, perhaps, that it is our heart, we find, if we are looking properly, Christ dwelling there because the love of Christ is straightening out our hearts[36] as they cling, in faith, to his wounds, blood, and death. Where is the boundary between our heart and the heart of Christ? We are being assimilated to himself, "divinized," "transfigured," such that, in the purifying love of Christ, we are becoming Christ, though always as members and never as Head. Where is "the self" that is independent, that is decipherable as a text, without Christ? The boundaries we had hoped were so reliable have become gloriously fuzzy as we look for a separate person, and find only one, Head and Members, the whole Christ, into which we are being transformed. The Way and the Goal are one.

The Psalms tell us to *Seek God's face evermore* (Ps. 104:4, Vulgate), but when, in the eschaton, the fullness of vision is given to us, will we still need to seek? In the *trin.*, Augustine comments on this Psalm passage by indicating that "faith seeks, understanding finds, ... and again, understanding still goes on seeking the one it has found," because that is:

> ... how incomprehensible things have to be searched for, lest the man who has been able to find out how incomprehensible what he is looking for is should reckon that he has found nothing.[37]

But does this include even the eschatological state, when faith is no longer necessary and is replaced by vision? Commenting on this Psalm text in a sermon, Augustine asks:

> May we think, perhaps, that even when we do see him face to face, as he is, we shall still need to search for him, and search unendingly, because he is unendingly lovable? Even now we can say to someone who is present, "I'm not looking for you," meaning, "I do not love you." Conversely, if someone is loved with the love of choice he is sought even when present, as long as our love is everlasting love, lest he become absent. When we love another, even when we can see that person, we never tire of the presence of the beloved, but want him or her to be present always. This is what the psalm conveys by the words, *Seek his face always*; let not the finding of the beloved put an end to the love-inspired search; but as love grows, so let the search for one already found become more intense.[38]

Even when we have vision, there is no "self" with a stable boundary at which one might gaze securely, but an ongoing transformation, and ongoing enlargement of the heart,[39] ongoing and increasing reference to the Love which is the highest *res*. "Vision" is here contextualized and relativized by "love." What love is that? The love to which we cannot make reference apart from the Scriptural images[40] of the suffering of Christ. Even in his resurrection body, Christ keeps his wounds, and likewise the resurrection bodies of his martyrs have their wounds preserved, if glorified.[41] Augustine's insistence on the preservation of these bodily wounds is his way of saying that cosmic mindfulness of the sufferings of Christ persists into eternity because there is no love greater than the transforming, enlarging, growth-fostering love represented and effected by that suffering. The Body of Christ, both in Head and in Members, keeps its wounds intact. If we have a self, it is one that is eternally stigmatized and thus eternally becoming as it learns ever-more fully of its own true significance, its own true reference, its own true identity, in the love of Christ. Then we will praise, and sing "Alleluia!" But now, for the time being, the more self-aware we become, the more we are compelled to cry out, "Help! Lord, Save!"; and then, in gratitude, even for crumbs from whole loaf that is Christ's, "Lord, Thank-You!"[42]

Acknowledgments

An earlier version of this chapter was published as Cavadini, J 2007. The darkest Enigma: Reconsidering the self in Augustine's Thought. *Augustinian Studies* 38: 119–132.

Notes

1 This is especially true in literature that treats Augustine as a philosopher in the history of philosophy. Taylor (1989) talks about "Augustine's turn to the self" (131). Augustine "introduced the inwardness of radical reflexivity and bequeathed it to the Western tradition of thought," a "fateful" step, namely, "to make a turn to the self in the first-person dimension crucial to our access to a higher condition" (132); and "the road from the lower to the higher, the crucial shift in direction, passes through our attending to ourselves as *inner*"(129, original emphasis). "Facing the right field" is what is decisive for spiritual vision. "The struggle is over the direction of our gaze," that is, inward (129). "Augustine shifts the focus from the field of objects known to the activity itself of knowing …. To look towards this activity is to look to the self, to take up a reflexive stance" (130).

"[R]adical reflexivity takes on a new status, because it is the 'space' in which we come to encounter God, in which we effect the turning from lower to higher" (140). The implicit assumption of this work and others like it is that Augustine's "philosophy" can be decoupled from his theology of the Incarnation and his ecclesiology. It is that decoupling, or the assumption that his so-called inward turn can be decoupled from his Christology and ecclesiology without losing anything essential, that "leads" to Descartes (and so sees in Augustine the forbear of Descartes).

2   The last chapter of Stock (1996) is devoted to the *De Trinitate* (*trin.*), but entitled "The Self" (243). In a subsection called "The Reader and the *Cogito*," indicating that Stock mostly follows the line laid out by Taylor, we can read, "Augustine has no term for the elusive notion of the self," and yet that does not seem to provide a caution against investing too much in making one's approach too dependent on this idea as a central interpretive device: "Yet, throughout the later books [of the *trin.*], there is no doubt that [Augustine's] principal concern is with the self as the intrinsic nature operating in each of us, that is, the source of permanence that we know to exist apart from the transitory constituents of our understanding" (260). The "self" is a stable entity which, as "in neoplatonism" (269), participates in a "gradualist scheme of religious enlightenment" (276). Despite the disclaimer on page 273 about the differences between Augustine and "purely philosophical thinkers" such as Plato and Descartes, this idea of a stable entity, the "self," participating in a gradual "enlightenment" that it, as a persisting entity, simply receives, almost cancels out entirely the idea of transformation which seems to be the essential burden of books 13 and 14 of the *trin.* For Stock, the dramatic "narrative" of philosophical ascent is essentially the same in Augustine as in earlier philosophers; the "narrative" does not change. Reading Scripture provides some external source of "purification" that contributes to an ascent whose basic narrative is already well-trodden: "Time's relationship to eternity is therefore a question of purification in which applications of one's readings of scripture play the principal role in disciplined ascent" (278), and in which the Incarnation itself almost seems to be reduced to a figure for the individual self in ascent (see the next sentence, 278).

3   *conf.* 10.6.8, "quid autem amo, cum te amo? ... lucem, vocem, odorem, cibum, amplexum interioris hominis mei." Latin text in CCSL 27, here at 159, lines 7, 14–15 (hereafter, CCSL 27, 159.7, 14–15); translation from Boulding (1997), 242.

4   See, for example, the prologue of Origen's *Commentary* on the Song of Songs, chapter 2, translated by Lawson (1956), 25–30, where all five spiritual senses are covered.

5   *conf.* 10.6.9, Boulding (1997), 243; CCSL 27, 159.32: "et direxi me ad me et dixi mihi, 'tu quid es?'"

6   *conf.* 10.17.26, Boulding (1997), 254; CCSL 27, 168.1, 2–3.

7   "In [Augustine's] doctrine, radical reflexivity takes on a new status, because it is the 'space' in which we come to encounter God, in which we effect the turning from lower to higher" (Taylor [1989], 139–140). Cary (2000) takes this in an emphatic direction that almost literalizes the metaphor: "For the striking and new thing about Augustinian inwardness is the conception of an inner space that one can enter and look within" (49); "the self" which Augustine "invented" is a private inner space, above which the inner eye, if turned in the right direction ("in and up," following Taylor), can see God: "Augustine's inward turn requires a double movement: first *in* then *up*. In contrast to Plotinus, the inner space of the Augustinian soul is not divine but is beneath God, so that turning into the inside is not all there is to finding God. We must not only turn inward but also look upward, because God is not only within the soul but also above it. In the interval between the turning in and looking up, one finds oneself in a new place, never before conceived: an inner space proper to the soul, different from the intelligible world in the Mind of God. The soul becomes, as it were, its own dimension – a whole realm of being waiting to be entered and explored" (39).

8   Boulding (1997), 243.

9   "Et respondi, 'Homo.' Et ecce corpus et anima in me mihi praesto sunt, unum exterius et alterum interius .... Homo interior cognovit haec per exterioris ministerium; ego interior cognovi haec, ego, ego animus per sensum corporis mei. Interrogavi mundi molem de deo meo, et respondit mihi, 'Non ego sum, sed ipse me fecit'" (CCSL 27, 159.32–34, 160.40–43).

10   The English word "oneself" can make it sound even more like Augustine is teaching a doctrine of a reified, abstract "self" which everyone has and owns. Again from *conf.*, "Is hearing the truth about oneself from you anything different from knowing oneself?" (10.3.3, Boulding [1997], 238, CCSL 27, 156.9), where the word "oneself" corresponds only to the Latin third-person reflexive pronoun "se."

11   "This is the soul's ugliness, not being pure and unmixed, like gold, but full of earthiness; if anyone takes the earthy stuff away the gold is left, and is beautiful, when it is singled out from other things and is alone by itself. In the same way the soul too, when it is separated from the lusts which it has through the body with which it consorted too much, and freed from its other affections, purged of what it gets from being embodied, when it abides alone has put away all the ugliness which came from the other nature" (see Plotinus' *Ennead* 1.6.5, translated by Armstrong (1966), 249). Also, "Go back into yourself and look; and if you do not yet see yourself beautiful, then, just as someone making a statue which has to be beautiful cuts away here and polishes there and makes one part smooth and clears another till he has given his statue a beautiful face, so you too must cut away excess and straighten the crooked and clear the dark and make it bright, and never stop working on your statue till the divine glory of virtue shines out on you, till you see self-mastery enthroned upon its holy seat. If you

have become this, and see it, and are at home with yourself in purity, with nothing hindering you from becoming in this way one, with no inward mixture of anything else, but wholly yourself, nothing but true light…." (*Ennead* 1.6.9, translated by Armstrong [1966], 259).

12 Augustine, *trin.* 14.17.23, here translated by Hill (1991), 389–390.

13 *trin.* 15.8.14, "quod nos sumus," translated by Hill (1991), 405.

14 *trin.* 15.9.15, "Aenigma est autem, ut breviter explicem, obscura allegoria," translated by Hill (1991), 407.

15 Hill (1991), 407, translating, "Sanguisugae erant tres filiae."

16 *trin.* 15.9.15, "Quid ergo est allegoria, nisi tropus ubi ex alio aliud intelligitur," translated by Hill (1991), 407.

17 See *trin.* 15.27.49, where Augustine explains that, if the "acies mentis," the keenness of the mind, is to "exercise" itself on the highest part of the human being, the mind itself, in a way that is useful for coming to see in some way the supreme, inexpressible, and unchangeable nature which is God, has to be governed by the rule of faith. The mind is not interpretable as an "image," as an allegory, without the rule of faith, just as Scripture, according to the *doctr. chr.*, is not interpretable apart from the rule of faith, and this applies in particular to figurative or allegorical passages (cf. also *trin.* 15.28.51).

18 In *trin.* 15.23–24.44, Augustine, who has the Platonic philosophers in mind here, points out that those who can see their own minds, and can see in it the trinities he has been indicating all along, but who do not understand their mind as an *image*, do not see through their minds the Trinity of which their minds are images. They do not, therefore, "refer" the image to its proper referent, that which it signifies, which they can only "see" indirectly, by a kind of "inference" or "interpretation" or "conjecture" from what they see: "per quod tamen speculum et in quo aenigmate qui vident, sicut in hac vita videre concessum est, non illi sunt qui ea. quae digessimus et commendavimus in sua mente conspiciunt; sed illi qui eam *tamquam imaginem* vident, ut possint ad eum cujus imago est, quomodocumque *referre* quod vident, et per imaginem quam conspiciendo vident, etiam illud videre *coniciendo*, quoniam nondum possunt facie ad faciem" (my emphasis). It is almost as though one "reads" the soul by the same "rules" that apply to the reading of Scripture.

19 See *trin.* 1.4.7, which summarizes the Catholic faith "on the Trinity which God is," and 1.7.14 on the "canonica regula" (characterized as such at *De Trinitate* 2.1.2) which allows one to interpret in a Catholic way Scriptural passages about Christ which might indicate he is "less" than the Father and so imply an Arian doctrine of God.

20 This is the advice that Augustine gives to those who can see the mind, but do not see it as an image. The point is not further, even more rigorous, introspection, but faithful discipleship in accordance with the rule of faith (*trin.* 15.24.44).

21 Matters taken up in *trin.* 13.10.13–18.23.

22   *conf.* 7.20.26; *trin.* 4.15.20. At *trin.* 4.15.20–17.23, Augustine notes drily that the Platonists and those like them were able to see with the eyes of their minds the incorporeal substance of God, but of course could not see historical events that were provided by God as the prophets could. Augustine comments on the philosophers as spiritual adepts, who "ridicule" or "deride" ("derident") the simple Christian believer and so constitute themselves as a spiritual elite, proud of their spiritual accomplishments precisely as accomplishments. Though genuinely adept, since they have been able to attain to a vision of "the light of unchanging truth" in "however small a measure," and have indeed "understood to the best of their ability the eternity of the creator," they have nevertheless not been able to match the gifts of the prophets. Their contemplative grasp on "the eternity of that spiritual and unchanging nature" was not such that "they could see in the wisdom of the Creator and ruler of the universe the rolled up scrolls of the centuries (*volumina saeculorum*) which *there* already are and always are, but *here* only will be and so are not yet; or that they could see there the change for the better not only of the minds but also of the bodies of human beings, each to its proper perfection," nor were they worthy of having such things shown to them by angels. What the spiritually adept cannot see, in other words, is the economy of God's love, and it is that economy which they disdain and reject. If they could have gazed more "firmly" or more "constantly" (*constanter*) or even perhaps more "closely" (rather than from afar), they would have noticed God's Love, the economy in the mind or wisdom of God. In a sense, the philosophers, because they were not humble, lacked imagination. The destiny that God's love has in store for us is unimaginable; faith is what begets imagination in an unsuspected destiny planned by the love of God. To ignore the economy, to try to peer beyond or behind it to "the self" that is independent of God's economy, is pride. It is to reject God's love and to hold God distant.

23   At *conf.* 7.20.26, Augustine describes his prideful state as being interested in joining the spiritual elite, known for their wisdom, "Iam enim coeperam velle videri sapiens plenus poena mea et non flebam, insuper et inflabar scientia. Ubi enim erat illa aedificans caritas a fundamento humilitatis, quod est Christus Iesus?" (CCSL 27, 110.11–14). Cf. *trin.* 4.17.23, where Rom. 1:20 is used to describe the philosophers who "call themselves wise," and who want to be regarded as authorities even on temporal matters such as the possibility of the resurrection of the body (see 4.16.21).

24   *en. Ps.* 67.32, where Mt. 15:27–28 is cited. See also *en. Ps.* 1 on Ps. 58:15, the image of Saul become Paul as a wolf who became a dog. The usefulness of these images is unfortunately marred by an ugly anti-Jewish context.

25   *en. in Ps.* 40:2, translated by Boulding (2000), 227.

26   Ibid., sec. 1.

27   *conf.* 10.3.4, "sed auris eorum non est ad cor meum, ubi ego sum quicumque sum," translated by Boulding (1997), 239.

28   *conf.* 1.1.1.

29   See *urg.* 55.56.

30   *cont.* 1.2, trans. Hunter (1999), 192.

31   *urg.* 54.55, translated by Hunter (1999), 104.

32   The translation of Boulding (2001, 63–64) exaggerates the "inner place" character of the soul: "Forte iste, ut dixi, fugerit ad conscientiam suam, ibi aliquantum desertum invenerit ubi requiesceret. Sed illa dilectio conturbat eum; solus erat in conscientia, sed non solus in caritate; intus consolabatur conscientia, sed forinsecus tribulationes non relinquebant" (CCSL 39, 664.2–6).

33   Boulding (2001), 64: "nihil tibi restat nisi exclamare: *Domine, pereo.* Porrigat manum ille qui fluctus calcat intrepidus, sublevet trepidationem tuam, firmet in se securitatem tuam, alloquatur te intus, et dicat tibi: Me adtende, quid pertulerim" (CCSL 39, 664.9–13).

34   Boulding (2001), 64: "Merito ergo forte turbatur cor tuum, quia excidit tibi in quem credideris; intolerabiliter pateris, quia non venit tibi in mentem quid pro te pertulerit Christus. Si in mentem non tibi venit Christus, dormit: excita Christum, recole fidem. Tunc enim in te dormit Christus, si oblitus es passiones Christi; tunc in te vigilat Christus, si meministi passionum Christi. Cum autem pleno corde intuitus fueris quid ille fuerit passus, nonne aequo animo et tu tolerabis, et fortasse gaudens, quia inventus es in aliqua similitudine passionum regis tui?" (CCSL 39, 664.22–31).

35   *en. in Ps.* 108:32, "cor est tamquam hominis medium …. Habitat enim Christus per fidem in cordibus nostris" (CCSL 40, 1600.20, 22), translated by Boulding (2003), 259.

36   See *en. in Ps.* 77:10, "The human heart is crooked in itself, but God is straight. If our heart clings closely to him, as to an unchangeable rule, it too can be straightened. But in order to keep with him, and thus be straight, it must approach God, not by walking towards him but by faith," translated by Boulding (2002), 101.

37   *trin.* 15.2.2, translated by Hill (1991), 395–396.

38   *en. in Ps.* 104:3, translated by Boulding (2003), 186: "An forte etiam cum facie ad faciem viderimus eum sicuti est, adhuc perquirendus erit, et sine fine quaerendus, quia sine fine amandus? Dicimus enim etiam praesenti alicui: Non te quaero; id est, non te diligo. Ac per hoc qui diligitur, etiam praesens quaeritur, dum caritate perpetua, ne fiat absens, agitur. Proinde quem quisque diligit, etiam cum eum videt, since fastidio semper vult esse praesentem, hoc est, semper quaerit esse praesentem. Et nimirum hoc est: *Quaerite faciem eius semper*, ut non huic inquisitioni, qua significatur amor, finem praestet inventio, sed amore crescente inquisitio crescat inventi" (CCSL 40, 1537.31–41).

39   On this image of enlargement of the heart, see *en. in Ps.* 4:2.

40   Perhaps one could usefully think of this economy of images as the equivalent of the "supernatural" in Augustine.

41   *ciu.* 22.19, on the wounds of the martyrs.
42   I would like to thank Nancy Cavadini, Cyril O'Regan, Jean Porter, and Dan Sheerin who read earlier drafts of this chapter. I have also benefited from listening to the comments of Michel Barnes, Peter Brown, Philip Cary, Paul Griffiths, Charles Matthewes, and other members of the original audience who heard this as an oral presentation. Where I have ignored their good comments, I have done so at my own risk.

References

Armstrong, A. H., trans. (1966) *Plotinus: Enneads*, vol 1. Loeb Classical Library, 440. Cambridge, MA: Harvard University Press.

Boulding, Maria, O.S.B, trans. (1997) *Confessions. WSA I/1*, edited by John E. Rotelle. Hyde Park, NY: New City Press.

Boulding, Maria, O.S.B, trans. (2000) *Expositions on the Psalms 33–50, WSA III/16*. Hyde Park, NY: New City Press.

Boulding, Maria, O.S.B, trans. (2001) *Expositions on the Psalms 51–72, WSA III/17*. Hyde Park, NY: New City Press.

Boulding, Maria, O.S.B, trans. (2002) *Expositions on the Psalms 73–98, WSA III/18*. Hyde Park, NY: New City Press.

Boulding, Maria, O.S.B, trans. (2003) *Expositions on the Psalms 99–120, WSA III/19*. Hyde Park, NY: New City Press.

Cary, Philip (2000) *Augustine's Invention of the Inner Self*. Oxford: Oxford University Press.

Hill, Edmund, O.P., trans. (1991) *The Trinity, WSA I/5*, Brooklyn, NY: New City Press.

Hunter, David G., trans. (1999) *Marriage and Virginity, WSA I/9*. Hyde Park, NY: New City Press.

Lawson, R. P., trans. (1956) *Origen. Commentary on the Song of Songs*, Ancient Christian Writers 26. New York, NY: Newman Press.

Stock, Brian (1996) *Augustine the Reader*. Cambridge, MA: The Belknap Press of Harvard University Press.

Taylor, Charles (1989) *Sources of the Self: The Making of Modern Identity*. Cambridge, MA: Harvard University Press.

8

The Sacramentality of Marriage in the Fathers

I told a colleague recently that I was working on an essay on the sacramentality of marriage in the Fathers. My colleague responded by saying that would be a short essay. In a way, I can see the point of this quip. The patristic period was not exactly the golden age of marriage, if one is looking for a widespread, rich tradition of reflection on the religious or theological significance of marriage. As Brown (1988) has shown, there was an emphasis on asceticism and the single life in many of the earliest Christian communities.[1] Marriage often came to seem at best a kind of given, a fact of life, not worthy of a great deal of reflection, and at worst an ambiguous good or even an evil. Even some orthodox writers – Tertullian in his Catholic phase, for instance – seemed to wonder how good an alternative marriage really could be, if it were only good in comparison to an evil, that is, as an alternative to "burning."[2]

Nevertheless, the canonical Gospels do not disparage marriage, but rather defend it as established by God and, if anything, argue that it should be restored to the pristine purity it had when it came forth from the hand of the Creator. Marriage in the canonical Gospels is used by Jesus as a suitable and even preferred image for the proclamation of the kingdom of God, even if at the same time there is reserved a place of admiration for those who leave marriage and family behind to follow their itinerant Lord, the Son of Man, who "had no place to lay his head" (Mt. 8:21). Paul's letters seem to reflect this tension

Visioning Augustine, First Edition. John C. Cavadini.
© 2019 John Wiley & Sons Ltd. Published 2019 by John Wiley & Sons Ltd.

between an appreciation for marriage, on the one hand, and a recognition that all things connected with the flesh and this world have been relativized by the prospect of the imminent return of the Lord in glory.[3]

As the return of the Lord was prolonged, the elements that Paul held in tension seem to have come somewhat undone and were represented in different strands of the later Pauline tradition. Deutero-Pauline texts such as Ephesians and later the Pastorals developed a robust appreciation for what Augustine would even later call the "good" or the "excellence" of marriage, while the apocryphal *Acts of Paul* embraces an almost heroic ideal of asceticism that borders on the disparagement of marriage. In the radical Pauline heretic Marcion, this disparagement passed over into outright rejection. Other sects and movements that emphasized the impending return of the Lord, who thought of the church as essentially the church of the martyrs in the face of a hostile empire, also disparaged marriage.[4] This was probably, in part, a reaction against the spirituality reflected in the Pastoral Epistles, which not only endorses marriage as a good but also verges on canonizing received, non-Christian wisdom about the ordering of households, presenting an almost too settled Christianity. These Christians were perhaps content to pattern the ordering of their households after their non-Christian, post-Augustan neighbors in order to please them. It is sometimes hard, looking back on these texts, to discern what elements are proclaimed as essential to an understanding of marriage as a good established by God and what are apologetic concessions to the Roman way of doing things in the face of suspicion and persecution.

For the most part, orthodox Christians did continue to defend the goodness of marriage, based on passages such as 1 Cor. 7 and Eph. 5:21–33. Their articulation of the ideals of married life often drew heavily on earlier philosophical ideals, Stoic in particular, "Christianizing" these ideals with greater or lesser success. These philosophical ideals generally regarded marriage from an ascetic perspective, emphasizing that sex is for procreation only, devaluing physical beauty, and disapproving of passion. Clement of Alexandria is a good second-century example of an exponent of civilized, philosophical sex.[5] Clement remarks, for example, that it would be difficult for a wife to continue to respect her husband if he conducted himself in an undignified way during sex. Clement instructs couples not to have sex "during the day, nor … after coming home from church, or from the marketplace or early in the morning like a rooster."[6] Brown (1988) warns against reading too much into these observations, which may strike contemporary sensibilities as odd. Clement's overall vision, of a partnership of husband and wife who serve Christ together in an age when they might both be called upon to be martyrs, is very compelling. The family served as a center of prayer and presumably a source of strength.[7] Clement's married Christian sage was not cold or gloomy and could regard sex and family, when taken up into the civilizing arts that were meant to enhance and nurture the educated life, as entirely positive, though there is no developed theory of what we would call the sacramentality of marriage per se.

John Chrysostom's preaching, at least in his own later years, may offer one of the most potentially appealing versions of this Christianized philosophical view of marriage.[8] Chrysostom has a rich appreciation for the love that should obtain between husband and wife. Although the wife is to submit to her husband, Chrysostom emphatically distinguishes her submission from the submission of a slave to a master. "What sort of union is it" he asks rhetorically:

> … when the wife trembles before her husband? What sort of pleasure will the husband himself enjoy, if he lives with a wife who is more a slave than a free woman?[9]

The wife is not a slave, but a "second authority," having "authority and honor equal to the husband's in many respects," but with the husband having something additional – it is he who is particularly charged with the well-being of the household, with its proper ordering.[10] Chrysostom understands this to mean that the husband is responsible to lead in the matter of love, because Eph. 5:25 instructs him to love his wife as Christ loves the Church, and Eph. 5:28 explains that this means that husbands should love their wives as much as their own flesh.[11] Husbands who would like their wives to obey them must lead in and with love, overlooking irritations that accumulate day to day and renouncing contempt. No matter how unappreciative or foolish or unattractive his wife may be, she could not, Chrysostom drily remarks, be as distant from the husband's imagined ideal as the Church was from Christ, who nevertheless espoused her and loved her.[12] A well-ordered household with the husband at the head should be one in which the spirit of love has overtaken the whole. When the husband can say that he, like Christ, loves his wife as much as his own body, he can then expect the obedience appropriate to a wife (as distinguished from the obedience appropriate to a slave, to which he is not entitled). The husband's authority as "head" does not authorize him ever to resort to violence or threats of violence, but rather to treat his wife as though he has been entrusted with the care of a "sacred image."[13] Such a household – where the love of the wife is worth more than anything else to the husband, and where children are loved for her sake, and not more than she is[14] – such a household would be filled with the mutual submission of husband and wife, enjoined by Eph. 5:21, and would be a "marriage that is according to Christ," "entirely spiritual, when the soul is united to God in an ineffable union which He alone knows."[15] Perhaps we would locate the sacramentality of marriage in Chrysostom in a statement such as this. Leading in love, the husband's headship, and therefore his received cultural authority, is transformed into a kind of submission, while the wife's subjection becomes a being-received-in-love and a loving in return.

Chrysostom imagines that living in such a household would afford a deep and satisfying pleasure to anyone who was a member of it. Unlike some of the other more "philosophically" minded theorists, Chrysostom in his later years does not seem as invested in disparaging the pleasure of sex. Perhaps he imagines that the pleasure of sex would be part of the pleasure of a larger spiritual enterprise. Perhaps we are not unjustified in thinking that, for Chrysostom, the pleasure of sex in Christian marriage is felt as the pleasure of being at home in a household configured by the love of Christ for the church. If this is correct, it would seem to be a true sublation of *eros* into *agape*.[16]

Of course, the "philosophical" ethic of marriage is bound to seem austere insofar as it eschews many pleasures that were commonly thought (and probably are commonly thought today) to be innocent enough in themselves – wealth; ostentation (including gold jewelry, makeup, and perfume); extravagant clothing (as opposed to simple elegance); dancing; and so on. And Chrysostom seems to envisage a situation – although it is not intrinsic to marriage as he describes it – where the husband is older than the wife and serves as her teacher in this kind of philosophical life:

> From the very first evening that he receives her into the bridal chamber, he should teach her self-restraint, moderation, how to live a holy life, rejecting the desire for money at the very outset, as soon as she comes through the door. He should instruct her in philosophy and advise her not to have pieces of gold dangling from her ears ... or strewn about the bedroom.[17]

In practice, Chrysostom's ideal marriage may have seemed rather confining, especially to women, just another variant on codes of household management that emphasized the power of men over women and nobility over slaves. And yet, perhaps this aspect of the ideal is more accidental than essential to it. Again, if there is a sacramentality to marriage in Chrysostom's ideal, could we not say that it is to be located in the way in which such notions as leadership and obedience cease being absolute quantities determined by cultural standards at large, but rather are recontextualized against, and relativized by, the love of Christ for the Church? Chrysostom's preaching suggests an ideal of marriage that, at least theoretically, has gone beyond the mere recommendation of a previously extant philosophical or economic ideal for Christian couples, to a point where the essential character of married life cannot be understood apart from reference to the love of Christ for the church. It therefore becomes capable of imaging and representing that love:

> What sort of children do you think will come from such parents? ... What will happen to everyone else who comes near them? Surely, they too will be filled with countless blessings.[18]

As appealing as it may have seemed, not everyone who defended the good of Christian marriage in antiquity was as sanguine about such an ideal. Augustine, for example, would likely have felt that it left largely unexamined some fundamentally problematic realities of human life. It would have struck Augustine as too ready to accept the sexual drive as unproblematically positive (even if in need of philosophical restraint), and as too eager to project an equally unproblematic straight line from *eros* to an uncomplicated domesticity. Augustine is as aware as anyone of the goodness and pleasure of domestic and family life and often comments on the enjoyment a father has in uttering nonsense words to his little son, or that a mother might have in pre-chewing little bits of food for her baby.[19] He is not above bragging about his own son, Adeodatus, years after his death.[20] He has obviously kept track of his own common-law wife, and he states his admiration for the celibate life she took up after returning to Africa, in contrast to his own miserable lapse into fornication while awaiting his formally arranged bridal prospect to reach legal age. Augustine seems to call himself an adulterer, later on, for leaving his concubine and immediately embracing another.[21] He comments, too, on the obviously welcome and desirable pleasures of endearment and affection between husband and wife.[22] He is not unaware or unapproving of the kind of love that Chrysostom highlights.

And yet, that love figures hardly at all in his extensive and impressive body of writing on marriage and related topics. To Augustine's mind, there is something naive about a view of marriage that treats sexual desire as a relatively uncomplicated *eros* that education and ascetic living can easily channel into the pleasures of home and family. For Augustine, sexual desire as we know it now is anything but uncomplicated. To people accustomed to thinking that sexual desire and the pleasure it seeks are obvious and uncomplicated goods that contribute, in a straightforwardly positive way, to the bonding and happiness of a married couple, Augustine's views will look pessimistic. Yet, Augustine would probably insist that it is simply realistic. Sexual pleasure is not a fixed quantity, unambiguously and obviously good as we experience it in a fallen world.[23] Rape, presumably, is pleasurable for the rapist, and husbands are not immune from the pleasure of violent sex just because they are married, and the elements of violence contributing to the pleasure of sex may be subtle enough. Pleasure of any kind (or pain, for that matter) is not simply a physical reality or a given for Augustine, but rather is a function of deep prior commitments of the human spirit, of the "heart." The heart that is configured by pride, that is, love of self over God, will take greatest pleasure in its own use of power, whether that is exhibited overtly in rape or in such less obvious forms as narcissistic self-admiration for one's (supposed) excellence as a lover, married or not. Such pleasures are not innocent and ultimately break down communion of persons rather than contribute to it. The heart that is configured by humility, that is, love of God above all, on the other hand, will find pleasure in creatures, including other people, as a reflection of the glory of the Creator and not as opportunities to exercise and admire its own power and ability, that is, as occasions of the reflection of one's own glory.

This means that any given emotion, such as joy or fear, is in itself neutral, but can be felt differently depending upon the fundamental configuration of the will.[24] The humble person does not give up feeling joyful, but feels joyful in loving God and neighbors, while the prideful person feels joy in exercising his or her own power in preference to the love of God and neighbor. Unfortunately, in fallen human beings, all emotions and desires are formatted or configured to pride, at least at first. No descendent of Adam can say with certainty that any anger that he or she feels is more righteous than self-interested, that his or her sadness is perfectly conformed to the sadness of Christ in the Gospels and bears no trace of envy or selfishness; certainly no fallen human being can claim that his or her desire for sex is free of what Augustine calls "lust." Lust is a desire for sexual pleasure that is pleasure in one's own power or ability independent of the love of God and neighbor; pleasure, for example, in domination, manipulation, or use of the other for self-admiration or gratification, rather than wondering joy in the presence of the other as a creature of God and, as such, a form of praise of God. The latter way of feeling would always be loving, ready at any second to interrupt sex (for example) without regret and with joy in favor of a greater demand of love that might present itself, and so the desire for sex would never outstrip reason or freedom. Lust, by contrast, is always at least partly self-absorbed, anxious for gratification even if in competition with other demands of love, and so lustful desire for sex is always, to the extent that it is lustful, unfree, a kind of "goading" or compulsion that intrudes itself regardless of the demands of love or justice. Lust qua lust, in the Augustinian sense, is not a good and can never be made a good. If it became something good, it would cease to be "lust." That does not necessarily mean it would cease to be sexual desire or that sex would cease being enjoyable, but the source of pleasure or enjoyment would be freedom, humility, and love, with no trace of self-absorption or self-admiration or other seeds of violence as an admixture.

Augustine, accordingly, thought of the Christian life as a journey of healing or purification of the heart, one that entailed leaving behind the pleasures of pride and complacency and learning the new pleasures of humility and love. Christian life is life in transition, a life that is a struggle, described in Gal. 5:17 as the opposition of the desires of the "spirit" and of the "flesh." One learns to replace the pleasures of the flesh, meaning all pleasures configured by pride, with the pleasures of the spirit, meaning all pleasures configured by charity or love.[25]

> As long as the spirit has desires opposed to the flesh, this work goes on with great intensity; perverted pleasures, lust, and base carnal impulses are resisted with the gentle joy of sanctity, the love of chastity, spiritual energy and the prized virtue of continence.[26]

"Continence" in Augustine is not the name of sexual renunciation but the name of the Christian life, the life in transition and healing, a matter of the heart, not dependent upon any particular bodily state,[27] and ultimately a gift from God.[28]

Chrysostom's view of marriage envisions the husband taking the lead in creating a transformation in his wife, implying that the superiority of the husband's education and training is sufficient for his own transformation as well. Augustine from the time of the *Confessions* never implies that education or philosophical discipline on its own is enough for the healing or purification he has in mind. In fact, a good education and the discipline and prestige that goes with it can more likely become the occasion for pride than a formation in humility. Nor is Augustine inclined to imply that the husband, as the male or older spouse, is likely to have the kind of moral advantage whereby he could be the primary agent of the Christian life of transformation for his wife. From an Augustinian view, Chrysostom's idea of marriage almost verges on the sacramentality of the husband, who occupies the place of Christ vis-à-vis his wife and household, rather than the sacramentality of marriage, strictly speaking.[29] For Augustine, the transformation of desire is not in the first place a matter of education, either of oneself or, especially, of one spouse by the other, but rather of *incorporation*. Incorporation as a member of the church into the body of Christ is also, at least incipiently, an incorporation into Christ's way of feeling, a configuration to his way of loving. It is impossible to acquire a complete picture of the "sacramentality of marriage" according to Augustine without considering first this primary notion of transformation-in-incorporation, especially because Augustine's favorite biblical passages for explaining it are passages associated with marriage.

In his *Enarrationes in Psalmos* (*en. Ps.*), Augustine frequently comments to his listeners – so frequently that he expects them to know it before he says it – that the voice speaking in the Psalms is always Christ's voice, even when the psalmist's voice is saying something that would seem unbecoming of Christ. Augustine's listeners knew why this could be true, namely, because in the Psalms sometimes Christ speaks in the voice of his members, the members of his body, and sometimes in the voice of himself, the Head. In a famous passage, Augustine is explaining that the title of Ps. 30 implies that the psalm was spoken in fear, and he then goes on to explain:

> Whose fear? Christ's certainly …. He who deigned to assume the form of a slave, and within that form to clothe us with himself, he who did not disdain to take us up into himself, did not disdain either to transfigure us into himself, and to speak in our words, so that we in our turn might speak in his. Facing death, then, because of what he had from us, he was afraid, not in himself, but in us. When he said that his soul was sorrowful to the point of death, we all unquestionably said it with him. Without him, we are nothing, but in him, we too are Christ.[30]

It is the "bond of charity" that links the Head and members so intimately into one body, that made the Head cry out, "Saul, Saul, why are you persecuting *me*" (Acts 9:4) when Saul was obviously persecuting not the risen Jesus, but his members on earth.[31] The charity or love of the Incarnation is compassion so radical that it generates a solidarity in which the Head takes on the sufferings of his members and speaks in their voice, on their behalf, and in so doing "transfigures" the members into himself, identifying with them completely. Augustine points out that the Father never forsook the Son, even in the Crucifixion, and yet the Son cried out, "Oh God, my God, why have you forsaken me?" – speaking the psalm verse in our flesh, making our situation of abandonment by God because of our sin his own, and yet in making this cry his own, he was "transfiguring it."[32] Our voice, our fear, our desolation, taken up by Christ's compassion, becomes his, and our fear is transfigured so that, when we give voice to it, our speech is Christ's, that is, it is a remembrance of and an invocation of his compassion. Our very fear can be the place of contact with Christ's compassion. "This is the wonderful exchange, the divine business deal, the transaction effected in this world by the heavenly dealer."[33] Voicing our own desolation, we are at the same time voicing Christ's solidarity with our desolation, and so, at the same time, at least in faith and in hope, we are voicing our joy at being the objects of such compassion.[34] We are, at least incipiently, feeling the joy of being espoused by Christ. "By a great sacrament (Eph. 5:31), these two were united in one flesh."[35] The Incarnation is the great "mystery" or "sacrament" in which Christ espoused the church by taking on our flesh.

Augustine's favorite way of speaking of this intimate unity of Head and body, the church, is to say that they are "two in one flesh" (Mt. 19:50). This way of talking, Augustine notes, is not meant to apply only to an ordinary human marriage, because Paul says that the two in one flesh, the spouses in a marriage, "are a great mystery (*sacramentum*), but I am referring it to Christ and the Church" (Eph. 5:31–32). "So," Augustine goes on to remark, "out of two people, one single person comes to be, the single person that is Head and body, Bridegroom and bride."[36]

It is interesting and significant to note that, unlike his spiritual "father" Ambrose and unlike Origen before him, Augustine almost never refers to the individual soul as a "bride" of Christ. Ambrose used the wedding imagery from the Song of Songs to refer as much to the relationship between the individual soul and the Word of God as to the relationship between the church and the Word, but Augustine leaves this former dimension of the allegory almost completely behind.[37] "There are many churches, but one Church; many believers, but one bride of Christ."[38] Or, in the words of St. Paul, which Augustine cites, "As the body is a unit and has many members, and yet all the members of the body, many though they be, are one body, so too is Christ" (1 Cor. 12:12).[39] The bond of charity does not only link the Head with the members individually, but the members with each other. Our relationship with Christ is ecclesially mediated: in the unity with each other, which is founded in and configured to the charity of Christ, we know ourselves as beloved by Christ as by a spouse. None of us alone can claim the titles of "spouse" or "bride" because we do not know ourselves as such apart from the charity that binds us all together. That binding charity is not something we could have created for ourselves or drawn from the innermost resources of our being with a lot of education and effort, but is the love of Christ that prompted the "great sacrament" of the Incarnation, the assuming

of human nature into a nuptial union of two in one flesh. We experience ourselves as loved with a spousal love in our experience of the
Church, of the unifying love that was Christ's "voluntary sleep" on
the cross, giving being to the Church from his wounded side as Eve
came forth from Adam's side:

> "I have the power to lay down my life, and I have the power to take it
> up again. No one takes it away from me; but I lay it down of my own
> accord, that I may take it up again" (Jn. 10:18). They disturbed him, but
> he lay down to sleep (cf. Ps. 56:5). In this respect, Adam was a type of
> Christ. God sent a deep sleep upon Adam, in order to fashion a wife
> for him from his side. Was God unable to make a wife for the first man
> by taking her from his side while he was awake? ... Because in Christ's
> case, a bride was made for him as he slept on the cross, and made from
> his side. With a lance, his side was struck as he hung there, and out
> flowed the sacraments of the Church.[40]

The "voluntary sleep" of Christ, that is, his utterly freely willed
death on our behalf, both is and represents a love so strong that it
shows that Christ actually did care about us as much as a man cares
about his own flesh, just as Paul invites husbands to think about their
wives. We experience this same sense of being cherished as a man
cherishes his own flesh, namely, according to Ephesians, as a spouse,
precisely *as* members of the church united in charity. We experience
the "marrying" love that prompted the Incarnation in the first place
as members of the church. In other words, the primary place to experience Christ's spousal love is in the church, simply as a member
bound to all others, not in marriage.

Being a member of the body of Christ, his bride, is, then, to be
configured to the spousal love of Christ for the church. This does not
mean that individually we are fully conformed to the love of Christ,
and the feelings, emotions, and affections that are formed by that
love, but rather that we are members of a body whose very identity
is that love, and that we are each of us in the process of being transformed more and more fully by that love as we interact with each
other. It is a process of our hearts being conformed to the "deep
heart" of Christ. Augustine comments on Ps. 63:18 ("The just one
will be joyful in the Lord, and will hope in him; and all the upright
of heart will be commended"), saying that the Lord "represented" or

"transfigured" us in himself, bearing our heart "within his own," and that now we are instructed to correct our hearts by the rectitude of God's eternally straight heart.[41] This means, among other things, not looking self-righteously and enviously at persons we imagine are more evil than ourselves who are certainly prospering more than we ourselves, wondering why God does not chastise and punish them. That is the kind of "crookedness" of heart that needs correction. We experience the love of God in Christ as a quality of love extended to our neighbor, on the one hand a suffering, but on the other a joy because we are "yielding to the heart of God." It is a joy experienced in faith and hope. It is learning to feel a new kind of joy or pleasure.

One may think that, up to this point, we have not seen much, strictly speaking, about the sacramentality of marriage itself, but that is only true if one is looking for a Scholastic-style theory of sacramentality, an explicit concept of efficacious sign. The Fathers work in images as much as they do in concepts. Hunter (1999) points out that "Augustine's discussion of the sacrament of marriage must be clearly distinguished from later Christian formulations," and that in Augustine "[t]he 'sacrament' in Christian marriages refers to the sacred mystery or symbolic meaning that is found in the indissolubility of the marital relationship."[42] He seems to be implying, and in this he is right, that Augustine does not have an explicit theory of marriage as an "efficacious sign" that not only signifies but also makes present Christ's love for the church to the spouses.

Yet, one can, I think, also exaggerate the differences too much if one is not careful to include a broader range of evidence from the world of imagery that Augustine creates around this topic.[43] Scholastic sacramental theology does not come out of nowhere. If we are to see it as an authentic development of earlier theology, we must be as attentive to the underlying continuities in doctrine as we are to the differences in formulation and style of thinking. In Augustine's case, to say that the two-in-one flesh of marriage is an image or a sacred sign, a "sacramentum" or mystery bearing representation of the unity of Christ with the Church such that the Church is Christ's bride, is to have said a lot already about marriage as a "sacrament" even in our later sense of the term. If we can learn so much about the Incarnation, Passion, and Resurrection of Christ − the paschal mystery − from reflecting on the unity of husband and wife and from using spousal imagery for its various moments, then we have also already learned a lot about how marriage is sacramental for Augustine.

For one thing, even if one cannot squeeze a full-blown Scholastic theory of sacramentality out of Augustine's rich and textured imagery, it is not enough to say that marriage is simply and only a sign of something other than itself. One could not learn so much about the reality it signifies if it did not in some way truly make present the reality it signifies, namely, the transformative and healing love of Christ for the church. If this is not recognized as often as it could be, it is because Augustine's theology of marriage is mostly separated by commentators from his ecclesiology. But they are joined precisely by the spousal imagery drawn from Scripture, namely Genesis, the Gospel of Matthew, and the Letter to the Ephesians, among others. Augustine's theory of marriage is often thought of as somewhat pessimistic or thin, but that again is because it is almost always separated from the ecclesiology that reveals and constitutes its true depth. The sacramentality of marriage in Augustine is entirely derivative of his ecclesiology. The primary place, or logically prior place, where the transforming spousal love of Christ is encountered is in one's membership in the Church, and not in marriage. Nevertheless, that encounter is made present for married Christians in and through their mutual incorporation into each other as "one flesh." They find Christ's Church-forming love, his "spousal" love, in their bond to each other.[44]

In Augustine, this is expressed, almost paradoxically, by the image of the virgin bride. The church is virginal because of the purity of Christ's love, which forms the Church. Married Christians participate in that virginity, not in virtue of a frame of mind they have acquired through education or philosophical training, and certainly not because they are physically virgins, but because they are incorporated into Christ:

> The whole Church, of which they [widows] are members, is itself his spouse, because by the integrity of her faith, hope and love she is a virgin, not only in holy virgins but in widows and the married faithful too.[45]

Married Christians participate in the virginity of the bride of Christ in virtue of their baptism. And yet, they have this participation not simply because they are baptized, but because marriage affords them a way of life that mediates the "healing" or pure, transforming love that is the origin of the church in the first place. It mediates the "virginity" of the bride to those who are not virgins and who continue to have sex. If it is not too cute to put it this way, marriage is the sacrament that allows Christians to have sex and not lose their virginity. That is the "excellence" of marriage.[46] It is a transformation-in-incorporation. Marriage is a state of life, a "gift from God," in which the "two in one flesh" of the literal marriage bond form a special, small Christian community in which to experience the "marrying love" of Christ, the pure and purifying love of the Incarnation. Note that this is not a special, romantic love different from the love bonding all members of the church, but rather it is *that* love that marriage mediates or makes present for the spouses. Marriage does not isolate them from the church or set up a community that is competing with the larger church, but rather makes the community of the two spouses authentically ecclesial, a "domestic church," to import a later phrase. It may be that the spouses do have a special, natural affection for each other, and such natural happiness that comes from this friendship is all to the good, but that is not what makes marriage "sacramental" in Augustine.[47] Rather, that natural affection is itself transformed or taken up into the higher love that is the bond between all Christians in the Church. This natural affection or friendship has nothing in it that is intrinsically sacramental, though, as part of God's good creation, it can be molded by and transformed by the sacrament into an ecclesial reality, into a mystical participation in the body of Christ. Augustine's theology of marriage is entirely dependent upon his theology of the Church.[48]

It is easy to be misled by the seemingly minimalist language that Augustine applies to marriage. In an era of especially heightened ascetic sensibility that prompted Manichees and even an otherwise orthodox doctor of the Church (Jerome) to disparage marriage, Augustine defended it as good, though a lesser good than consecrated virginity or widowhood.[49] True, marriage is a state of life, Augustine always insists, for the weaker sort of Christian who cannot manage celibacy.[50] It is a "cure for weakness, and in some cases a source of comfort for human nature."[51] The "comfort" comes in such things as "living with one's husband for a long time and having children," the "natural happiness" that Anna, the prophetess, was denied because her husband died when she was young.[52] Marriage provides a way of life that takes up this "natural happiness" into the body of Christ, so that one experiences all of the joys and comforts proper to natural happiness as part of or in the context of one's incorporation into a new society, the new body, even if this is an incorporation in a lower or lesser place:

> How great is the excellence in the fidelity of married women, that is to say Christian and religious married women, can be concluded from the fact that, when he was commanding them to flee from fornication (and certainly he was addressing married persons), he said, *Do you not know that your bodies are members of Christ?* (1 Cor. 6:19, 7:34). So great is the excellence of Christian marriage, therefore, that they are even members of the body of Christ. Nevertheless, while the excellence of chastity in widowhood is greater, it does not follow that in this state of life a Catholic widow is something greater than a member of Christ, but among the members of Christ she occupies a place superior to that of the married woman.[53]

In Augustine, "fornication" refers to sex with a prostitute (as here) or between unmarried persons, but it also always refers metaphorically to a turning away from God's embrace. Fallen sexual desire, that is, "lust," *is* a desire to turn away from God's embrace and be joined to the body of those who are turned away, toward incorporation into the world, the network of relations and identities configured by pride. "Lust," for Augustine, once again, is not simply a biological desire for an uncomplicated, physical pleasure, but is a desire for an exclusive identity apart from God, an identity wholly in the world. It is the desire for the pleasure of constructing one's identity exclusively as a cultural project, rather than receiving it first and foremost from God, as a creature of God. This desire does not go away simply because one is married. But marriage turns the evil of lust into a "good use," without making it, qua lust, good. It turns fallen sexual desire, and the community of two it creates, unbelievably and wondrously, into a locus of continuing incorporation into Christ's body, even if it remains, strictly speaking, a community generated by lust. In marriage, lust itself is exercised within the healing bounds of continence. The fact that lust qua lust does not become good is grounds for a continuing formation in humility, lest one regard one's incorporation into Christ as an achievement of one's own, a natural achievement of human nature. Lust issues in bragging.[54] Married love is founded in humility, and so in confession and gratitude.

We can look a little more closely at how this works, using Augustine's idea of the three "goods" of marriage. Marriage turns the evil of lust into a good use, and even sexual pleasure that is indulged simply for the pleasure and not for the procreation of children is "pardonable because of the good there is in marriage" as long as there is no intention to thwart the procreative effect of intercourse.[55] Having children is a natural good, the original and primary intention of the Creator in making human beings "male and female," so intercourse that is open to procreation respects the Creator's intention and is an implicit confession of the goodness of God, a training in humility and praise.

The fidelity of the spouses to each other, meaning both that they do not have sex with anyone else and that they do not abstain from sex except by mutual agreement, is the second good of marriage. Restricting sex according to the norms of procreation and fidelity is a form of chastity, a discipline which is the form that "continence" takes in married people.

> Continence in marriage usually allows some freedom to … carnal desires,[56] but it reins them in and keeps them under control. Not even in marriage are they let go with unlimited freedom. They are limited either by what is required because of the weakness of one's spouse … or to what is appropriate for the purpose of having children …. In so doing, that is, controlling carnal desire in married couples, and placing certain limits on it, and bringing a certain order to its lively and unruly stirrings by imposing definite limits, it uses the evil in people for good. It makes them good and wants to make them perfect.[57]

As already mentioned, continence is primarily a spiritual good, not a physical good.[58] It is another name for the process and the progress of the healing and purification of desire that we receive when configured to Christ. *The church is subject to Christ*, it says in Eph. 5:24, but this does not indicate that the church is perfected now, without spot or wrinkle, but that it is being perfected both in married persons who are sexually active within the bounds of the goods of marriage, and in celibate persons. This is the body that cries out with one voice in the Psalms, to the one who *heals all our infirmities* (Ps. 103:3). "Christ heals these [carnal] desires in those who belong to him," and Augustine is clear that this means both sexually active married persons and celibates, married or single.[59]

Marriage is a way of life instituted in particular as a "cure for weakness," but this is more than it seems at first, because as such it images the whole Christian life, which (as we have seen) is one continual healing and purification in Christ. The openness to procreation and the fidelity of the spouses are not healing because they are ascetical enterprises undertaken out of a desire to live philosophically, but because they are the expressions of being incorporated into Christ, into his healing love, first at baptism and then by marriage. This is where the third good of marriage comes in, its indissolubility or permanence of commitment. It is this good especially that carries the "sacrament" or mysterious signification of the love of Christ for the church and conveys it to the other two goods.[60] A couple might be "two in one flesh" at the time of intercourse, but the indissolubility of marriage makes this "two in one flesh"-ness a permanent condition, a matter not simply of the body but of the spirit. It is not sexual union, per se, that signifies the "two in one flesh" that is Christ and the church, but the permanent intimacy of life, body, and spirit that characterizes a Christian marriage in particular and so enables it to carry this significance.[61] It is not significant because it is an extra, added-on element of ascetic effort, but *because* of the union of Christ and the church, because it is a configuration of the couple to that larger mystery and so the presence of it in *their* flesh and spirit. In their married life, their hearts are being ever more closely configured to the love of Christ for the church, and that is what all of their "use" of marriage means.

How far can that configuration go? The only limit on it is that the spouses cannot be literally virgins.[62] But, Augustine comments, there are the beatitudes, and married persons can grow in perfection of these, and there is martyrdom, and the married have been martyrs, and one can never know from one's way of life, married or celibate, who at any given time is actually ready to endure martyrdom.[63] Of two people, one married and one celibate, it could be the married person, and martyrdom is a greater perfection, Augustine reminds us, than virginity.[64] Celibacy is more prone to pride than is married life. There is no doubt in Augustine's mind that consecrated virginity ranks higher than marriage, yet he comments that, apart from Christ and the Virgin Mary, there is no way of knowing whether, in fact, those with the highest reward will be married persons or virgins. Also, although the life of consecrated virginity is higher than marriage, there is ultimately no higher way of describing the good of virginity or celibacy except by describing it in terms of marriage imagery, – that is, of the permanent intimacy of Christ and his spouse the church, and of the ongoing configuration of this bride, in the person of all who are members, to her spouse. Without this imagery, celibacy itself has no language to interpret its own significance and would be forced back merely onto the language of philosophical discipline and self-perfection. Marriage is a *visible* sign of the purifying love of Christ for the Church. For that reason, and because, as a visible sign, it *presents* an encounter with that love for those who are married, it can also serve as a symbol for other ways of life in the Church in which that love can be found. That is why marriage is "sacramental," while, paradoxically, the higher way of life of virginity is not.

Augustine has been criticized frequently because he could find no positive place for sexual pleasure in a marriage, but the sacramentality of marriage should not, in Augustine or anywhere else, be a function of the contribution of sexual pleasure, but of Christ.[65] Marriage, in restraining and channeling lust, does promote the healing transformation of prideful pleasures into pleasures of justice and charity. As mentioned earlier, lust in marriage is exercised within the healing boundaries of married continence, and so within the framework of healing, purifying love. Lust is not the principle of its own healing and can contribute nothing to the good of the married partners – yet, exercised in the boundaries of married continence, it is perhaps worn down by the glacial pressure of married continence. For Augustine, this does not mean that sexual desire is ever free of lust in this life, just like all fallen emotions are never quite free of disordered passion. What sex feels like as this transformation takes place is left largely to the imagination in Augustine. It must, at least, mean learning to take pleasure in humility and all of its fruits. Sex that is truly humble may not seem pleasurable in the first instance to those whose desires have not been configured by marriage, Christ's sacrament, into the love that gave its life for someone ugly and undesirable and hostile. One does not "lust" after such pleasure, yet it is highly desirable, a true joy and real pleasure, greater than any that "lust" can promise or provide, and one may, in fact, experience it now, even if only (or mostly) "in faith and in hope."[66]

Brief Afterword on a Contemporary Application

The "theology of the body" that was so creatively articulated by Pope John Paul II as a way of offering a robust account of the meaning of Christian marriage in the idea of the "nuptial meaning" of the body, its fundamental orientation to self-donation as symbolized and enacted in permanently committed sexual union that is open to procreation, is a true theological contribution to Christian reflection on marriage. It draws on a Thomistic sensibility more than an Augustinian one, and perhaps does a much better job than Augustine does in accounting for the "positive" role of sexual intercourse open to procreation in marriage. Yet, not all theologies can have all goods; perfectly orthodox theologies can have differing strengths that complement one another. Augustine's view is probably more suspicious of the perceived pleasure of "self-donation," which, just as much as the celibacy of a proud virgin, can be a pleasure of pride without even realizing it.

Without disparaging the goodness of the body or of procreation, Augustine locates the sacramentality of marriage more firmly in the good of Christian fellowship in the Church. For the same reason that Augustine's theology of marriage will look very different, in the end, from Chrysostom's, it will look different from similar efforts, medieval or modern, to Christianize a philosophical or educational ideal, whether that is Aristotelian or "personalist." For one thing, for Augustine, there is no question that the husband in a particular marriage has or mediates the place of Christ, in the sense that he is the agent of transformation or purification, or that he is more the "donor" and less the "receiver." Both husband and wife are members of the one body, the bride of Christ; both are profoundly receivers before they are anything else. It is in the first place as members of the church, bound to all others in charity, that they are configured to Christ's transforming and purifying love. Members of the church are not, in the first place, souls in individual relation with the Word of God, but rather members of each other in the flesh that the Word "married" in the Incarnation. This flesh now signifies Christ's love, and one is configured to it by incorporation, not in the first place by education, effort, or gendered bodily form. Marriage mediates to the spouses in a more immediate way, and in a way that is predicated on the possibility of sexual intercourse, the same love that characterizes and binds all members of the body to all others.

Further, if sexual desire in Augustine is a much more ambiguous affair than in Thomas or in the theology of the body he has inspired, it may make it easier to find a pastoral approach that understands the intractable problems that may arise in matters sexual. Sexual desire is not as self-evidently and unassailably positive, and its expression not as straightforwardly uncomplicated, as more "positive" views sometimes make it seem. These positive views may lend themselves, without the intention of doing so, to harsher pastoral expectations (if it is so straightforward, then it's *your* fault if you cannot get it right) or to unnaturally idealistic or romantic expectations in those about to be married, which could end up in serious disillusion and rejection of the whole Catholic idea of marriage. Foregrounding the issue of "healing," where that means a slow, patient formation in the humility of Christ, in the purifying love of the Incarnate, may not be such a terrible pastoral strategy in an age where everyone is convinced that anything that feels good is in fact evidently good, and where gratification, or an enthusiastic feeling of "self-donation," cannot always be called forth. Without making the roles of men and women in sex and reproduction interchangeable, and without removing the good of reproduction as intrinsic to marriage, Augustine finds a way to make the "self-donation" of the spouses a function not primarily of natural inclination, but of the long, hard, purifying pedagogy in the loving humility of Christ, which begets the only true joys.

I do not want to speak against the theology of the body, which I admire as John Paul II preached it (as opposed to the versions of it found in some of its proponents less learned than he was). But I would argue that, as with any theology that is necessarily limited in some ways and superior in others, it can benefit from a complementary spirituality based on the Augustinian view. This complementarity should be seen as positive, and as something worthy of development in its own right.

Acknowledgments

An earlier version of this chapter was published as Cavadini, J. C. Fall (2008) "The Sacramentality of Marriage in the Fathers." *Pro Ecclesia* 17 (4): 442–463. © Rowman & Littlefield Publishing Group.

Notes

1   Brown (1988).

2   See, for example, Tertullian, commenting on 1 Cor. 7:9 in *To His Wife* 1.3: "Scripture says that *it is better to marry than to burn*; but what sort of good, I ask you, can that be which is such only when it is compared to what is bad?" In Le Saint (1951), 13, even more forcefully stated at *Exhortation to Chastity* 3 (Le Saint [1951], 47), though this somewhat negative assessment is balanced by the closing peroration of *To His Wife* on the beauties of Christian marriage, in the face of which "Christ rejoices" (2.8; Le Saint [1951], 35).

3   Paul was concerned "not to sweep away the structures of the pious household," yet "[m]arriage, like household slavery, was a 'calling' devoid of glamour. It did not attract close attention as the present age slipped silently toward its end" (Brown [1988], 54, 57).

4   The New Prophecy (Montanists, especially as exemplified by Tertullian), Marcionites, Encratites, and Valentinians (from a very different point of view) all had relatively negative views of marriage (see Brown [1988], 76–82, 83–121). The evidence of the *Martyrdom of Saints Perpetua and Felicitas* shows that even married women bearing children could receive the gifts of the Spirit and become spiritual leaders, but this does not seem to be a gift thought of as mediated by marriage per se. Brown hints that Perpetua's courage and poise was in part a reflection of her status as a matron: "A *matrona* to the last, 'with shining face and quiet poise' she asks for a hairpin so her free flowing hair will not be mistaken as mourning but the fact that she is married seems mostly unremarkable to the ancient editor of the text" (Brown [1988], 75).

5   "Clement's ideal of the Christian life was permeated by a deep sense of the service of God … combined with an awareness of the presence, in the soul of the believer, of His Word, Christ – an intimate companion …. To do justice to this notion, and to the program of lifelong moral grooming that it implied, Clement fell back instinctively on the Stoic views which, along with Platonic metaphysics, were part and parcel of the intellectual *koinè* of the age" (Brown [1988], 128).

6   Clement of Alexandria, *The Instructor* 2.96. Translated by Hunter (1992), 45. Hunter's introduction is a very helpful theological overview of the developments and views regarding marriage in the patristic period. On the incorporation of Stoic ideals into Christian understandings of marriage, see 7–9. Clement's use of philosophical ideals is, however, in the service of defending particularly Christian notions such as the good of the world precisely as *creation*, as implied by Brown, and noted by Hunter (15) against the disparagement of the goodness of creation by Encratites and Gnostics alike. Brown argues that Clement goes further than the pagan moralists by attempting to regulate the etiquette of intercourse, but he points out that that was because Clement had to defend intercourse against attacks from hostile pagans. His point was to show that Christians behaved philosophically even in sex.

7   Brown (1988), 134–136.

8   I am following Hunter here, who deemphasizes the more negative views that Chrysostom held and preached in his earlier days, views that are more to the fore in Brown's (1988) treatment (e.g. at 309, "John's was a bleak and deliberately atomistic vision that has elicited little sympathy from modern readers"). Hunter (1992) notes that, in his *Homily 20 on Ephesians*, "Chrysostom evidences little of the mistrust of human sexuality that characterizes so much of the Christian literature of this period (and that characterized Chrysostom's own early writings). On the contrary, Chrysostom speaks of the desire (eros) that draws two human beings together as the creation of God and as the highest form of human love (*Homily 20.1*). Rather than develop a sexual asceticism, Chrysostom focuses on the problem of attachment to money" (19–20). For an extended statement of a more sympathetic view, see Ford (1995). Cattenoz (1993), while not on the topic of marriage itself, offers a good resource for continuing reflection. Brown's view builds on the earlier treatment offered by Clark (1983); see, more recently, Clark (1994).

9   John Chrysostom, *Homily 20 on Ephesians* (translated at Hunter [1992], 80). It is interesting that Jerome, perhaps a seemingly unlikely candidate, can take this one step farther. Commenting on Eph. 5:33, he notes, "*The woman, however, fears her husband.* If fear of God, because of fear of punishment, disqualifies the one who fears from being perfect, how much more imperfect will be the wife who fears, not only God, but also her husband? Because of this it should be asked whether *wife* and the *fear* of a *wife* should be understood in a literal sense, since frequently wives are found to be much superior to husbands at ordering them, and running the house, and educating the children, and maintaining family discipline, while the husbands live in luxury and pursue mistress after mistress. Whether wives of such caliber should rule, or fear, their husbands, I leave to the reader's judgment." *Commentary on Ephesians* 3.5, translated by Halten (1999), 249–250.

10   "The wife is a second authority; she has authority and honor equal to the husband's in many respects. But the husband has something more. His special concern is the well-being of the household" (*Homily 20.6 on Ephesians*, translated by Hunter [1992], 87).

11   John Chrysostom, *Homily 20.3 on Ephesians* (translated by Hunter [1992], 82).

12   John Chrysostom, *Homily 20.2*, "*Husbands*, he says, *love your wives, as Christ has loved the church.* You have seen the measure of obedience; now hear the measure of love. Would you like your wife to obey you as Christ? Then you must care for her, as Christ does for the church. Even if it is necessary to give your life for her, even if you must be cut into a thousand pieces, even if you must endure any suffering whatever, do not refuse it. Even if you do suffer like this, you will never suffer as much as Christ did. For you are doing it for one with whom you are already joined, but he did it for one who rejected him and hated him" (translated by Hunter [1992], 79–80).

178 Visioning Augustine

13 John Chrysostom, *Homily 20.7 on Ephesians* (translated by Hunter [1992], 90).
14 John Chrysostom, *Homily 20.8 on Ephesians* (translated by Hunter [1992], 93).
15 John Chrysostom, *Homily 20.5 on Ephesians* (translated by Hunter [1992], 85).
16 See Benedict XVI (2006), *Deus Caritas Est* 1.7, on the relation between *eros* and *agape*.
17 John Chrysostom, *Homily 20.7 on Ephesians* (translated by Hunter [1992], 90).
18 John Chrysostom, *Homily 20.9 on Ephesians* (translated by Hunter [1992], 96).
19 For example, at *cat. rud.* 10.15.
20 See *conf.* 9.6.14.
21 In *conf.* 6.15.25, it is obvious that Augustine knows what has happened to her and where she is. Brown (1988), 393, points out that the case, raised in *b. coniug.* 5.5, of the man who dismisses his concubine only to live and have sex with another woman, is Augustine's own condemnation of himself. Augustine judges that such a man is an adulterer against the concubine.
22 In *ciu.* 19.12, Augustine notes the miserable condition of the mythic Cacus, "who had no wife with whom to exchange endearments, no children to play with when little or to give orders to when they were a little bigger, no friends with whom to enjoy a chat." Translated by Bettenson (1972). See also *en. Ps.* 40, sec. 5, for another example. Translated by Boulding (2000a), 230–231: "A good man finds rest in his own home, in his household, his wife and children, in his modest way of life, in his smallholding, in the young plants he has set with his own hands, in some building that has been put up through his initiative. Innocent people find their relaxation in things like these."
23 I tried to take up this topic in an earlier essay – Cavadini (2005, reprinted as Chapter 6 of this volume) – and the comments that follow on lust and sexual pleasure are treated in greater length there.
24 As explained, for example, in *ciu.* 14.6.
25 Passages dramatizing the opposition of flesh and spirit from Gal. 5:17 are common in Augustine. The most famous is in *conf.* 8.5.10–12. In *ciu.* 14.2–3, Augustine is insistent that "flesh" in the Pauline verse does not mean "body"; the body is not the source of sin, but the soul, and some of the pleasures of the "flesh" have nothing to do with the body (such as envy; see also *cont.* 4.11; 9.22). The *en. Ps.* often take up Gal. 5:17 into Augustine's preaching.
26 Augustine, *cont.* 14.31 (translated in Hunter [1992], 214–215).
27 *cont.* 1.2–2.5: "It follows that the purity that is exercised in controlling the reproductive organs, which is what is usually meant by the word 'continence' used in its literal sense, suffers no violation or infringement, if the more perfect continence we have been speaking about at length is maintained in the heart" (translated in Hunter [1992], 194).
28 Married life is a gift of God, even as the single (celibate) life is (Augustine cites 1 Cor. 7:7 as his authority), and both offer continent ways of life – that is, ways of life in transition and transformation from pride to humility.

29 Augustine did believe that Eph. 5:22–23 meant that the wife was to be subor-
    dinate, that is, obedient, to the husband, but he does not picture Christ's saving
    work as somehow being mediated to the wife through the husband (see *cont.*
    9.23, one of Augustine's strongest statements of the superiority of husband to
    wife on the pattern of Christ and the church and spirit and flesh, and yet, there
    is no indication of the husband as therefore the agent of transformation of his
    wife in any intrinsic way).

30 *En. 2 in Ps. 30*, sec. 3 (translated by Boulding [2000b], 323).

31 *En. 2 in Ps. 30*, sec. 3 (translated by Boulding [2000b], 323).

32 *En. 2 in Ps. 30*, sec. 11 (translated by Boulding [2000a], 331).

33 *En. 2 in Ps. 30*, sec. 3 (translated by Boulding [2000a], 323).

34 In the second exposition of Ps. 31: "God scourges every son whom he acknowl-
    edges (cf. Heb. 12:6). Every single one? Yes .... Even the only-begotten Son
    himself, he who was sinless, even he was not exempt. The only-begotten Son
    himself, bearing your weakness and representing you in his own person, as the
    Head which included the body in itself, even he was deeply saddened in his
    human nature as he approached his passion, in order to give you joy. He was
    saddened that he might comfort you" (*En. 2 in Ps. 31*, sec. 26, translated by
    Boulding [2000a], 387).

35 *En. 3 in Ps. 30*, sec. 1 (translated by Boulding [2000a], 334).

36 *En. 3 in Ps. 30*, sec. 4 (translated by Boulding [2000a], 324).

37 So, frequently, in his *De Isaac vel Anima* (*On Isaac, or, The Soul*). Translated by
    McHugh (1972).

38 *En. in Ps. 64*, sec. 14 (translated by Boulding [2001], 281).

39 *En. in Ps. 30*, sec. 4 (translated by Boulding [2001], 324).

40 *En. in Ps. 56*, sec. 11 (translated by Boulding [2001], 111–112).

41 *En. in Ps. 63*, sec. 18 (translated by Boulding [2001], 262).

42 Hunter (1999), "General Introduction," 18.

43 On this point, Schmitt (1983) offers a view that states the basis for continuity
    (298–301). See especially, on page 299, "C'est. le moment de se rappeler que,
    suivant la perspective platonicienne plus or moins inhérente à la structure men-
    tale d'Augustin, une figure n'est. jamais pure représentation d'une réalité, mais
    déjà, en quelque sort, participation à cette réalité. Plus qu'une image 'concep-
    tuelle' de l'union du Christ et de l'Eglise, la vie conjugale chrétienne fournit de
    cette réalité surnaturelle une image 'virtuelle', dynamique."

44 This point is made nicely, in somewhat different language, by Schmitt (1983):
    "Par le baptême, les époux sont déjà introduits dans la réalité de ce mystère
    auquel ils participent l'un et l'autre comme membres du Corps du Christ. Leur
    mariage développe ce double caractère christique et ecclésial qui les marque et
    les incite à imiter d'une manière spéciale cette mystérieuse alliance. C'est.
    en référence à celle-ci que l'union des chrétiens tire son excellence et sa
    valeur surnaturelle. Plus qu'un 'bien,' même le plus éminent du mariage,

le 'sacramentum' christo-ecclésiale représente, en vertu du baptême qui le sous-tend, le point ultime de référence et le principe de cohérence de toute la doctrine augustinienne du mariage chrétien" (298).

45   *b. coniug.* 10.13 (translated by Hunter [1999], 121).

46   See *b. coniug.* 10.13, "it is unthinkable that the holy widows see Christ as their second husband. He was already their spouse, not physically but spiritually, before that, when they were faithful and submissive to their husbands (1 Pt. 3:5–6). The whole Church, of which they are members, is itself his Spouse, because by the integrity of her faith, hope and love she is a virgin, not only in holy virgins but in widows and the married faithful too. The apostle says to the whole Church, of which they are all members, *I have prepared you to present you to the one husband, Christ, as a chaste virgin* (2 Cor. 11:2). He, whom even in the flesh his mother could conceive without defilement, knows how to make it possible for that virgin spouse to bear children without being defiled" (translated by Hunter [1999], 121).

47   See *b. coniug.* 9.9 (translated by Hunter [1992], 40), "Undoubtedly we should take note that God gives us some benefits that are to be sought after for their own sake, such as wisdom, health and friendship, and others that are necessary for the sake of something else, such as learning, food, drink, marriage and sleeping together. Some of these, such as learning, are necessary for wisdom; others, such as food, drink and sleep, are necessary for health; others, such as marriage and sleeping together, are necessary for friendship. The latter also contribute to the continuation of the human race, in which loving relationships are of great benefit."

48   Another way of putting this is offered by Schmitt (1983), who points out that it is the state of incorporation into Christ, following upon Baptism, that confers upon Christian marriage its sacramental signification of the nuptial mystery of Christ and the church. He talks about Baptism and Christian marriage as a kind of double symbolism for the one fundamental mystery of Christ's nuptial relationship to the church: "Il s'agit fondamentalement du même mystère considéré sous un double symbolisme, similaire et complémentaire. Ceci nous permet d'entrevoir que, dans la pensée d'Augustin, c'est. dans sa relation au baptême, qui introduit le chrétien dans la mystère du salut, que le mariage trouve fondamentalement sa signification de 'sacramentum'" (257).

49   Hunter offers a good introductory sketch to the way in which Augustine's *On the Excellence of Marriage* (*De bono coniugali*) steers a middle course between the positions of the monk Jovinian, who regarded marriage as in every way equal to a life of consecrated virginity, and the disparagement of marriage evident in Jerome's earlier reply to Jovinian. See Hunter (1999), 14–16, 29–30, and Hunter (1992), 20–22.

50   See *b. coniug.* 10.10, "It seems to me, therefore, that at the present time the only ones who should marry are those who are unable to be continent, in accordance with that advice of the same Apostle" (translated by Hunter [1999], 42).

51　*b. uid.* 8.11 (translated by Hunter [1999], 120).

52　*b. uid.* 13.16 (translated by Hunter [1999], 123–124).

53　*b. uid.* 3.4 (translated by Hunter [1999], 114).

54　There is an unforgettable image of this bragging depicted in *conf.* 1.18.28 and 2.3.7. On fornication as a metaphor for turning away from God, see Cavadini (2003), reprinted as Chapter 4 of this volume.

55　*b. coniug.* 4.5 (translated by Hunter [1999], 115).

56　Augustine knew this was usually considerable freedom: see *b. coniug.* 13.15 (translated by Hunter [1999], 45): "Yet in private conversations, either with married persons or those who have been married, have we ever heard any people give any indication that they never have relations with their wives except with the hope of conceiving?"

57　*cont.* 12.27 (translated by Hunter [1999], 212).

58　Abstaining from sex, or from adultery if married, is not enough to make it true continence. Continence is a matter of intention. See, for example, *cont.* 12.26–27 (translated by Hunter [1999], 211–212).

59　See *cont.* 11.25 for these points and quotes (translated by Hunter [1999], 210).

60　*b. coniug.* 7.6–7 (translated by Hunter [1999], 38–39).

61　Pagan marriages only have the first two "goods" – that is, at their best, they are simply exercises in philosophical asceticism, though Augustine later modified this view somewhat (see Hunter [1999], 59 n. 18).

62　Virgins, both men and women, boys and girls, can follow the Lamb "wherever he goes" (Rev. 14:4), because by virginity they follow him both "in body and heart, wherever he goes" (*uirg.* 27.27; translated by Hunter [1999], 85), and not just in heart.

63　See *uirg.* 28.28 regarding the Beatitudes, "The rest of the faithful, therefore, who have lost bodily virginity, must follow him, not wherever he goes, but wherever they can. They can, however, go everywhere, except when he walks with the honor of virginity." Augustine then goes through all the Beatitudes, and concludes, "Those who imitate him in these respects, in that way are following the Lamb. No doubt even married people can follow those footsteps; even if they do not put their feet exactly in the same footprints, at least they walk the same path" (translated by Hunter [1999], 85–86).

64　*uirg.* 44.45 (translated by Hunter [1999], 98): "how does the virgin know whether, perhaps, because of some hidden spiritual defect, she is not yet ready for martyrdom, whereas the other woman, whom she delights to think is her inferior, is already able to drink the cup of the Lord's humility …? … How can she know whether perhaps she is not yet a Thecla, but the other woman already is a Crispina?"

65　This is the position of Brown (1988), 402. Hunter (1999), 19, agrees and extends the point, saying that Augustine "could find no truly positive role for sexuality and procreation in the Christian dispensation." He does not explain what a "truly positive role" might be. It is true that, for Augustine, procreation does not make married women equal to those who are consecrated virgins, for procreation is common to Christians and non-Christians alike, and "one does not give birth to Christ, but Adam" (*uirg.* 6.6). Before the Incarnation, physical conception and birth was a necessary prophetic sign, because the Jewish people as a nation had to be built up in order to bear prophetic witness and, in the end, give rise, physically, to the Savior (*uirg.* 9.9, etc.). But, since the Incarnation, it is no longer strictly speaking necessary for Christians, since there are so many people of so many races being born who can be reborn spiritually (see *b. uid.* 8.11, etc.). "The essential good of marriage is indeed always good; but for the people of God it was once an obligation of the law, while now it is a cure for weakness, and in some cases a source of comfort for human nature" (*uirg.* 8.11, already quoted in part earlier). It is only because procreation is a genuine and unquestionable good, *even* after the Incarnation, that marriage can hold any kind of a cure for weakness, and no form of Christian life can offer anything greater, in one way or another, than such a "cure." Procreation does not in itself confer holiness; it is not the sacrament itself; and marriages that are non-procreative through no intentional fault of the spouses are still valid and beneficial to the spouses, but that is only because marriage of itself is ordered to the good of procreation, and even the unintentionally childless respect that ordering. On the point of the "positive" role of sexual pleasure in marriage, see also Cavadini (2005), reprinted as Chapter 6 of in this volume.

66 I would like to thank Nancy Cavadini, Cyril O'Reagan, and Jean Porter for kindly reading and commenting on an earlier draft of this chapter. I also profited from the comments of those at the seminar on the Sacramentality of Marriage held at the University of Notre Dame in October 2005. Of course, mistakes that remain are my own responsibility.

References

Benedict XVI (2006) *Deus Caritas Est.* Vatican City: Libreria Editrice Vaticana.

Bettenson, Henry, trans. (1972) *Concerning the City of God against the Pagans.* Harmondsworth, Middlesex: Penguin Books (repr. 1987, 2003).

Boulding, Maria, O.S.B., trans. (2000a) *Expositions on the Psalms 1–31, WSA III/15.* Hyde Park, NY: New City Press.

Boulding, Maria, O.S.B., trans. (2000b) *Expositions on the Psalms 33–50, WSA III/16.* Hyde Park, NY: New City Press.

Boulding, Maria, O.S.B., trans. (2001) *Expositions on the Psalms 51–72, WSA III/17.* Hyde Park, NY: New City Press.

Brown, Peter (1988) *The Body and Society: Men, Women, and Sexual Renunciation in Early Christianity.* New York: Columbia University Press.

Cattenoz, Jean-Pierre (1993) *Le Baptême, Mystère Nuptial.* Venasque: Editions du Carmel.

Cavadini, John C. (2003) "Book Two: Augustine's Book of Shadows." In *A Reader's Guide to Augustine's Confessions,* edited by Kim Paffenroth and Robert P. Kennedy, 25–34. Louisville, KY: Westminster John Knox.

Cavadini, John C. (2005) "Feeling Right: Augustine on the Passions and Sexual Desire." *Augustinian Studies* 36: 195–217.

Clark, Elizabeth (1983) *Women in the Early Church.* Wilmington, DE: Michael Glazier.

Clark, Elizabeth (1994) "Ideology, History, and the Construction of 'Women' in Late Ancient Christianity." *Journal of Early Christian Studies* 2: 155–184.

Ford, David C. (1995) *Women and Men in the Early Church: The Full Views of St. John Chrysostom.* South Canaan, PA: St. Tikhon's Seminary Press.

Halten, Thomas, trans. (1999) *The Human Couple in the Fathers,* introduction and notes by Giulia Sfameni Gasparro, Cesare Magazzu, and Concetta Aloe Spada. New York: Society of St. Paul.

Hunter, David G., trans. and ed. (1992) *Marriage in the Early Church.* Minneapolis, MN: Fortress.

Hunter, David G., trans. (1999) *Marriage and Virginity, WSA I/9.* Hyde Park, NY: New City Press.

Le Saint, William P., trans. (1951) *Tertullian. Treatises on Marriage and Remarriage, Ancient Christian Writers 13.* New York, NY: Newman Press.

McHugh, Michael P., trans. (1972) *Saint Ambrose: Seven Exegetical Works, FC 65.* Washington, DC: Catholic University of America Press.

Schmitt, Emile (1983) *Le Mariage chrétien dans l'oeuvre de Saint Augustin: Une théologie baptismale de la vie conjugale.* Paris: Études Augustiniennes.

9

Eucharistic Exegesis in Augustine's
Confessions

Introduction

Perhaps the title of this study will impress the reader as implausible at
best and as incoherent at worst. After all, the *Confessions* (*conf.*) grants
the Eucharist relatively scant mention, and even this is only fleetingly
in the last three books,[1] the same place where we encounter the most
sustained project of exegesis in the entire work, the interpretation of
the Creation narrative in Gen. 1:1–2:3. On the other hand, Bochet
(2004) has recently argued that, despite the fleeting mention of
Augustine's baptism – at 9.6.14 – the exegesis of book 13 is a kind of
sustained reflection on the life of the baptized as life in the Spirit, and
of life in the Spirit as a life of growth and spiritual development. This
point of view is urged against the Donatist idea of a more definitive,
and, from Augustine's point of view, a more static, perfection granted
at baptism. Bochet (2004) has argued that the baptismal liturgy of the
Easter vigil, with its Scripture readings and particular rites, is a crucial
"place of engenderment" of the allegory of book 13, with its
prominent juxtaposition of the creation narrative with Pauline texts.[2]
To this should be added O'Donnell's (1992) reminder that the
(sometimes) scant overt references to the liturgy in the text can be
deceiving relative to its importance for Christians in Antiquity.[3]

One reason why the Eucharist can seem almost incidental to the
narrative of *conf.* is that, except in association with Monica (cf. 6.2.2),

Visioning Augustine, First Edition. John C. Cavadini.
© 2019 John Wiley & Sons Ltd. Published 2019 by John Wiley & Sons Ltd.

it is not mentioned explicitly until after the narration of Augustine's baptism. In fact, the association with Monica continues in the sustained narration and reflection upon Monica's last request of Augustine, namely, that he remember her at the altar of the Lord wherever he may be.[4] For Monica, as Augustine presents her, the altar of the Lord, not a gravesite, is the true locus of memory. Augustine mentions her burial, but the principal feature in the narrative of burial is the notice that the "sacrifice of the price of our redemption was offered for her"[5] there before her body was placed in the grave. This is the only report in *conf.* of Augustine participating in Mass on a specific occasion.

Later on, Augustine emphasizes that Monica was not concerned with having a "special monument (*monumentum electum*)," and that, indeed, the only remembering of her that she wanted was at the altar ("tantummodo memoriam sui ad altare tuum fieri desideravit"). She herself had bound her soul to the "sacrament of the price of our redemption (*pretii nostri sacramentum*)," by the "bond of faith (*vinculo fidei*)," never having missed even one day of Mass. She knew, Augustine says, that from the altar the Holy Victim is dispensed ("altare ... unde sciret dispensari victimam sanctam"), the one in whom we have our victory over the Enemy, the one who paid the price (*pretium*) of his own innocent blood for us.[6] In one of the most moving passages of *conf.*, Augustine asks rhetorically, "Who will refund him his innocent blood? Who will return to him the price he paid for us in order to take us away from him?"[7] That price cannot be repaid by anyone who might wish to take us away from him because there is nothing else to equal the worth of this freely-given, gratuitous gift. "He owed us nothing,"[8] so this "price" is an entirely unmerited, and, as such, an entirely unimaginable, mercy. We have our victory in the one who paid this price because he, the one who "hung upon the tree," is now seated at the right hand of the one to whom *conf.* is addressed, the Father, where he "intercedes for us."[9] Because of this intercession, we can hope that mercy will triumph over judgment.[10]

At the Intersection of Memory and Hope

In these reflections, the Eucharist appears at the intersection of memory and hope. In fact, it is the sacrament of a whole economy of mercy that forms memory in hope. The Eucharist is the sacrament of the price paid by the Word made flesh, and those bound to the Eucharist by the bond of faith cannot be "wrenched away" from the Father's protection, for there is nothing greater than the price of Christ's innocent blood, no claim or power, of "lion or dragon,"[11] stronger than that mercy. Thus, the person bound to the Eucharist in faith is bound to a memorial of God's mercy that configures or even defines all of one's own memory, which is to say, one's identity, and impels it into hope. We can recognize this, indeed, as the dynamic of the so-called ascent or vision at Ostia, earlier in book 9, where Monica and Augustine were, in the spirit of what I would call Eucharistic remembering, speaking about "forgetting what lay in the past, and stretching out to what was ahead" (cf. Phil. 3:13) in order to inquire about what the eternal life of the saints would be like (9.10.23). After that vision, Monica realizes she has no further stake in this world and her hope lies in God's mercy beyond death. That is why the narrative of the vision so easily passes into the narration of her last request: to be remembered at the altar of the Lord.

The Eucharist is thus a properly eschatological sacrament that mediates an identity suffused with hope in God's economy of mercy instead of in one's own ability to create an identity out of whole cloth. As he recounts her life, Augustine refers to Monica as a virtuous "servant of God,"[12] raised in a kind of "domestic church," to use the contemporary expression,[13] a "peacemaker,"[14] merciful, and forgiving of others from her heart.[15] Yet, even her mercy was a gift to her from God. Even the mercy of the merciful is not a unilateral achievement of identity creation. Their mercy is itself a mercy extended by God, something given to them, for which the only appropriate response is gratitude. *Conf.* 9.13.35 is a kind of celebration of mercy in which Augustine recounts his mother as one of the "merciful" to whom the Beatitudes (cf. Mt. 5:17) promise mercy, and yet there is no one truly merciful who is not already the beneficiary of God's mercy. They cannot place that hope in their own mercy; their only hope is in the intercession of that "healing remedy who hung upon the tree, the medicine for our wounds who intercedes for us." In fact, Augustine here asks God to hear him "through (*per*)" that healing remedy.[16] If even Monica's virtues are gifts of God, her life cannot have been so perfect that she could claim it as a settled achievement, a self-made and self-perfected identity.

And, indeed, she will not claim, Augustine tells us, that she has no debts to pay. On the contrary, when the devil accuses her, she will reply that her debts have been paid by the innocent blood of Christ.[17] In asking that she be remembered at the altar where the sacrifice of that price is offered, where the sacred Victim is dispensed and one can be bound sacramentally to his sacrifice, she is asking that her life be remembered within the compass of this mercy and the hope it portends. Even Monica's life is not a self-evidently settled achievement that one can look upon with any assurance, except by remembering and invoking the mercy of God dispensed from the altar. At the end of book 9, Augustine the bishop leaves his readers, fellow members of the Church whom he serves in episcopal ministry with "heart and voice and pen," at God's altar remembering Monica by praying for her. "So may the last request she made of me be granted to her more abundantly by the prayers of many, evoked by my confessions, than by my prayers alone."[18] Augustine has rhetorically evoked the Eucharistic community, sacramentally formed in the memory of the price of our redemption. Formed in that memory, they can pray in hope, united with the intercession of Christ.

Remembering the Dead and the Dead Remembering

Looking back in this light, we can recognize more clearly some of Augustine's earlier narrative adumbrations of the communion formed in Eucharistic memory and hope. Book 9 as a whole is the book of memory of the dead: one by one, Augustine remembers Verecundus, his patron (9.3.5–6); Nebridius, his friend (9.3.6); Adeodatus, his son (9.6.14); and Monica, his mother (9.11.27). He remembers with special affection Nebridius, his "sweet friend" and God's adoptive son, who lives now, Augustine is sure, in "Abraham's bosom."[19] There, whatever else it may mean, Nebridius is happy, able to put his mouth to God's fountain and to drink in wisdom without end directly from God instead of having to settle for whatever answers Augustine was able to give him, as in the days when he was alive on earth. And yet, Augustine cannot believe that his friend, though drinking in wisdom directly from God and so completely happy, can have forgotten him: "Yet I cannot believe," Augustine writes, "that he is so inebriated as to forget me (*ut obliviscatur mei*), since you, Lord, from whom he drinks, remember us" (cum *tu, domine … nostri sis memor*).[20] Nebridius, though drinking in the incorporeal wisdom of God, is not beyond the economy of God's remembering. He is not beyond the economy of memory. God's mindfulness of all of us is, one could say, constitutive of the wisdom Nebridius is drinking in. Certainly, that wisdom is not something separate from God's remembering. By the end of book 9, the reader also knows that this mindfulness is expressed by the intercessory prayer of Christ at God's right hand.[21] Significantly, it is here, in recounting Nebridius' participation in the mindfulness of God, that the reader is reminded of just what God's remembering involves. Nebridius, Augustine recounts, had, before his conversion, fallen into the error of believing that the flesh of God's Son, who is Truth itself, was only a phantasm, an apparition or a fake.[22] It is the truth of this flesh that Nebridius came to believe in, and thus he became acquainted with what the true mindfulness of God entails. His original Christ was no proper subject in the economy of memory, no proper historical agent. Though Nebridius is now in Abraham's bosom, he has not found a wisdom above the economy of God's mindfulness. He has not found a wisdom that can leave this economy behind in forgetfulness.

Trinitarian Mindfulness

Further, Augustine's ensuing narrative of his recitation of Ps. 4 is also a meditation on this economy of mindfulness or memory. Having lost his voice and his heart as a rhetorician, Augustine, in reciting the Psalm out loud, recovers his voice and his heart, transfixed by God's arrows, that is, by God's words in Scripture and by the charity they communicate (9.2.3). He travels the way of the affections laid out in *doctr. chr.*[23] He feels a new kind of anger and a new kind of sweetness and joy in his heart.[24] The anger is at his own sins and the joy is at God's mercy. Augustine reads Ps. 4 as an exercise in the mindfulness of God's mercy. Augustine reads v. 1[25] as a plea for God's mercy, while in the very same breath there is a confession of the mercies that God has already had on him. Verse 1 offers a prayer for mercy based on the mindfulness of mercy. Here is the intersection of hope and memory that, by the end of book 9, we will recognize as Eucharistic mindfulness or Eucharistic remembering.

Augustine confesses that saying the words of the Psalm caused him to shudder with awe, in hope and exultation at God's mercy, "at your mercy, Father,"[26] as he puts it. By explicitly invoking the Father, Augustine indicates that the mercy he is remembering is the very mercy that unfolded in the Trinitarian economy of salvation, and that the revelation of this mercy is at one and the same time the revelation of the Trinity. As the Psalm goes on, it causes Augustine to remember his life in a specific way, that is, as having "loved emptiness and chased falsehood."[27] And yet, even this history of fallenness is itself already inscribed in a prior narrative of mercy:

> I, certainly, had loved emptiness and chased falsehood, and you, Lord [=Father], had already glorified your Holy One, raising him from the dead and setting him at your right hand, whence he could send the Paraclete, the Spirit of Truth from on high, as he had promised.[28]

The narrative of God's free mercy is the economy of the Trinity. This Trinitarian economy is the economy of God's mindfulness or remembering. "Be sure of this," the Psalm enjoins as it goes on, "the Lord has glorified his Holy One" (Ps. 4:4).[29] Here, Augustine is remembering himself remembering:

> For so long, I had been anything but "sure," and "had loved emptiness and chased falsehood," and so I trembled as I heard these words, for they are addressed to the kind of person I was remembering myself to have been.[30]

The memories are in sharp contrast and, as he writes, he remembers his remembering as painful.[31] If any Manichees, who, as Augustine sees them, still loved emptiness and chased falsehood, could have witnessed Augustine's painful remembering, he knows that God the Father would hear them when they cried out to him for his mercy, "because he who for us died a true death in the flesh now intercedes with you [Father] on our behalf."[32]

As we have seen, by the end of book 9, this interceder is further identified as the very one whose mercy is measured by the price he paid for it, his own innocent blood, of which the Eucharist is the sacrament. The Trinitarian mindfulness that was so moving to Augustine as he read Ps. 4 out loud is, by the end of book 9, revealed

also as a Eucharistic mindfulness or remembering. For, being bound
sacramentally to the "price" of Christ's innocent blood is being bound
sacramentally to the mindfulness or remembering of God, which is
revealed in the Trinitarian economy. This Trinitarian economy is the
framework for mercy, and a revelation of the very being of God as
Trinitarian. It is the Christian Trinity, not simply the Plotinian One,
that is "id ipsum,"[33] the foundation of being itself, as the Psalm goes
on to recall, and, in this memory of love at the foundation of being,
one can "rest and fall asleep," for we know that this God will "show us
good things" (9.4.10–11). After his narration of his reading of the
Psalms, the next thing that Augustine chooses to narrate, though
surely it was not the very next thing in the sequence of time (as
Augustine himself seems to indicate), is a "wondrous speediness of
God's mercy (*misericordiae tuae mirabilem celeritatem*; cf. 9.4.12)" in the
healing of a toothache. It is important to Augustine that this "sign
(*nutus*)" be directed to the health of his physical body, for God is a
God of every level of healing (*salutis omnimodae*), and it is because
Christ had true flesh that even a healing in the economy of flesh can
stand as a sign for ultimate salvation, of God's remembering.

Thus, from the retrospect of the end of book 9, we can recognize
its exegesis of Ps. 4 as Eucharistic exegesis, as exegesis arising from a
kind of "memoria formata," which is perhaps what the image of the
heart pierced by God's love is meant to symbolize.

Let me note one more thing before we take our leave of book 9.
Famously, this book's opening section is the only place in *conf.* where
Augustine addresses Christ directly, and, like the mention of his
baptism, it is famous not only for its rarity but because it is so fleeting
(9.1.1).[34] It serves here to set into relief, by contrast, the standard
addressee of Augustine's *conf.*, who is thus not generically God or the
Lord, but God the Father. Christ is mentioned here as the Redeemer,
the "true and highest sweetness"[35] who could satisfyingly take the
place of the fleeting and inconsequential sweetnesses afforded by the
triple sins of 1 Jn. 2:16, to which Augustine had clung for so long. This
sweetness is God's mercy, true flesh and blood who truly died for us
and now intercedes for us. It is by addressing the Father that Augustine
invokes this sweetness, this economy of mercy, for to address the
Father is to respect the Trinitarian economy of salvation and to invoke
it. This address does not make *conf.* less Christological; on the contrary,
it makes it more so. "Confession" is a way of remembering that is

Eucharistic, that is formed in the memory of the one who paid the price of his innocent blood and now intercedes for us at the right hand of the Father. Augustine's prayer, uttered in the Spirit, in its address to the Father, is joined to this prayer of Christ. The whole of *conf.* is an exercise in Eucharistic remembering, though we do not grasp that fully until Augustine is able to recount his baptism and then his own participation, as a baptized Catholic, in the Eucharist at his mother's graveside.

Sacrament of Truth

We noticed in the preceding text that Augustine alludes to his role as bishop in the Church at the end of book 9, and that, in so doing, he evoked the presence of the Eucharistic community. Augustine sees to it that this community persists in attendance throughout the rest of *conf.* by featuring it prominently in book 10. Book 10 emerges out of book 9's ascent to the Eucharistic altar. It emerges out of Eucharistic remembering, in the midst of the Eucharistic assembly, all evoked by Augustine's skillful rhetoric. Book 10 will continue and deepen this Eucharistic remembering. It is explicitly addressed not only to God but also spoken "in the ears of believing men and women … your sons and my masters," those whom God has ordered Augustine to "serve."[36] "To those, then, such people as you command me to serve, I will disclose myself not as I have been but as I am now, as I am still."[37] This will not be for them the same as hearing the truth directly from the fountain of wisdom, as Nebridius now hears it, but, in a sense, the Eucharistic community serves as a sacrament of such direct infusion by God's truth. "Love believes all," Augustine quotes 1 Cor. 13:7, "at least among those who are bound to each other by charity … whose ears are open by charity."[38] This is the charity we encounter so often in Augustine's other works, even at this period,[39] the charity which binds all the members of the Church into one Christ, Head and Body. None of those so bound to Augustine "have laid their ears to my heart, though it is only there that I am whoever I am," and yet Augustine is sure they will believe him and know him when he confesses to God in their presence, "because charity, in which they are good, tells them that I am not lying when I confess about myself; that very charity in them believes me."[40] Clearly, we are a long way from *sol.*, that is, from the late 380s. Augustine does not need to "flee into solitude"[41] to face the truth or to tell it. The community formed by the blood of Christ, by his mercy, his charity, is a kind of sacrament of truth; the charity defining the community permits truthful conversation. Book 10 therefore is formed in the same Eucharistic remembering that we encountered in book 9, and this act of remembering is now more emphatically evoked as a specifically ecclesial act. Book 10 ends with Augustine the bishop mindful of the "price" paid for him, the innocent blood of Christ, "in whom are hidden all the treasures of wisdom and knowledge" (cf. Col. 2:3), locating himself again in the midst of the Eucharistic community:

> I am mindful of the price paid for me, and I eat it, I drink it, I dispense it to others, and as a poor man I long to be filled with it among those who are fed and feasted. And then do those who seek him praise the Lord (cf. Ps. 21:27).[42]

Those who seek the Lord by a Eucharist[ic] act of remembering, of memory, praise the Lord because they find him, in memory, as the mercy that is the sure basis for hope. There is no God behind, beyond, or above the mercy that is mediated in the sacrament of our redemption and encountered in the mutual bonds of charity that bind the whole Church. The citation of Ps. 21:27 in association with the skillful rhetorical evocation of the bishop in the midst of the Eucharistic community creates an *inclusio* of the whole so-called autobiographical part of *conf.*: this Psalm was first and only cited in the opening lines of the whole work[43] and, after this, is not cited again. We are invited to believe that, in the Eucharistic community, whose very defining feature is nothing other than God's mercy, we can seek God in such a way that our seeking will succeed to the praise that, according to the opening lines of the work, will delight our restless heart.[44]

I believe that these reflections should temper, at least somewhat, the overly individualistic interpretations of *conf.* that seem to pop up from time to time. It is true that in book 10 we find ourselves in the presence of some of the most beautiful and intimately interior individual apostrophes, such as the prose poem "Late have I loved you" (cf. 10.27.28). But, as intimate as these exchanges with God truly are, they are not private: "I confess not only before you in secret exultation tinged with fear and secret sorrow infused with hope, but

also in the ears of believing men and women," including those who
have died and those not yet born, as Augustine notes in a passage
already cited earlier (cf. 10.4.6). In fact, they are all the more intimate
for not reflecting the one-on-one bridal mysticism that Augustine
could easily have inherited from Ambrose. Instead, this discourse of
love, and the experience it reports, is mediated ecclesially and shaped
Eucharistically. The mysticism that ensues (if that is the right word) is
not simply private and interior, but arises as the bonds of charity
among the members of the one Body, the Spouse, are purified and
perfected.[45] Augustine is certainly aware of God's mercy on his behalf,
but what mercy is this other than the price of Christ's blood that
defines the whole Eucharistic community? Augustine is aware that he
is the subject of *this* love, the love that binds a people and that re-casts
Augustine's whole identity Eucharistically. The person who is able to
say, "I love you, Lord ….You pierced my heart with your word, and
I fell in love with you,"[46] whose heart is transfixed by the charity proclaimed in God's word, is the one aware of his heart transfixed by the
price of his redemption, the same price paid for everyone and the
price that binds all into one Body. Awareness of the *pretium* is not
awareness of an individual love affair with God, but of a mercy that
forms an eschatological people. Aware of oneself as a subject of this
love, one can afford an expression and experience of intimacy with
God that is, paradoxically, all the more intimate for not being private.
The paradigm for such a paradoxical experience in *conf.* is the
conversation at Ostia, where Augustine and his mother have an
intimate experience of the hope towards which the Eucharist impels
them, even as and throughout the entire time that they are talking
with each other.[47]

Ascent to Mercy

We can observe more closely the structure of the ascent to God
through memory that Augustine undertakes in book 10. Like all
ascents patterned after the Neoplatonic spirituality of inwardness, it is
a path of deepening self-awareness, and "remembering" is not simply
an act of recalling the past – though that is involved – but, rather, of
encountering and identifying oneself. Can one ascend beyond
"memory" to God? Or, more precisely, can one ascend beyond

memories (plural), beyond the acts enacted and defined in body and time, to a self-awareness that no longer finds anything self-defining in body and history? If so, that would be what Augustine calls "pride" (but not necessarily what Plotinus would call "pride"), because it would involve the attempt to ignore or rise above the "price of our redemption," which took place in "true flesh" and blood. It would mean rising above and beyond Eucharistic remembering. This does not mean that Eucharistic remembering would not involve a certain inwardness or what later becomes known as the "interior life." Rather, it means ascending to deeper awareness of oneself as a subject of the mercy that is dispensed in the Eucharist and which creates a community bound in charity. In book 10, Augustine "ascends" to God's mercy. One can therefore evoke the most intimate self-revelations before God and yet confess them publicly because everyone involved, as a member of the Eucharistic community, is defined by the same unimaginably priceless mercy; beyond that, no one has anything to brag about. The intimacy with God is, in a sense, mediated by intimacy in truth and love with those whose lives are defined by that mercy and bound together through the price of our redemption that is "dispensed" from the altar.

The examination of conscience that Augustine shares with the community in book 10 has appeared over the years to many readers as excessively individualistic and obsessive. Yet, what it attempts to convey rhetorically is not obsession; rather, it is a radical awareness of a change that is in progress, of undergoing transformation. God dwells in memory as truth,[48] but how? How can one afford to look at the truth about oneself? How can one afford to face the "bitterness" of recollection? Only if the awareness of truth is simultaneously the awareness of the "sweetness" of God's mercy. Upon moving into his examination of conscience, Augustine says, "On your exceedingly great mercy rests all my hope. Give what you command, and then command whatever you will."[49] This is not a comfortable self-awareness. It is the self-awareness of one whom God is transforming "by faith and by [his] sacrament."[50] And this is not an awareness of oneself merging into God as though God's agency were all. Even that would probably be more comfortable! Rather, it is the awareness of one who, by God's gift, is in medias res, "making progress towards God,"[51] who can "exult" though "with trepidation," at what God's gift has achieved in him, and yet "deploring how unfinished" he is and hoping that God's mercy will perfect him.[52] Confession such as this can only bear to be uttered when one is, like Monica, bound by faith to the sacrament that defines the very boundaries and contours of memory. How otherwise could one bear to confess such a state – baptized, but so short of perfection, and knowing one has indeed made genuine progress, but refusing to claim that progress as ultimately one's own achievement and always seeking perfection itself as a gift? How otherwise could one bear to admit to awareness ("memory") of, and then to confess, such a state except by clinging to the sacrament of the price of one's redemption "in the midst of those who are fed and feasted?" Awareness of one's sinfulness and one's all-too-easy liability to temptation can prompt a paralyzing obsession that would drive a kind of escapism. But Eucharistic remembering permits obsession to become confession in the midst of the Church. Each account of temptation in book 10 rises or ascends to the confession that Augustine is dependent upon God's mercy.[53] And, frequently, each seemingly obsessive and individualistic account of temptation finds expression in an appeal to the "right hand" of God, namely, to the intercession of Christ.[54] Augustine prays "as one of the weaker members of His Body," but indeed as a member of His Body. And, as a member of the Eucharistic community, one is formed into the prayer of Christ the Head, He "who has *overcome the world.*"[55] Each account of temptation is an experiment in truth-telling that can only happen as a confession of God's mercy, as an evocation of the economy of mercy of which the Eucharist is the primary sacrament. Each meditation and confession is an ascent in memory to mercy and hope.

This means, ultimately, an ascent to the Trinity. We have already seen this in a preliminary way in book 9. In book 10, however, it is even more explicit and precise. A Eucharistic mindfulness, when deepened in the ascending course of self-awareness, is a mindfulness of the economy of salvation mediated by the Eucharist. The "price of my redemption," which "I eat and drink," is "*God's equal, God with God, and with him one only God.*"[56]

> How you loved us, O good Father, who spared not even your only Son, but gave him up for us evildoers! How you loved us, for whose sake he who deemed it no robbery to be your equal was made subservient, even to the point of dying on the cross.[57]

The hymn at Phil. 2:6–8 is, perhaps, for Augustine, the most important Trinitarian passage in the Bible. It is this very one who *did not deem it robbery to be equal to God*, who is victor and victim, priest and sacrifice, who "intercedes for us." There is no God to ascend to beyond the Trinity. There is no essence into which the Trinity resolves itself, which can be glimpsed behind and apart from the Trinitarian economy of love and mercy. God is always the God who "remembers" for the One who is equal to the Father has ascended with His own true flesh. There is no essence of being that leaves the economy of revelation, mercy, and memory behind, and can define God in purely philosophical terms, without reference to this economy and the true flesh in which it was enacted. At most, you can have a distant vision,[58] so distant that it misses the most important feature of God, his love and mercy.

Eucharistic Exegesis

Thus, one proceeds forward from book 10 with an invocation of Eucharistic remembering as inherently Trinitarian, as Trinitarian mindfulness. The exegesis of Gen. 1:1–2:3 that will occur in books 11–13 will thus be again a kind of "Eucharistic exegesis." Seen from the memory that is configured by the Trinitarian, Eucharistic mindfulness to which we ascended at the end of book 10, the origin of the world can be seen to be the same gratuitous Trinitarian love that also gives rise to redemptive mercy.

Book 11 is the Book of the Father and book 12 the Book of the Son, but it is especially in book 13, the Book of the Spirit,[59] in which one can see what I mean when I call the exegesis of books 9–13 "Eucharistic." Book 13 begins with an invocation of God's mercy: "Upon you I call, O God my mercy (cf. Ps. 58:18), who made me and did not forget me when I forgot you."[60] This is the very beginning of the book, and it contains the dynamic of the whole book, and indeed the whole of *conf.*, in a nutshell. God is "mercy," known as such because He did not "forget" Augustine when Augustine had forgotten God. God's "remembering" is God's mercy. Book 10 led us on an ascent to Eucharistic mindfulness of this "remembering"; and now, from that vantage point, we will see that this very mercy is what "made" the whole world (Augustine the creature serves as a synecdoche here).

Following the invocation, the opening chapters of book 13 sum up the results of the previous two books. All the language of "beginning," and time itself, are contextualized, one might even say *relativized*, in the gratuitous, merciful remembering of God and in our Eucharistic remembering of God's remembering:

> What advance claim did heaven and earth have upon you, when you made them in the Beginning? Let your spiritual and corporeal crea-tion speak up and tell us what rights they had. In your Wisdom you made them...[61]

This is a sentiment that includes both the formless matter called "earth" and the inchoate spiritual creature called "heaven" in Gen. 1:1.[62] This "Beginning" is the "same Word ... who, being in the *form of God*, is equal to you."[63] The citation from Philippians reminds us that we have met that Word before – He's the one who emptied himself to become the price of our redemption, dispensed from the altar. If creation is accomplished through this Word, it is not through any need or necessity on God's part,[64] but through the same gratuitous love that occasioned God's "remembering." The motive for creation is seen through and in the "remembering" of God's gratuitous redemptive mercy. To say this is also to say that the world is created in the same Spirit as it was redeemed, in the "charity of Christ," the very "charity" of God that has been "poured out into our hearts through the Holy Spirit who has been given to us" (cf. Rom. 5:5).[65] In the allegory, which begins at 13.12.13,[66] because the Holy Spirit thus "hovered over the waters" of our darkness, because God's "mercy did not forsake us in our misery,"[67] we "remembered [God] ... we called [God] to mind in that mountain which, though lofty as yourself, was brought low for us"[68] – that is, in the Word who became flesh for us. Eucharistic remembering is accomplished in the Spirit, sent by the Father "through Christ who ascended on high,"[69] in his true flesh, promising us the same resurrection of the flesh.[70] Thus, in our conversion, "was light made."[71] The spiritual growth of the Church – that is, the Eucharistic community – can be recounted using the "figures" of the Hexameron Creation narrative in Genesis because it is the work of the same Trinity that was active in the work of creation.

To put it another way, the doctrine of creation is a figure cast by the abiding "light" of Eucharistic awareness of God's mercy, which is irreducibly Trinitarian. Cast as a "figure" by the narrative of the growth of the Church in the Spirit, we can "understand" the creation narrative, because we can see in creation not impersonal emanation or any kind of mythological struggle, but the same mysterious gratuity of love and mercy that we see in that which is "figured." To put it even more precisely, it is from the perspective of the Spirit-filled person, whose mind is formed in Eucharistic remembering by the charity poured out into his or her heart, that one can truly ascend to "see" creation. In this mysterious reality borne within oneself, one can begin to have a glimpse into the origin of the world. Augustine, still addressing the community of charity that he had addressed in book 10, the Eucharistic community, is asking them to reflect in faith on the gift of charity they have been given.

The Light of Faith

As Augustine tries to puzzle through the mystery of the Trinity, of how the Three can be One God, he finds that he cannot resolve the Trinity to something other than itself, to something behind it or above it, for there is nothing above God's mercy.[72] And thus, he is led to meditate in faith[73] on the work of the Spirit in the Church using the Creation narrative as a figure. Faith is the "lamp" that permits us to resist resolving the Trinity into some essence beyond itself, to resist settling for a premature vision of a distant God with no evident memory at all. Resisting this premature vision in favor of the fullness of vision promised eschatologically is the work of love "proceeding forward" by the light of Eucharistic faith. The ascent to the Trinity achieved in book 10 can only proceed forward by and in faith.[74]

Homo Spiritalis

Perhaps the most interesting point in the allegory is the discussion of Gen. 1:24–27, the creation of the "living soul"[75] that becomes the human being made in the "image and likeness of God." In the allegory, the "dry land" separated from the waters of the world is the Church. Nourished by the preaching of the Word and by the celebration of the Eucharist,[76] the Church brings forth the "living soul" bearing within it the beasts of the earth, the cattle after their kind, and the snakes and creeping things, that is, the emotions or "motions of the soul,"[77] that can, if wrongly directed, give rise to concupiscence of the flesh, to *curiositas*, and to *ambitio saeculi*. But these emotions can be reformed so that they are "shape[d] no longer to the standards of this world" (cf. Rom. 12:2), but rather in imitation of others who have learned to direct these emotions to good ends.[78] When such a person has matured, under the influence of the Spirit, to the point that Rom. 12:2 calls "the renewal of your minds," that is, to the point where he or she can make spiritual discernments or judgments independently of the good example of others, he or she becomes the *homo spiritalis*, corresponding, in the allegory, to the human being made "in the image and likeness" of God.[79] Such a person is sufficiently formed in the Eucharistic remembering of God's mercy that he or she can begin to see himself or herself as made in the Trinitarian likeness.[80] This is the most interesting point of the allegory, because it is at this point that the literal and the figurative interpretations coincide. It is the nodal point of the allegory. In the Spirit-filled person, we see, as fully as we can, what it means to *be* in the image and likeness of God, to be the subject of God's creative love. The Spirit-filled person *is* the image and likeness of God, as close as we can see it, being perfected, being fully formed. Can we perhaps even say that he or she is being fully created? The Spirit-filled person fulfills the intention that God had for Creation all along. Such a person is so filled with love and so loving that he or she can look on creation and see it as God sees it – namely, as "exceedingly good."[81] In the Spirit-filled person, it is God who is seeing the world, as Genesis says, and who sees that it is good. Augustine pictures God saying, "What you see through my Spirit, I see."[82] It is not simply an act of faith, but, indeed, a work of love, to be able to look out on the world and see it as God sees it, namely, as "exceedingly good." The one who sees the world as God sees it sees it from the perspective of a heart formed in mercy. However, this is not a mercy of our own devising. The person whose heart is formed in the Eucharistic memory of Christ's love by the Holy Spirit can bear to see how precious the world is (in the sense of "worth the price," in God's eyes). It is really a different way of seeing, formed by the Holy Spirit. One who sees the world in this way can bear to look out over creation and see that it is "good," and "recognize" God in His works,[83] resisting the Manichaean temptation to be "displeased at [God's] works,"[84] owing to the (alleged) presence of substantial evil therein. The person whose heart is formed by the Spirit in the Eucharistic remembering of God's mercy sees the world in the original love in which it was created, and therefore "sees" that it is "good." Such a person will also be able to understand the creation narrative of the Hexameron.

Eucharistic exegesis of the creation narrative thus enables one to see the economy of redemption as, in a way, not merely the restoration, but the completion of creation.[85] And, the more keenly we are aware of God's mercy, the more keenly we are aware that we see that completion now only in hope of the perfection of the work of His mercy in the eternal Sabbath.[86] Until then, God's work of Creation will not have been fully accomplished – but, thankfully, God's "mercy endures forever."[87]

Acknowledgments

An earlier version of this chapter was published as Cavadini, J. (2010) Eucharistic Exegesis in Augustine's Confessions. *Augustinian Studies* 41: 87–108.

In addition to the memory of Fr. Thomas F. Martin, O.S.A. (*Beati misericordes*, Mt. 5:7), this chapter is dedicated to the Most Rev. Michael D'Arcy, Bishop of the Diocese of Ft. Wayne-South Bend, *dispensator sacramenti tui* (10.31.41).

Notes

1 Cf., for example, 13.21.29 and 13.23.34.
2 Bochet (2004); cf. esp. 261: "La liturgie baptismale nous est. donc apparue comme un des 'lieux d'engendrement' de la lecture de la Genèse qu'Augustin développé dans le livre XIII des *Confessions*."
3 See, for example, O'Donnell (1992), "Introduction and Text," 1:xxviii–xxix, noting esp. the following: "Few modern scholars (indeed, few moderns of any persuasion, *including* the most ardent proponents of a traditional doctrine of tran-substantiation) hold a view of the importance and efficacy of cult acts that even remotely approaches the visceral reverence for cult that all late antique men and women felt"; and yet, "[i]n all the years after his baptism and ordination, in all the five million surviving words of his works, Augustine never describes or discusses the cult act that was the centre of his ordained ministry," due to the custom of secrecy attaching to virtually all late antique cults.

4   See *conf.* 9.11.27 (edited in CCSL 27, 149): "… tantum illud vos rogo, ut ad domini altare memineritis mei, ubiubi fueritis." Boulding (1997) translates this as: "One thing only do I ask of you, that you remember me at the altar of the Lord wherever you may be" (230). In what follows, I have used Boulding's translation throughout. Where her translation is modified, it will be noted.

5   Ibid., 9.12.32 (CCSL 27, 149): "… offerretur pro ea. sacrificum pretii nostri …."

6   These texts are all from ibid., 9.13.36 (CCSL 27, 153).

7   Ibid. (CCSL 27, 153): "Quis ei refundet innocentem sanguinem? Quis ei restituet pretium, quo nos emit, ut nos auferat ei?" This translation is my own.

8   Ibid. (CCSL 27, 154): "… non debens …."

9   Ibid. 9.12.35 (CCSL 27, 153): "… medicinam vulnerum nostrorum, quae pependit in ligno et sedens ad dexteram tuam te interpellat pro nobis."

10   See, ibid.: "Superexultet misericordia iudicio …"; cf. Jas. 2:13.

11   Ibid., 9.13.36 (CCSL 27, 153): "Ad cuius pretii nostri sacramentum ligavit ancilla tua animam suam uinculo fidei. Nemo a protectione tua dirumpat eam. Non se interponat nec vi nec insidiis leo et draco …."

12   For one example, see, ibid., 9.8.17 (CCSL 27, 143): "… famula tua …."

13   Ibid. (CCSL 27, 143): "… in domo fideli, bono membro ecclesiae tuae." For the phrase "domestic church," see *Lumen Gentium* 11, as cited in the *Catechism of the Catholic Church* (1994), section 1656.

14   Ibid., 9.9.21 (CCSL 27, 146): "… inter dissidentesque atque discordes quaslibet animas, ubi poterat, tam se praebebat pacificam …."

15   Ibid., 9.13.35 (CCSL 27, 153): "Scio misericorditer operatam et ex corde dimisisse debita debitoribus suis …."

16   Ibid., 9.13.35 (CCSL 27, 153): "Exaudi me per medicinam …."

17   Ibid., 9.13.356 (CCSL 27, 153–154).

18   Ibid., 9.13.37 (CCSL 27, 154): "Et inspira, domine meus, deus meus, inspira seris tuis, fratribus meis, filiis tuis, dominis meis, quibus et corde et voce et litteris servio, ut quotquot haec legerint, meminerint ad altare tuum Monnicae, famulae tuae … ut quod a me illa poposcit extremum uberius ei praestetur in multorum orationibus per confessiones quam per orationes meas …."

19   Ibid., 9.3.6 (CCSL 27, 136): "Et nunc ille vivit in sinu Abraham. Quidquid illud est., quod illo significatur sinu, ibi Nebridius meus vivit, dulcis amicus meus, tuus autem, domine, adoptivus ex liberto filius: ibi vivit …."

20   Ibid. (CCSL 27, 136): "Iam non ponit aurem ad os meum, sed spiritale os ad fontem tuum et bibit, quantum potest, sapientiam pro aviditate sua sine fine felix. Nec eum sic arbitror inebriari ex ea., ut obliviscatur mei, cum tu, domine, quem potat ille, nostri sis memor …."

21   See the texts cited supra; for example, in n. 8.

22   See, ibid., 9.3.6 (CCSL 27, 135–136): "ut veritatis filii tui carnem phantasma crederet."

23 *doctr. chr.* 1.17.16 (edition in BA 11.2, 96): "via … affectuum …" This text is a corrected version of that found in CCSL 32.

24 *conf.* 9.4.10 (CCSL 27, 138): "Legebam: 'Irascimini et nolite peccare' [cf. Ps. 4:5] et quomodo movebar, deus meus, qui iam didiceram irasci mihi de praeteritis …"; 9.4.9 (ibid.): "Inhorrui timendo ibidemque inferui sperando et exultando in tua misericordia, pater …." The phrase "joy in my heart" comes from Ps. 4:7; see 9.4.11 (ibid., 139): "dederas *laetitiam in corde meo* …." If we include the mention of "dolor" (cf. 138: "in dolore recordationis meae"), then we may note that this context contains all four classical passions or emotions: anger, fear, joy, and sadness.

25 Ibid., 9.4.8 (CCSL 27, 137): "Cum invocarem, exaudivit me deus iustitiae meae; in tribulatione dilatasti mihi. Miserere mei, domine, et exaudi orationem meam …"; cf. Boulding's (1997) translation: "When I called on him he heard me, the God of my vindication; when I was hard beset you led me into spacious freedom. Have mercy on me, Lord, and hearken to my prayer" (215).

26 Ibid., 9.4.9 (CCSL 27, 138): "in tua misericordia, pater …."

27 Ibid.: "dilexeram enim vanitatem et quaesieram mendacium …."

28 Ibid. (the following continues directly from where the last note left off): "Et tu, domine, iam magnificaveras sanctum tuum, suscitans eum a mortuis et conlocans ad dexteram tuam, unde mitteret ex alto promissionem suam, paracletum, spiritum veritatis …."

29 Ibid.: "Et scitote, quoniam dominus magnificavit sanctum suum …."

30 Ibid.: "… et ego tandiu nesciens vanitatem dilexit et mendacium quaesivi et ideo audivi et contremui, quoniam talibus dicitur, qualem me fuisse reminiscebar …."

31 Ibid.: "… in dolore recordationis meae…."

32 Ibid.: "… quoniam vera morte carnis mortuus est. pro nobis qui te interpellat pro nobis …." Note that an allusion to Rom. 8:34 is provided in the *apparatus fontium*.

33 Ps. 4:9, as cited at ibid., 9.4.11 (CCSL 27, 139): "O in pace! O in id ipsum! O quid dixit: obdormiam et somnum capiam?"

34 Ibid. (CCSL 27, 133): "… quod subderem cervicem leni iugo tuo et umeros levi sarcinae tuae, Christe Iesu, adiutor meus et redemptor meus …."

35 Ibid., 9.1.1 (CCSL 27, 133): "Quam suave mihi subito factum est. carere suavitatibus nugarum, et quas amittere metus fuerat, iam dimittere gaudium erat. Eiciebas enim eas a me, vera tu et summa suavitas, eiciebas et intrabas pro eis omni voluptate dulcior, sed non carni et sanguini, omni luce clarior, sed omni secreto interior, omni honore sublimior, sed non sublimibus in se …." Boulding (1997) translates these lines as: "How sweet did it suddenly seem to me to shrug off those sweet frivolities, and how glad I now was to get rid of them – I who had been loath to let them go! For it was you who cast them out and entered yourself to take their place, you who are lovelier than any pleasure,

though not to flesh and blood, more lustrous than any light, yet more inward than is any secret intimacy, loftier than all honor, yet not to those who look for loftiness in themselves" (209–210). Boulding suggests the allusion to 1 Jn. 2:16 on 210 at n. 8. The centrality of this passage for the thought and structure of *conf.* is emphasized by O'Donnell (1992); for example, see 1:xxxv (n. 3). See also Crosson (1989).

36   Ibid., 10.4.6 (CCSL 27, 157): "… ut … confitear non tantum coram te secreta exultatione cum tremore et secreto maerore cum spe, sed etiam in auribus credentium filiorum hominum …. Hi sunt servi tui, fratres mei, quos filios tuos esse voluisti dominos meos, quibus iussisti ut serviam …."

37   Ibid. (CCSL 27, 158): "Indicabo ergo talibus, qualibus iubes ut serviam, non quis fuerim, sed quis iam sim et quis adhuc sim …."

38   Ibid., 10.3.3 (CCSL 27, 156): "Sed quia caritas omnia credit, inter eos utique, quos conexos sibimet unum facit, ego quoque, domine, etiam sic tibi confiteor, ut audiant homines, quibus demonstrare non possum, an vera confitear; sed credunt mihi, quorum mihi aures caritas aperit …." The allusion to 1 Cor. 13:3 and 7 simultaneously alludes to Paul's theology of the one Body bound by love – that is, the Church. Note too that, just as the self-disclosive part of the narrative actually begins, Augustine calls attention to himself as "dispenser of [God's] sacrament," *dispensator sacramenti tui* (see, ibid., 10.30.41 [CCSL 27, 176]), thus once again invoking his manner of speaking as one within and to the Eucharistic community.

39   See, for example, *doctr. chr.* 1.16.15 (BA 11.2, 96).

40   *conf.* 10.3.4 (CCSL 27, 157): "Dicit enim eis caritas, qua boni sunt, non mentiri me de me confitentem, et ipsa in eis credit mihi …."

41   Ibid., 10.43.70 (CCSL 27, 193): "… fueram fugam in solitudinem …."

42   Ibid. (CCSL 27, 193): "Cogito pretium meum et manduco et bibo et erogo et pauper cupio saturari ex eo inter illos, qui edunt et saturantur: et laudant dominum qui requirunt eum …." The translation given is a modified version of Boulding's (1997). Specifically, "pretium" is emphasized and translated consistently with the places in which it appears in book 10. O'Donnell (1992) comments on this passage as follows: "Whatever is incomplete about this encounter with Christ [through ascent of the soul] is brought to fulfillment in Bk. 9, through baptism (9.6.14), and culminates at the end of Bk. 10, where Augustine closes the central book of the work with a passage of such dense Eucharistic imagery that it may best be thought of as perhaps the only place in our literature where a Christian receives the Eucharist in the literary text itself" (1:xxxvii, n. 3).

43   1.1.1 (CCSL 27, 1): "Et laudabunt dominum qui requirunt eum."

44   Ibid.: "Tu excitas, ut laudare te delectet, quia fecisti nos ad te et inquietum est. cor nostrum, donec requiescat in te."

45   See again *doctr. chr.* 1.16.15 (cf. n. 39 supra): "Est enim ecclesia corpus eius, sicut apostolica doctrina commendat (cf. Eph. 1:23), quae coniux etiam eius dicitur

(cf. Eph. 5:24ff.). Corpus ergo suum multis membris diversa officia gerentibus (cf. Rom. 12:4), nono unitatis et caritatis tamquam sanitatis adstringit. Exercet autem hoc tempore et purgat medicinalibus quibusdam molestiis, ut erutam de hoc saeculo in aeternum sibi copulet coniugem ecclesiam non habentem maculam aut rugam aut aliquid eiusmodi" (cf. Eph. 5:27, with reference to Sg. 6:9). Augustine reads the Song of Songs through the ecclesial theology of Ephesians, rather than the more individualistic mysticism of Ambrose as found in, for example, his *De Isaac vel anima*.

46   10.6.8 (CCSL 27, 158): "Percussisti cor meum verbo tuo, et amavi te." Cf. 9.2.3 (ibid., 134): "Sagittaveras tu cor nostrum caritate tua, et gestabamus verba tua transfixa visceribus," which may be translated as: "With the arrows of your charity, you pierced our hearts, and we bore your words within us like a sword penetrating us to the core."

47   On this episode, see O'Donnell (1992), 3:127–129 (n. 3), and Cavadini (1996).

48   Cf. *conf.* 10.24.35 (CCSL 27, 174).

49   Ibid., 10.29.40 (CCSL 27, 176): "Et tota spes mea non nisi in magna valde misericordia tua. Da quod iubes et iube quod vis." This final sentence occurs elsewhere in *conf.*, for example, 10.37.60 (CCSL 27, 188).

50   Ibid., 10.3.4 (CCSL 27, 156): "... mutans animam meam fide et sacramento tuo ...." This is probably a reference to baptism.

51   Ibid., 10.4.5 (CCSL 27, 157): "... quantum ad te accedam munere tuo ...."

52   Ibid., 10.30.42 (CCSL 27, 177): "... exultans cum tremore in eo, quod donasti mihi, et lugens in eo, quod inconsummatus sum, sperans perfecturum te in me misericordias tuas usque ad pacem plenariam, quam tecum habebunt interiora et exteriora mea, cum absorpta fuerit mors in victoriam." Cf. 1 Cor. 15:54.

53   For concupiscence of touch, see, ibid., 10.30.42 (CCSL 27, 177): "... sperans perfecturum te in me misericordias tuas ...."; for concupiscence of taste, see 10.31.45 (179): "... da quod iubes et iube quod vis." This is a phrase that, as we have already seen, is associated with God's mercy; for concupiscence of smell, see 10.32.48 (181): "Vna spes, una fiducia, una firma promissio misericordia tua." For concupiscence of hearing, see 10.33.50 (182): "... miserere et sana me ...."; for concupiscence of sight, see 10.34.53 (184): "... tu euellis, domine, euellis tu, quoniam misericordia tua ante oculos meos est. Nam ego capior miserabiliter, et tu euellis misericorditer ...." If we move beyond concupiscence of the flesh for each of the five senses, to, for example, *curiositas*, see 10.35.57 (186): "... et una spes mea magna valde misericordia tua," an idea echoed a few lines later at 10.36.58: "... aut aliquid nos reducet in spem nisi nota misericordia tua, quonaim coepisti mutare nos?" For *ambitio saeculi*, see 10.38.63 (189): "... quaerens misericordiam tuam ...." (note also that the phrase "da quod iubes et iube quod vis" occurs at 10.38.60 [188]). Observing that each of these examinations of conscience, that is, of memory, are mini-ascents to God's mercy, makes the closing sections that follow all the more forceful, for, in these sections,

Augustine summarizes the whole examination of conscience (cf. 10.41.66; ibid., 191) and ascends to the definitive form of God's mercy, the Mediator between God and humankind (10.42.67; ibid.), who is equal to God and yet mortal like us (10.43.68; ibid., 192), who intercedes for us (10.43.69; ibid., 193), and who redeemed us with the price of his blood, now dispensed and received in the Eucharist (10.43.70; ibid.). Finally, note the mention of God's "unfathomable mercy (*secreta tua misericordia*)" (192) as that which sent the Mediator in the first place, so that what is revealed in the economy of the Incarnation and is dispensed in the Eucharist is this mercy. The ascents to God's mercy are thus recapitulated in these sections as all moments in one grand ascent to the Eucharist.

54 This is less frequently mentioned than God's mercy, but is still prevalent enough to characterize the examination of conscience. There is at least one invocation for each of the three types of temptation. For concupiscence of the flesh, see 10.31.44 (178): "… invoco dexteram tuam …." and 10.31.47 (180): "… et interpellat te pro peccatis meis, qui vicit saeculum (cf. Jn. 16:33), numerans me inter infirma membra corporis sui …." For *curiositas*, see 10.35.56 (185): "… obsecro te per regem nostrum …." For *ambitio saeculi*, the invocation is in the transition to the summary statement and is in the past tense. See 10.41.66 (191): "Ideoque consideravi languores peccatorum meorum in cupiditate triplici et dexteram tuam invocavi ad salutem meam."

55 *conf.* 10.31.47 (CCSL 27, 180); for the Latin, see n. 54.

56 Ibid., 10.43.68 (CCSL 27, 192): "… quia aequalis deo et deus apud deum et simul unus deus" (cf. Phil. 2:6 and Jn. 1:1). The emphasis has been added.

57 Ibid., 10.43.69 (CCSL 27, 192–193): "Quomodo nos amasti, pater bone, qui filio tuo unico non pepercisti, sed pro nobis impiis tradidisti eum! Quomodo nos amasti, pro quibus ille non rapinam arbitratus esse aequalis tibi factus est subditus usque ad mortem crucis …" Cf. Phil. 2:6 and 8.

58 Famously, at *conf.* 7.20.26 and 7.21.27.

59 See O'Donnell (1992), 3:251, n. 3.

60 *conf.* 13.1.1 (CCSL 27, 242): "Invoco te, deus meus, misericordia mea, qui fecisti me et oblitum tui non oblitus es."

61 Ibid., 13.2.2 (CCSL 27, 242): "Quid enim te promeruit caelum et terra, quae fecisti in principio? Dicant, quid te promeruerunt spiritalis corporalisque natura, quas fecisti in sapientia tua …."

62 See, ibid.,13.2.3 (CCSL 27, 243): "Quid te promeruit materies corporalis, ut esset saltem invisibilis et incomposita, quia neque hoc esset, nisi quia fecisti? … Aut quid te promeruit inchoatio creaturae spiritalis, ut saltem tenebrosa fluitaret similis abysso, tui dissimilis …?"

63 The passage cited in the previous note continues: "… nisi per idem verbum converteretur ad idem, a quo facta est, atque ab eo inluminata lux fieret, quamvis non aequaliter tamen conformis formae aequali tibi?"

64 Even the initial, inchoate life of the spiritual creature was due to God's grace: "... ut et quod utcumque vivit et quod beate vivit, non deberet nisi gratiae tuae ...." See, ibid., 13.3.4 (CCSL 27, 243). See also, ibid., 13.4.5, where Augustine remarks: "What, then, would have been lacking to that Good which is your very self, even if these things had never come to be at all, or had remained in their unformed state? It was no need on your part that drove you to make them, but out of your sheer goodness ...." This translation is a modified version of that of Boulding (1997). See 344–345 (n. 4). For the Latin, see CCSL 27, 244: "Quid ergo tibi deesset ad bonum, quod tu tibi es, etiamsi ista vel omnino nulla essent vel informia remanerent, quae non ex indigentia fecisti, sed ex plenitudine bonitatis tuae ...."

65 Here, Augustine is explaining why, in Gen. 1:2, the Holy Spirit is said to hover "above the waters" when there is no question of physical location. He answers, in part, that it is from the "supereminence" of love, which is poured out into our hearts from God, and which love draws us upward. See *conf.* 13.7.8. For the Latin of the passages translated in this context, see CCSL 27, 245. The text of Rom. 5:5 is: "quia caritas tua diffusa est in cordibus nostris per spiritum sanctum, qui datus est nobis."

66 While it is important to note that Augustine does not mark the beginning of the allegory and that he only rarely mentions the fact that he is interpreting allegorically or figuratively (cf., e.g., *conf.* 13.24.37 [CCSL 27, 263–264]: "allegorice" vs. "proprie," and "figurate," and 13.34.49 [CCSL 27, 272)]: "figurationem"), Augustine does not draw much attention to the difference between the "proper" or literal interpretation and the "allegorical" or "figurative" interpretation, because this is not simply an allegory of arbitrary correspondence between one narrative (creation) and another (redemption). Rather, it is because, in some ways, there is only one narrative of God's creative and redemptive mercy.

67 Ibid., 13.12.13 (CCSL 27, 248): "Sed quia spiritus tuus superferebatur super aquam, non reliquit miseriam nostram misericordia tua ...."

68 Ibid. (CCSL 27, 248): "... commemorati sumus tui, domine ... de monte aequali tibi, sed parvo propter nos ...."

69 Ibid., 13.13.14 (CCSL 27, 249): "... in voce sua; in tua enim, qui misisti spiritum tuum de excelsis per eum, qui ascendit in altum ..." Note too, the references to Rom. 12:2, 1 Cor. 14:20 and Gal. 3:1, which Augustine has just quoted, as well as his assertion that Paul did not speak these words in his own voice.

70 See, ibid., 13.14.15, which speaks of "... God ... who will breathe life even into our mortal bodies through the Spirit who dwells in us (cf. Rom. 8:11) and has been mercifully hovering over the dark chaos of our inner being." For this, see Boulding (1997), 353. For the Latin, see CCSL 27, 250: "... deum meum, qui vivificabit et mortalia corpora nostra propter spiritum, qui habitat in nobis, quia super interius nostrum tenebrosum et fluuidum misericorditer superferebatur." The mention of the resurrection body is important because, just as Christ's flesh

is a living memory, in heaven, of the economy of salvation, so even when we reach the eschatologically promised vision, our own very being, thanks to our bodies, will be a living memory of our death and of the mercy of God who raised us.

71 Ibid., 13.12.13: "... and you said, 'Let there be light; repent, for the kingdom of heaven is near, repent, and let there be light' (cf. Gen. 1:3 and Mt. 3:2 and 4:17) .... Disgusted with our darkness, we were converted to you, and there was light" (cf. Gen. 1:3). For this translation, which is a modified version of Boulding's (1997), see 350–351. For the Latin, see CSEL 27, 248: "... et dixisti, Fiat lux; paenitentiam agite, appropinquavit enim regnum caelorum, paenitentiam agite; fiat lux .... et displicuerunt nobis tenebrae nostrae, et conversi sumus ad te, et facta est lux."

72 See 13.12.12, where Augustine takes a moment to review explicitly the Trinitarian mystery which he has raised for our consideration ever since he ascended with us to the Eucharistic mindfulness of book 12. He directs our attention to the Trinitarian image within ourselves, but notes that the proper conclusion to be drawn from this consideration is how different the Trinity is from ourselves. It is easy to resolve the triad of one's own being, knowledge, and will into a unity. But for the Holy Trinity, "[Are not] the simplicity and the complexity reconciled in some way beyond our comprehension?" – making it presumptuous to make any assertion about it: "... an utrumque miris modis simpliciter et multipliciter infinito in se sibi ...?"; "Quis ullo modo dixerit? Quis quolibet modo temere pronuntiaverit?" (CCSL 27, 248). Henry Chadwick notes the allusion to Plotinus, *Enneads* 6.8.17.25, that is present here, and then summarizes: "The One is wholly self-related." He also sees an allusion to *Enneads* 6.5.9.35, in connection with which he observes: "It possesses multiplicity 'by itself and from itself.'" For this, see Chadwick (1991), 280, n. 15. Even if these allusions are intentional, it does not necessarily indicate that Augustine believes Plotinus has a precise understanding or version of what Christians mean by the Trinity. The point is that this is as far as one can get through precise philosophical language. Unless one is content to remain at this distance, the only alternative is to accept the Christian revelation, and proceed forward in faith, which is what Augustine does next. Bringing up the philosophical aporia serves to demonstrate the rationality, if you will, of proceeding forward in faith; it is not meant to demonstrate the independent sufficiency of philosophical reflection on the Godhead. On the contrary, it serves as the springboard for the faithful consideration of the mighty works of the Spirit of God, the Spirit of Christ, as the fulfillment of God's works of mercy.

73 In the passage just cited in n. 72, that is, at 13.12.13 (CCSL 27, 248), we read: "Procede in confessione, fides mea; dic domino deo tuo: sancte, sancte, sancte (cf. Is. 6:3 and Rev. 4:8), domine deus meus, in nomine tuo baptizati sumus, pater et fili et spiritus sancte, in nomine tuo baptizamus, pater et fili et spiritus sancte (cf.

Mt. 28:19), quia et apud nos in Christo suo fecit deus caelum et terram (cf. Gen. 1:1), spiritales et carnales ecclesiae suae, et terra nostra antequam acciperet formam doctrinae, invisibilis erat et incomposita (cf. Gen. 1:2) et ignorantiae tenebris tegebamur (cf. Ps. 54:6) ...." This is the allegory's point of origin. In other words, in order to find out more about the Trinity, one has to consider the merciful work of the Trinity in redemption, deepening the Eucharistic mindfulness one has already achieved if one has followed Augustine. Dipping back into philosophy will neither reveal this mercy nor cause us to "see" it.

74   In the figure, the darkness of our ignorance has been formed by teaching or doctrine (see 13.12.13, cited in n. 73 supra), and "made light" by the Spirit who has inspired our repentance and faith and made us "light in the Lord" (*lux in domino*); 13.12.13 (CCSL 27, 248). "Et tamen adhuc per fidem, nondum per speciem," alluding to 2 Cor. 5:7, means that, even though we are now "light in the Lord," we still walk by faith, and not by sight. Boulding (1997), 351, n. 4, translates this as: "But as yet we know this only by faith, not by anything we see"; and Chadwick (1991), 280, n. 72, as: "Nevertheless, we still act on faith, not yet on sight." However, to me, it seems preferable to fill out the terse Latin with the idea of "walking," consonant with the allusion to 2 Cor. 5:7. Later, but still in this same discussion of faith, Augustine preserves the implied metaphor when he imagines his faith scolding his own temptation to slide back into the abyss whence it came: "But my faith takes it to task, that faith which you have kindled, lamp-like, on my nocturnal path ...." (13.14.15; cf. ibid., 250: "Dicit ei fides mea, quam accendisti in nocte ante pedes meos ...."). The point is not an absolute contrast between faith, which is inferior, and vision, which is superior, but rather between the distant vision afforded by contemplation of philosophical aporiae on their own, and the "light" which faith *adds* to such a situation, so that we may walk onward to a fuller, eschatological vision in which what faith now sees, namely God's mercy, remains as part of the vision. Faith is itself a "light," and the presence of the Spirit in us makes us "light" already: "By this [dwelling of the Spirit in us] we have received, even on our pilgrim way, the pledge (cf. 2 Cor. 1:22 and 5:5) that we are children of the light already. We may only be saved in hope (cf. Rom. 8:24), but we are at home in the light and in the day ...." (13.14.15; cf. ibid., 250: "Vnde in hac peregrinatione pignus acceptimus, ut iam simus lux, dum adhuc spe salvi facti sumus et filii lucis et filii diei ...."). Leaving faith behind would mean leaving behind the Spirit of God Himself, and so would be a rejection of the Trinity, not an apprehension of the Trinity, and the acceptance of a distant vision, too far away to "see" the wonderful works that God has done.

75   *conf.* 13.21.29 (CCSL 27, 257): "... animam vivam ...."

76   Ibid. (CCSL 27, 258).

77   Ibid., 13.21.30 (CCSL 27, 259): "Motus enim animae sunt isti in allegoria ...." Boulding (1997), 363, translates this as "... impulses of the soul ...." and

comments in a note that "[t]he three classes of animals created on the same day as human beings are taken to represent the three temptations of 1 Jn 2:16, which parody the Trinity: Father, Spirit, Son" (cf. n. 185). The reference to the Trinity is helpful; however, the three animals do not, precisely, represent the three temptations, but "motions of the soul" which can be bad if they turn into the passions represented in 1 Jn. 2:16, but these very same emotions can be good if used in imitation of Christ, as Augustine explains in the next section (cf. 13.21.31). Thus, it seems as though a neutral word for the Latin "motus," such as "motion" or "emotion," is a better translation. Here, *conf.* anticipates the teaching of Augustine in *ciu.* book 14. For more on this, see Cavadini (2005), reprinted as Chapter 6 of this volume.

78   Ibid., 13.21.30 (CCSL 27, 258–259).

79   Ibid., 13.22.32–23.33 (CCSL 27, 260–262).

80   Ibid., 13.22.32 (CCSL 27, 260). Perhaps there is an inference that the *homo spiritalis* is able to contemplate the image of the Trinity within himself or herself because of the work of the Spirit that is transforming him or her. Perhaps this is the germ of the theory of the renewal of the image that is so important in *trin.* book 14.

81   Ibid., 13.18.43 (CCSL 27, 267): "Et uidisti, deus, omnia quae fecisti, et ecce bona ualde, quia et nos uidemus ea, et ecce omnia bona ualde" (cf. Gen. 1:31).

82   Ibid., 13.29.44 (CCSL 27, 268): "… quae uos per spiritum meum uidetis, ego uideo …" See also the discussion at 13.31.46, which concludes thus of those contemplating creation in the Spirit of God: "If, then, seeing something in God's Spirit, they perceive it to be good, it is evidently not they, but God, who sees that it is good." For the Latin, see CCSL 27, 269: "… ita quidquid in spiritu dei uident quia bonum est., non ipsi, sed deus uidet, quia bonum est."

83   Ibid., 13.30.45 (CCSL 27, 269): "… te cognoscunt in eis" (eis = "opera tua").

84   Ibid. That given in the text follows Chadwick's (1991) translation, 300, n. 72. For the Latin, see CCSL 27, 268: "… displicent opera tua …."

85   Note, for example, the way in which the summary of the literal exegesis in 13.32.47 is followed, and, seemingly, completed, by the summary of the figurative exegesis in 13.33.48. This makes the whole discussion seem like one continuous narrative.

86   When God will finally "rest" in us – that is, when God's work of love in us is finally complete (cf. 13.37.52): "And then you will rest in us, as now you work in us …." For the Latin, see CCSL 27, 272: "Etiam tunc enim sic requiesces in nobis, quemadmodum nunc operaris in nobis …."

87   Ps. 136 (refrain; the Vulgate has "misericordia"; the King James Version has "mercy").

References

Bochet, Isabelle (2004) *"Le firmament de l'écriture": L'herméneutique augustinienne.* Paris: Institut d'Études Augustiniennes.

Boulding, Maria, O.S.B., trans. (1997) *Confessions. WSA I/1,* edited by John E. Rotelle. Hyde Park, NY: New City Press.

Catholic Church (1994) *The Catechism of the Catholic Church* Vatican City: Libreria Editrice Vaticana.

Cavadini, John C. (1996) "The Food of Truth." In *Labors of the Heart: Mission and Ministry in a Catholic University,* edited by Mark L. Poorman, 55–66. Notre Dame, IN: University of Notre Dame Press.

Cavadini, John C. (2005) "Feeling Right: Augustine on the Passions and Sexual Desire." *Augustinian Studies* 36: 195–217.

Chadwick, Henry, trans. (1991) *Confessions.* Oxford: Oxford University Press.

Crosson, Frederick (1989) "Structure and Meaning in St. Augustine's *Confessions.*" *Proceedings of the American Catholic Philosophical Association* 63: 84–97. Reprinted in *The Augustinian Tradition,* edited by Gareth B. Matthews, 27–38. Berkeley and Los Angeles: University of California Press, 1990.

O'Donnell, J. J., trans. (1992) *Augustine: Confessions,* 3 vols. Oxford: Clarendon Press. [Volume 1 is a translation of the text. Volumes 2 and 3 are O'Donnell's extensive commentary.]

10

Spousal Vision

A Study of Text and History in the Theology of Saint Augustine

I

In the beginning of *de ciuitate dei* (*ciu.*), Augustine announces the subject of his work, namely:…

> to defend (*defendere*) the most glorious City of God, both as it is living by faith in the course of time, a pilgrim among the impious, and in the stable security of its eternal seat, which it now awaits through patient endurance.

Augustine goes on to remark that, in order to accomplish this task, he will not be able to "pass over in silence whatever that the plan and logic of the task," that is, the defense of the city of God, "stipulates to be said about the earthly city." This city is one that, "in its desire for domination is itself dominated, even when peoples are enslaved to it, by the lust of domination itself."[1] In the whole of *ciu.*, there are few passages that are more familiar than this one, yet it is probable that we only rarely if ever hear it fully. It is interesting to note that a discussion of the earthly city is not the primary aim of *ciu.*, but, because it is something which is required by the primary subject matter, it "must not be passed over in silence." From the very outset of the treatise, discussion of the earthly city is secondary and derivative to discussion of the "most glorious City of God."

Visioning Augustine, First Edition. John C. Cavadini.
© 2019 John Wiley & Sons Ltd. Published 2019 by John Wiley & Sons Ltd.

II

It is not really hard to see why this should be true, for the earthly city, as such, cannot be detected apart from its contrast to the city of God. The earthly city is characterized by its desire to dominate and enslave nations or peoples, a project most fully realized in empires. But, surely, the imperial enterprise is visible enough in human history apart from discussion of the city of God! The empires are indeed all too visible. They are not hidden in the least! And Augustine will use the Roman historians to good effect in demonstrating the reality of imperial ambition and its consequences. But the "earthly city," the *ciuitas terrena* as such, that is, *as* the "earthly city," cannot be seen in any way – even analytically – apart from the perspective afforded by discussion of the city of God, because it has no identity that can be discerned, described, or discussed apart from the contrast with the heavenly city that is afforded by "the Scripture of [God's] people."[2]

We learn later that the earthly city can be named as such, but this is only because scripture affords us enough perspective to provide it with a name: "Babylon." "Babylon" is the name of the historical capital of the Assyrian empire, as Augustine points out (albeit incorrectly) in *ciu.* 16, and yet the name is lent to the whole earthly city: "Thus in Assyria," Augustine comments, "the dominating power of the impious city prevailed. Its capital was Babylon whose name, 'Confusion' (*confusio*), is most apt for the earthborn city (*terrigenae ciuitatis*)." As such, the name becomes transferrable: "This took place about 1,200 years before the foundation of Rome, the second Babylonia, as it were, the Babylonia of the West" (cf. 16.17).[3] As Augustine points out here and elsewhere, confusion is never visible as such apart from its contrast with order. Even the circumstances of Babylon's founding (and especially the resultant confusion of languages) evoke a contrast, since the original language, Hebrew, remained unconfused among the forbears of Abraham. The earthly city can never be seen as such in this world, hence the ambiguity attendant on Augustine's use of the denomination "earthly city": it sometimes seems to be a synonym for an actual empire, especially Rome, and sometimes it seems to be a more generic designation. This is because it can only be "seen" in this world as one or another successful imperial project. Assyria is not itself the earthly city; rather "in Assyria the ungodly city exercised predominant power." But the "city" of which Assyria is only an outcropping or example is, as a whole community, no community; it is Babylon, or simply, "confusion." Like a cosmic black hole, the earthly city cannot be seen. Only the plumes of light that come from the stars caught in its undertow, in this case, the undertow of the *libido dominandi*, can be seen. Only the empires can be seen, and it is they that write history.

<h1 style="text-align:center">III</h1>

The secondary or dependent status of the discussion of the earthly city is explicitly featured in the later books of *ciu*. Having already shown the origin (*exortu*) of the two cities in "the angels ... and in the first two human beings," in books 11–14, Augustine, as he begins book 15, undertakes a discussion of the "development" (*excursus*) of the human component of these cities, "two classes (*genera*) of the human race," "one comprised of those who live according to man (*secundum hominem*), the other of those who live according to God (*secundum Deum*)," two "fellowships" (*societates*) of human beings, which, Augustine says, he "calls two cities, speaking mystically" (*mystice*).[4] This "excursus" occupies the whole of time, the whole of the "era" or "world" (*uniuersum tempus siue saeculum*) in which there are mortal human beings, that is, the whole of human history.[5] Augustine is using the scriptures to help him track human history as the course of the two cities. Scripture offers an account of some historical events, and it enables one to speak "mystically" about them because it enables one to see their meaning, otherwise obscure, hidden in the all-too-visible and "confusing" drama of empires. Both the "events" (*gesta*) in question and the written accounts of the events (*conscripta*) "are always to be referred to Christ and His Church, which is the City of God."[6] There probably were righteous people between the time of Noah's sons and Abraham, but they are not recorded in scripture because, Augustine remarks, it is not the point of scripture simply to offer an historical register, but a narrative with a purpose:

> It would take too long, and it would represent historical diligence more than prophetic providence. Accordingly, the writer of these holy Scriptures (or rather the Spirit of God through him) is concerned not only with narrating past events (*narrentur praeterita*) but also announcing

future events (*futura*), though only those things which pertain to the City of God. For everything that is here said about those human beings who are not its citizens is said with this purpose, that it may show up to advantage, may be thrown into relief, by contrast with its opposite (*ut illa ex comparatione contraria uel proficiat uel emineat*).[7]

The point is that a prophetic reading of history enables its meaning, overshadowed by the grandiose transactions of empire,[8] to be seen. The course of the city of God is revealed and, in the process, so is the earthly city, but by contrast. Thus, discussion of the earthly city in the Bible is secondary to discussion of the city of God, and Augustine's own account follows suit.

IV

In book 18, after a long hiatus, Augustine self-consciously returns to the topic of the "other city," as he calls it, in order to emphasize its contrastive and subordinate character when compared to the city of God. He notes that his silence about the "other city" in the closing sections of book 16 and throughout book 17 was intentional, in order:

... first to bring out more distinctly the development of the city of God by describing its course, without interruption from its contrary, that other city (*a contrario, alterius ciuitatis*), from the time when God's promises began to be more explicit.

But now he intends to outline the progress of that other city, enough, at least, so that "readers may observe both cities and mark the contrast between them."[9]

Reading the history of the earthly city as Augustine narrates it there, one has the initial impression that it is simply like reading the history of the world, human history as such. It seems so unremarkable and so derivative[10] that one feels justifiably tempted simply to skip book 18 and get to "the good stuff" of book 19. Indeed, had we forgotten that the narratability of something called the "city of this world" was itself remarkable and "mystical," we would be unimpressed by the story of the "society of mortals," still "linked by a certain communion in nature" from the time of book 12,[11] the point at which this communion was first mentioned as part of Augustine's recounting of creation.[12] Now this communion in human nature is seen only dimly, limned as a communion in pursuit of dominance on the one hand, or, barring that, in the preference of subjection and slavery to death – for the losers – on the other.[13] The result, Augustine notes, is that – though all are subject to God's providence – some nations have established empires, while others are dominated by the empires. All this just sounds like human history without remainder. However, those who are aware of the pilgrim city, the city of God, can see that history cannot so simply be reduced to this history of striving for domination. This is only a partial account, and that of which it is a history has a name, the city of this world or the earthly city:

> Now the society whose common aim is earthly advantage or desire, the community which we call by the general name of "the city of this world (*ciuitas huius mundi*)," has been divided into a great number of empires; and among these we observe that two empires have won a renown far exceeding that of all the rest. First was the Assyrian Empire; later came that of the Romans.[14]

The empires, especially Assyria and Rome, are visible enough, but the city of this world, as such, can only be seen "*mystice*," in contrast with the city of God. It cannot be seen on its own as one thing because it is intrinsically fragmented, with no real identity of its own, except "confusion."

It is interesting to see how Augustine recounts secular history. In book 18, he uses as sources, not primarily the Bible, but the secular historians and other secular literary sources or Christian texts derived from them.[15] Here, the Bible is used mainly to map the history that the Bible relates onto the context of the secular history that the non-biblical sources relate, so that we can see the way that "Babylon progresses, along with the City of God, a pilgrim in this world," with a view to contrasting the two (*ciu.* 18.2). As early as book 11, the biblical text has served the wider purpose of providing the narrative of the origin and development of the city of God with which, by contrast, something called the "earthly city" can appear and have a narrative that transcends the narratives of each particular empire or would-be empire. Apart from that, what we find are only the individual narratives of empire, irreducible to each other, each vying, as it were, to order the world and to dominate the other. Furthermore, it is interesting to see how, in Augustine's account, each imperial narrative is also irreducibly intertwined with myth. Not even Augustine can recount the history of these empires without reference to their myths as such. Even though many of these myths can be, and actually have been, demythologized by secular historians so as to show that the gods are illusory or were just deified human beings all along – or, as in the case of Romulus, even though it is actually known by everyone that the "god" in question was originally human – these histories cannot be told without also recounting the myths.[16] Even more, the myths, even when known to be false, are enforced on those who are subject to the empire in question.[17] There is no imperial history without the myth because there is no true rationale for any particular empire; each is actually motivated by the desire to dominate and, even more importantly, each is completely a function of the desire to dominate, since the earthly city is the one that, even in its domination, is itself dominated by the lust for domination. There is no "myth" that allows one to tell universal history. That is the function, as a byproduct, one might say, of the story of the city of God; the story of the city of God is the prophetic denunciation of myth; it is the anti-myth with reference to which one can release universal history from its fragmentation into the various mythic narratives of empires.

V

Augustine explains the persistence of myths in the imperial histories – despite their evident falsity – by tying them to the worship of the gods in the public cults and to the way they are presented in obscene stage shows. Augustine's protest against the obscenity of the staged presentations of the myths is one of the most persistent features of *ciu.*; indeed, it is almost a leitmotif throughout. On Augustine's account, not only is empire intrinsically idolatrous, empire is also intrinsically pornographic. Those creating empires are dominated, Augustine says, by the lust to dominate. That is what they have in common, there is nothing rational at the basis of these projects of domination, essentially no "accounting" or "recounting" of them that would distinguish one from another. This is why the attempt to rationalize empire by historical narration really becomes an attempt to replace history by myth. Empires are founded in the "confusion" of the desire to dominate by those who are already shamefully dominated by that desire. And to justify themselves, to raise themselves above the level of shameful "confusion," to erase the evidence of the irrational lust to power which causes shame, they mystify themselves as they tell their own story. The pornographic style of empire is related to this. Using the history of only one group of people to divinize and worship certain human beings as that group rises to power distorts the meaning of the human person to meet the end of domination. Even when the myths are known to be false, the pornographic character of their representation ensures that the imperial dissembling that they encode remains alive in the hearts of citizens.[18] Augustine points out the irony that people live by myths even though they are known to be false. They survive as a commitment to a view of history obsessively recreated by the lust of those watching the pornographic performances.

VI

Augustine invites us to explore the relationship between empire and the pornographic. Let us recall the first instance of the earthly city, later actually named "Confusion," but having roots in the *confusi*,[19] as Augustine calls them, the first human couple, who were confounded and shamed as they discovered their own nakedness. Let us also recall how they reached this state. If we go back to book 14, we realize that Eve, according to Augustine, was truly fooled by the devil, who had commandeered the serpent for this very purpose. Adam, however, is not fooled. Augustine does not exculpate Eve, but hers is not the decisive sin. The defining moment is when Adam fully and deliberately decides – despite *not* being deceived – to disfigure by sin the spousal fellowship that he and Eve had already been given by God. Augustine puts this decision in slightly different ways as he narrates, but they are all variations on the theme of *superbia*: Adam, even before accepting the forbidden fruit, had fallen into the posture of a "self-pleaser," one who puts love of self above love of God. He "lifted up his heart" to himself instead of to God; in other words, he worshipped himself. Augustine comments that, having defected from the love of God, Adam supposed that "he was only a venial transgressor if he did not desert the one companion (*sociam*) of his life even if it involved him in a companionship (*societate*) of sin."[20]

Commentators have generally been harsh on Augustine for seeming to imply that Adam should have abandoned Eve rather than enter into a *societas* characterized by sin. But Augustine's description of the alternatives would seem to be made from inside the psychology of Adam, that is, from within his heart, which had already begun to be evil, even before accepting the fruit from Eve. It is true that Adam preferred to enter a fellowship of sin rather than to abandon Eve, but, in fact, these were not the only alternatives available to him. This is the way Adam, already a self-pleaser, constructed them. Adam already has the lack of imagination, and, thus, the carelessness, that afflicts all of the complacent and proud. What does not occur to Adam, who has learned to lift up his heart to himself instead of to God, is that, in some way, he could sacrifice himself for his wife in order to save her from the devil who had obviously fooled her (albeit through her own pride), instead of letting her stay in his thrall, thus sacrificing their companionship to Adam's own pride. He should have had mercy on her. Sacrifice is mercy, and, in *ciu.*, mercy is the true worship of God,[21] though this worship is precisely what is refused by those who deny their heart to God.

That Adam had some alternative is clear from the contrasting story of the second Adam. Christ did not abandon us, and, though he joined us sinners, he did not enter into a fellowship of sin with us. He was prepared, in mercy, to sacrifice his own life for Eve, now in the person of the Church, the new Eve (which presumably includes the old Eve). Adam had the chance, it would seem, to somehow "save" Eve by his own compassionate mercy, but he preferred to take advantage of Eve, committing himself to the complacent truncation of the imagination, the "myth" of the false alternatives. Part of his construction of these false alternatives is revealed in the story he tells God in order to explain what happened. As Augustine sees it, Adam blamed Eve, expecting that God would judge her and vindicate him[22] – a version of the primal myth of empire invoking the divine as being on one's side. Like the literary presentations of human suffering that, as Augustine explains in *Confessiones* (*conf.*),[23] invite a false compassion in order to displace the true compassion of self-sacrifice, Adam, in following Eve into sin, enacts a simulacrum of mercy justified by a myth.[24] Moreover, in ratifying and consummating Eve's original sin, Adam *transformed it into original sin* in the strict Augustinian sense.

Original sin is the sin of *Adam* (*ciu.* 14.11), namely, the *willing of and the creation of a fallen solidarity*. It is the solidarity itself that falls and that thus loses its capacity to be narrated except by a contrasting solidarity which reveals the "nakedness" of the first solidarity, its cohesion as forced, as "confusion." And, as such, it must be covered up by myth.[25]

VII

If one goes back even further in *ciu.*, to book 12, one will recall that Augustine noted the distinction between the creation of human beings and that of the other animals. Human beings were created out of one human being (*hominem … unum ac singulum creauit*), Adam, whereas the other animals were created by commanding many to come into existence at once. Augustine notes that some of these animals are of a solitary habit and others gregarious (*congreges*), preferring to live together in flocks or herds. But the specific social character of human beings is distinguished from these latter by scripture's unique account of the creation of human beings from one human being:

> [I]n this way the unity of human society (*societatis unitas*) and the bonds of human sympathy (*uinculumque concordiae*) would be more emphatically brought home to man, if human beings were bound together not merely by likeness in nature but also by the feeling of kinship.[26]

A little later, as already noted,[27] Augustine comments that the human race is, "more than any other species, at once social by nature (*sociale natura*) and quarrelsome by perversion," and, further, that the creation of the human race out of one human being, from whom would be propagated a multitude, should serve as a salutary reminder to preserve "a harmonious unity in plurality."[28] The fact that the woman was made from the man is therefore an indication that human solidarity is not accidental; on the contrary, it is intrinsic to human beings:

> And to this end, when he created the woman who was to be coupled with the man (*uiro*, for the first time), he decided not to create her in the same way as he created man himself (*ipsam … ipsum*). Instead he made her out of him (*ex ipso*), so that the whole human race should spread out from the one original human being (*ex homine uno*).[29]

This is done not only in view of the biological unity of the human race, but with a view to their eventual fellowship with the society of angels (*sanctis angelis in aeterna pace sociandum*),[30] which means that there is a prelapsarian eschatology implied in the creation of human beings from one *homo*, and the creation of Eve, in turn, from that one *homo*. It is precisely the creation of Eve from Adam that signifies the distinctiveness of human solidarity. Thus, in this way, it is originally spousal. Augustine goes on to comment that "the fact that the woman was made for him out of his side also signifies how affectionate (*cara*) should be the union (*coniunctio*) of husband and wife."[31] It does not signify the domination of either spouse.

Augustine promises further discussion of this "prodigy," namely, that the woman was created from the side of the man (*ex latere uiri femina facta sit*), and what it prefigured.[32] This he takes up in book 22, when he comes to discuss whether women will retain their sex in the resurrected body. This is an open question in patristic theology and one that some remarkable theologians, for example, Gregory of Nyssa, resolved by noting that the reproductive organs would not be present in the resurrection body.[33] But Augustine's question is not simply whether the reproductive organs would be present, but *which* reproductive organs – that is, whether women would become men. The textual occasion for treating the question arises from scriptural passages from Ephesians and Romans which indicate that we are to attain to the "perfection of manhood (*in uirum perfectum*), the stature of the full maturity of Christ," "conformed to the image of God's Son."[34] Augustine points out, famously, that, although all defects will be removed from the resurrected bodies of the saints, the sex of women is not a defect but nature.[35] In other words, the woman is not a lesser version, a deformed or vitiated male, but has a beauty of her own that will be renewed and redeemed as such. Human solidarity is not intrinsically male; instead, it is intrinsically or irreducibly spousal. The eschatological vindication of the integrity of women is the vindication and fulfillment of the spousal significance of human solidarity. Human solidarity is not based on imperial homogenization. But what exactly is it based on? Where can the imagination turn if it wants to see human history in its *original* nakedness, before the shame of the "confusion" it fell into and before the shamelessness of imperial mythmaking that covered it? We do not want our nakedness exposed! How can we resist covering it up with just another myth? How can we move beyond the complacency of Adam's lack of spousal imagination?

VIII

In book 12, as already noted, Augustine had commented that the original creation of Eve from Adam was an indication of the natural solidarity of the human race, and, as such, an indication of the eventual fellowship and solidarity we would have with the angels. There was thus an eschatological signification contained in the original spousal solidarity, a signification of grace.[36] After the Fall, this significance is retained; but now, it is only a prophetic "prefiguration" of redemption in Christ. The passage cited earlier from book 22 continues:

> Now in creating woman at the outset of the human race, by taking a rib from the side of the sleeping man (*uiri dormientis*), the Creator must have intended, by this act, a prophecy of Christ and his Church. The sleep of that man (*sopor uiri*) clearly was (*erat*) the death of Christ, whose side, as he hung lifeless on the cross, was pierced by a lance, whence flowed blood and water. We know these are the sacraments by which the Church is built up (*aedificatur*).[37]

Among other things, this passage sharply contrasts Adam's self-interested lack of imagination for what it was and, in doing so, lays out a vista for our own imagination. If Adam had been less complacent, if he had not preferred to be a "self-pleaser" but had sacrificed that desire and clung to God in true worship, as did the good angels, he would have been able to imagine another alternative besides the false dichotomy of abandoning his wife or disfiguring their spousal companionship by exploiting her vulnerability and assuming divine vindication in blaming the victim. He would have seen the sacrificial reference of his and Eve's own irreducibly gendered bodies, signifying a human solidarity based in the sacrifice of one's pride in the worship of God. He would have seen it in his own person in relation to his spouse, for the mystery of "Christ and his Church, which is the City of God ... has never failed to be foretold in prophecy from the beginning of the human race."[38]

Commenting on the foolish and embarrassing nakedness of the drunken Noah in front of his sons, Augustine sees in it a foreshadowing of the nakedness of Christ on the Cross:

> "He was drunk" – that is, he suffered – and "he was naked"; for then his weakness was laid bare, that is, was made evident. As the Apostle says, "he was crucified through his weakness" (cf. 2 Cor. 13:4). And that is why he also says, "the weakness of God is stronger than men and the foolishness of God is wiser than men" (cf. 1 Cor. 1:25).[39]

Christ accepts our nakedness, not an imaginary noble nakedness, but a nakedness that can be figured by the embarrassing predicament of Noah who got himself drunk and exposed his nakedness. Christ assumes *our* nakedness, puts himself in the foolish position of having no imperial narrative to hide it. This is not a pornographic nakedness, but the vulnerability of the would-be spouse before the brutal myths that deny there is any such thing as the spouse. This nakedness is weakness. From the perspective of "Babylon," of "confusion," someone should cover that nakedness with a myth, or, at least, with the concomitant pornography that makes of nakedness a shameless imperial entertainment.[40] In Christ, God has foolishly taken on the shame of our nakedness, but as the "Wisdom" by which the world was created, and not as myth. Christ, without cause for shame, accepts the shame we deserve out of love, and, thus, the weakness he exhibits has a narrative hidden – because it is "foolishness" – to the imperium, the narrative of the spouse. This embarrassing nakedness is our own nakedness, or what we have made out of nakedness, transfigured, to borrow an expression,[41] and it provides our imagination with all it needs to deflate all imperial mythmaking and to tell a different story, to re-narrate the story of human solidarity from the start.

If we are to recover the imagination to do so, we ourselves must, like the good sons of Noah, cover the nakedness of Christ not with myth but with honor. Augustine explains that Shem and Japheth's taking a garment and turning their backs on the nakedness of Noah is a figure of Christ's nakedness being in the past for us, honored by remembering it, by accepting a place in the narrative it makes possible. We have to take on the shame and embarrassment of "nakedness," of feeling as though we have no narrative because we have given up Babylon's claim that only an imperial myth is a real narrative. We have to be willing to sacrifice the narratives that clothe our nakedness with glory and prestige, even if it is the glory and prestige of claiming the purity of the victim. There is only one pure Victim, and he is also the one true Priest, the teller of the story, and we have to let his foolish nakedness define us. The question then becomes: How do we "escape from the midst of Babylon"[42] but not from history?

IX

Augustine continues from the passage cited earlier from *ciu.* 22.17, finding significance in the very word used to describe the creation of Eve from Adam:

> This word, *aedificatur*, is the precise word used in Scripture of woman's creation; it says not that God "formed," or "fashioned" a woman but that "he built [the rib] up into a woman." Hence the Apostle also speaks of the "building up" of the Body of Christ, which is the Church.[43]

Employing imagery from Eph. 4:12–13, Augustine explains that our coming into the perfection of the "perfect man (*in uirum perfectum*)" has nothing to do with all of us becoming men; rather, it is about the "building up" of the church, head and body together (*uir perfectus, caput et corpus*), and this body consists of all the members "who will be completed in their own time." This is a process that is taking place in history, over time, as people are added to the church:

> Meanwhile, while the Church is being built up, members are added to the body every day, to which Church it is said, "You are the Body of Christ and each of you members"[44] … and again, "We being many, are one Bread, one Body" (1 Cor. 10:17).

It is a true historical process occurring in and through the visible, sacramental life of the Church "by which the Church is built up." The sacraments are the efficacious presence of Christ's spousal love. The mechanism of their efficaciousness is not specified or, rather, it is specified precisely in historical, not imperial, terms. Christ's spousal love is active as an historical, not imperial, agent, an agent of his nakedness and not of a myth. It is "mysteriously," that is, "sacramentally" (one could even use "foolishly" as a synonym), efficacious, building up a visible solidarity of people whose only demarcations are the sacraments themselves. This is a people to whom Christ's nakedness has been sacramentally mediated, whose solidarity and identity is defined by Christ's spousal love alone, a visible foolishness, a nakedness, in that sense.[45]

This solidarity, or foolishness, is denoted by the word "sacrifice" because the church has no other identity apart from the sacrificial love of the Bridegroom, and no other unity apart from that imparted by his sacrifice. As Augustine writes in a famous passage from book 19:

> [I]t is we ourselves, we, his City, who are his best, his most glorious sacrifice. The sacrament of this sacrifice we celebrate in our oblations, familiar to the faithful, as we have maintained in the previous books.[46]

In claiming this identity by the use of ("we"), Augustine is not indulging in the presumption that he or any of his readers are saved. He is not saying they are members of the city of God in its eschatological clarity or perfection and, thus, no longer on the pilgrimage of trial and purification. Rather, it is a claim that the identity of the city of God is irreducibly a nakedness, irreducibly a foolishness, irreducibly Eucharistic. There is no other true "we" except for the "we" formed by the visible Eucharistic body. Any other attempt to say "we" will evoke imperium, the myth that covers nakedness. "We" cannot narrate an identity or claim a unity based on any achievement (whether exterior or interior), characteristic, right-eousness, skill, nationality, or anything else. And yet, there is a "we," and it refers to a visible, historical body, the presence of the city of God in history in the only way it can truly be present in history: free-ing history from imperial mythmaking by and through its very presence.

How do people make the sacrifice that Adam should have made? When they allow themselves to be "built up" into a "we" − not by their achievements, including especially their spiritual achievements, would-be achievements, prestige, or skill, but by "the sacraments" that poured forth from Christ's sleeping nakedness. We make the sacrifice that Adam should have made when we honor this nakedness by letting it tell the story that defines how we say "we," honoring the sacramentally demarcated church as the presence of the spouse in history. Seeing the spouse, in fact, *is* seeing Christ; for seeing this body is to see the nakedness of Christ, the embarrassing foolishness that takes away our shame at having no narrative but myth and that enables us to resist replacing it with myth. To narrate the history of this body is inevitably to narrate the story of a sacrifice made in love, of one who did not abandon the spouse, who did follow us into sin, but not into a "companionship of sin." The true spouse had more imagination than that. His love was such that he, while having no sin, mixed himself irrevocably with us sinners without being distinguishable as such – and thus his nakedness. As Augustine quotes the prophet Isaiah, "as a sheep is led to the slaughter, and as a lamb before its shearer is dumb, so he did not open his mouth. In his humiliation, he was denied justice."[47] He did not try to construct a self-justifying narrative, though he had no sin; in fact, he spoke no narrative. He thereby transfigures the "shame" of the fallen nakedness, shame at being exposed without a self-justifying myth, into the glory of being his own nakedness, the glory of feeling or, at least, of actually being loved.

He thereby releases the narrative of world history from the grip of competing imperial myths and allows these all to be seen "mystically" as of one piece, as Babylon. According to Augustine, what the prophet Isaiah says, he says to the Church:

> Do not be afraid because you are made ashamed … for you will forget your endless shame, and you will not remember the reproach of your widowhood. Because it is the Lord who made you; his name is the Lord of Hosts; and he who rescues you, the God of Israel, will be called the God of the whole earth.[48]

If we do not try to rise above the self-giving, spousal love of Christ by holding out for a better spouse, by holding out for one that is not so obviously mixed, we make the sacrifice that Adam should have made. And, as a result, we can begin to see history more clearly. Looking back at history, we can see the spouse clearer and clearer if we do not disdain the present church but see with the eyes of the Bridegroom. We see the scandals,[49] the divisions, the bad leadership, as well as the good examples, the unity, and the good leadership – but we see it with the Eucharistically formed, sacrificial love of the Bridegroom.[50] In the struggle to love, the scales are slowly removed from our eyes. We can begin to see that love has been an historical agent from the very beginning. The imperial lie that love does not exist and does not act in history, that only force will prevail and that only prestige matters, is slowly uncovered as the myths that have disguised the lie are dismantled and the pornographic spell that enabled it to shamelessly teach that love (such as the woman given to Adam) is too vulnerable to matter, that there is no spouse, and that the only ones who make history are those who conquer, is broken.

We can begin to read history this way when we read it, as it were, with the spousal vision afforded by the biblical text. We begin to see that the self-emptying love of God has never been absent from history, but, as self-emptying, it is "hidden," as Augustine puts it, "in the shadows" of imperial bombast. It is emptied to the point where it does not take over, but acts in and through the freedom of true historical agents which remain historical agents. Noah's nakedness, for example, seems an unlikely image for the representation of Christ. Neither Saul nor David nor Solomon are particularly prepossessing as moral personages. None of them seem fit to represent Christ. But they do not serve as figures because of their evident personal fitness; rather, they serve because God has chosen to use them, without taking over their freedom. That prophetic figures have an intrinsic, not accidental, difficulty of interpretation means it requires a sacrifice to see them. They must be seen with "spousal vision." Adam is a good example of someone who, because it would have meant a sacrifice, was not able even to "read" the figure he bore in his very own person.

X

God's kenotic love is also present in the text of scripture, "for Scripture is concerned (*consultum*) for man," and its use of language is determined by that concern.[51] Commenting on the story of Noah's ark, Augustine has occasion to remind his readers that the books which have been preserved for so long and which were so carefully transmitted could not have been written for no purpose or simply in order to be consulted for *res gesta*, historical facts. Why would we need to know that there were included two of each unclean species and seven of each clean species, unless there were some significance in the details beyond the mere facts? And yet, it is equally important that it *is* events that are narrated. The narration means that scripture is not just a text of figurative meanings, but has the character of interpreting history itself.[52] Augustine is concerned about preserving "the truth of the history" because scripture is not simply a symbolic narrative of inner truths but a narrative that permits one to see what history really is:

> The Scriptural narrative ... gives an account of the succession of kings and of their achievements and the events of their reigns; and yet a careful examination of the narrative, with the help of God's spirit, reveals it to be more concerned – or at least not less concerned – with foretelling the future than with recording the past.[53]

In other words, the scriptural narrative shows that these and other events "are always to be interpreted with reference to Christ and His Church, which is the City of God," as cited earlier. If the Song of Songs "voices a kind of spiritual delight felt by holy minds in the marriage of the king and queen of that city, namely, Christ and the Church,"[54] it can also stand in for the whole of scripture, which shows us the key to demythologizing history away from the myths of empire. The key to demystifying empire is to approach history not by trying to seize it for oneself and by finding pleasure in the conquest, but by allowing a different pleasure to arise, the delight in the marriage of Christ and the Church, and to feel pleasure at seeing history re-invested with its true spousal significance. Uncovering the "allegorical draperies" of the text and, with it, of history means not doing away with history, but seeing in it the active presence of love. Any other way of reading history or of narrating it, including the ways practiced by the enlightened philosophers, will be captured by the tractor beam of imperializing myth.

XI

Books 15–18 of *ciu.* are rarely studied. This is perhaps because the typologies, which seem so obvious to Augustine, seem so useless and artificial to us moderns. If this is so, why might it be the case? In part, Augustine would answer by acknowledging that he may not be correct about all the typologies that he uses.[55] Another part of the answer might be that he would like us, as his readers, at least to consider that we have already – and a little too readily – bought into the myth of empire. Perhaps we do not actually believe that love is operative in history; or, perhaps, we believe that it is operational but only as a "spiritual reality," and, thus, we do not "see" it because we are both offended by the mixed character of the body that is said to fulfill the prophecies and offended by the figures of prophecy fulfilled in her. Perhaps we have a view of the Church, of prophecy, and of the fulfillment of prophecy that is too triumphalistic. On all levels, we want something that is clear and unmixed, something not in the shadows but in the open. We seek to eschew what the Bridegroom did not, namely, mixed company. We cannot forget that his case was even more extreme than ours, precisely because, in his, it was the sinless one who mixed himself in with us sinners. If we do not eschew what the Bridegroom did not, if we allow ourselves to live in mixed company, configured to the nakedness of Christ mediated through the sacraments, we will begin to see the whole world and its history differently. We will see the love of God operative where we did not expect to see it, where we do not see, or, at least, do not want to see such love, preferring to justify ourselves instead. Seeing the bride with the eyes of the Bridegroom would be to accept the self-emptying, spousal love he offers, bearing patiently the failings of other Christians and praying even for those outside the Church who are its enemies. Thus, the Church would be a sacrament not only unto itself but unto the world. If we can see with eyes formed by the Bridegroom's love, configured to the sacrifice of Christ in the Eucharist, we will see that the Eucharist forms and marks a solidarity that is being built up and can be narrated, not by adding another imperial myth to compete with the others, but by showing all of the myths up for the cynicism and complacency they have exhibited since the time of Adam and Eve. This is to see history released from domination by the lust for domination. Is that not the point? This is not a narrative of another holy empire, but a narrative of freedom emerging from the captivity of empire, a narrative, as Augustine has insisted from his very first page, of pilgrimage.[56]

Acknowledgments

An earlier version of this chapter was published as Cavadini, J. (2012) Spousal Vision: A Study of Text and History in the Theology of St. Augustine. *Augustinian Studies* 43: 127–148.

Notes

1   The text of *ciu.* employed in what follows is that of CCSL 47 and 48. Unless otherwise noted, the translation is that of Bettenson (1972), with occasional adjustments. The best brief commentary on the *ciu.*, complete with an excellent bibliography, is O'Daly (1999). On the idea of contrast, see 164, though here the emphasis is the other way around, highlighting the city of God by contrasting it with its opposite. See also 53–66 on "The Theme of the Two Cities."

2   *ciu.* 1. praef. (CCSL 47, 1): "scriptura populi sui," the antecedent of "sui" actually being "rex … et conditor ciuitatis huius, de qua loqui instituimus."

3   Ibid., 16.17 (CCSL 48, 522): "In Assyria igitur praeualuerat dominatus impiae ciuitatis; huius caput erat illa Babylon, cuius terrigenae ciuitatis nomen aptissimum est, id est, confusio." See also *ciu.*16.4, on Gen. 11:1–10, the tower of Babel, which Augustine says is Babylon or "Confusion"; *ciu.* 16.11, where the same equation is made, noting that Hebrew was the original language from which the others were confused, leaving God's people with their language unaffected. *Ciu.* 17.16 interprets the "queen" of Ps. 45:10–17 as "Christ's Church, wedded to so great a husband by a spiritual marriage and a divine love." Augustine comments: "This queen is Sion, in the spiritual sense … Jerusalem in the same spiritual sense, which is a point on which I have already said a great deal. Her enemy is Babylon, the city of the Devil, whose name means 'confusion.'" When Augustine says he has already discussed this point a great deal, he is referring to *ciu.* 15.2, where he interprets the allegory of the two women from Gal. 4:21–5:1 as a reference to the two cities. Later on, in book 15, the city of God is called "Christ's Bride" (*ciu.*15.22, "sponsa Christi" [see CCSL 48, 488]; see also *ciu.* 17.20, on the Song of Songs). The reader is intended to "hear" this designation as an overtone even in the shorthand of other passages, such as *ciu.*18.35, where "Zechariah says of Christ and the Church, 'Rejoice greatly, daughter of Sion! Shout for joy, daughter of Jerusalem! See, your king is coming to you, a righteous king and a savior'" (Zech. 9:9). This king is the same bridegroom-king of Ps. 45. Isaiah prophecies about the bride also – we are expected to hear the reference to her in Augustine's citation of Isa. 54:1–5, which Augustine interprets as an allusion to the Church figured in the barren woman who will bear many more children than those who did not have the reproach of being barren. Such passages also show that the feminine pronoun so often used to refer to the Church or to the city of God in books 15–18 is not simply an impersonal grammatical gender dependent on the grammatical gender of the noun *ecclesia*. The contrast Jerusalem/Babylon, with the heavenly analogue of the former being the bride of Christ, also evokes the book of Revelation (see O'Daly [1999], 53–54, n. 1). At *ciu.* 14.28, Augustine recalls the distinction between the two cities made in the preface, adding that these two cities are distinguished by two kinds of love, in one the lust for domination, in the other the love which generates mutual subjection in service: this passage is recalled in *en. Ps.* 125:3, "Duas istas ciuitates faciunt duo

amores: Jerusalem facit amor Dei, Babylonem facit amor saeculi" – a parallel pointed out by F.-J. Thonnard in the BA edition of *ciu*. See BA 36, 745 at n. 43.

4　*ciu*. 15.1 (CCSL 48, 453), recalling language from 11.1 and elsewhere. On the structure of the work, see O'Daly (1999), 67–73, n. 1.

5　*ciu*. 15.1 (CCSL 48, 453).

6　Ibid., 16.2 (CCSL 48, 500): "ad christum et eius ecclesiam, quae ciuitas dei est, esse referenda."

7　Ibid., 16.2 (CCSL 48, 500–501): "nimis longum fieret, et esset haec historica magis diligentia quam prophetica prouidentia. illa itaque exequitur litterarum sacrarum scriptor istarum uel potius per eum dei spiritus, quibus non solum narrentur praeterita, uerum etiam praenuntientur futura, quae tamen pertinent ad ciuitatem dei; quia et de hominibus, qui non sunt ciues eius, quidquid hic dicitur, ad hoc dicitur, ut illa ex comparatione contraria uel proficiat uel emineat."

8　Cf. ibid., 18.1: "The City of God developed not in the light, but in the shadow."

9　Ibid. (CCSL 48, 593): "ut ambae inter se possint consideratio legentium comparari."

10　Not to mention "unwieldy, disorganized, and out of place." For this description summarizing critics' views, see Lee (2011), esp. 563. Despite its title ("Republics and their Loves: Rereading *City of God* 19"), this essay is in fact the best recent discussion of both *ciu*. 18 and 19; it also contains a complete guide to all of the relevant literature.

11　*ciu*. 18.2 (CCSL 48, 593): "societas ... mortalium ... unius ... eiusdemque naturae quadam communione deuincta."

12　Ibid., 12.23 discusses human nature, emphasizing its natural solidarity. In 12.28, it is expressed in this way: "For the human race is, more than any other species, at once social by nature and quarrelsome by perversion." See CCSL 48, 384: "nihil enim est quam hoc genus tam discordiosum uitio, tam sociale natura." It almost seems that 18.2 picks up here, that is, where 12.28 left off, with books 13–14 describing the "uitium" of original sin and with books 15–17 describing the intertwined course of the two cities, but with book 18 focusing squarely on the human community as it is, that is, united by a vitiated nature and, as a result, unable to achieve its natural social calling except in continual attempts at subjugation.

13　Ibid., 18.2 (CCSL 48, 593): It is the "uox naturae" which proclaims that subjugation is preferable to annihilation.

14　*ciu*. 18.2 (CCSL 48, 593): "sed inter plurima regna terrarum, in quae terrenae utilitatis uel cupiditatis est diuisa societas (quam ciuitatem mundi huius uniuersali uocabulo nuncupamus), duo regna cernimus longe ceteris prouenisse clariora, assyriorum primum, deinde romanorum."

15　For Augustine's reliance on Eusebius and Jerome, see Lee (2011), 566, and the literature he cites there (n. 10).

16　In the case of Romulus, Augustine comments in *ciu*.18.24 (amplifying the remarks in 3.15, and preparing for those in 22.6) that Cicero regarded the

elevation of Romulus into the ranks of the gods as a very special mark of affection, since it happened not in primitive times of susceptibility to illusion and
ignorance, but in the enlightened times of educated people. This elevation
occurred as the result of Romulus's disappearance during an eclipse of the sun,
a regular eclipse (see 3.15), which was mythologized into a prodigy by its association with the disappearance of Romulus. The story that Romulus was suck-
led by a she-wolf may be true, as a special dispensation of God's providence
(18.22), but it was mythologized as a prodigy that showed Romulus was conceived by Mars (ibid.), and this myth was handed on as tradition such that the
community "drank in this superstition with its mother's milk" (22.6). In other
words, even Cicero had to find a way to put a positive spin on the deification
of Romulus because he could not adequately find a way of praising Rome and
her founding without doing so, and Augustine himself would not be telling the
history of Rome if he did not repeat this myth and offer a way of reading it that
explained its staying power. In a broader sense, since the earthly city is a "city of
demon worship" (18.41), some of the myths intertwined with the histories are
actually based upon events that were sponsored by demons – for example, the
transformation of Diomedes's men into birds, in order to mislead the Greeks
into thinking Diomedes became a god (18.19 and 18.16–17, cf. in general
10.11–12, 16). It is the idolatry of the earthly city that makes it susceptible to
such demonic tricks. The very name of the city of Athens is associated with a
myth which is implicitly repeated every time the city is named, and it is impossible to disentangle myth and history because some of the events involved in
the competition between Athena and Poseidon were actual events initiated by
demons, even though the irrationality of the outcome should have curbed the
credulity of the citizens (18.9). In any event, the point is that Augustine cannot
report the history of the earthly city, in this case Athens, without referring to
the myths in which the history is inextricably interwoven (nor can Varro! – see,
e.g. 18.10–11). The case is similar for Serapis in Egypt (18.5). However, in other
instances, there is no demonic interference, just the credulity of those who are
amazed at the talents or gifts of certain people, as in the case of Phegous in
Greece and Isis in Egypt (18.3), Prometheus and Atlas, Mercury and Minerva
(18.8), Apollo, Bacchus, etc. (18.13). Saturn, though originally a human being,
is enshrined in the national epic, the *Aeneid* (18.15; cf. *Aen.* 8.321–325). "How
should we react to all of these accounts?" – Augustine asks, specifically with
regard to the stories of prodigies worked by demons, but also, I think, with
regard to the whole structure of mythologized history which they support.
"And what can we say, except that we should 'escape from the midst of Babylon'
(18.2, Isa. 48:20), by clinging to the Mediator, advancing by the steps of faith
which 'becomes active in love'" (ibid.; cf. Gal. 5:6). The pilgrimage away from
the credulity caused by the lust for domination is in the love that forms
the Church. Little by little, that love enables the soul to be released from the

attachments causing the credulity, and it allows one to see history truly. In short, it is love that demythologizes history.

17   *ciu.* 22.6, etc.

18   See ibid., 18.13 and 18.24. Such passages only serve to recall the discussions in books 6 and 7 regarding the obscene stage plays and public rituals associated with the cult of the various deities, many of which are mentioned again in book 18.

19   After sinning, Adam and Eve experience the loss of control of their bodies as well as novel, unbidden movements due to lust, which renders them "self-conscious and embarrassed" in Bettenson's (1972) translation of "adtentos" and "confusos," which means one is embarrassed because one is confused – that is, "confounded." Cf. *ciu.* 14.17 (CCSL 48, 440): "And so they recognized they were naked, stripped, that is, of that grace which prevented their bodily nakedness from causing them any embarrassment (*confunderet*)." Later in the same section, we read "proinde confusi inoboedientia carnis suae." Bettenson (1972) translates "confusi" as "embarrassed," which, while not inaccurate, does not quite capture the fact that it indicates the embarrassment that comes from being confused or stymied. "Confounded" seems more appropriate. Augustine is borrowing from the translation of Genesis that he is reading: "Nudi errant, et non confundebantur" (cf. Gen. 2:25, cited at *ciu.* 14.17 [CCSL 48, 439]). See also "confusa" at *ciu.* 14.21 (CCSL 48, 443), where it modifies "libidine" itself, meaning that the lust was jumbled, disordered, confused, and, therefore, compelled them to cover up. The embarrassment arises from confusion and disorder.

20   *ciu.* 14.13 (CCSL 48, 435). Those who are "*sibi placentes*, self-pleasers," are those who "lift up their hearts (*sursum habere cor*)" – referring to the liturgical phrase "*sursum corda*" – "each to himself (*ad se ipsum*)," an act which belongs to "pride (*superbiae*)." Cf. esp. 435, lines 30–32. For the claim that both Eve's and Adam's sins are functions of pride, see 434, lines 3–6.

21   This has already been made clear in book 10.4–6.

22   See *ciu.* 14.11: Adam was not seduced as Eve was; he knew what he was doing was sinful, but he erred "about the kind of judgment that would be passed upon his allegation that 'The woman you gave me as a companion, she gave it to me, and I ate.'" Adam expected himself to be excused for a small sin and Eve to be blamed for the debacle.

23   Cf. *conf.* 1.13.20–21 on pitying and weeping for Dido at the expense of a true assessment of one's own state.

24   This is the primal sin of the Roman Empire, which wishes to hear the account of the merciful God, who "'resists the proud but gives grace to the humble' quoted in its own praise: 'To spare the conquered and beat down the proud,'" thus perverting the worship of God, which is mercy, to its own glory or self-worship. The Roman Empire is one big idol, a false image of true mercy (*ciu.* 1. praef., citing Prov. 3:34 from the LXX [cf. 1 Pet. 5:5 and James 4:6], as well as *Aeneid* 6.853). See Cavadini (2012).

25 After all, how could Adam have sacrificed that to which he has lifted up his heart? It would mean sacrificing his "god." Adam must keep alive his commitment to himself as his own founding principle, as the source of his own coherence, though he has abandoned all coherence in preferring himself to the true God. He must now control the narrative, control the fact that there is no narrative. He must construct a mythological narrative to cloak his destruction of the genuine narrative. He must give the fallen "community" story. This means he must dominate the narrative. His decision to remain with Eve is not a self-sacrificing, tortured descent into a companionship in which he hates to leave Eve alone. That would conflict with everything Augustine has already told us about pride. Nor is it even really a decision – Adam has already made his decision interiorly. He is now free only to sin. He goes with the flow of false alternatives. He has an interest in dominating the spousal community. Eve's interior decision to disobey God has made her vulnerable, but the original sin, one might say, is not finalized until it has corrupted not only human individuals but human community – that is, until Adam decides to take advantage of Eve's having been seduced. Here is the primordial instance of empire. Interestingly enough, it is construed spousally, if one can call something so loveless and cynical as "spousal." We may plausibly imagine that Adam re-configures sex, and the marriage it consummates, to an experience of the pleasure of domination and the corresponding pleasure of submitting to domination. Here is the connection between pornography and empire.

26 *ciu.* 12.22 (CCSL 48, 380): "eo modo uehementius ei commendaretur ipsius societatis unitas uinculumque concordiae, si non tantum inter se naturae similitudine, uerum etiam cognationis affectu homines necterentur." Cf. *ciu.* 14.1 and 14.22.

27 Cf. n. 12 supra.

28 *ciu.* 12.28 (CCSL 48, 384): "nihil enim est quam hoc genus tam discordiosum uitio, tam sociale natura …. in multis concors unitas seruaretur."

29 Ibid., 12.22 (CCSL 48, 380): "quando ne ipsam quidem feminam copulandam uiro sicut ipsum creare illi placuit, sed ex ipso, ut omnino ex homine uno diffunderetur genus humanum."

30 Ibid., 12.23 (CCSL 48, 380).

31 Ibid., 12.28 (CCSL 48, 384): "quod uero femina illi ex eius latere facta est, etiam hic satis significatum est quam cara mariti et uxoris debeat esse coniunctio." Cf. *ciu.* 14.22 (CCSL 48, 444).

32 Ibid., 12.28 (CCSL 48, 384).

33 See, for example, Gregory of Nyssa, *Dialogue on the Soul and the Resurrection,* where Macrina, in her final speech, agrees with Gregory's suggestion that the resurrected body will not have the trappings of mortality, the accretions to the body that are necessary for "sexual intercourse, conception, parturition, impurities, suckling, feeding, evacuation …" etc. For this translation, see Moore and Wilson (1893).

34 *ciu.* 22.17 (CCSL 48, 835), citing Eph. 4:13 and Rom. 8:29.

35 Ibid.

36 Cf. the use of *gratia* at *ciu.* 12.23 (CCSL 48, 380).

37 *ciu.* 22.17 (CCSL 48, 835–836): "ut enim in exordio generis humani de latere uiri dormientis costa detracta femina fieret, christum et ecclesiam tali facto iam tunc prophetari oportebat. sopor quippe ille uiri mors erat christi, cuius exanimis in cruce pendentis latus lancea perforatum est atque inde sanguis et aqua defluxit; quae sacramenta esse nouimus, quibus aedificatur ecclesia."

38 Ibid., 16.2 (CCSL 48, 500): "christum et eius ecclesiam, quae ciuitas dei est … cuius ab initio generis humani non defuit praedicatio."

39 Ibid. (CCSL 48, 500): "inebriatus est, id est passus est, et nudatus est; ibi namque nudata est, id est apparuit, eius infirmitas, de qua dicit apostolus: etsi crucifixus est ex infirmitate. unde idem dicit: infirmum dei fortius est hominibus, et stultum dei sapientius est hominibus."

40 Note the comment of Frye (1971), 178: "One sometimes gets the impression that the audience of Plautus and Terence would have guffawed uproariously all through the Passion."

41 The expression comes from *Enarrationes in Psalmos*, the most famous example being *en. Ps. 30, s.* 2.3. Section 4 of that sermon demonstrates the close connection between the image of bride and the image of body as images for the Church in Augustine's ecclesiology. See also Cameron (1997), and, idem, (2005).

42 See n. 15.

43 *ciu.* 22.17 (CCSL 48, 836): "aedificauit eam in mulierem." Cf. Gen. 2:22.

44 1 Cor. 12:27. Note that, at other places, for example, *s.* 213.7.7, this verse is associated with the sacraments (here, baptism). In *s.* 272 (a brief homily without editorial section divisions), 1 Cor. 10:17 and 12:27 are used together to indicate the forming of the one body through the Eucharist.

45 May we say that seeing the Church is the closest we can come to "seeing" grace in this world?

46 *ciu.* 19.23 (CCSL 47, 694): "nos ipsi sumus" – but note that there is a typographical error in line 182, where "non" is printed in place of "nos."

47 Ibid., 18.29, citing Isa. 52:14–53:12, the fourth "servant song." In this passage, the servant has no outward characteristics that would distinguish him from the wicked, and he is buried with evildoers, as vulnerable as a lamb about to be shorn of its wool (stripped).

48 Ibid. (CCSL 48, 620–621): "ne timeas, quoniam confusa es … quoniam confusionem aeternam obliuisceris et opprobrium uiduitatis tuae non eris memor. quoniam dominus faciens te, dominus sabaoth nomen ei; et qui eruit te, ipse deus israel uniuersae terrae uocabitur." Cf. Isa. 54:1–5.

49 The purification of the Church can be understood as a purification of the way the members of the Church, such as Augustine, speak the word "we." It is easy to oversimplify this process of purification conceptually by thinking of it as a

process of mere separation. The "we" of the Church is purified by eliminating some of those who now say "we" but who will not finally say "we." It's impor- tant to keep in mind that they will be eliminated because, in the end, they will not *want* to say "we" except in the way that the community that is no com- munity, the earthly city, says "we." Of course, a separation will occur, but the purification of the way the Church says "we" is also a purification of the way the elect say it. *Everyone* says "we" with mixed motives, including the elect, who, as much as anyone else, say it out of an interior mixture of motives. They are as "mixed" interiorly as the Church is "mixed" exteriorly, and so, when they say "we," they do not say it perfectly either. The two ways of being "mixed," inte- riorly and exteriorly, are related. In *en. Ps. 99.9*, while commenting on Song of Songs 2:2, "like a lily in the midst of thorns, so is my beloved amid the daugh- ters," Augustine asks who are the daughters and who are the thorns before commenting that the thorns are thorns by their behavior, even though they are also daughters by the sacraments. He goes on to gloss his comment with Ps. 55:12–14 (cf. 54:13–15 LXX) – verses about betrayal by a companion. He notes: "Is there any place to which a Christian can withdraw, to get away from the distress caused by false brethren? Where is a Christian to seek refuge? What is he to do? Should he seek lonely places? Scandals (*scandala*) pursue him there. Is a man or woman who is making progress to seek solitude, where there will be no one at all to put up with (*patiatur*)? But what if such a person was himself impossible to put up with, before he had begun to improve? If he thinks that because he has made some progress he cannot be expected to tolerate anyone else, his very intolerance proves that he has made no progress at all …. Is there nothing in you that anyone else has to bear with? If there really is nothing, I am amazed. But if there is nothing, that means you must have all the more strength to put up with other people …. 'But I can't,' you answer. That means there are things in you that are a trial to other people. 'Bear with one another in love' (cf. Eph. 4:2)." This translation is Boulding's (2003), 20; for the Latin, see CCSL 39, 1398. Augustine goes on to point out that even joining a monastic community will provide no refuge for the one who does not want to say "we" prop- erly – that is, to "bear with one another in love." All of these people one wants to escape from are siblings ("daughters") by the sacraments, and that is the only reliable basis for saying "we." It is also what mediates the purification of "we." The sacramentally defined visible Church is what mediates the purification of the "we" of the church. It cuts against the grain of those – all of "us" – who do not want to "bear with one another in love." The interiorly mixed state of the city of God on pilgrimage in this world is a theme forcefully present in *ciu*. 19.27, where it is the occasion for all of its members to cry out, "forgive us our debts, as we forgive our debtors" (cf. Matt. 6:12). The mixed character of the Church is also the subject of *ciu*. 18.49–51. Both the evil and the good swim inseparably together in the dragnet of the Gospel, to be separated only when the shore is reached (18.49). In the meantime, the good are grieved by the defamation of the Christian name by wrongdoers in the church and the difficulties that heretics create for evangelization. Yet, this grief profits those who grieve, because it issues from a love which makes them hate the thought that the scandal-causing wrongdoers and heretics should perish or hinder the salvation of others. It gives way to consolations of joy at their recovery from error (18.51). In other words, even those heretics who persist in heresy so far as to "part company with the Church (*foras exeuntes*)" (see CCSL 48, 649), and even the gravest evildoers who can be said to "persecute" the Church by their behavior or error, cannot be assumed to be reprobates and must remain the beneficiaries of the love that trains the Church in patience, benevolence, and beneficence.

50 It is undoubtedly true for Augustine that, as Cameron (2012) has brilliantly reminded us, "Christ meets me everywhere" (vi). It is just as likely, or even more likely, however, that we will meet Christ first in the person of his spouse, the Church, and perhaps that is a much more difficult meeting than is meeting him "everywhere," even if that "everywhere" is limited to "everywhere" in scripture (the title of the book comes from *c. Faust.* 12.27). But Augustine's point is that encountering the Church *is* to meet Christ in person, such is the unity of Head and Body in one conjugal flesh! There is no seeing Christ without seeing the spouse, because, without seeing the spouse, we do not see Christ's love which created her as spouse; we experience only our own attempts at feeling righteous, at imagining what the spouse would look like if her identity were based on her (our) merits. Thus, there is no seeing the spouse unless she is seen as Adam should have seen Eve, that is, with the eyes of the Bridegroom. Adam should have acted in accordance with the prophetic sign that he himself, together with Eve, represented. Instead, he invented empire.

51 *ciu.* 15.25 (CCSL 48, 493). In part, this means that scripture narrates historical events, some of which have a mysterious, figurative significance, while the narration as a whole is meant to highlight the figures: "It is only the strings of the lyre, and of other similar musical instruments, that are designed to produce the music; but to effect the result the other components are included in the framework of the instruments. These parts are not struck by the player, but the parts which resonate when struck are connected with them. Similarly, in prophetic history some things are recorded which have no prophetic significance in themselves; but they are there for the significant events to be attached to them, moored to them, as we might say." For this, see *ciu.*16.2 (CCSL 48, 501).

52 This is a point that Augustine repeats not only in the context of commenting on Noah's Ark but also at several points in this section of *ciu.* Scripture prophesies by historical events (17.8), that is, by the way it narrates them. And the result is that we can, for example, recognize in Solomon a foreshadowing of Christ. The reverence of David for the person of Saul, carefully narrated by scripture in such a way that also emphasizes the fact that Saul is David's enemy,

shows that the person of Saul bears a significance that transcends his immediate role in history (17.6).

53   *ciu*. 17.1 (CCSL 48, 551): "ipsa scriptura, quae per ordinem reges eorumque facta et euenta digerens uidetur tamquam historica diligentia rebus gestis occupata esse narrandis, si adiuuante dei spiritu considerata tractetur, uel magis uel certe non minus praenuntiandis futuris quam praeteritis enuntiandis inuenietur intenta."

54   *ciu*. 17.20 (CCSL 48, 589): "canticum canticorum spiritalis quaedam sanctarum est uoluptas mentium in coniugio illius regis et reginae ciuitatis, quod est christus et ecclesia." God's providential guidance of earthly kingdoms is not opposed to the free will of historical agents. In *ciu*. 5.1, Augustine makes the distinction between chance, fate, and providence. And he makes it clear that God's providence is not a disguised version of the myth of fate. After rejecting astrology, he says that God is not, in effect, a higher version of astrology, and that correct belief in him does not mean that he takes the place of the stars in causing human beings to act in certain ways. Instead, God's freedom and God's providence is the reason that there can be any history. Note the dismissal of the various mythological accounts of history, in contrast to the narrative of Israel, in *ciu*. 4.34, the passage that immediately precedes the opening of book 5.

55   Augustine, for example, will take credit for only "varying degrees of success" in his discernment of the typologies. See *ciu*. 16.2 (CCSL 48, 500): "alius alio magis minusue congruenter."

56   I owe a special debt of gratitude to Nancy Cavadini for her help with this chapter. I would also like to thank Patout Burns, Robin Jensen, Gregory Lee, Jim Lee, Cyril O'Regan, John Sehorn, and James Wetzel for helpful comments on an earlier version of this chapter (though any problems that remain are, of course, attributable only to me!). This chapter was finished on February 28, 2013, the last day of the pontificate of His Holiness Pope Benedict XVI, and it is dedicated to him with love and gratitude.

References

Bettenson, Henry, trans. (1972) *Concerning the City of God against the Pagans.* Harmondsworth, Middlesex: Penguin Books (repr. 2003).

Boulding, Maria, O.S.B., trans. (2003) *Expositions on the Psalms 99–120, WSA III/19.* Hyde Park, New York: New City Press.

Cameron, Michael (1997) "Transfiguration: Christology and the Roots of Figurative Exegesis in St. Augustine." In *Studia Patristica 33*, edited by E. A. Livingstone, 40–47. Leuven: Peeters.

Cameron, Michael (2005) "*Totus Christus* and the Psychagogy of Augustine's Sermons." *Augustian Studies* 36: 59–70.

Cameron, Michael (2012) *Christ Meets Me Everywhere: Augustine's Early Figurative Exegesis.* Oxford/New York: Oxford University Press.

Cavadini, John C. (2012) "Ideology and Solidarity in Augustine's *City of God*." In *The Cambridge Companion to Augustine's City of God*, edited by James Wetzel, 93–110. Cambridge: Cambridge University Press.

Frye, Northrop (1971) *Anatomy of Criticism.* Princeton: Princeton University Press.

Lee, Gregory W. (2011) "Republics and their Loves: Rereading *City of God* 19." *Modern Theology* 27: 553–581.

Moore, William and Henry Austin Wilson, trans. (1893) *Select Writings and Letter of Gregory, Bishop of Nyssa.* Nicene and Post-Nicene Fathers 5, edited by Philip Schaff and Henry Wace. Buffalo, NY: Christian Literature Publishing Co.

O'Daly, Gerard (1999) *Augustine's City of God: A Reader's Guide.* Oxford: Clarendon Press.

11

Trinity and Apologetics in the Theology of St. Augustine

I

This chapter aspires to make a modest contribution to the study of the book *De Trinitate* (*trin.*) by St. Augustine, by way of suggestion, though in a somewhat curious way. I hope to clarify some of the issues of intention and character of the *trin.* largely by studying not that work, but another of Augustine's major works, the *City of God* (*ciu.*). Because the largest concentration of patristic theology on the Trinity is in works directed against heretical Christians, such as Tertullian's *Adversus Praxeam*, Athanasius' *Orations*, or Hilary's *De Fide*, and, indeed, in part, Augustine's *trin.*, we have come to think of the Trinity as a subject mainly for intra-Christian theological conversation. We can forget that the Trinity was also a subject taken up in ancient apologetics. One need only recall Justin Martyr's exposition and development of his *Logos* theology in his *First* and *Second Apology* as one of the most brilliant illustrations of how true this is. Justin, on the one hand, wants to show how faith in Christ is, with the philosophers and against pagan mythology, on the side of "reason" or *logos*, and yet he also wants to show, against pagan philosophy, how the doctrine of "Reason" Incarnate does not leave one with a "religion within the limits of pure reason alone," as though "Reason" itself could be fully known apart from Christ. Rather, the Incarnation of the Logos reveals the philosophical reasoning of even someone as great as Socrates as

---

Visioning Augustine, First Edition. John C. Cavadini.
© 2019 John Wiley & Sons Ltd. Published 2019 by John Wiley & Sons Ltd.

merely a "seed" of something whose full stature cannot be imagined apart from Christian faith that "Reason" became Incarnate in Christ, suffered and died for us.[1] Faith in Christ permits a new form of worship, fully rational and demythologized, replacing the sacrificial cults of the gods of the myths, but not reducible to any pagan philosophic practice either, because it involves a true sacrifice of narrower forms of reason, in gratitude for Reason fully revealed as divine self-offering.[2] It is in order to explain this new form of worship, to disprove the charge of atheism, that Justin is ultimately required to explain who, exactly, the Logos is – and that means Trinitarian theology – *en route* to describing the new form of worship which is identical with the Eucharist.

This is no less true as we move forward to the third century, with Origen's *Contra Celsum*, or indeed to the fifth, with Augustine's *ciu.* These, the two most magnificent works of Christian apologetics left to us from the patristic period,[3] both feature significant discussion of the mystery of the Holy Trinity, and within the confines that Justin had already laid out. Origen, for example, needs to show how Christian teaching about the Logos gives Christianity a natural affinity with philosophical wisdom of the past, and yet how Christian belief in the Incarnation of the Logos distinguishes it irrevocably both from pagan mythologies of divine generation and from any philosophy that does not recognize the divine *philanthropia* revealed in Christ.[4] The same double movement observable in Justin is evident here, and we will find that, in Augustine's *ciu.*, the case is no different. An exposition of Trinitarian theology is required to distinguish Christian teaching from myth, and thus align it with the best instincts of philosophic culture, and yet, at the same time, to show that it cannot be derived from the teaching of the pagan philosophers, but rather requires a revision in philosophical thinking and practice. Of course, the detail regarding the Trinity offered in these apologetic discussions is not at the level we would expect in a work that features a treatment of the mystery of the Trinity as its central subject. Still, discussions of the mystery of the Trinity in apologetic contexts are not irrelevant for helping us to understand something of what is at stake for each author in the more focused polemical or systematic treatments where there is shared material, logic, or argument. I believe this is the case both for Origen's Trinitarian teaching and for Augustine's, but here, of course, I will be concentrating on Augustine.

It is especially useful in the present context to remember that the works of the ancient apologists almost always had a mixed audience in mind. The ancient apologies were directed especially at those along the borders of Christian faith, either pagans who had made inquiries or who were regarded as potential prospects for conversion, or Christians who found themselves tempted by the arguments of pagan critics.[5] In such a context, it is probably better to talk about strategies of persuasion, of the use of shared rhetorical convention and philosophical wisdom, to help leverage and secure Christian commitment, rather than to think in terms of the contrast between "natural" and "revealed" theology that has more of a place in later systematic or scholastic theology. Such a contrast belongs to a period when there was no longer an independent and influential pagan culture whose criticisms needed to be answered by leveraging common ground – without at the same time reducing Christian faith to the results of argument or to non-Christian philosophical wisdom. It may surprise us to think that the ancient apologist could have expected to generate some kind of understanding of the Trinity among non-Christians, or that some of the same strategies of persuasion could be addressed both to Christians and non-Christians on such a central Christian dogma as the Trinity. But it may be that our readiness to use such categories as "natural knowledge of God" anachronistically has blinded us to the genius of these ancient strategies of persuasion and clarification, and kept us from learning as much as we can from them.

In any event, I believe something can be gained from looking again at some of the most prominent themes in Augustine's *trin.* from the perspective afforded of a review of those themes as they are present in the *ciu.*, not principally because the texts from the *ciu.* give us more information about what Augustine thought about the Trinity, but because we may learn something from seeing these themes in an overtly apologetic context intended for a mixed audience of those along either side of the border of Christian faith.

Augustine provides an especially likely case for such a study because one finds a considerable amount of overlapping material between the *trin.* and the *ciu.* There is an extensive discussion of the Trinity itself in book 11 of the *ciu.* with significant follow-up in book 12 and preparation in book 10. Both the *trin.* and the *ciu.* have important discussions of mediators, true and false, of the economy of theophany, angelic miracle and demonic prodigy, of prophecy, of true and false worship of God, and of the image of the Trinity in human beings and its "footprints" in all of creation. Augustine himself connects the two treatises by cross-reference of the *ciu.* in the *trin.* (13.12).

However, these discussions, in the respective treatises, are something like inverse images of each other. In the *ciu.*, the focus is on the polemic against polytheistic worship and the Platonic inconsistency in recognizing the true God, but nevertheless supporting the public cults. Discussions of what the true worship of God is, and of biblical teaching on Creation, as well as theophany and miracle, are also featured. These contextualize the discussions of the Trinity and of human beings as created in the (specifically) Trinitarian image of God. In the *trin.*, the situation is reversed. Here, the focus is on the Trinity and on the Trinitarian image of God in human beings, which is the context in which discussion of the other themes comes up. But it is interesting to notice that, though the relative proportion of the treatment topics is vastly different, these topics are present in roughly the same sequence or order in both treatises.[6] There is no reason to think that the logic governing the sequence present in the *ciu.* has been rendered inoperative in the *trin.*, even as some of its potentiality, undeveloped in the *ciu.*, has emerged and developed more fully in the *trin.* in conversation with other Christians, heretical and Nicene. Studying this logic of exposition in the *ciu.* can, I believe, enable us to use what are "minor" themes in the *trin.*, but "major" themes in the *ciu.*, to help us understand better the intention and scope of the *trin.* These themes, because they are in the minor key as it were, have sometimes seemed to be digressive or difficult to relate to the larger whole, and sometimes, even when it is understood they are not digressions, the account offered of their integration seems artificial or stilted.

Why not let Augustine's own logic provide the connections? My thesis is that his logic is more visible in the apologetic treatise, where the doctrine of the Trinity is included as part of a critical effort to distinguish Christian belief and worship from pagan belief and worship, even as it is also part of an appeal to the seeds of reason present in pagan culture (to use Justin's phrase) that can provide some sort of access for critics or inquirers to what Christians actually believe. In the *ciu.*, the doctrine of the Trinity requires and in turn underwrites a cosmology and anthropology that, despite major points of contact or access, are ultimately incommensurate with any of the accounts on offer in pagan imperial culture, because all of these accounts, be they philosophical, political, or mythological, endorse or at least countenance polytheistic worship. The anthropology that is expressed in the doctrine of human beings as bearers of the Trinitarian image of God, and its relation to the doctrine of the Trinity itself, is especially clear in the polemical context of the *City of God* "*Against the Pagans*." There is no reason to suppose that this relation changes in any significant way in the treatise on the Trinity, which developed in roughly the same, long, period. There is also no reason to suppose that the same strategies of persuasion associated with the Trinitarian material in the *ciu.* cannot shed light on Augustine's intention in the *trin.*, or that the mixed audience effect has been so left behind that it does not function at all in the latter text.

In fact, it is notoriously difficult to say who the intended audience of the *trin.* may be. To whom is the treatise directed? It certainly sends mixed messages. Among others, we encounter the "brethren" who ask questions and demand answers from the one whose office as bishop makes him their servant.[7] But Augustine also says he is writing to people, on the other hand, "who do not *hunger and thirst for justice* (Mt. 5:6), but are well fed and have more than enough," who do not seek God beyond the corporeal imaginings (*phantasma*) of their minds.[8] Who are these people? It could be a description of Augustine himself taken from passages in the *Confessions* (*conf.*) describing him before his conversion.[9] And, though he has been "roused by the Holy Spirit" and sees his own deficiencies in the "light of God," he is still prey to such imaginings.[10]

Among other people Augustine explicitly intends to address are unspecified persons who "have contempt for the starting point of faith."[11] Who are they? Could they be, to some extent, anyone who picks up the treatise? From a non-Christian who had perhaps begun to inquire into the faith but left it behind, to a professed believer who may underestimate the "contempt" for simple faith in his or her own heart? Who is it who needs a course of reasoning (*rationem*) to show them how unfit they are to see God, and so persuade them to "return" to "the starting point of faith"?[12] Further, is the audience made up of those who have yet to be persuaded of how much God loves us? Or those who are so persuaded?[13] And who would belong to either group? Could Augustine even have in mind anyone who thinks "they can purify themselves for contemplating God and cleaving to him by their own power" (4.20)? And if so, would these only be pagan philosophers, people like Porphyry, or could this be a tendency hidden in even some of the most zealous Christian seekers? Unspecified "Arians" are mentioned (5.4, 6.,1 along with Arius himself, 6.10) and "Eunomius" and his followers (15.38) – are these also addressed? If so, it cannot be taken as any kind of determinative description of the audience for whom this is intended. The sheer brilliance and hard work required to clarify, after centuries of study, some of the polemical contexts out of which portions of the argument arise show, in a way, how much the treatise is rhetorically constructed to elude a precise designation of the addressee, to be, in effect, one step removed from the particular contexts which may have given rise to strands of its thought.[14]

All in all, Augustine's studied reticence to declare a particular, specific audience as his addressee has the effect of highlighting all us "readers"[15] as a collection of people who share in common the need for conversion of some sort, loosely speaking, on either side of the border of Christian faith in the face of the "difficulty" of the task of seeking God. We are all dwarfed by this difficulty – and I say "we" advisedly because Augustine writes intentionally with future readers[16] in mind who may be seeking God and yet know nothing of the specific contexts in which some of the arguments were generated.

Could this indeterminacy of address be a more significant dimension of the treatise than hitherto realized? In its own way, it is a function of the greatness of the mystery of God which Augustine has allowed to pervade the text. The indeterminacy of address in a way represents the purity of the "light of God" in which we are all to learn to see ourselves better. Before the difficulty of the mystery of God, it is the great need for "conversion" that any of us has, on either side of the border of Christian faith, that is emphasized. This discourages triumphalism even as it does not relativize the Christian proclamation which defines the very greatness and uniqueness of the mystery of God in the first place. No reader is allowed to think that the treatise points to someone else, some audience well-defined by Augustine, and not him or herself, believer or non-believer.

Perhaps the reader will indulge a somewhat arresting analogy. In "The Iliad, or the Poem of Force," Simone Weil suggests that the greatness of the *Iliad* is to be found in the "extraordinary sense of equity which breathes through the *Iliad*," and makes it difficult to know which side, if any, is favored, Greek or Trojan. There is no triumphalism.

> Nothing precious is scorned, whether or not death is its destiny; everyone's unhappiness is laid bare without dissimulation or disdain; no man is set above or below the condition common to all men.

What accomplishes this is a "note of incurable bitterness that continually makes itself heard, though often only a single word marks its presence," a bitterness "that proceeds from tenderness and that spreads over the whole human race, impartial as sunlight." This marks the greatness and the uniqueness of the *Iliad*: "Such is the spirit of the only true epic the Occident possesses."[17] Hill (1991), one of the persons of our time most intimately and most affectionately acquainted with Augustine's *trin.*, makes a similar judgment when he comes to identify its successors: "[Augustine] did not, unfortunately, have any real successors" despite the dependence that many later and wonderfully brilliant theologians had on his text.[18] Could this be related to the "light" of God's greatness and truth that the author allows to "spread" over the whole treatise, "impartial as sunlight," gently revealing the need for conversion, for seeking, indeed for begging, in all of us, the author included? The work indeed "scorns nothing precious," using it, instead, to leverage an awareness of the greatness of the mystery of God, and yet never letting any such awareness pass as a settled achievement that can stand up and call attention to itself in the light of that mystery. Before that mystery, we are all cast simply as "human beings who seek God" (2.1). However we answer this question, and whatever we think of this analogy, we have perhaps done enough to justify the approach taken, in an experimental fashion, in the present chapter.

II

The doctrine of the Trinity is discussed explicitly and most fully in *ciu.* book 11, but book 10 provides a thorough preparation for this discussion in its explanation of the person of the Mediator. In a way, this is already a full-blown discussion of the Trinity, since Augustine has to make it clear that the true Mediator is, *in the form of God*, one God with the Father,[19] in order to differentiate him from the various kinds of angelic or daimonic mediators claimed by polytheist cults that are endorsed even by Platonist philosophers. The various prodigies and theophanies revealed in Scripture are part of an angelic economy of mediation that points to and is fulfilled in the revelation and true worship of the one Mediator the angels themselves worship.[20] As already noted, it is interesting that this is roughly the same structure that we find in the *trin.*, where, before the main discussion of the doctrine of the Trinity in itself and the proper language to use in expressing the Trinitarian relations in books 5–7, there is an extensive discussion of theophany and mediation. As in the *ciu.*, this discussion already is, in effect, a discussion of the Trinity because of the need to differentiate the true and final Mediation from both earlier anticipations and false mediation of the demons, supported by philosophers under the guise of theurgy.[21] Discussion of the economy of salvation is, in both texts, already Trinitarian, and precedes any discussion of the doctrine of the Trinity in itself. Book 10 is the culmination of the first "half" of the *ciu.*, in which Augustine undertakes to demonstrate that the gods of the pagan pantheon are not to be worshipped either for temporal benefits (books 1–5) or for spiritual or eternal benefits (books 6–10).[22] Book 10 is the conclusion more particularly of a discussion begun in book 8, where Augustine first takes up what he always regarded as the most glaring inconsistency in Platonic theology, namely, that, although they knew the one true God, they nevertheless defended the polytheistic practice of worshipping many gods, a concern that goes all the way back to Justin and ultimately to St. Paul. Exposition of this inconsistency is very frequently accomplished with the help of Rom. 1:19–22, as at *ciu.* 8.10.[23] Because they teach that there is one God who made heaven and earth,[24] the Platonists are the philosophers with whom Augustine has chosen to discuss the question of the second five books of the first part of the treatise, namely, "whether, for the sake of happiness which is to come after death, sacred rites are to be performed for the one God or for many."[25] They are targeted for discussion because they "have held, concerning the true God, that He is the author of all created things, the light by which things are known, and the good for the sake of which things are done,"[26] corresponding to the triune character of philosophy in physics, logic, and ethics, which Plato brought together for the first time,[27] because he had discovered, either from reading Scripture (see Section 8.11), or *being understood from the things which are made* (Rom. 1 :20), God as the "First Principle of things (*rerum principium*), which was not itself made and by which all things were made,"[28] the light of our minds, by which we learn all things,[29] and the true and highest good:

> But Plato says that the true and highest good is God, and he therefore wishes the philosopher to be a lover of God; for philosophy aims at the happy life, and he who loves God is happy in the enjoyment of God.[30]

After naming all those, from Aristotle to Plotinus, Iamblichus, Porphyry, and Apuleius, who can assent to these ideas, he notes, "Yet all these, and others who were of the same school, and, indeed Plato himself, held that sacred rites should be performed in honor of many gods."[31] As he proceeds with his analysis of Platonic discussions of theurgy and the polytheistic cult, he is aware that there are various degrees of endorsement of these practices, but what is most glaring to Augustine is the fundamental inconsistency that seems to cleave Platonic thinking in two, as a kind of late antique version of what Sartre was later to call "bad faith."

Augustine's most sophisticated opponent, as he sees it, is Porphyry, whose position Augustine begins to engage at *ciu.* 10.9, and who continues to occupy Augustine's attention for the rest of book 10. Porphyry does endorse theurgic sacrifice, but in a hesitating, tentative way, according to Augustine, as helpful in purifying the "spiritual" part of the soul, by which images of corporeal things can be seen, though not for purifying the higher, "intellectual" part of the soul. Theurgy thus enables the soul to see the gods of light, but not to make the last stage of the return to the one God.[32] Porphyry seemed to have believed that philosophers need not engage in theurgy, because they do not have need of the purification it can offer. To lesser souls, theurgy can offer a purification which is beneficial, even if not the ultimate purification afforded by the practice of philosophy. Not even sacrifices offered to the sun and the moon, conceived of as high and good gods, can afford that, and so human beings are not ultimately purified by sacrifices offered to any of the gods, since the sun and the moon would be the highest.[33] They are purified, instead, by the *principia*, or principles. "And," says Augustine:

... we know what he, as a Platonist, means by the *principia*. For he here refers us to God the Father and God the Son, Whom he calls in Greek the Intellect or Mind of the Father.[34]

The Platonists seem to have some kind of natural knowledge, as we might call it, of the Trinity, that includes even the Holy Spirit in some way:

> Of the Holy Spirit, however, he says nothing, or nothing clearly; for I do not understand what he means when he speaks of some other being holding an intermediate place between these two (*quem alium dicat horum medium*).

He thinks Plotinus' teaching is clearer:

> For if, like Plotinus, when the latter is discussing the three principal substances (*de tribus principalibus substantiis*), Porphyry had wished us to understand this third as being the soul of nature (*animae naturam*), he surely would not have given it a place intermediate between these two: that is, between the Father and the Son .... No doubt he spoke as he was able or as he wished. We, however, say that the Holy Spirit is the spirit not of the Father only, nor of the Son only, but of both.[35]

Augustine goes on to note that philosophers can use words as they please, "but we are obliged by religious duty to speak according to a fixed rule, lest verbal licence beget impious opinions concerning the matters which our words signify."[36] Augustine next introduces the proper precision to be observed when speaking of the Trinity, in a passage reminiscent of the *trin.*:

> When we speak of God, therefore, we do not say that there are two or three *principia*; nor are we at liberty to say that there are two or three gods. Speaking of each – of the Father, the Son, and the Holy Spirit – we confess that each individually is God; but we do not say, as the heretical followers of Sabellius say, that the Father is the same as the Son, and that the Holy Spirit is the same as the Father and the Son. Rather, we say that the Father is the Father of the Son, and that the Son is the Son of the Father, and that the Holy Spirit is the spirit of both the Father and the Son, but is neither Father nor Son. It was then truly said that only by a *principium* can a man be cleansed; but the Platonists are incorrect in speaking of *principia* in the plural (*pluraliter*).[37]

But this is not merely a technical or an innocent mistake. It is a distortion that proceeds from the endorsement of polytheistic worship:

> Porphyry, however, was in subjection to envious powers. He was ashamed of them, but he was too much in awe of them to speak freely against them. And so he refused to understand that the Lord Christ is the *Principium* by Whose incarnation we are cleansed. Indeed, Porphyry held Him in contempt because of the flesh He took in order to become a sacrifice for our cleansing. It was because of his pride that Porphyry did not understand this great mystery (*magnum ... sacramentum*).[38]

But not to understand this great *sacramentum* is also, then, not to understand the Trinity. By refusing to recognize Christ "as the *Principium*," Porphyry misapprehends the Trinity. Later, using a Greek expression, Augustine repeats the claim that Porphyry recognizes ultimate purification can come only from what he calls the "*patrikos nous*," that is, Augustine adds, "the mind or intellect of the Father, which is conscious of the Father's will."[39] But Porphyry misunderstands the Trinity because he "does not believe this is Christ." The reason, again, is pride:

> [Y]ou despise Him because of the body that He received from a woman, and because of the shame of the Cross. Your exalted wisdom (*excelsam sapientiam*) rejects such lowly and abject things, and looks to higher regions (*de superioribus*).[40]

Passages such as this one are sometimes read as though Porphyry's mistake is merely that he did not see the Incarnation, that is, that the Son was Incarnate in Christ – as though he had an accurate understanding of the Trinity, but just did not see the economy. Clearly this is an incorrect interpretation of the passage. He can "see" the Son, the *patrikos nous*, but he just cannot accept that He/It would become Incarnate. But, to the contrary, not "believing" that this Mind or Intellect is Christ, is not to "see" this Mind correctly. It is to see something, true, but only in a distant and shadowy way:

> You proclaim the Father and His Son, Whom you call the intellect or mind of the Father, and between these two you place a third, by Whom we take it that you mean the Holy Spirit; and, as is your

custom (*more vestro*), you call these three gods (*tres deos*). Thus far, though your use of words is incorrect, you do to some extent see as it were a kind of shadowy image of what we should strive towards (*qual-itercumque et quasi per quaedam tenuis imaginationis umbracula, quo niten-dum sit*). You do not, however, wish to acknowledge (*agnoscere*) the incarnation of the immutable Son of God, by which we are saved and through which we are able to come to the things we believe or in some small way understand. You see after a fashion (*utcumque*), although at a distance, and with clouded vision (*etsi de longinquo, etsi acie cali-gante*), the country in which we should abide; but you do not hold fast to the way that leads to it.[41]

There is perhaps no more familiar comparison in the Augustinian analysis of Platonic theology than that the Platonists see the fatherland at a distance and yet do not embrace the way to get there. Here, this is specifically applied to the Trinity. Passages like this are sometimes interpreted to mean that Platonists have a kind of natural knowledge of the Trinity, as I have already noted, and that all they really lack is acceptance of the way there. But, while partially correct, in that the Platonists indeed do see the "fatherland" but do not hold to the way there, this view does not fully take into account Augustine's claim that, when it comes to the Trinity, what the Platonists see is distorted.[42] How could it be anything different? If they do not contemplate in faith "the grace of God in Jesus Christ our Lord, and that incarnation of His, by which He took on the soul and body of a man! … the supreme example of grace," if they do not see that "the only Son of God, remaining immutable in Himself, put on humanity and bestowed upon mankind the Spirit of His Love through the mediation of a Man,"[43] then they do not *see* the Trinity. If one rejects the Mediation, one is rejecting the true Trinity and cannot see the kind of God the real God is. The most essential features of God's gracious action in mercy are rejected, and so are the most essential features of God as Trinity which make such a Mediation possible. From such a "distance" as they are observing, pridefully refusing the nearness of God in the Incarnation, the Platonists see a plurality of *principia* without evident, precise relation. They see "gods," not "God," "substances" and not the one substance of the irreducible Three. There is indeed some kind of knowledge of the Trinity available to the philosophers, though it is difficult to know if it should be called "natural knowledge" or some kind of awareness through grace,[44] yet it is corrupted and distorted by pride. Far from serving any kind of salvific purpose, it configures the philosophers to the condemnation issued by Paul in Rom. 1:19–21.

Further, the Platonist rejection of the humility of God in the Incarnation means not simply the rejection of a "way" that is somehow separate or separable from God, but a rejection of God Himself, a rejection of the Trinity, one of whose consubstantial and equal persons, defined by immutable relation to the Father, *is* the way. Rejecting the way is rejecting God, refusing to worship Him, the true Trinity. Rejecting the Mediator is rejecting, not one *principium* out of three, but *the Principium*, God Himself. Thus, their distant and distorted vision is not the result of a neutral misfortune, as though these virtuous and noble philosophical observers just happen by bad luck to be a little too far away to both see and possess what they see. The distant and distorted image represents a vested interest in distance and so in distortion – the vested interest which Augustine always calls "pride." (There is really no seeing past this "pride" to speculate what may or may not have been "naturally" visible without it, since such speculation is itself subject to prideful distortion.)

For Augustine, the case of Porphyry is perhaps the clearest and most poignant case, for, as Augustine analyzes it, Porphyry does see the need for grace. One could imagine that awareness of distance could take the form of an awareness of a need for something that one cannot supply oneself. Porphyry loved the truth enough to correct Plato where he thought Plato was in error (10.30), and he loved it enough to try to correct the errors of some of the theurgists (Anebo, 10.11). If Porphyry has "natural knowledge" of anything that is accurate and true, it is natural knowledge of the lack and the need implied in awareness of something you want that is distant. Porphyry seems to see that this distance requires assistance:

> You confess that there is such a thing as grace, however; for you say that it has been granted only to a few to reach God by the power of their intelligence. You do not say, "It has pleased only a few," or "Only a few have wished," but "It has been granted only to a few." Beyond doubt, then, you acknowledge the grace of God, not the sufficiency of man (10.29).

And yet Porphyry rejects the grace when it is offered because it conflicts with his own Platonic teaching about bodies, which makes the Word's humble acceptance of a body appear too humiliating for philosophical wisdom to accept (10.29). It reveals the prideful, vested interest of the philosophers in wanting to be "wise and strong in themselves" (10.28), rejecting such "lowly and abject things" as the Cross, that is, rejecting the nearness of God that grace actually offers. Invested in the distance of God from themselves, a distance which represents the attainment they have yet to achieve, they are coarsened by this refusal, made insensitive to the gratitude they owe to God for the grace even of this distant knowledge. This refusal enables them to continue to claim to be "wise" *instead of glorifying God and giving thanks*, instead, that is, of worshipping God. By refusing to accept the "medicine" that the simple Christian does not "blush" to accept, refusing to build on the "gift" that God has given them and the indications they should have had of Him from philosophy itself (10.29), the Platonist philosophers "are not healed; rather, they fall into a still more grievous affliction,"[45] and that seems to be the inability even to imagine that the true God can be worshipped, that there could be some kind of cult of this God, and one available to everyone. Porphyry bemoans the lack of a "universal" way for salvation, insensitive to the love and mercy that is being lavished on the world from the Cross, dividing salvation up between those who can purify themselves, and those who must resort to the deceptive consolations of the demons through theurgy. Philosophy corrupted by pride believes it can purify itself by its own strength; "worship" is for those who are not strong enough to purify themselves, and must have recourse to whatever ambiguous help the "gods" can offer by way of theurgy.

And at issue, as noted, is indeed the refusal to worship God. What, then, exactly is worship? Augustine began to argue early in book 10 that what uniquely characterizes worship is sacrifice.[46] The only way to worship God is through sacrifice, and, for a rational creature – even the unfallen angels, who, together with holy men and women, are "the one City of God, which is His living sacrifice and His living temple"[47] – that means not simply offering sacrifices, but *being* a sacrifice.[48] If the philosophical rejection of the Mediator entails the rejection of the true worship of God, then, for the philosopher himself, this also entails a refusal to offer himself as a sacrifice. The philosopher can have his cleansing on his own, so sacrifice is not necessary for him. His philosophical achievement in the knowledge that there is only one true God also leads him, if he is honest as Porphyry, to understand that the mythological gods are only demons, and that sacrifices to them are ineffectual for salvation, and any benefit they may confer is at best dubious, given the source. Yet, the desire to be called "wise" as an end in itself nevertheless coarsens one with *curiositas* so that one can learn and then seem to be an "expert" in the theurgic arts, pleasing those who have the same vice of *curiositas* or hoping to arouse it in others.[49] The class of those who cannot purify themselves by philosophy are thus established by the pride and *curiositas* of the philosophers as a lower class of people, encouraged to indulge in theurgy, to render sacrifice to beings whom the philosophers know are not truly divine and who actually accept sacrifice only because they are prideful and know it is due to the one true God alone:

> Those deceitful and proud spirits who demand such sacrifice for themselves do so for no other reason than that they know it to be due to the true God ....They delight not in the smoke of carcasses, but in deceiving and subjecting to themselves the soul of the suppliant whom they hinder from drawing near to the true God, preventing him from offering himself as a sacrifice to God by inducing him to sacrifice to other gods.[50]

They are thus prevented from offering themselves as a sacrifice to God, which would, presumably, enable them to see through the whole charade and say, "Where is the wise? Where is the scribe? ... the foolishness of God is wiser than men; and the weakness of God is stronger than men" (1 Cor. 1:20ff, at 10:28).

For Augustine, the Platonic endorsement of the economy of polytheistic sacrifice, all the while knowing the one true God, amounts to a systemic displacement of sacrifice from one's person, that of the philosopher and that of the simpler seeker, onto an exterior economy of sacrifice that has nothing to do with offering oneself but rather with refusing to offer oneself. The Psalmist recommends that the goal of human life be to "draw near to God" (Ps. 73:28).[51] But the Platonists do not have a cult for the one true God that is other than philosophy itself. For the few, there is this way of attainment by one's own power; for the many, there is an authoritative recommendation, at least, to the economy of sacrifice to the so-called gods (10.27). These so-called gods are actually demons, for no good "angel" or "god" would ever accept sacrifice, which they know is due only to God. Thus, Platonic spirituality, characterized by a fundamental inconsistency, boils down to the delivery of philosophy into an economy of pride, manifested in a sacramental system of deflection of sacrifice from oneself, such that one is never the sacrifice, but rather the master of the economy of sacrifice. Philosophical achievement liberates one from the necessity of sacrifice, and the philosopher is rewarded with vision: you can indeed begin to see a God, one who is enough like the real God to justify arrogating to oneself, for one's philosophical achievement, the title "wise," but a "god" who does not relate to sacrifice at all, but to achievement and its reward, glory. This is a God who must remain distant, whose distorted vision is an image of the distortion in the philosopher's own soul, and whose threeness could be seen itself as a distance to travel and so something to attain, and so the spirituality of attainment is written right into the Godhead. It is a convenient distortion of the real Trinity.[52]

From this perspective, what Christ brings is not simply "faith," as a kind of stopgap that helps us perform the purification we should have been able to do ourselves, until we can finally get strong enough to do it ourselves, but rather the end of the economy of attainment and displacement. Christ brings true worship. That is his most important work. Instead of displacing sacrifice away from himself, he becomes a sacrifice:

> Hence, the true Mediator, the man Jesus Christ, became the Mediator between God and man by taking the form of a servant. In the form of God, He receives sacrifice together with the Father, with Whom He is one God. In the form of a servant, however, He chose to be a sacrifice Himself, rather than to receive it, so that not even in this case might anyone have reason to think that sacrifice is to be offered to a creature, no matter of what kind. Thus, He is both the priest who offers and the sacrifice which is offered.[53]

Augustine has already thoroughly explained that the true sacrifice, the "interior" sacrifice, or sacrifice of oneself, is not self-destruction, but is any "work of mercy" or "act of compassion" performed for God alone and with no ulterior motive, seemingly for nothing.[54] Only someone fully equal to God, himself God, however, could have no possible ulterior motive, since God needs nothing to increase His happiness. Thus, the sacrifice of the Mediator is the truest possible "work of mercy" or "act of compassion," and hence worship. It makes true worship possible again for everyone through their participation in this one true sacrifice. That participation occurs through the sacramental economy by which the Mediator forms the Church – in particular, the Eucharist. Continuing the passage cited earlier:

> And He intended that the daily sacrifice of the Church should be the sacrament of this *res* [i.e. of Christ's being both priest and oblation]. For the Church, being the Body of which He is the Head, is taught to offer herself through Him.[55]

It would be a mistake to take a sentence like this as offering a fully articulated theory of sacramental causation such as we find in Thomas Aquinas, and yet it is also a mistake to see in the Eucharistic economy simply an exterior sign of something that takes place essentially on the "inside," with no essential relation to the sign. Again:

> This is the sacrifice of Christians: *We, being many, are one body in Christ* (Rom. 12:4). And this also, as the faithful know, is the sacrifice which the Church continually celebrates in the sacrament of the altar, by which it is shown to the Church that she herself is offered in the offering that she makes to God.[56]

No theory of sacramental causation is offered, but that does not mean that some kind of causation is not implied here, for example, in the word "in" (*in ea re*). The Church is shown that she herself is offered *in* what she is offering, and in that offering the unity of the Church is effected. The visible Church is, in that sense, a sacrament itself, since it is a *societas* defined by no other demarcation except Christ's compassion, His mercy, His sacrifice, which can only be present "mysteriously," "sacramentally," and not in an individual spiritual achievement, even if that is given the name "faith." Faith is important, true, but it is important because it enables one to participate in the true sacrifice of Christ by being formed Eucharistically into the unity of the Church, by being formed into one Body, through and in the Eucharist. As Augustine says in book 4 of the *trin.*, in a passage which could equally have come from the *ciu.*, the devil has very few followers left nowadays, as more and more people leave behind his sacred rites, and "acknowledge the price paid for them [his just blood unjustly shed, 4.17], and drink it with devout humility, and putting all their trust in it forsake their enemy."[57] "Acknowledging the price paid for us" entails "drinking it." In drinking, one puts all one's trust (*fiducia*) in this price and leaves the "enemy" behind along with his false economy of achievement and displacement. Being formed ever more perfectly into the compassion of Christ, one is formed ever more fully into unity with all the members of the one Body, reformed away from the world, *transformed in the renewing of our mind*, presenting ever more completely our bodies and ourselves as a living sacrifice.[58] In the Eucharist, the exterior economy of sacrifice is thus recovered from the "bad faith" of the Platonist split of an interior spiritual economy of attainment from an exterior economy of displacement, and reconnected to the one economy of true worship that permits and actually *is* true purification or transformation. Not only does this not involve fleeing from the body, it involves the formation of a new Body, the Body of Christ, which will persist into eternity.[59] "Drawing near" or "cleaving" to God is our good, according to the Psalm – and Plato too! – but this means sharing in the love of God through the Holy Spirit, in fellowship with all others who draw near to God, and so, in the practice of true worship, we come to be aware of the Trinitarian economy as an economy of love, gratitude, and thanksgiving for the good example of others[60] and for the hand of compassion that was stretched out to us.[61] It is in fulfilling the requirements of true worship from Rom. 1:20, "glorifying God and *giving thanks*," that we come to know that the true Trinity is beyond the limited vision attained in Platonic practice.

III

Moving into book 11 of the *ciu.*, the first book of the second part of the treatise, we encounter a sustained treatment of the doctrine of creation based on the account given in the first chapter of Genesis, *en route* to explaining the "origin, progress and merited end of the two cities."[62] In the *ciu.*, as elsewhere in Augustine, the seventh day of God's rest is interpreted as indicating the purpose of creation, and in particular that of human beings. God's "rest" is the attainment of creation to its ultimate end; we human beings "become" God's rest in an eternal Sabbath of praise, that is, of worship.[63] It is only from the perspective of true worship now, then, that we can truly see the purpose and character of creation.

Augustine reminds us right at the outset of book 11 that the main issue at stake in the difference between the two cities is, in fact, the issue of the true worship of God:

> The citizens of the earthly city prefer their own gods to the Founder of this holy city, for they do not know that he is the God of gods. Not of false gods, however ... who seek divine honors from their misguided subjects. Rather, He is the God of pious and holy gods, who take delight rather in submitting themselves to One than in subjecting many to themselves, and in worshipping God than in being worshipped in place of God.[64]

In terms of the argument at this point in the *ciu.*, Augustine has established that we can see the true Trinity only from the perspective of true worship. Since this Trinity is the One Creator, it is also only from that perspective of true worship that we can understand creation. We can understand that true creative activity is an act of the Trinity and has a Trinitarian structure. We can see that all of creation bears some trace of its origin in the Trinitarian creative act, and we can see that we ourselves, human beings, in particular, have been created in the image of the Trinity. This cannot be fully known apart from revelation, or fully seen apart from the perspective of true worship in which the image is reformed and we are gradually transformed into God's "rest." Such is the logic that we find reproduced in the *trin.*, though here in the *ciu.* it is very compressed, as it is in service of the larger project of discussion of the origin and ends of the two cities. Still, one moves from a consideration of the economy of salvation, as a series of theophanies and signs pointing to the coming of the Mediator, with concomitant clarification of Trinitarian doctrine, and then to the establishment of true worship in the sacrifice of the true Mediator. The discussion moves on to a more technical articulation of the Trinity in itself. It is the Eucharistic awareness of God, already implicit in the act of *giving glory* and *thanks* that is Eucharistic worship, which enables and requires this technical precision, and grows into a concomitant awareness of oneself as a creature and, indeed, image.[65] From the perspective of revelation and true worship, we are now able truly to *glorify God* (Rom. 1:21) and so to see Him as Creator, and ourselves as creatures, in a way that leaves behind all the strategies of alienation and displacement of sacrifice represented at their most sophisticated by Platonism and, on a lower level, by the pagan cults underwritten by the philosophers.

What begins to emerge from the perspective of true worship is that Platonism by contrast has, or at least underwrites, a "cloudy vision" not only of God the Creator, but of His act of creation. We have already noted earlier that, in book 8, Augustine invokes a considerable degree of common ground with the Platonists, in which the doctrine of creation is especially featured. In book 11, where Augustine is discussing the creation of the angels, he is able to use that common ground effectively to argue that all created natures are good, against the position of the Manichees. But as the discussion is continued into book 12, where the creation specifically of human beings is the subject, questions arise. The discussion of creation concludes amidst remarks such as the following:

> There are, however, those who believe, with their master Plato, that all mortal creatures – among whom man holds the pre-eminent place, akin to the gods themselves – were created not by that supreme God by Whom the world was made, but by other, lesser gods, created by Him and acting with His permission or at His command [see *Timaeus* 41c]. If these persons could only be rid of the superstition which causes them to seek to justify the offering of rites and sacrifices to such gods as though they were their creators, they would also easily shake off the error of this opinion.[66]

The primary error is cultic and in the order of worship. The truth is that these "gods," or angels, themselves "gratefully ascribe their own existence to the same God,"[67] and this means desiring not our worship, but to be formed with us into a living sacrifice of praise.[68] This means also refusing to agree that an angel, instead of God, is the creator of our bodies, such that the body becomes not truly part of God's intention for human beings, but a kind of "prison," and these so-called creators actually "jailors," "forgers of shackles and chains." Here is the compromise with myth that philosophy, devoid of true worship, is willing to make.

Let the Platonists therefore either desist from threatening us with our bodies as the punishment of our souls, or cease from preaching that we are to worship as gods those whose work upon us they exhort us to flee and evade by all means in our power.[69]

The Platonic ambivalence about the body translates into a disfigurement of the soul as it is encouraged to engage in worship almost as an act of hatred of ourselves as embodied creatures, since the body is the most obvious impediment to the technology of spiritual attainment.

But the order of creation as it came from the hand of God is not an order of unfreedom or shackling, but an order of freedom, that has its origin in the absolutely mysterious freedom of God, who creates not out of necessity or through any non-divine intermediary, but in his Word, co-equal to Himself. This is the same extraordinary and unimaginable freedom we see in the choice of the Word to empty himself and become, himself, a sacrifice. In true worship, we see the world from the perspective of this freedom, unconstrained and acting only out of goodness. Augustine pictures us asking, of any created reality, "Who made it? By what means did He make it? And, Why did He make it?" – with the answer:

> It is the Father of the Word Who said, Let it be. And that which was made when He spoke was beyond doubt made by means of the Word. Again, when it is said, "God saw that it was good," it is thereby sufficiently signified that God made what He made not from any necessity, not because He had need of any benefit, but simply from His own goodness: that is, so that it might be good .... And if this goodness is rightly understood to be the Holy Spirit, then the whole Trinity is revealed to us in the works of God.[70]

We see the world, the whole world including the physical reality, marked by the sign of this mysterious freedom beyond which one cannot find a cause or a rationale.

> As we run over all the works which He has established in a wonderful stability, let us consider His footprints (*vestigia*), as it were, more deeply impressed in one place and more lightly in another, but distinct even in those things which are below us.[71]

Even physical, inanimate reality bears the "footprints" of its creation in freedom and for freedom, for, in their measure, number, and weight, there is something that is truly itself and not something else, truly something, and, in its weight, a kind of love that is a complete self-expression for this kind of thing. Though not an "image" of God, it is still marked by the "big bang" of its origin in the loving freedom of the Trinity.

So much the more does the human being, made, Scripture says, in God's image, bear these marks. The image is an image because it is the lineaments of a truly created freedom, free not by analogy but, actually, in its ability to exist, to understand, and to love, and yet it is still an image, not equal to God. It has existence, but is not self-existent or the author of its own nature.

> If we were the authors of our own nature (*natura*), we should have generated our own wisdom (*sapientiam*) also, and should not require to reach it by teaching (*doctrina*); that is, by learning it from elsewhere. Our love (*amor*), too, going forth from ourselves and returning to ourselves, would be enough to make our lives blessed, and would need to enjoy no other good. But now, since our nature has God as the author (*auctorem*) of its being, we must beyond doubt have Him as our teacher (*doctorem*), that we may be truly wise; and Him also to bestow spiritual sweetness (*suavitatis intimae*) upon us, that we may be blessed indeed.[72]

Only a Trinitarian account of God generates an irreducible account of human freedom, one that does not fragment into pre-philosophic or extraphilosophic myth on the one hand, or into philosophical cloudiness on the other. The image is a sort of needy correspondence, a freedom whose freedom is an "image" of an unimaginably greater freedom and love that guarantees it as free, and only in relation to which (really, to Whom!) this freedom is actually available and actualized. This is created rather than uncreated freedom, the soul requiring God to be free as God is, and the rest of creation bears the marks of this "need," of the dependence of created freedom on the uncreated. The soul, as "image":

> ... is not equal to God; indeed it is very far removed from Him; for it is neither co-eternal with Him, nor, to express the whole matter briefly, is it of the same substance as God. It is, however, nearer to God in nature than anything else made by Him, even though it still requires to be reformed and perfected in order to be a still closer likeness.[73]

We have already seen that this re-formation is accomplished in true worship, in the participation in the greatest free act imaginable, the compassionate choice of the Word to be made flesh and to justify us by His blood as members of the one Body. The human being becomes more and more "like" God, the more it is formed and renewed in the compassion and mercy of the Redeemer, that is, in His sacrifice, and this is to become freer and freer. The image perfected is the "just man" whose justice is a function not of narrow human devising but of the mercy of God revealed in Christ.

IV

As noted, we can see, in this sequence of books 8–12 in the *ciu.*, roughly the same progression of topics as in the *trin.*, from the examination of the economy of theophany and mediation in *trin.* books 1–4, itself already a clarification of Trinitarian language, but leading to an even more precise focus on the clarification of Trinitarian language in light of this economy in books 5–7, to the contemplation of the Trinity as Creator and the creation as stamped by the irreducible mystery of freedom that is the Trinity, including most especially the image of God which is in human beings. If the *trin.* re-balances the detail and the focus, still, the logical interconnection, and even, in a rough way, the sequence of the same topics in the *ciu.*, are not jettisoned.[74] The basic logic is that the doctrine of the Trinity properly articulated makes possible a complete doctrine of creation. This includes a doctrine of the human creature that emphasizes freedom in mercy and compassion, and a necessary course of growth and renewal in mercy and compassion that is our growth in freedom. This occurs in true worship, which binds us into the communion of the one Body. The Eucharistic sacrifice is, in fact, ordered toward communion with other human beings, such that growth in freedom is growth in communion and growth in communion is growth in freedom.

What does this say for the interpretation of the *trin.*? For example, what of the detailed, lengthy examination of the interior "image" of God that we find discussed in books 8–10 and 14–15? Is this a solipsistic, ultrainteriorized monadic spirituality that eschews the economy and seeks, in a way, to rise above it?[75] It is rather an attempt to show the reader "something they cannot deny,"[76] something they can become aware of independent of their own possible assent to Christian faith, namely, themselves remembering, understanding and loving, the indelible mark of the Trinitarian creator on all of us, and, in a different way, even on our bodies and the "outer man."[77] But this is only to put the reader, in effect, into the place where Augustine's rhetorical artistry in the *ciu.* puts Porphyry, on the verge, so to speak, of conversion, and held back only by his pride. It is to rhetorically position the reader that way, to help him or her find himself or herself a "dark enigma" that cannot be interpreted apart from Scripture, and cannot be clarified except through true worship. In the words of the *ciu.*:

> Contemplating His image in ourselves (*in nobis autem ipsis eius imaginem contuentes*), therefore, lets us, like that younger son of the Gospel, come to ourselves, and arise and return to Him Whom we had forsaken by our sin (Lk. 15:11–12). In him, our being (*esse*) will have no death, our knowledge (*nosse*) will have no error, and our love (*amare*) will know no check. In our present state, we believe that we possess these three not on the testimony of others, but because we ourselves are aware of their presence, and because we discern them with our own most truthful inner vision (*interiore ... aspectu*). We cannot, however, know of ourselves how long they will continue, or whether they will ever cease, and what will be the outcome of their good or bad use. Hence, we seek the testimony of others, if we do not already have it.[78]

"Inner vision" cannot be denied, but it is not enough. In fact, under the guidance of the apologist, it only poses the question. More precisely, the focus of the inner vision to which the reader is invited is conjured by the apologist from the perspective of revelation.[79] Only from the perspective of revelation can one be invited to see one's own mind, which one cannot in itself doubt, for the "image" and the "enigma" it is.[80] What one "cannot doubt" is then used by the apologist to leverage also this very awareness in the reader, namely, in order to show that awareness of that very thing, which we cannot doubt, is in fact awareness of oneself, as, without revelation, an unanswerable question, uninterpretable, like an obscure text. For the pagan inquirer or critic, this could be enough to provide the occasion of conversion. For the Christian reader, this provides a kind of "understanding" of Christian teaching which enables him or her to be able to confidently answer the pagan critic with the truth. And yet, the Christian reader is not himself or herself immune from the need for conversion, broadly speaking, conversion not just to a deeper intellectual assent to the truths of faith, but to the awareness of their own pride, their own temptation to accounts of the world and human being which are just Christianized versions of the triumphalist complacency of late antique imperial culture.[81] If any of us, pagan or Christian, while being exercised in this inner vision, with the help of grace, *come to ourselves*, we will "arise and return to Him Whom we had forsaken by our sin," and we will embark upon, or persevere more strongly in, the course of healing humility that is the Eucharistic life.

Interior vision, at that point, becomes the awareness of oneself worshipping God, that is, awareness of oneself as sacramentally bound in a *societas* defined by no other qualification, cultural status, or accomplishment which might serve the glory of *emporium*, but rather by Christ's sacrifice alone. It is awareness of oneself as a kind of question continually being posed, and continually being answered in the immolation of self that is one's sacramentally conferred identity as incorporated into the one sacrifice of Christ. Perhaps it is a little like the alternating "evening knowledge" and "morning knowledge" of the unfallen angels throughout the 6 days of creation.[82] It is the awareness of oneself continually as a temptation to pride, and the continuing immolation of self in refusing to accept the temptation by clinging to the blood of Christ, the price of our redemption. For we have our "morning knowledge" only in our true worship in and of Christ. This is the awareness of oneself that is truly the awareness of the image *as* an image, that book 14 of the *trin.* presents, the "worship"[83] that is true wisdom, ever more deeply clinging to the blood of Christ, the "price of our redemption," which means ever more deeply aware of one's sacramentally conferred identity as a member of the one Body, and one's whole life as Eucharistic. We are always directed back to the economy of salvation.[84]

The apologetic double effect of the *ciu.* is alive and well in the *trin.*, not only in the early books, but even more forcefully, perhaps, in the very books which have been supposed to be most pertinent to the converted Christian. Besides the indications of a "mixed" audience already mentioned earlier, large sections of books 13 and 14 have the apologetic feel to them that we can recognize from our examination of the *ciu.* Almost the whole first half of book 13 is taken up with demonstrating that, from the point of view of revelation, the pagan philosophical quest for happiness is self-defeating because "human argumentation (*humanis argumentationibus*)"[85] can succeed only in getting to some notion of the immortality of the soul, only to stumble on the problem of the soul's relation to the body. If one does not have the proper faith and the concomitant worship of God the Creator, one will not be able to find a stable immortality for the soul because the "shackling" that the body is will always threaten it, as Augustine explained in *ciu.* 12. It is exactly this issue of the status of the body that Augustine identifies as his only explicit point of contact between the two treatises.[86] Augustine the "apologist" has, in both texts, leveraged an account of shared wisdom about happiness into a persuasive strategy for accepting what faith proclaims about the resurrection of the body:

> This faith of ours, however, promises on the strength of divine authority, not of human argument, that the whole man, who consists of course of soul and body too, is going to be immortal, and therefore truly happy.

Lest we despair of this, *the Word became flesh*:

> For surely if the Son of God by nature became son of man by mercy for the sake of the sons of men … how much easier it is to believe that the sons of men by nature can become sons of God by grace and dwell in God; for it is in him alone and thanks to him alone that they can be happy, by sharing in his immortality; it was to persuade us of this (*propter quod persuadendum*) that the Son of God came to share in our mortality.[87]

Who needs this persuasion? Any pagan inquirer or critic, just as in the *ciu.*; and yet, what Christian can believe he or she is persuaded enough? Is there any Christian not tempted by pride to find a spiritual immortality that nature alone can attain? That does not require such a complete sacrifice of the self to grace? In other words, to the sacramental worship of the Church, the *societas* or *familia* that is defined not by nationality or sex or spiritual awareness or accomplishment but mysteriously – "sacramentally" – by Christ's love? Those who "philosophized without the Mediator" inevitably fell into false worship (13.24, with the citation of Rom. 1:20, 23). Augustine presents an argument for the "faith that purifies the heart" (13.25). In reviewing this argument in book 14, Augustine says that his aim in book 13 was to "commend faith itself."[88] To whom? There is no need to be a Christian to receive this argument as intelligible, and to be persuaded of the need for faith. Christians receiving it, on the other hand, "understand" that their own faith is the answer to centuries of spiritual quest, which that quest could not produce or imagine on its own terms, and that it is this faith, and not an independent "understanding," that is the answer. We all need to be turned back to the "initium fidei" in some way.[89] Book 14 ends by citing the *Hortensius* of Cicero, to show the inadequacies of mortals, desiring immortality, relying upon reason alone without faith in the Mediator.[90]

And thus, in Book 14, we find that the image of God is most especially located not simply in the triad of memory, understanding, and love, but in remembering, understanding, and loving God – that is, in true worship:

> This trinity of the mind is not really the image of God because the mind remembers and understands and loves itself, but because it is also able to remember and understand and love him by whom it was made. And when it does this it becomes wise. If it does not do it, then even though it remembers and understands and loves itself, it is fool-ish. Let it then remember its God to whose image it was made, and understand and love him. To put it in a word, let it worship (*colat*) the uncreated God.[91]

This is to cling to God,[92] which we know from *ciu.* requires sacrifice; let it *not be conformed to the world, but reformed in the newness of mind* (14.22, citing Rom. 12:2, the passage associated with the Eucharist in *ciu.* 10.6). Let it cease to cling to any "understanding" or "knowledge" as spiritual accomplishment. If not a believer, let it become a believer; if a believer, let this "understanding" be ever more purified by the sacrifice of true worship instead of becoming a substitute for it.

If the logical sequence of the thought of books 8–12 of the *ciu.*, present and relatively intact in the *trin.*, has not lost the apologetic critique offered to pagan philosophical reason from the perspective of faith and true worship, it does not mean that the other emphasis in ancient apologetics is lost, namely, an appeal to shared ground in reason as offering an unbeliever, with the proper guidance, some

helpful access to Christian faith, such that the diligent exercise of
reason might lead one to see the reasonableness of converting. Surely
the *trin.* is not intended primarily for pagans thinking of converting.
Yet, that does not mean that the apologetic themes we have noticed
from the *ciu.* cease to function apologetically and that the treatise has
no accessibility or useful intelligibility to the non-Christian, even as
it offers something useful to Christians by the same "apologetic"
strategy.[93]

For one thing, discourse on the Trinity, present in the *ciu.* and with
significant similarities to what we find in the *trin.*, seems to Augustine
accessible enough to pagans – not, of course, to Porphyry, who, as
Augustine notes, is dead, but to non-Christians who admire Porphyry
and on that basis have refused to become Christians.[94] Like Justin and
Origen and others before him, Augustine attempts to leverage what
reason can share between Christians and non-Christians as an occasion
for conversion, and there is no reason to think that these apologetic
tonalities have dropped out of the picture. The textual evidence from
the *trin.* would argue that they have not, and that the double effect we
can see from *ciu.* is instructive for how the treatise functions for
Christians.[95] For Christians are poignantly convicted of the need for
ongoing conversion if the same arguments that can convince pagans
are also useful for providing "understanding" for Christians. Christians
should, therefore, not pride themselves, even on their own conversion.

But furthermore, who knows whose will is fixed in love? And who
knows who needs to be persuaded to love God? What Christian is
there who can claim complete and perfected conversion, or even
observe this within himself or herself?[96] Our awareness of our own
transformation is mediated by, and, one might almost say, takes its
content from, our being sacramentally incorporated into the one
Body, and thus from our status as a "member."[97] But our membership
is based on no discernible human achievement: that is the point of
leaving behind the Platonist divorce of an interior economy of
attainment from an exterior economy of sacrifice. There is no purity
of light or love within that is so clearly discernible that *it*, rather than
simple membership in the visible Church, becomes the criterion for
belonging. That would still be, in a way, displacing sacrifice from
oneself. Participation in the sacrifice of Christ, such that one actually
becomes oneself a sacrifice, is mediated only in the sacramental
formation of a Body in which one is genuinely mixed in with some

who will not be saved, and that may in fact be oneself! It comes with no guarantee. One cannot hold out for any marker that is not sacramental, for that would be to displace the sacrifice of Christ away from oneself, ultimately, in favor of some clearly discernible spiritual attainment of one's own.

Rowan Williams' (1993) famously commented that, in Augustine's *trin.*:

> ... the image of God in us, properly so called, is not "the mind" in and to itself ... but the mind of the saint – the awareness of someone reflectively living out the life of justice and charity[98]

This is beautiful and undoubtedly true, but, perhaps in spite of itself, it can slip almost imperceptibly into underwriting a split between the awareness of an inner process of transformation and renewal in faith, and an exterior economy of membership in the Church. One looks for a "reflective" awareness of love and renewal that is somehow additional to and deeper than one's simple awareness of oneself as a member of the visible *societas* of the Church.

But who then is the saint? Whose conversion away from pride is so complete that they are not beset by the temptation that felled Porphyry only in Christian terms, such that one's voluntary poverty, or one's willingness to give one's son or daughter to the life of virginity, or even one's willingness to die for the faith, offers an occasion for pride and not humility?[99] Who is the Christian whose very "understanding" of the mystery of the Trinity is not always in danger of lapsing back into an awareness of an accomplishment in which he or she can take pride? Where is the Christian whose self-awareness is not always in danger of lapsing back from "evening knowledge" into the "night" of the fallen angels? Paradoxically, something so august as awareness of the Trinity is coincident with and can never depart from one's simple awareness of the flesh of Christ – that is, of one's own incorporation into the visible Church. Paradoxically, far from cutting oneself off from the world, awareness of oneself as incorporated into the visible Church as incorporation into a "mysterious," that is, "sacramental," economy of salvation is the awareness of a mystery at work that transcends and defeats all language of spiritual accomplishment and makes one's flesh, available, in Christ, as bread for the life of the world.[100] Is that not, in the end, the only thing that can lend perspective on, and so challenge, the hegemonic claims that beset the human person from any and all of the kingdoms of this world? Is that not, in the end, the best apologetic of all?[101]

Acknowledgments

An earlier version of this chapter was published by John Wiley & Sons, Ltd. as Cavadini, J.C. (2012) "Trinity and Apologetics in the Theology of St. Augustine." *Modern Theology* 29: 48–82. doi:https://doi.org/10.1111/moth.12001.

Notes

1 See, for example, *Second Apology* 10, for a summary statement of the Logos Incarnate, His superiority to all human teaching, and the merely partial grasp of Him even in someone like Socrates. His relation to God is discussed in *Second Apology* 6. Plato had a doctrine of the Trinity that was a deficient imitation of biblical teaching (*First Apology* 59–60), which is given earlier in the text (13, 22–23, 32–33), and reviewed later (63). Myths are a demonic distortion of the doctrine of the Logos, the Son of God (54), and the Trinity (64).

2 Baptism fulfills the prophecies of Isa. 1:16–20 (*First Apology* 61), and so exposes as distortion and myth the sprinklings of pagan ritual (62) and the mythology that distorts the Trinity (64). Only those "illuminated" by Baptism (61) can see the truth of the Eucharist, which presupposes the Incarnation of the Logos and is truly His body and blood (66). After initiation in baptism and Eucharist, life is such that "for all that we receive we praise the Creator of all through His Son Jesus Christ and through the Holy Spirit" (67). The Mithraic sacrificial rites are a contemporary re-mythologization of worship (66), a demonic disfigurement of the Eucharist. Translations of Justin from Barnard (1997).

3 Chadwick (1953) invites the comparison: "In the history of the intellectual struggle between the old and the new religion the *Contra Celsum* is of the first importance, comparable only with Augustine's *City of God*" (xiii). Bourret (1976) echoes this judgment (207).

4 For example, see *Contra Celsum* 6.63–72. Origen corrects mistaken notions that Celsus has about the Logos-Son and the Spirit, clarifying notions of Incarnation by distinguishing it from the mythological ideas Celsus imagines Christians to believe, and also clarifying the nature of true worship. The same concern about true worship is evident at *Contra Celsum* 8.12–14, which takes up the relation between the Father and the Son, each considered an "hypostasis." At *Contra*

Celsum 5.39, Origen is distinguishing the way in which Christians call the Logos a "second God" from the mythological worship of polytheism. See also, ibid., 2.9 and 2.31.

5   With regard to Origen: by the time Origen writes, Celsus is long dead, and Origen explicitly writes, at the request of his patron Ambrose, in case there are believers whose faith might "be shaken and disturbed by the writings of Celsus" (*Contra Celsum* P.4), and he intends it "either for those entirely without experience of faith in Christ, or for those whom the apostle calls *weak in faith*, for he says this, *Him that is weak in faith receive ye* (Rom. 14:1)." That is, it is intended for (somewhat sympathetic?) non-Christians and for those whose faith might be troubled by such cultured despisers of Christianity as Celsus. See Frede (1999). With regard to Augustine, see especially van Oort (1991), esp. 165–175; and also O'Daly (1999), 36–38. Both apologetic treatises have a critical dimension and a constructive dimension. In Augustine, this is a structural feature of the text, with *ciu.* books 1–10 the critical and 11–22 the constructive. In Origen, the two are not separated structurally, but Origen calls attention to them in a lengthy comment as he begins book 4 of the *Contra Celsum* (4.1).

6   The overall movement is from a consideration of the economy of redemption to a consideration of the Trinity in itself, especially in its contrast with created being. In both texts, the two discussions are not independent, they are mutually implicated; the latter has roots in and arises out of the former. *Ciu.* 10 (completing the argument begun in books 8–9) provides a discussion of the economy of salvation, which is, at the same time, a discussion and clarification of the doctrine of the Trinity, just as in books 2–4 of *trin*. *Ciu.* 11 takes up, in the context of discussing the act of creation, the utter uniqueness of the nature of God the Creator, a Trinity of Persons which is nevertheless wholly simple and undivided. *Trin.* 5–7 takes up the same topic, though in inverse proportions, with the discussion of the uniqueness and simplicity of God's nature front and center, with some discussion of the act of creation (e.g. *trin*. 7.12, 6.11–12, 5.12–17 [in the discussion of the senses of "origin"]) in that context. The Trinity is *simplex*, and so Father and Son, together with the Holy Spirit, are one God, in such a way that each is God in himself but all three are not three Gods or three Omnipotents, but one God (*ciu.* 11.10, 11.24; cf. *trin*. 5.9, giving rise to the long discussion concluding at the end of *trin*. 7.6). The plural is to be used of the word "person" (*ciu.* 11.10 with contrast to Sabellius; 11.24; *trin*. 5.10 with contrast to Sabellians; 7.7–11). Properties of the persons are mentioned briefly at *ciu.* 11.24, more extensively at *trin*. 6.11, with discussions of the Holy Spirit as the holiness of both Father and Son (*ciu.* 11.24, *trin*. 6.7). God's simplicity involves an absolute contrast to creatures, for, in creatures, qualities inhere in substance or nature, whereas in God, to be good, wise, great, God, etc., is the same as to be (*ciu.* 11.10, expanded throughout *trin*. from 5.3–5 [there are no accidents in God] to 7.2 and 7.10, with the constant refrain that to be X is the same as to be, for God; see *trin*.

5.11, 6.5–8, 6.11, 7.1 etc.). God is immutable in the act of creation since it was not created in time (*ciu.* 11.6, 11.21, *trin.* 5.17; note the coincident point about God's knowledge and creation at the end of *ciu.* 11.10 and *trin.* 6.11), and the co-eternity of the Son and Holy Spirit guarantee that the relations of origin do not involve change either (*ciu.* 11.10, 11.24; *trin.* 5.6, etc., including, in both texts, the distinction between what is said of a Person *ad se* and what is said *relative* or *ad alteram*). In both texts, the uniqueness of God's being is compared and contrasted throughout to the likenesses and unlikenesses to God that can be seen in creation, and this applies to all creatures (*trin.* 6.11–12; *ciu.* 11.24–25, 27), and in a special way to the image of God that is in human beings (*trin.* 7.5, 12; *ciu.* 11.26, 28). Both texts emphasize the need for the renewal or regeneration of the image. If the *ciu.* enjoins us to consider all of creation, and, in particular, to gaze at the image in ourselves, with the benefit of knowledge about it given by revelation (11.28), the *trin.* takes up this exhortation in 7.5 and 7.12, then expanded into the extended discussion of books 8–10, 14–15.

7 As at *trin.* 3.1, "fratribus autem non valeam resistere iure quo eis servus factus sum flagitantibus ut eorum in Christo laudabilis studiis lingua ac stilo meo quas bigas in me caritas agitat maxime serviam." Latin text from CCSL 50, 127, lines 17–20; cf. 1.5, which mentions "conversations with the brothers" as a possible source of correction for any errors (*per fraternas sermocinationes*, CCSL 50, 34, line 45). Translations from the *trin.* are taken from Hill (1991), sometimes with adjustment, as here.

8 *trin.* 4.1, CCSL 50, 160, lines 24–27.

9 There are many possible examples to offer, but see the summary description at *conf.* 7.1.1 of Augustine's struggle against the *phantasmata* of corporeal images. See CCSL 27, 92, lines 1–27 ("phantasmata" at line 15).

10 *trin.* 4.1, looking especially at CCSL 50, 159–160, lines 7–23, 27–29.

11 "fidei contemnentes initium," *trin.* 1.1, CCSL 50, 27, line 3. They are "deceived by an immature and perverse love of reason (*immaturo et perverso rationis amore falluntur*)," ibid., lines 3–4.

12 Augustine sums up his intentions with regard to such people: "… with the help of the Lord our God, we shall undertake to the best of our ability to give them the reasons they clamor for, and to account for (*eam imsam quam flagitant … reddere rationem*) the one and only and true God being a trinity …. In this way … they may actually come to realize (*reipsa experiantur*) that that supreme goodness does exist (*esse illud summum bonum*) which only the most purified minds can gaze upon, and also that they are themselves unable to gaze upon it and grasp it for the good reason that the human mind with its weak eyesight cannot concentrate on so overwhelming a light, unless it has been nursed back to full vigor on *the justice of faith* (Rom. 4:13) ….We shall go on to accommodate these garrulous rationalizers who have more conceit than capacity ….We shall do them such a service, perhaps, that they are able to discover reasons they can have

no doubt about (*ut inveniant aliquid unde dubitare non possint*), and so … they will sooner find fault with their own minds than with the truth itself or our arguments. In this way … they may return to the beginning and right order of faith (*atque ita … ad initium fidei et ordinem redeant*), realizing at least what a wholesome regimen is provided for the faithful in holy Church…." (*trin.* 1.4, CCSL 50, 31, lines 1–3, 6–11, 13–21). That is where Augustine locates himself, "in familia Christi tui, … inter pauperes" who are seeking in praying, himself as bishop begging for bread that he might serve others, all too conscious of his own susceptibility to error, given the difficulty of the quest and the weakness caused by sin. This is where Augustine would like all of his readers to be, seeking by begging for bread *in familia Christi* (*trin.* 4.1, CCSL 50, 159–160, lines 22–23).

13   *trin.* 4.2; cf. 13.13.

14   The polemical context of some sections of the *trin.* has been brilliantly clarified in a series of articles by Barnes. See Barnes (1993) and (1999). But see also Madec's (2000) helpful reminder: "Le *De Trinitate* est. un ouvrage de recherche, répondant à l'exhortation du psalmiste: 'Cherche toujours son visage,' (Ps. 104 [103]. 4; [*De Trinitate*] 1.3.5)" (60). See also, ibid., 53–57, on the lengthy time of composition.

15   The very first word of the text refers to the one about to read it ("*Lecturus* haec quae de trinitate disserimus," *trin.* 1.1, CCSL 50, 27, line 1, my emphasis). Such emphatic notice directly to an unnamed reader is rare in Augustine. The audience constructed as "the reader" retains a prominent presence throughout. The whole of *trin.* 1.5–6 is addressed to "Quisquis haec legit" (CCSL 50, 32, line 1, insistently repeated at CCSL 50, 32, line 11, "quisquis…. Legit"; 32–33, lines 17–18, "[lector] ponat librum meum vel etiam … abiciat"; 33, line 32, "Quivero haec legens") in the context of forming a collaborative pact with the reader in the face of the grave difficulty of the subject at hand, "for nowhere else is a mistake more dangerous, or the search more laborious, or discovery more advantageous" (*quia nec pericu losius alicubi erratur, nec laboriosius aliquid quaeritur, nec fructuosius aliquid invenitur*, 32, lines 9–11, with a kind of emphatic reprise at *trin.* 3.2). The constant address to the reader emphasizes the extreme difficulty of the task, which relativizes even the difference between author and reader as both fellow seekers. As the difficulty of the search increases, Augustine's appeal to the reader intensifies, to the point of asking the reader's forgiveness for any failure in expression or understanding on Augustine's part, and assuring forgiveness for any slowness (*tarditatem*) in the reader – *trin.* 5.1 ("Ab his etiam qui ista lecturi sunt…," CCSL 50, 206, lines 13–17). The fact that many of these references are in the prologues to the early books, most likely added at a late point in composition, show that they reflect Augustine's thinking about the work as a whole. One should also notice that Augustine is constantly mentioning his "slower readers" (beginning with the *tardiores*, at *trin.* 1.6, CCSL 50, 34, line 49),

even using such mentions to mark strategic, structural decisions, made out of consideration for them (at *trin.* 10.19, on behalf of the *tardioribus*, the turn to the "outer man" is made, and book 11 is straightaway begun almost as a sort of detour, CCSL 50, 332, line 18; cf. *trin.* 14.10, "legentium … tarditatem," CCSL 50A, 435, lines 59–60; cf. *trin.* 14.20, ibid., 448, line 78). By the time Augustine recounts this "detour" in book 15, it is made simply on behalf of the "reader," unqualified (*trin.* 15.5, CCSL 50A, 466, line 84). The "slower reader" has become almost a sacrament of the "slowness and weakness of the human mind" (*trin.* 15.49, CCSL 50A, 530, line 44) before the difficulty of the search. Even to "careful and intelligent readers" (*illis qui haec diligenter atque intelligenter legent, trin.* 15.45, CCSL 50A, 524, lines 22–23), what is most apparent is the extreme difficulty of seeing the Trinity with any clarity, in this case why the Holy Spirit is not a son, though he proceeds from the Father. Throughout, the "reader" is the audience as a shadow cast from the perspective of the severe difficulty in the search for God.

16 At *trin.* 1.5, Augustine envisages a situation where a reader may have a criticism, but he, Augustine, may not be alive ("si in hac vita maneo," CCSL 50, 33, line 35).

17 Quotations from Weil (1986; original French from 1941); quotes taken from pages 190, 188, and 191.

18 Hill (1991), 56.

19 See, for example, at *ciu.* 10.20, "Unde verus ille mediator, in quantum formam servi accipiens mediator effectus est. Dei et hominum, homo Christus Iesus, cum *in forma Dei* sacrificium cum Patre sumat, cum quo et unus Deus est, tamen *in forma servi* sacrificium maluit esse quam sumere, ne vel hac occasione quisquam existimaret cuilibet sacrificandum esse creaturae," CCSL 47, 294, lines 1–6.

20 The economy of miracle, prodigy, and theophany is discussed beginning at *ciu.* 10.7 and continues through 10.18, with a summary comment in 10.32. *Ciu.* 10 seems to assume the results of the discussions at *trin.* 2–3 regarding the theophanies and other Old Testament prodigies. *Ciu.* 10.8, for example, assumes the results of the inquiry in *trin.* 2.10.19–12.22 and 3.11.26–27, namely, that it was angels who appeared to Abraham and to Lot and to the other patriarchs, a point made also at *ciu.* 10.13, extending the point to include all the patriarchs and Moses too, as well as the prodigies before the whole people on Mt. Sinai. As Augustine concludes in *trin.* at 2.17.32 and 3.11.22–27, these were worked through angels or other creatures "serving the Creator." In both texts (see *trin.* 2.16.27), the request of Moses to see God face to face (Exod. 33:13) is interpreted as a realization on Moses' part that he had never seen God in His essence, but only as represented by a creature.

21 See the passage cited from Bochet (2012), in n. 74. The reader may wish especially to compare the discussions on purification or purgation of the soul in *ciu.*

10.28–29 with that at *trin.* 4.1.3–2.4, where purification of the soul cannot even be explained without explaining who the Word of God is who becomes Incarnate to purify us. In both texts, it is the humility of the Word of God that is emphasized as cleansing, but this humility cannot be understood unless one understands just who the Word is, and what His status is as God. The polemic in the *trin.* against theurgy (at *trin.* 4.8.12–10.13) entails an explanation of the true sacrifice of the true Mediator, and how that Mediator is equal to the Father. This discussion is comparable to the more extensive critique of theurgy in *ciu.* 10.

22   See, for example, *ciu.* 10.32, at CCSL 47, 314, lines 180–184.

23   After an extensive discussion, from *ciu.* 8.1 to 8.10, emphasizing the Platonist philosophers as those who have come the closest to Christian doctrine in natural and moral philosophy and logic, Augustine in *ciu.* 8.10 sums up this agreement using Rom. 1:19–20 and reiterates it forcefully, but he also uses Rom. 1:21–22 to state their error: "Novit [homo Christianus] sane etiam ipsos [Platonicos philosophos], in quibus errant, cavere; ubi enim dictum est, quod per ea, quae facta sunt, Deus illis manifestavit intellectu conspicienda invisibilia sua; ibi etiam dictum est. non illos ipsum Deum recte coluisse, quia et aliis rebus, quibus non oportebat, divinos honores illi uni tantum debitos detulerunt: *Quoniam cognoscentes Deum non sicut Deum glorificaverunt aut gratias egerunt…*," *ciu.* 8.10, CCSL 47, 226, lines 19–25, with the quotation of Rom. 1:20–21 continuing to line 30.

24   "Ideo quippe hos potissimum elegi, quoniam de uno Deo qui fecit caelum et terram, quanto melius senserunt, tanto ceteris gloriosiores et inlustriores habentur…," *ciu.* 8.12, CCSL 47, 229, lines 11–14.

25   "utrum propter felicitatem, quae post mortem futura est, uni Deo an pluribus sacra facere oporteat," ibid., lines 9–10. Translation modified slightly from Dyson (1998). In general, I have used Dyson's translation, supplemented by consultation with Bettenson (1972, repr. 1984, 2003) and, infrequently, my own renderings. I have not noted these adjustments unless it seemed necessary to call attention to an issue of interpretation affecting my argument.

26   *ciu.* 8.9, "de Deo summo et vero ista senserunt, quod et rerum creatarum sit effector et lumen cognoscendarum et bonum agendarum," CCSL 47, 225, lines 1–3. At *ciu.* 8.5, God is called "rerum auctorem" (CCSL 47, 221, line 39), and only later, in 8.5 (ibid., 222, line 71), "creator," when Augustine is speaking in his own person of his own teaching.

27   *ciu.* 8.4, CCSL 47, 220, lines 24–33.

28   *ciu.* 8.6, CCSL 47, 224, lines 47–48, 49–51.

29   *ciu.* 8.7, "lumen autem mentium esse dixerunt ad discenda omnia eundem ipsum Deum, a quo facta sunt omnia," CCSL 47, 224, lines 18–20.

30   *ciu.* 8.8, "Ipsum autem verum ac summum bonum Plato dicit Deum, unde vult esse philosophum amatorem Dei, ut, quoniam philosophia ad beatam vitam tendit, fruens Deo sit beatus qui Deum amaverit," CCSL 47, 225, lines 46–49.

31 *ciu.* 8.12, "Sed hi omnes et ceteri eius modi et ipse Plato diis plurimis esse sacra facienda putaverunt," CCSL 47, 229, lines 28–30.

32 *ciu.* 10.9, "Nam et Porphyrius quandam quasi purgationem animae per therugian, cunctanter tamen et pudibunda quodam modo disputatione promittit; reversionem vero ad Deum hanc artem praestare cuiquam negat;…utilem dicit esse mundandae parti animae, non quidem intellectuali, qua rerum intellegibilium percipitur veritas, nullas habentium similitudines corporum; sed spiritali, qua corporalium rerum capiuntur imagines. Hanc enim dicit per quasdam consecrationes theurgicas, quas teletas vocant, idoneam fieri atque aptam susceptioni spirituum et angelorum et ad videndos deos," CCSL 47, 281–282, lines 13–16, 21–27. Cf. the description of the *teletai* at *trin.* 4.10.13, CCSL 50, 178–179, lines 1–34.

33 *ciu.* 10.23, "Dicit etiam Porphyrius divinis oraculis fuisse responsum nos non purgari lunae teletis atque solis," CCSL 47, 296, lines 1–2, with relevant information from lines 3–5 and 6–8.

34 Ibid., "dicit…principia posse purgare….Quae autem dicat esse principia tamquam Platonicus, novimus. Dicit enim Deum Patrem et Deum Filium, quem Graece appellat paternum intellecturm vel paternam mentem," CCSL 47, 296, lines 6, 8–11.

35 Ibid., lines 13–17, 19–21.

36 Ibid., "Nobis autem ad certam regulam loqui fas est, ne verborum licentia etiam de rebus, quae his significantur, impiam gignat opinionem," CCSL 47, 297, lines 23–26.

37 *ciu.* 10.24; see CCSL 47, 297, lines 1–11. Note the mention of Sabellius (cf. *trin.* 7.4.9). The Trinitarian discussion is meant to be heard both by Christians and by pagans. On language about the *principium*, compare *trin.* 5.13.14–5.14.15, CCSL 50, 220–223, which argue at length for the same point, namely, that *principium* is to be used in the singular when speaking of the Trinity.

38 *ciu.* 10.25.

39 *ciu.* 10.28, "Ignorantium certe et propter eam multa vitia per nullas teletas purgari dicis, sed per solum p*atrikon noun*, id est. paternam mentem sive intellectum, qui paternae est. conscius voluntatis," CCSL 47, 303, lines 18–21.

40 *ciu.* 10.28, CCSL 47, 303, lines 21–23, "Hunc autem Christum esse non credis; contemnis enim eum propter corpus ex femina acceptum et propter crucis opprobrium, excelsam videlicet sapientiam spretis atque abiectis infimis idoneus de superioribus carpere," with Dyson's translation slightly adjusted.

41 *ciu.* 10.29, CCSL 47, 304, lines 1–11.

42 Thus, here I find myself reluctantly disagreeing with the view of Brachtendorf (2000) when he comes to treat the relevant passages in *ciu.* 10.23 and 29 – see especially 8–13.

43 *ciu.* 10.29, CCSL 47, 304, lines 20–23; 305, lines 29–31.

44 On this point, the reflections of Madec (2000) seem on point, for one thing, noting that whatever of the Trinity that Porphyry has seen, it is due to the grace

of Christ, whether Porphyry likes it or not, all the while cautioning us not to read back into *trin.* the difference between "philosophy" and "theology," especially insofar as that is thematized by the parallel scholastic distinction between "natural" and "supernatural" (see especially at 69–73, 78). For an intriguing attempt to negotiate this problem of natural knowledge of the Trinity in Augustine, with special reference to the *trin.*, using the idea of "implicit knowledge," see Brachtendorf (1998).

45   *ciu.* 10.29, CCSL 47, 307, lines 107–109.

46   *ciu.* 10.4.

47   *ciu.* 12.10.

48   *ciu.* 10.25 notes that the holy angels "do not wish that we would sacrifice to them, but that we might *be* (*simus*) with them a sacrifice to God," my translation and emphasis, CCSL 47, 300, lines 73–74, 75–76. *Ciu.* 10.6 points out that this applies both to the body, which, according to Rom. 12:1, is to be a "living sacrifice," as well as the soul, to which is directed Rom. 12:2, so that "the soul itself may become a sacrifice (*sacrificium*) when it directs itself to God in order that, inflamed with the fire of his love, it may receive His beauty and be pleasing to Him, losing the form of worldly desire and being reformed immutably by its submission to him," see CCSL 47, 278, lines 18–24. Rom. 12:2 is also used to describe the transformation of the image of God from deformity in *trin.* 14, where the idea of the gradual renewal of the image is discussed, a renewal to be enjoyed by those who are "holding fast to the faith of the Mediator" in the worship of God (see *trin.* 14.16.22, CCSL 50A, 451–454, lines 1–66; *trin.* 14.17.23, ibid., 454–455, lines 1–37).

49   *ciu.* 10.27 and 28, CCSL 47, 302, line 37; and 303, line 13.

50   *ciu.* 10.19, CCSL 47, 294, lines 24–25, 29–33. The false gods have at least this in common with the true God: it is not the matter of the sacrifice they seek, but what it signifies and effects in the soul of the worshipper – but the sign and the thing signified are not so easily separated, as implied in the good angels' refusal to accept either, as mentioned in *ciu.* 10.26.

51   *ciu.* 10.3, 10.6, 10.18, 10.25, 12.9.

52   See Cavadini (2007), reprinted in this volume.

53   *ciu.* 10.20, see at CCSL 47, 294, lines 1–7.

54   *ciu.* 10.6.

55   *ciu.* 10.20, "Cuius rei sacramentum cotidianum esse voluit ecclesiae sacrificum, quae cum ipsius capitis corpus sit, se ipsam per ipsum discit offerre," CCSL 47, 294, lines 7–9, taking "cotidianum" with "sacrificium," disagreeing with Dyson (1998), 422, who takes it with "sacramentum." Dyson's translation assumes that the Eucharist itself is not a sacrifice, but only the "sign" of one (as he translates "sacramentum"); the sign can be daily, but the sacrifice is ongoing and interior, he seems to indicate. But Augustine is perfectly comfortable using the language of sacrifice in connection with the Mass, as his usage at *conf.* 9 shows abundantly

(see Cavadini [2010], reprinted as Chapter 9 of this volume). Bettenson (1972) seems to agree, translating, "the daily sacrifice of the Church" (401).

56   *ciu.* 10.6, "Hoc est sacrificium Christianorum: *multi unum corpus in Christo* (Rom. 12:5). Quod etiam sacramento altaris fidelibus noto frequentat ecclesia, ubi ei demonstratur, quod in ea re, quam offert, ipsa offeratur," CCSL 47, 279, lines 52–55. Other usage in the *ciu.* reveals some kind of sacramental causation in Augustine's thinking, however implicit. For example, at *ciu.* 22.17, "For the man's [Adam's] sleep was the death of Christ, from Whose side, pierced with a spear as He hung lifeless upon the cross, there flowed forth water and blood, which we know to be the sacraments by which the Church is built up (*quae sacramenta esse novimus, quibus aedificatur ecclesia*)," CCSL 48, 835–836, lines 19–22. The ablative of agency with the passive voice claims a kind of sacramental efficacy, even if it is not specified precisely how it works. Again, at *ciu.* 15.26, "And the door which was set in the side of it [the ark] clearly represents the wound made in the side of the Crucified when it was pierced with a spear, which is indeed the way of entrance for those who come to Him, because from that wound there flowed the sacraments in which believers are initiated (*quia inde sacramenta manarunt, quibus credentes initiantur*)," CCSL 48, 495, lines 23–26. Even with the weaker translation of *quibus*, "in which," as opposed to a more instrumental translation, "by which," there is evidently something that happens as a result of the sacraments of initiation. At *ciu.* 17.20, Augustine comments on the banquet of Wisdom in Prov. 9, referring that banquet to the table "furnished with wine and bread," and he adds that "to become a guest at that table is to begin to have life (*participem autem fieri mensae illius, ipsum est incipere habere vitam*)," the implication being that participation in the Eucharist is participation in the Wisdom of God. This seems confirmed as Augustine comments on Eccl. 8:15, "There is nothing better for a man than that he should eat and drink." Augustine applies the comment to the Eucharist, to the "sharing of this table (*participationem mensae huius*) which the Priest Himself provides, the Mediator of the new covenant according to the order of Melchizedek, the table furnished with His body and blood," namely, "that sacrifice which has superseded all the sacrifices of the old covenant, which were offered as a foreshadowing of that which was to come … for, instead of all those sacrifices and oblations, His body is offered, and served up to the partakers of it (*corpus eius offertur et participantes ministratur*)," CCSL 48, 588, lines 73–91 (cf. *ciu.* 16.22, on the prefiguration of the Eucharist in the sacrifice of Melchizedek). Participation in the sacramental table at which the sacrifice of Christ's body and blood is offered is efficacious, in some way, in granting life. Finally, to return to book 10, at *ciu.* 10.19, Augustine discusses why visible sacrifice should be offered to God, instead of just offering a "pure mind and a good will" (could this be what the philosophers think?), and why, in sacrificing, we offer the visible sacrifice *only* to the true God (cf. *ciu.* 10.26). The visible sacrifice signifies the invisible sacrifice of ourselves, and yet the invisible sacrifice is not enough, and perhaps is

not even complete *as a sacrifice*, without the visible sacrifice which signifies that what is happening invisibly is indeed a sacrifice. If the visible sacrifice were easily dissociable from the invisible sacrifice, there would be no problem offering it to another god. Even here, there is an element of efficacious causality implied. Would it be alright to reject the Eucharistic sacrifice in favor of simply an invisible offering? Apparently not.

57   "agnoscentibus gentibus et pia humilitate bibentibus pretium suum, ejusque fiducia deserentibus hostem suum," with "pretium" referring back to "suo [the Lord's] justo sanguine," *trin.* 4.18 and 17, CCSL 50, 184, line 76; and 185, lines 84–85.

58   *ciu.* 10.6, making use of Rom. 12:1–5 throughout.

59   As explained at *ciu.* 22.18.

60   See *ciu.* 8.27.

61   See *ciu.* 10.24; Augustine speaks simply of the Incarnation as the hand stretched out to us, but this is clearly an image of *misericordia*.

62   *ciu.* 11.1. O'Daly (1999) notes that, despite the plan of the work indicating a new section here, "the continuity between this new section of the work and what went before is greater than Augustine's scheme suggests," indicating a continuous sequence of thought (135).

63   *ciu.* 22.30 treats the eternal Sabbath rest and praise of God.

64   *ciu.* 11.1; see CCSL 48, 321, lines 16–19, 23–25.

65   See n. 6.

66   *ciu.* 12.25, CCSL 48, 381, lines 2–9.

67   *ciu.* 12.26, CCSL 48, 382, lines 23–26.

68   *ciu.* 10.7, cf. 12.9.

69   *ciu.* 12.27, CCSL 48, 383–384, especially lines 10–18.

70   (As narrated in Scripture, we must add.) *ciu.* 11.24.

71   *ciu.* 11.28, CCSL 48, 348, lines 36–39; cf. *ciu.* 11.24.

72   *ciu.* 11.25, CCSL 48, 345, lines 39–47.

73   *ciu.* 11.26, CCSL 48, 345, lines 1–7, "Et nos quidem in nobis, tametsi non aequalem, immo valde longeque distantem, neque coaeternam et, quo brevius totum dicitur, non eiusdem substantiae, cuius Deus est, tamen qua Deo nihil sit in rebus ab eo factis natura propinquius, imaginem Dei, hoc est illius: summae trinitatis, agnoscimus, adhuc reformatione perficiendam, ut sit etiam similitudine proxima." The progression of thought here, though very compact, is similar to the progression of thought in the summary at *trin.* 15.10 (we really are an image), 11–13 (but the dissimilarity is very great), 14 (not only intrinsically but because it is in need of reformation).

74   This point is made, in a somewhat different way, by Bochet (2012), with regard to book 3 of the *trin.*: "Face aux ariens, il fallait établir que, dans les théophanies, ce n'est pas le Fils qui s'est rendu visible dans son essence divine: le Créateur a utilisé des anges pour signifier aux hommes un message; le Fils n'est donc pas

inférieur au Père. Mais le rôle ainsi conféré aux anges risquait alors d'en faire des intermédiaires nécessaires à la création et au salut et de cautionner par là même les thèses des platoniciens : Augustin se devait donc de discuter directement Porphyre et les platoniciens afin de lever tout ambiguïté." She continues later on to note that Augustine's use of some Platonic philosophy requires that he show his rejection of their religion in an absolute way: "Mais cet usage même de la philosophie des platoniciens imposait en retour qu'Augustin marque sans équivoque qu'il ne partageait pas pour autant leur religion. Il lui fallait souligner l'opposition du christianisme au platonisme en matière de médiation religieuse" (97).

75   LaCugna's (1991) critique, for example (see 103). LaCugna's critique is a more measured and qualified version (with even some positive appreciation, e.g. on 367, 323) of the critique of Gunton (1990), with both ultimately reflecting the critique of du Roy (1966).

76   See n. 12. The language of discovering something about which one cannot doubt is echoed most closely in the *trin.* at 10.14 with regard to "living, remembering, understanding, willing, thinking, knowing, judging," and, from these, in 10.17 are selected the triad of remembering, understanding, willing.

77   The *"vestigia"* or footprints of the Trinity in sensible things are treated in book 11 of the *trin.*, just as in book 11 of the *ciu.*, as antecedent to a consideration of the "image" within. *Trin.* 11.1 introduces the discussion of the *vestigia* (CCSL 50, 333–334, lines 1–35) in the "outer man" as propaedeutic to a consideration of the inner image, comparable to the movement from *ciu.* 11.27 to the passages I have cited from *ciu.* 11.28 (corresponding to note 57, which in the text of Augustine immediately precedes that in note 64). *Trin.* 11.8 evokes very beautifully the way in which there is nothing at all created that does not bear some likeness to God, and, just as in *ciu.* 11.24, 27–28, this is linked to the reason for creation, namely, the supreme goodness of God (CCSL 50, 343–344, lines 51–55, 1–41).

78   *ciu.* 11.28, adjusting Dyson's (1998) translation (on 488) slightly; CCSL 48, 348, lines 39–50.

79   Hill (1991) notes, "[B]y the end of Book X Augustine has completed his construction of the Trinitarian image in man, which is so designed that it does throw light on the processions which constitute the trinity in God. I say 'construct' advisedly, first because he is clearly being selective in his use of psychological activities, and is tailoring his selection to meet the requirements of the linguistic standards set in Books V–VII…" (54). Also see the *note complémentaire* of Agaësse in BA 16: "Il n'y a donc qu'une image de Dieu : inchoative dans la création, pervertie dans le péché, rénovée dans la justification, achevée dans la vision. Mais ces différents états ne s'expliquent que par leur relation mutuelle. L'image inchoative ne se comprend que par son ordination à l'image parfaite,

comme l'image pervertie ne se comprend que par ce qui subsiste en elle de l'image primitive. Nous sommes dans une perspective qui se réfère au point de vue de Dieu sur l'homme et toutes les expériences humaines ne sont interprétées qu'à la lumière de la Révélation" (632). Ayres (2010) in his recent book seems to align himself with these positions, for example, when noting that "… the language of Trinitarian faith is a guide for the exploration of the mind," with reference to book 9 (see 293).

80　On this point, see *trin.* 15.44; in more detail, see Cavadini (2007), especially at 126 (reprinted as Chapter 7 of this volume; at page 143).

81　As an example, see especially *ciu.* 5.18, where the *exempla* of the pagan heroes are addressed to Christians, warning them not to use their own ascetic or spiritual gifts as though they were accomplishments undertaken for the purpose of seeking praise or glory. On this point, see Cavadini (2012).

82　See *ciu.* 11.7, where Augustine discusses the character of a creature's self-knowledge: "In comparison with the Creator's knowledge, the knowledge of the creature is like a kind of evening light (*vesperascit*). But when our knowledge is directed to the praise and love of the Creator, it dawns and is made morning (*lucescit et mane fit*); and night never falls while the Creator is not forsaken by the creature's love. Accordingly, when Scripture enumerates those days in order, it never includes the word 'night.' It never says, 'There was night,' but, *The evening (vespera) and the morning were the first day*; and so too with the second, and so on. And, indeed, the knowledge which created things have of themselves is, so to speak, shadowy until they see themselves in the light of God's wisdom and, as it were, in relation to the art by which they were made. Therefore, it can be called *evening* more suitably than 'night' (*nox*). Yet, as I have said, morning returns when the creature returns to the praise and love of the Creator. When it does so in the knowledge of itself, that is the first day" (CCSL 48, 327, lines 18–31). See also *ciu.* 11.29, CCSL 48, 349, lines 10–13, 30–32.

83　"*Dei cultus*," *trin.* 14.1, CCSL 50A, 421, lines 10, 25, 27; cf. *trin.* 12.22, to which Augustine himself here refers us (see CCSL 50, 375, lines 22–23).

84　See Cavadini (1992), esp. 109 (reprinted as Chapter 1 of this volume; at ##).

85　*trin.* 13.12, CCSL 50A, 398, line 1.

86　Ibid., lines 11–12.

87　Ibid., 398–399, lines 13–16, 23–31.

88　*trin.* 14.3, "ipsam praecipue fidem commendare curavi," CCSL 50A, 424, line 68.

89　"To know how the godly are to be assisted … and how the attacks of the ungodly upon [faith] are to be met," the double thrust of apologetic (*scire quemadmodum hoc ipsum et piis opituletur et contra impios defendatur*, *trin.* 14.3, CCSL 50A, 424, lines 65–66).

90 *trin.* 14.26, "ista sola ratione … sine fide mediatoris," CCSL 50A, 459, line 66.

91 *trin.* 14.15, CCSL 50A, 442–443, lines 1–10, citing Job 28:28, here as "Ecce dei cultus est sapientia," lines 9–10.

92 *trin.* 14.20, "ei … inhaerere," CCSL 50A, 448, line 84; "cum illi … adhaeserit," ibid., line 86, recalling Ps. 73:28, which figured so prominently in *ciu.* 8–10, and is cited at *trin.* 6.7, CCSL 50, 235, lines 14–15.

93 One may, on the one hand, agree with the comments of a recent excellent monograph on the *trin.*, and yet, at the same time, wonder if it edges toward overstatement: "Since the will is never neutral, we are either moving away from God, or discover that we have been snatched away from this aversion, from the devil's power, from the blindness of our covetousness and pride, from the bleakness of our despair and granted the grace of conversion, of moving towards God through the charity poured out in our hearts through the Holy Spirit given to us. The novelty, the strangeness, the gracious character of this love is such that it becomes the most eloquent indication of the renewal brought about by Christ's salvation and of its Trinitarian character …. *Love comes first* to the point that such talk makes sense only once it has become a *reality* already. Augustine's *trin.* is not destined for people who need to be converted, to be persuaded to love God. His reader has to be someone who already knows, already sees, already loves out of God's love" (Gioia [2008], 300).

94 *ciu.* 10.29.

95 What I have been calling the double address of the *trin.* is particularly visible in sections 15.48–50 (noted, in somewhat different words, by J. Moingt in BA 16, note 66, on 660–661). After citing a lengthy section from one of his own *Tractates on the Gospel of John*, which attempted to explain why the Holy Spirit is said to "proceed" and not to "be born," Augustine says, "I have transcribed this from that sermon into this book but of course I am not addressing unbelievers in this passage but believers" (*Haec de illo sermone in hunc librum transtuli, sed fidelibus, non infidelibus loquens*, CCSL 50A, 530, lines 36–37). This implies that Augustine believes that here he is speaking, at least in part, to unbelievers. Seeming to recall the preface, where he addressed those who contemned the "initium fidei," he now asks why they would not "believe" what Scripture says about the Trinity instead of asking for the "most stringent proof" (*liquidissimam reddi sibi rationem*, ibid.). He has now shown them their own incapacity, without faith, to see what they would like to see. Thus, "when they have placed their unshakable trust in the holy scriptures as the truest of witnesses, let them pray and seek and live rightly, and in this way take steps to understand." Let them join Augustine in "that tavern to which that Samaritan brought the man he found half-dead" (*trin.* 15.50, CCSL 50A, 532, lines 77–78), let them become members of the "familia Christi" as Augustine is (*trin.* 4.1). As for those who are believers already, Augustine's soul, addressed in the soliloquy of section 50, stands in for all. Let Augustine's soul, and all Christians, recognize if they can the

difference between begetting of the word and the procession of love in the image which is the mind, and, if with Augustine, they are unable to fix their gaze in stable contemplation, but are troubled by bodily images, let them recognize their weakness, and let the understanding they have received prompt them to humility and to prayer. In closing the book with a prayer, Augustine brings both kinds of readers to the point where argument has done all it can do, and now one must beg God for what one is looking for (*trin.* 15.51): "Let me remember You, let me understand You, let me love You. Increase these things in me until you refashion me entirely" (*trin.* 15.51, CCSL 50A, 534, lines 21–23).

96   Gioia's (2008) position, cited in n. 93, if pushed too far, could be taken to imply a state where one can almost verify one's own status as being renewed, being sanctified, from the quality of love and gratitude that one is aware of in oneself.

97   I wonder if Gioia's (2008) position, though willing to take over the language of the Church as the "location" of transformation, does not take the mysterious sacramentality of the Church seriously enough. The word "location" is cited by Gioia (2008), 21, from Ayres (1998), 126. While Ayres' article has many attractive features, I wonder if it is adequate to talk about the Church so emphatically as the "location" of purification or transformation without a corresponding and equally emphatic emphasis on its actual, mysterious, instrumentality. Of course, we are not ascending by our own efforts alone; it is the Head who is training the Body by an "*exercitatio* ... which will enable us to progress from our obsession with the material to greater contemplation of the presence of the creator," and this "*exercitatio* is undergone within the body of Christ" (131). Yet, this begs the question as to whether or not this path traveled, the paradigm of spiritual progress, is essentially the same ascent of purification proposed in Neoplatonists, only now the training is made possible by Christ who has also, in his dual structure of two natures, provided a "location" for this training in the Church, so that by faith we might advance from his visible human nature to his invisible divine nature. Ayres (2010) refers the reader back to this article (168, n. 87).

98   This is quoted by Gioia (2008), 19, as foundational for his own position. Williams' (1993) text goes on to say, "The saint's mind images God because its attitude to its own life has become indistinguishable from its commitment to the eternal good; when it looks at itself, it sees the active presence of unreserved charity." Both texts are from Williams (1993), 121–134, at 131. It is a very high standard for knowing oneself as the image of God if one must "see," when one looks at oneself, the presence of "unreserved" charity. This really would seem to describe only Christ – unless you can include those who can know themselves as Christ in the only way (and insofar as) we can know this, namely, by sacramental inclusion as members in one Body.

99   See n. 81.

100   For example, the connection between almsgiving and the Eucharist is evident in Augustine (see, e.g. *s.* 106.4; *En. 3 in Ps.* 103.13; etc.). More generally, see Anderson (2009), 148–149 (references to Ben Sira and Tobit) and 165–167 (Irenaeus). A more exhaustive discussion is in Anderson (2013). See also Anderson (2011).

101   I would like to thank Emmanuel Bermon and Gerard O'Daly, who invited me to participate in the colloquium "Le De Trinité de Saint Augustin: Exégèse, Logique et Noétique" at Université de Bordeaux 3 (June 2010), at which an earlier version of this chapter was read. I would like to thank Boyd Taylor Coolman, at whose invitation another version of this chapter was read at the Boston College Historical Theology Colloquium (July 2011). I would also like to thank Nancy Cavadini, Jim Lee, and Cyril O'Regan for assistance of various kinds, all crucial; and also the two anonymous readers for *Modern Theology*, who read with care. I hope all of them can see their influence in the present chapter without at the same time feeling responsible for the mistakes or distortions I have inevitably introduced. This chapter is dedicated to Bl. Mother Teresa of Calcutta, "saint of darkness" (from her letter dated March 6, 1962, and cited by Kolodiejchuk [2007], 230). Blessed Teresa of Calcutta, pray for us!

References

Anderson, Gary (2009) *Sin: A History.* New Haven, CT: Yale University Press.

Anderson, Gary (2011) "Is Purgatory Biblical?" *First Things* 217: 39–44.

Anderson, Gary (2013) *Charity: The Place of the Poor in the Biblical Tradition.* New Haven: Yale University Press.

Ayres, Lewis (1998) "The Christological Context of Augustine's *De Trinitate* XIII: Toward Relocating Books VIII–XV." *Augustinian Studies* 29: 111–139.

Ayres, Lewis (2010) *Augustine and the Trinity.* Cambridge/New York: Cambridge University Press.

Barnard, Leslie William, trans. (1997) *Justin Martyr. The First and Second Apologies,* Ancient Christian Writers 56. New York/Mahwah, NJ: Paulist Press.

Barnes, Michel René (1993) "The Arians of Book V and the Genre of *De Trinitate.*" *Journal of Theological Studies* 44: 185–195.

Barnes, Michel René (1999) "Exegesis and Polemic in Augustine's *De Trinitate* I." *Augustinian Studies* 30: 43–59.

Bettenson, Henry, trans. (1972) *Concerning the City of God against the Pagans.* Harmondsworth, Middlesex: Penguin Books (repr. 1984, 2003).

Bochet, Isabelle (2012) "La puissance de Dieu à l'oeuvre dans le monde: Le livre III du *De Trinitate* d'Augustin." In *Le De Trinitate de saint Augustin: exégèse, logique et noétique,* edited by Emmanuel Bermon and Gerard O'Daly, 67–97. Turnhout: Brepols.

Bourret, Marcel S.J., trans. (1976) *Origen. Contre Celse*, vol. 5. Sources Chrétiennes 227. Paris: Les Éditions du Cerf.

Brachtendorf, Johannes (1998) ""... *prius esse cogitare quam credere*': A Natural Understanding of 'Trinity' in St. Augustine?" *Augustinian Studies* 29: 35–45.

Brachtendorf, Johannes (2000) *Die Struktur des menschlichen Geistes nach Augustinus. Selbstreflexion und Erkenntnis Gottes in De Trinitate.* Hamburg: Felix Meiner.

Cavadini, John C. (1992) "The Structure and Intention of Augustine's *De trinitate.*" *Augustinian Studies* 23: 103–123.

Cavadini, John C. (2007) "The Darkest Enigma: Reconsidering 'the Self' in Augustine's Thought." *Augustinian Studies* 38: 119–132.

Cavadini, John C. (2010) "Eucharistic Exegesis in Augustine's *Confessions.*" *Augustinian Studies* 41: 87–108.

Cavadini, John C. (2012) "Ideology and Solidarity in Augustine's *City of God.*" In *The Cambridge Companion to Augustine's City of God*, edited by James Wetzel, 93–110. Cambridge: Cambridge University Press.

Chadwick, Henry, trans. (1953) *Origen. Contra Celsum.* Cambridge: Cambridge University Press.

du Roy, Olivier (1966) *L'Intelligence de la Foi en la Trinité selon Saint Augustin.* Paris: Etudes Augustiniennes.

Dyson, R.W., trans. (1998) *The City of God against the Pagans*, Cambridge: Cambridge University Press (repr. 2007).

Frede, Michael (1999) "Origen's Treatise *Against Celsus.*" In *Apologetics in the Roman Empire*, edited by Mark Edwards, Martin Goodman, Simon Price, and Christopher Rowland, 131–155. Oxford: Oxford University Press.

Gioia, Luigi (2008) *The Theological Epistemology of Augustine's De Trinitate.* Oxford: Oxford University Press.

Gunton, Colin (1990) "Augustine, the Trinity, and the Theological Crisis of the West." *The Scottish Journal of Theology* 43: 33–58.

Hill, Edmund, O.P., trans. (1991) *The Trinity, WSA I/5.* Brooklyn, New York: New City Press.

Kolodiejchuk, M.C. Brian, ed. (2007) *Mother Teresa: Come Be My Light: The Private Writings of the Saint of Calcutta.* New York, NY: Doubleday.

LaCugna, Catherine Mowry (1991) *God For Us: The Trinity and Christian Life.* San Francisco, CA: Harper.

Madec, Goulven (2000) "'Inquisitione proficiente': Pour un lecture 'saine' du *De Trinitate* d'Augustin." In *Gott und sein Bild: Augustins De Trinitate im Spiegel gegenwärtiger Forschung*, edited by Johannes Brachtendorf, 53–78. Paderborn: Ferdinand Schöningh.

O'Daly, Gerard (1999) *Augustine's City of God: A Reader's Guide.* Oxford: Clarendon Press.

van Oort, Johannes (1991) *Jerusalem and Babylon: A Study into Augustine's City of God and the Sources of His Doctrine of the Two Cities.* Leiden: Brill.

Weil, Simone (1986) "The *Iliad* or The Poem of Force." Translated by Mary McCarthy from the original French of 1941 and reprinted in *Simone Weil – An Anthology*, edited by Siân Miles, 162–195. New York, NY: Grove Press.

Williams, Rowan (1993) "The Paradoxes of Self-Knowledge in the *De trinitate*." In *Collectanea Augustiniana: Augustine, Presbyter Factus Sum*, edited by Joseph T. Lienhard, Earl C. Muller, and Roland J. Teske, 121–134. New York, NY: Peter Lang.

12

God's Eternal Knowledge According to Augustine

> What human being can know the design (*consilium*) of God? Who will be able to think (*cogitare*) what the Lord intends (*velit*)? For the thoughts of mortals are timid, and our attempts at discovery are uncertain. For the corruptible body weighs down the soul, and the earthly habitation depresses the mind as it thinks many things.[1]

This passage from the Wisdom of Solomon (Wis. 9:13–15), here taken from Augustine's citation of it at *City of God* (*ciu.*) 12.16, is perhaps the best summary of Augustine's teaching about God's eternal knowledge.[2] The most basic mistake that a human being can make, with reference to God's knowledge, is to underestimate the uniqueness and the superiority of God's mind, and to measure it unduly against a human standard. It is the articulation of this uniqueness that is the underlying theme of all of Augustine's discussions of the matter.

For Augustine, this will mean, ultimately, the insufficiency even of philosophy to provide an adequate account of what seems to be an almost uniquely philosophical topic, God's eternal knowledge. This is true despite undoubted areas of agreement between pagan philosophical teachings and Christian doctrine that can seem broad enough at first glance. Therefore, in our discussion of this topic, we have to be careful not to give the impression that what we are doing is separating out a stable body of philosophical teaching that will describe Augustine's

Visioning Augustine, First Edition. John C. Cavadini.
© 2019 John Wiley & Sons Ltd. Published 2019 by John Wiley & Sons Ltd.

thinking on the eternal knowledge of God, and that then whoever wants to move from philosophy to theology can proceed to what Christian revelation adds to this body of philosophical knowledge.

Agreeing with the Philosophers

Of course, Augustine himself tempts us to think this way. After all, who more than the philosophers have identified themselves with the transcendence of God invoked by the Wisdom of Solomon? The Platonists especially offer areas of agreement that evoke Augustine's wholehearted assent:

> These philosophers ... have been raised above the rest by a glorious reputation they so thoroughly deserve .... They recognized that no material object can be God; for that reason they raised their eyes above all material objects in their search for God. They realized that nothing changeable can be the supreme God; and therefore in their search for the supreme God, they raised their eyes above all mutable souls and spirits .... It follows that all these alike could come into being only through him who simply is (*ciu* 8.6).

The Platonists certainly have won their way to an awareness of the uniqueness and superiority of God, including, in some way, his transcendence over all changeable and mutable beings like ourselves. God is transcendent because He is utterly simple: for God, all God's attributes are identical with each other and with God's being, so that "for Him, to exist is the same as to live, to understand, to be happy." The twin hallmarks of the uniqueness of God's being are His immutability and simplicity.

> It is because of this [immutability and simplicity] that the Platonists realized that God is the creator from whom all other beings derive, while He is Himself uncreated and underivative (*ciu.* 8.6).

God's transcendence over all else that exists constitutes Him as their origin. This means that there exists in God the "original idea" or "form" (*primam speciem*, *ciu.* 8.6) of all things, the first, unchangeable, and therefore incomparable form of all things, the "first principle of things" (*rerum principium*). One could take this as a description of God's eternal knowledge: it is the eternal "idea" for all things that are not God. God is creator because His "idea" or "form" is what gives existence to everything else, insofar as everything must have form or idea to exist.

Participation in this form or idea is also the "light of the human mind, making possible every acquisition of knowledge" (*ciu.* 8.7). As the "idea" or "form" of the Good is itself the Highest Good, it is also the proper object of all loves. Plato has thus united all three branches of philosophy – natural, rational (logic), and moral – in the one transcendent source of them all. Accordingly, the Platonists:

> … acknowledge (*confitentur*) a God above every kind of soul, who made not only this visible world … but every kind of soul whatsoever, a God who makes the rational and intelligent soul blessed … by participation in his unchangeable and immaterial light (*ciu.* 8.2).

In a sense, then, seeing the physical world and sensing, interiorly, the world of soul and of mind, we are "seeing" the mind of God, the original idea according to which everything sensible has come into existence. We are, in a way, seeing the eternal knowledge of God, and we can "ascend" to a contemplation of God's mind as we contemplate all that is informed by His eternal idea. St. Paul leads us to expect that this would be the case. Augustine characteristically applies to the Platonists what Paul says in Rom. 1:19–20:

> … what is known of God is what he himself has revealed to them. For his invisible realities have been made visible to the intelligence, through his created works, as well as his eternal power and divinity (*ciu.* 8.6).

This makes it all the more tempting to see, in the doctrine of God's immutable simplicity, in the doctrine of God's "idea" as informing all of changeable and composite reality, a body of philosophical teaching that is detachable from what is known from revelation as independently true.

Beyond Agreement

We should be wary of this approach, however. In the *ciu.*, Augustine actually begins his discussion of the Platonist teaching as part of an extensive critique.

He opens book 8 by announcing his intention to discuss "theology" with the philosophers – and, he says, "I take this Greek word to signify reasoning or discussion regarding divinity (*de divinitate rationem sive sermonem*)" (*ciu.* 8.1). But his intention is not simply to discuss but to "refute all of the empty opinions (*vanas opiniones*) of the philosophers" insofar as they touch on "theology." This includes all the philosophers who "take it that there is a Divinity and that he cares for human affairs," among which the Platonists are the prime examples. Nevertheless, all these philosophers "do not consider that the worship (*cultum*) of one unchangeable God is sufficient for the attainment of a life of blessedness even after death, but suppose that for this end many gods are to be worshiped, gods who were created and established by him" (*ciu.* 8.1). It seems almost like a technicality, this lack of worship, one easily excised and entailing no inroads into the areas of agreed-upon teaching, namely, the existence of one true unchangeably simple God and his care for human affairs (providence of some sort).

But a little later on in the text, Augustine uses St. Paul again, this time to articulate his critique, continuing in Romans from where he left off in 8:6:

> For while the Apostle says that through his created works God has revealed to them his invisible qualities by making them visible to the intelligence, he says at the same time that they have not offered the right sort of worship to God himself, because they have transferred the divine honors, due to God alone, to other objects, which have no right to them. *Though having some acquaintance with God, they have not glorified him as God, nor have they given thanks to him; but they have dwindled into futility in their thinking (in cogitationibus suis) and their unwise (insipiens) heart is darkened. Claiming to be wise, they have become foolish (stulti) and have exchanged the glory of the incorruptible God for images representing corruptible man, or birds, beasts or snakes* (*ciu.* 8.10, Rom 1:21–22).

This analysis offers a more critical assessment of the philosopher's wisdom, indicating a "darkness" and a "foolishness" belying the claim to be "wise," a kind of pervasive vitiation of truth into futility and foolishness. There is probably no passage more characteristically associated with Augustine's critique of Platonism than this passage from Romans, because he saw (on the one hand) their undisputed awareness of the transcendence of God as source of all other beings, and (on the other hand) their willingness to countenance the worship of other gods, as a discrepancy so glaring that it called for closer inspection of the areas of agreement, to see how far there actually is agreement. And this is how the argument proceeds in the *ciu*. How close is the actual agreement, when examined from the perspective of biblical revelation?

A Test Case

It turns out that God's knowledge from all eternity, and its relation to temporal knowledge and events, is a perfect test case. As Augustine proceeds with his discussion of Creation, beginning in book 11, the issue is raised regarding how the eternal knowledge of God relates to the world of time and change. We have already seen that they are related because the world of time and change is, in a way, God's eternal "idea" realized in a temporal medium. Looking at it from the perspective of St. Paul, there is a formal, bare-bones accuracy about it, but there is in the teaching only an impersonal correspondence of type to archetype. There is no one to worship and no one to thank, and this "darkens" the truth seen, as though it were corrupted by a vitiating deficiency. As the biblical teaching on creation is exposited, the truth of the philosophical teaching stands out as a capacity to help explain the biblical teaching, to provide understanding of it. The philosophical teaching on its own is like a radioactive element with a short half-life. Its truth is a formality, an "idea," which gains material content only as it is used in the explication of revelation. Otherwise, its very formality is unstable, and it "dwindles to futility" in understandings that are false.

City of God Book 11: Creation

Book 11 begins the discussion of creation with an invocation of the authority of Scripture. Scripture's authority invites our trust concerning things which are out of reach (*remota*) both to our interior and exterior senses (*ciu*. 11.3). The mind must be trained and healed by faith so that it may be capable first of enduring, and then clinging to and enjoying the changeless light of God (*ciu*. 11.2). The Platonists may know the destination to which we must travel, but faith provides a pathway to the God of human beings through the human being who was God, *the Mediator between God and men, the man Christ Jesus* (*ciu.* 11.2, 1 Tim. 2:5). The Platonist philosophers are "nearer the truth than the others," but "they are a long way from it" (*ciu.* 11.5), and because they are a long way off, they see the only way that someone far away from something can see, without detail and distorted by the distance.

A close reading of Augustine's text shows that it is not, however, the sheer distance in itself that is distorting, but, we could say, Augustine charges the philosophers with an investment in the distance. The absolute difference between God, the eternally unchangeable, and changeable mortal creatures is a distance that it is the job of philosophers, so to speak, to manage. As professionals, as philosophers, they *"claim to be wise."* The very distance is an evocation of the difficulty of what they have accomplished in *"recognizing God"* and their pride in the accomplishment. In this dynamic, the Mediator becomes, as it were, a competitor, and so they want to push the Mediator out of the way as distasteful, unnecessary, or at best one way among others: they "consider that honors of worship should be paid to many gods." Even regarding the Mediator as one possible option among many is to push Him aside. What the philosophers refuse to recognize is that there is no pushing Him aside, because He is actually the goal as well as the way (*ciu.* 11.2). Accepting the mediation of the Goal-drawn-close would mean abandoning the prestige of arbitrating the distance: they *"recognize God,"* but *"they do not give thanks."* Faith will eventually give rise to vision, but faith-become-vision has the same content as when it was just faith, namely, the Mediator. For one thing, He never loses His humanity, as Augustine explains at length in book 22. For another, He is always the One eternally characterized by the graciousness revealed in that humanity, which is thus not extrinsic to His person. The graciousness and compassion is part of His eternal essence. Faith in the Mediator does not simply bring us where the philosophers have arrived at by their own effort, or would arrive at by their own effort eventually, because He is the content of that vision, and, insofar as it is a vision of the eternal knowledge of God, it includes that gracious character, inextricably tied to the Incarnation. It is a vision of the kind of God that willed to become Incarnate.

Continuing with the discussion in book 11, the basic point the philosophers see is that God's "idea," His knowledge, is eternal and immutable:

> It is not that God's knowledge varies in any way, that the future, the present, and the past affect that knowledge in three different ways. It is not with God as it is with us. He does not look ahead to the future, look directly at the present, look back to the past. He sees in some other manner, utterly remote from anything we experience or could imagine …. He sees all without any kind of change (*ciu*. 11.21).

This means that God's knowledge of temporal things exists independently of time: "God knows events in time without any temporal acts of knowledge, just as he moves events in time, without any temporal motions in himself" (*ciu*. 11.21).

In fact, if God's knowledge of creatures were not eternal, perfect, and unchanging, he would not have been able to produce the works he produced in their perfection, because he would not have known if he would have to add something to complete the perfection of his works after they were made (*ciu*. 11.21). In other words, you cannot add to God's knowledge, as it is eternally complete. "If God created knowingly, he created things which he already knew," and this has the surprising implication, Augustine says, that "this world could not be known to us, if it did not exist, whereas it could not have existed, if it had not been known by God" (*ciu*. 11.10). If there is a formal, philosophical common ground, it is this, though it is important to note that the common ground can be seen as such because the philosophical doctrines of God's unchangeability and simplicity are being used in the service of helping to understand biblical teaching.

God's *Consilium*: An Eternal Plan

The passage from the Book of Wisdom (9:13–15) quoted at the beginning of this chapter is a clue of what more is involved here, beyond the areas of agreement. God's eternal knowledge of the world is not simply the "objective" or "disinterested" knowledge of a living blueprint or a computer program. Augustine's fundamental starting point is, instead, the biblical notion of God's *consilium*, his "counsel" or "plan" or "design" in the sense of "intention": *What human being can know the design of God?* (Wis. 9:13). He appeals to this idea to answer criticisms of the biblical notion of creation.

Augustine mentions, without naming, a Manichaean criticism of the biblical story of creation, which in turn echoes the Epicurean criticism of philosophical versions of creation, such as the Platonic view: "Why did the eternal God decide to make heaven and earth at some particular time rather than before?" (*ciu.* 11.4). A Platonist defense, commonly accepted in other philosophical schools that held some kind of doctrine of creation, would be that there is no beginning of creation in time, but that the world, "in a way that is scarcely intelligible, is always being made." This protects God's immutability because it protects God from having a change of mind or a sudden new idea, and thus preserves God as Creator while rescuing the divine from the mythological.

But Augustine finds this defense inconsistent with the biblical idea of God's eternal "plan." If, as the Platonists will agree, the soul now experiences misery from which it needs liberation, the misery, at least, cannot be co-eternal with God and must be a novelty that God's eternal knowledge must still somehow accommodate. If one resorts to the idea of endless cycles of alternation between misery and liberation, one protects God's immutability at the expense of holding that there is no true novelty in the world and that everything exists in endless cycles (*ciu.* 11.4). But this is to condemn the soul to endless misery, because even in its temporary happiness it must look forward to a return to misery, or else is ignorant of its return, and thus its ignorance compromises its happiness. But if the liberation is final and complete, then once again there is a genuine novelty to account for.

Augustine uses the biblical idea of God's "plan" to press forward. If this liberation has no part in "God's eternal plan" (*in aeterno ... consilio*), then God is not the author of happiness, or else He just changed His mind. Thus, just as this genuine novelty could be part of God's eternal plan without altering its immutability, so the world could have been created in time "without any change in his eternal purpose and design" (*aeternum consilium voluntatemque*). The issue, then, is not simply God's knowledge, but God's intentions, God's "plan," God's integrated act of knowing and willing, reflected in a temporal world where genuine, permanent loss and gain is possible, where the soul can persevere and move permanently from mortal misery to immortal happiness, the world of history as we see it in the biblical narratives where God's plan is played out. Augustine, in this long passage, does not argue his way toward the existence of such a plan, but uses philosophical argumentation to help generate understanding of what such a plan might mean.

The philosophical defense stemming from cycles preserves the dependence of the world on God as a dependence on an eternal "idea" by imagining the world reproducing, in temporal modality, as an infinite series of cycles of the same events, the eternity of the idea. But, Augustine asks (using an analogy from space rather than time), what does this defense really gain over the Epicurean idea that the world is a mindless series of atomic combinations (*ciu*. 11.5)? Its very rationality, ironically, its attempt to abstract from history to protect God from the mythological depiction of a powerful divine agency who is changeable, acting within the world of time and space as part of that world, deprives that world of a true "plan" or story. But this is only something that can be glimpsed when one has a true "plan" with which to compare it. Augustine had insisted at the outset of the whole discussion that the belief that God made the world is nowhere better attested than in the Holy Scriptures (*ciu*. 11.4). This is not a throwaway line. The biblical notion of creation is one not simply of derivation from a transcendent source (something one can see in its sheer beauty, *ciu*. 11.4), but rather of an intentional plan, a true act that can be narrated (however mystically), the "beginning" not just of time and space but of a story, which, just as it had a true beginning, has a true end.

Augustine goes on to explain that, indeed, when the Bible says, "In the beginning God made heaven and earth" (*ciu*. 11.6), the word "beginning" indicates the creation of time itself – but not just as a formal condition of existence of something that is not God, but time as part of a *plan* where there will be genuine "stories" which will be brought to fruition in God's "rest," and, in that rest, we will be able to see how God's works have fulfilled the prophetic promise implied in the very notion of God's mysterious rest (*ciu*. 11.8). Time is thus not a byproduct of declension from eternity, but intended, planned, as the substrate of true history.

The issue available, then, for philosophical analysis is not simply the relation of eternal knowledge to temporal reality, but whether there is a real story to be told anywhere, and what that story might be. If a rational creature ever fell into misery, and was ever permanently restored by God to happiness, and if the philosopher will agree to this teaching, as Scripture proclaims, then the philosopher, Augustine says, will also agree, as already noted, that this happened "without altering the immutability of God's plan," meaning his "eternal plan" (*ciu.* 11.4). Thus, there is no myth, since the divine nature does not change. But because God's eternal knowledge, his "idea," is not simply an abstract impersonal awareness, but, by contrast, a "plan," there is no reduction to endless cycles.

Who? How? Why?

Augustine goes on to comment that, to the three questions regarding the creation of the world – Who? How? Why? – the answers from Scripture are "God," "Through his Word," and "It was good." Plato sees this: "the most valid reason for creating is that good works should be effected by a good God," and Augustine opines that he may have learnt this from reading Genesis, or simply, as Rom. 1:20 says, by seeing the invisible things of God from the creation. But Plato's understanding of what "good" means is abstract, or, we might say, philosophically constrained. This is clear if we follow out the Trinitarian implication of these questions, as Augustine does later in book 11:

> It was, of course, the Father of the Word who said, "Let it be made." And since creation was effected by his speaking, there can be no doubt that it was done by means of the Word. And the statement, "God saw that it was good" makes it quite plain that God did not create under stress of any compulsion, or because he lacked something for his own needs; his only motive was goodness; he created because his creation was good .... Now if this goodness is rightly interpreted as the Holy Spirit, then the whole united Trinity is revealed to us in its works. Hence comes the origin, the enlightenment, and the felicity of the Holy City constituted by the holy angels on high (*ciu.* 11.24).

The Word of God is identical with God's Wisdom, the "idea" through which all things were made (*ciu.* 11.4, 7, 10). The Trinitarian account of creation reveals the absolute freedom of God in creating, against such views as the Manichaean myth, which amounts to a declaration that God needed to create in order to restrain and contain incursions against Him by a primeval evil power (*ciu.* 11.22), as though God somehow matured through the process of combating evil. Nor did God need anything but His co-equal Word, nor have any other reason for creating than His own goodness, in the person of His Spirit (see *ciu.* 12.18 on how it is incorrect to speak of God's having or being in a "condition" [*dispositio*] as though something could be added to him).

Creation does not remedy a need that God has or add to God in any way, and so it is perfectly free to be itself, unconstrained by God's "needs." Creation everywhere bears the marks of the freedom in which it was created:

> Why, even the irrational animals, from the immense dragons down to the tiniest worms, who are not endowed with the capacity to think on those matters, show that they wish to exist and to avoid extinction .... And then there are the trees and shrubs. They have no perception to enable them to avoid danger by an immediately visible movement; but they send up one shoot into the air to form their crown, and to safeguard this they fix another shoot into the earth to form their root (*ciu.* 11.27).

These "traces" (*vestigia, ciu.* 11.28) of the Trinity exist even in inanimate objects "which shoot up aloft or sink down to the depths or hang suspended in between, so as to secure their existence in the situation to which they are by nature adapted" (*ciu.* 11.27). They are not free but by their "measure, weight and number," that is, in their having, even at a low level, an individual identity, they still trace out their origin in God's freedom, the freedom to be themselves and not a function of a great cosmic need. Human beings, of course, are not only "traces" but the very image of God's freedom, in created form (*ciu.* 11.26, 28). The beauty of the world is not simply the reproduction of an eternal "idea" but is a mark of its nature as a free gift which keeps "appearing" in a seemingly infinite mirroring of jubilant tracery:

> Nevertheless, although there is no kind of real knowledge in the senses of irrational creatures, there is at least something parallel to knowledge, whereas all other material things are called "sensible," not because they have senses, but because they are perceived by the senses ....Yet [plants and trees] and all other material things have their causes hidden in

nature; but they offer their forms to the perception of our senses, those forms which give loveliness to the structure of this visible world. It almost seems as if they long to be known, just because they cannot know themselves (*ciu.* 11.27).

The whole of creation is free to be itself, free for self-expression, and as such is one whole multifaceted refraction of the freedom of God which gave the universe, as it were, to itself.

City of God Book 12

More on the Trinity in the following text, but meanwhile, the problem of God's eternal knowledge and its relation to time comes back again with redoubled force in *ciu.* 12, because there the subject is specifically the creation of human beings, and there is no doubt from biblical revelation that this occurred not at the beginning of time, but at a definite moment in time, and so is a genuinely new act of God within time. It begs the question, why did God do this at that time, and not another. Why so late?

Various philosophical solutions include the idea that the human race, like the world itself, is actually eternal, though involved in an infinite cycle of growth and reduction, and so, in each cycle, the human race appears to arise recently from a few individuals at a given time (*ciu.* 12.10). In other words, the world itself has no beginning, a position refuted earlier in book 9 (*ciu.* 12.13, referring to 11.5). Another position is that there are, so to speak, an infinite number of beginnings of the world (matched by an equal number of destructions of the world); or that there is an infinite number of beginnings and endings of the same cycle of repeated events in one world (*ciu.* 12.15). These variations on the cyclic theories that we saw from book 9 are meant to reconcile the unchanging eternal knowledge of God with the changing events of time.

Augustine responds to this philosophically, at first, by arguing that this would mean that the immortal soul was forever alternating between "false bliss and genuine misery," since the soul that has achieved happiness after death is happy simply in ignorance of its coming return to misery or, even worse, knows the misery is coming, in the next cycle (*ciu.* 12.14). Reason, Augustine seems to think, can have a glimmer of the truth – it is not reasonable to think that "happiness" means something when you know there is no permanence or genuine fulfillment, no end to any story, in the universe. Reason can see that a happiness due to ignorance is not really true. But this argument from reason alone is really no proof, but an appeal to reason to see reason, to consider the position of revelation. Augustine builds up to an appeal to Scripture, "For Christ died once for all for our sins"; and "in rising from the dead he is never to die again: he is no longer under the sway of death" (*ciu.* 12.14, citing Rom. 6:9). Here is a declaration of an unrepeatable, unique event, the pivot on which all stories turn, as it were. In view of Romans 6:9, we must reject theories of cycles, including facile, philosophical interpretations of Genesis via Ecclesiastes (*ciu.* 12.14):

> It is no wonder that those theorists wander in a circuitous maze finding neither entrance nor exit, for they do not know how the human race, and this mortal condition of ours, first started, nor with what end it will be brought to a close. They cannot penetrate *the depth of God* (1 Cor. 2:10, *altitudinem*), the deep counsel by which, being himself eternal and without beginning, he started time and man from a beginning, and made man in time, as a new act of creation, and yet with no sudden change of purpose (*non tamen novo et repentino*) but in accordance with his unchanging and eternal plan (*inmutabili aeternoque consilio, ciu.* 12.15).

God's "plan" is not simply his eternal knowledge, but his knowledge as inseparably joined to his will, and, in that sense, one could say his purpose or intention, which, as God's and as utterly free, is unfathomable:

> Whose strength avails enough to plumb this unplumbable depth, to scrutinize the inscrutable depth by which God made man as a temporal being, when no man had existed before him, making him in time with no change of purpose (*non mutabili voluntate*) and multiplying the whole human race from that one man? (*ciu.* 12.15)

What one encounters, therefore, in any unique historical event, as such, is a depth of mystery that is unfathomable, resistant to philosophical analysis:

Let men form their opinions from their own thoughts, and theorize and argue as they please, but *According to your deep design (altitudinem tuam) you multiplied the sons of men* [Ps. 12:8], which no human being can discover (*nosse*). For it certainly is a profound mystery (*altum est*) that God always existed and yet willed to create the first man, who had never existed, at a certain time, without having altered his purpose and design (*consilium voluntatemque, ciu.* 12.15).

In the unrepeatable historical event, we find ourselves contemplating a reality which is unfathomable in its depth, because it is a trace or image of something unfathomable in its depth, of the mystery of God's freedom as that is expressed from all eternity in His "plan" or "counsel." This plan eternally contains a promise for human beings, that of eternal life, according to Titus 1:2–3, which – or really, Who – is the co-eternal Word of God, eternally predestined to be given to human beings (*ciu.* 12.17).

Is Meaning Dissolved by Infinities?

The objection is presented, ultimately coming from Aristotle, that "infinite things are beyond the comprehension of any knowledge" (*nulla infinita ulla scientia posses comprehendi*), meaning that no mind, even God's, can comprehend an infinite series such as the series of numbers, and that therefore God has a finite conception of everything he creates, but, to prohibit any inactivity on God's part, so that God is always active but not creating an incomprehensible infinity, what is created must be a finite set of events that repeats itself endlessly – cycles, again (*ciu.* 12.18). Augustine says that "faith ought to laugh at these theories, even if reason could not refute them," though he proceeds to show how reason can refute them. The main problem, again, is that these speculators:

> ... measure the utterly unchangeable mind of God (*mentem divinam omnino inmutabilem*), which can embrace any kind of infinity and numbers all the innumerable possibilities without passing them in sequence before its thought – they measure this mind by their own narrow and changeable human mind. The Apostle describes what happens to them: *Comparing themselves to themselves, they fail to understand* [2 Cor. 10:12].

When it occurs to their minds to do something new, they change their plans in so acting (*novo consilio faciunt*); for their minds are subject to change. Thus it is not really God whom they are thinking of, in this argument; they find that impossible, and instead they imagine themselves in God's place. And so they do not measure him by his own standard, but *themselves by themselves* (*ciu.* 12.18).

Apparently, as hinted at the beginning of this chapter, this replacement of God's mind for a more familiar human mind is a projection of which even the most sublime philosophers are guilty.

In any event, God's "rest" and "activity" are the same from God's point of view; God is never the passive subject of dispositions such as "rest," but he "knows how to be active while at rest, and at rest in his activity" (*novit quiescens agere et agens quiescere*), because "he can apply to a new work not a new design but an eternal plan" (*potest ad opus novum non novum, sed sempiternum adhibere consilium, ciu.* 12.18). There is no change of will or intention (*voluntas*) because, by the very same will that prohibited things from existing at an earlier point, they were brought into existence later. Augustine comments that God demonstrates in a wonderful way, to those capable of seeing it, his free, gratuitous goodness (*gratuita bonitate*) in creating, because he did not need creation before it was created, and it did not increase his happiness once created. We return, then, to the freedom of God as the basis for, and guarantee of, true, unique historical events, and the intrinsic wonder attaching to such events.

Still arguing back from reason, Augustine indicates that, according to Plato, God created the world using numbers, and Scripture agrees that God has set in order all things "by measure, number and weight" (Wis. 11:20). This implies that:

> ... every infinity is, in a way we cannot express (*ineffabili modo*), finite to God, because it is not incomprehensible to his knowledge (*scientia*), and every individual creature, no matter how many there are or how different they are from each other, is contained already in God's eternal prescience (*aeterna praescientia, ciu.* 12.19).

In other words, infinities do not defeat intelligibility. They may intimidate us into declaring that all temporal reality is cyclic, but they do not intimidate God, since they are relativized into intelligibility by

God's eternal plan. The uniqueness of history does not threaten the "reasonableness" of God, but rather God's reasonableness guarantees the intelligibility of even an infinite number of unique individuals and events.

Augustine continues to argue, again, from the unreasonableness of the position that there can ever be true happiness if there are cycles of alternating misery and release from misery. It is unreasonable, he suggests, to defend God's eternal knowledge of his works by requiring his creatures to conform to the supposed conditions for God to know them, and thus endlessly alternate between mortal misery and temporary release. This amounts to saying that our misery is continuous. A happiness that is ignorant of coming misery is false and deceptive. Augustine appeals to reason here, but again, it is not clear that the argument amounts to more than an appeal to the reasonable instincts of the philosophers (recalling the example of Porphyry which he first brought up in 10.30, who seems to have been persuaded by this kind of argument to disagree with what Plato was believed to have taught on the issue). The argument may not be intended to stand on its own, but to try to show at least the reasonableness of turning, against cycles, to the "straight way, which is Christ" (*ciu.* 12.21; cf. Jn. 14:6), and to the eternal life of the saints, which "refutes [the cycles] completely" (*ciu.* 12.20).

Further Trinitarian Considerations

In order to realize fully the implications for God's knowledge from all eternity, including God's self-knowledge, we have to turn back, momentarily, to the issue of the Trinity, beginning with the Incarnation. The Incarnation is one of those things that Augustine says we are "incapable of discovering by ourselves" both with our exterior and interior visions (*ciu.* 11.3), because it involves a truth of something God *did*, something God *became*. Augustine had explained already back in book 9:

> That Mediator, in whom we can participate and by participation reach our felicity, is the uncreated Word of God, by whom all things were created …. God himself, the blessed God who is the giver of blessedness, became (*factus*) partaker of our human nature (*ciu.* 9.15).

He remained (*mansit*) above the angels in the form of God, but willed (*voluit*) to be below the angels in the form of a servant, and in so doing he brings us not to the angels, but to the Trinity (*ciu.* 9.15). This "willing" is obviously part of God's eternal "plan" or "design," his eternal wisdom.

It is easy to miss the striking incongruities, or seeming incongruities, these passages on the Incarnation contain, exemplified most fully in the uses of the verb *facere*: God, who is unchanging, made the world (*fecit*), but himself is not made; and yet God "was made" or "became" (*factus*) something He had not been before, partaker of our human nature, at a particular point in time. The philosophical language we have seen so far cannot account for this. The God whom good philosophy describes as eternally unchangeable seems to have a narrative, if authoritative Scripture is to be believed. Here, in a nutshell, is an illustration of the way in which a philosophical account is true, namely, insofar as it helps to "understand" the biblical proclamation. In this case, the language of God's immutability serves to indicate, not to dissolve, the magnitude of the mystery of God, because the philosophical language does not have the last word and yet is not discarded. God's nature remains unchanged and unchanging, but there is still a narrative! Some*one* eternal has a narrative even if no eternal *thing* or *nature* changes. Some*one* eternal becomes something, something actually happens in time to this someone, and thus we come to the idea of the Trinity, and must, as we close, take up some of the relevant discussion in book 10.

The Mind of the Father

This someone is the Word, the original "idea," the "Mind of the Father" as Porphyry the Platonist would style it, who is some*one* in relation to Father and Holy Spirit (against the Sabellians), but not some*thing* different (*ciu.* 10.24; cf. 11.10). He is not a separate "principle" (*principium*), one of three, but, co-equal with Father and Holy Spirit, is *the principium* or first principle. He "assumes" a human nature, including the human soul, "in some unique and ineffable (*ineffabili*) manner," "remaining unchangeably (*incommutabiliter*) in his own proper being (*in se*)," thus giving his love (*dilectionis*) to human beings, by which they might come to him (*ciu.* 10.29). God does not change, and yet there is a story to be told, a genuine story, and it is about God's love.[3]

Eternal Folly

So are we now in a position to realize more fully what is involved in the eternal knowledge of God – keeping in mind that creation is accomplished in the eternal Word of God, that very same Word which is not one of three *principia*, but the *principium*, the one God Himself? The Word, equally the *principium* with the Father, *became flesh and dwelt among us* (*ciu.* 10.24, Jn. 1:14), "stretching out a hand" of compassion and mercy to those who lay fallen, in the offering of his life as a sacrifice in which he was himself both priest and victim (*ciu.* 10.20).

What kind of "wisdom" or "counsel" is this? The wisdom of this "plan" is *folly, stupidity, foolishness* (*stultitiam*), as Augustine asserts, making his own the words of St Paul:

> Where now is the wise man? The scribe? The debator of this world? Has not God made foolish the wisdom of this world? For since, in the wisdom of God (*Dei sapientia*), the world through wisdom did not know God, it pleased God through the foolishness of preaching to save those who believe. The Jews looked for powerful signs and the Greeks sought wisdom, but we preach Christ crucified, a stumbling block to the Jews and folly to the Greeks, but to those who have been called, both Jews and Greeks, Christ the power and wisdom of God. For the foolishness of God is wiser than men, and the weakness of God is stronger than men (1 Cor. 1:20–25, *ciu.* 10.28).

Augustine immediately goes on to comment that this "foolishness" of God "is in fact grace," "rejected as folly and weakness by those who think themselves wise and strong by their own virtue" (*ciu.* 10.28). In other words, it is rejected by those who are proud of the makeshift happiness that really is only an attachment to a denial of misery in virtue of relying on one's own wisdom and strength. But it takes misery, undisguised by philosophical illusion, to see the "folly" of the Cross and to accept it as wisdom, the "grace which heals the weakness of those who do not proudly boast of their delusive happiness, but instead make a humble admission of their genuine misery" (*ciu.* 10.28).

Porphyry, Augustine claims, perhaps as the most honest of the philosophers, does recognize the necessity of grace. In a passage commenting on Plato's assertion that no one can reach the perfection of wisdom in this life, Porphyry comments that "after this life, all those who live the life that is according to the intellect (*secundum intellectum*) will receive all that is needed for their fulfillment from the providence and grace of God" (*ciu.* 10.29). Porphyry can even see that this will mean a refutation of cycles of alternation between misery and (so-called) bliss, at least for some people (*ciu.* 10.31, with Augustine anticipating the arguments against cycles that he will make later in books 11 and 12).

And yet, this philosophical account of grace is, well, philosophical. It falls considerably short of the divine "folly." It is grace configured to the regime of "virtue and wisdom" of self-advancement, it is not "foolish" enough. It is grace for those who, in effect, deserve it, who have lived the life of the intellect, the life according to the "mind or intellect of the Father." We recall that the Platonic version of this mind is not the one first principle together with the Father, nor did it become Incarnate, something which nothing and no one could deserve no matter how virtuous or powerful, the supreme instance of grace and thus of the freedom of God. In this philosophical rendition of grace, the Platonic God is not "free," has no "plan" or design other than an impersonal "idea," no grace that would not undercut the "power and wisdom" of the philosopher, and certainly no such love. This "Mind" is not a "priest," in the sense of one who consummates a sacrifice, let alone the sacrifice too (*ciu.* 10.31). Thus, the eternal knowledge of God, as Augustine sees it, is, despite formal points of contact, very distant from the unbelieving philosophical conception of it even at its best.

In fact, at its best, the unbelieving philosophical view approaches its greatest distortion of the truth because it attempts to take over from God his freedom by construing that freedom as "folly," not wisdom, and by construing his love as "weakness," not "power," attempting, instead, to control His grace. To put it a different way, it is precisely the historical character of this grace that offends the philosophic sensibility, its opacity precisely as a concrete self-offering in history. "Why just now?" and "Why so late?" are the questions posed by the philosophers to the "plan" of the Christian God, which therefore cannot possibly be the sought-after "universal way for the soul's liberation" (*ciu.* 10.32), precisely because it is historically specified and located, instead of being something that is abstractable from time and history and, as such, eternal. Knowing God's eternal knowledge is to know the "great Teacher" (*ille magister*), God, who made himself contemptible in the

eyes of the proud who were too ashamed to admit they needed healing and to what extent. To know this God is to know a God eternally,
unchangeably, and irreducibly *foolish*, whose "plan," eternally present
to himself and immutable, is the "folly of preaching," the Cross of His
own sacrifice, a God who is, therefore, eternally willing this sacrifice
of his own life in history, as history, because anything else would be
less loving, less a self-gift. It would be myth, the suffering of the divine
nature. It would be Manichaeism, in which God is not truly free to
love, but is rather compelled to create as part of a strategy of self-
defense (*ciu.* 11.22).

The Twilight of the Gods

And what about philosophy? Philosophical doctrine, as a way of
helping to explain biblical teaching, helps in the critique of mythologies, such as Manichaeism presents. But on its own, does it really
deliver on its promise of a wisdom that leaves behind mythological
accounts of the world in its own reaction against the poets and the
gods? In Augustine's analysis, philosophy, at its very best, can banish
the poets and critique the mythological depiction of the divine; yet,
Augustine shows that it does this by dissolving history into endless
repetitive cycles of misery alternating with ignorant bliss, in order
to preserve an account of God's knowledge that is eternal and
unchanging. The price of God's eternal knowledge is the misery of
everyone else:

> It is intolerable for devout ears to hear the opinion expressed that after
> passing through this life with all its great calamities ... and we have
> arrived at the sight of God and reached our bliss in the contemplation of
> immaterial light through participation in his changeless immortality ...
> that we reach this bliss only to be compelled to abandon it, to be cast
> down from that eternity, that truth, that felicity, to be involved again in
> hellish mortality, in shameful stupidity, in detestable miseries, where
> God is lost, where truth is hated, where happiness is sought in unclean
> wickedness; and to hear this is to happen again and again, as it has
> happened before, endlessly, at periodic intervals, as the ages pass in
> succession; and to hear that the reason for this is so that God may be
> able to know his own works by means of those finite cycles with their

continual departure and return, bringing with them our false felicities and genuine miseries .... For this theory assumes that God can neither rest from his creative activity, nor grasp within his knowledge an infinity of things (*ciu.* 12.21).

The eternal knowledge of the philosophical God is threatened by history, and therefore this God, limited by history, must retreat from history. There is only one place to retreat from history – into myth. He is limited by his own transcendence. He turns out to be a more rarified version of the Manichaean God. History, in its every unrepeatable unique moment, at any time of which everything can be lost, hedges this God in, lest he be "contaminated" with it (*ciu.* 9.17, speaking of the flesh).

And so the gods, banished from the philosophical light, find themselves perfectly welcome in the twilight, where they are available to receive the sacrifices of theurgic worship. Even Porphyry knows that the benefits of theurgy are marginal at best and that the gods being cultivated are dangerous at worst, and yet the philosophical God is so weighted by his own transcendence that he cannot or will not intervene in history to relieve its misery. Someone has to do it, even as a palliative (not to say, opiate), hence the gods, and the Platonist countenancing of their worship. The philosophers' God turns out to be a projection of the philosophers' own minds. In arguing for cycles, "it is not really God whom they are thinking of ... instead they imagine themselves in God's place" (*ciu.* 12.18). Eager to *claim they are wise*, they imagine a God distant from history; in fact, they *keep* him distant from history by their theories, keen as they are to preserve their prestigious status as *wise*, as the arbiters of God's transcendence through their own virtue and wisdom:

> Thus all those who cannot approach to philosophic virtue (a lofty ideal to which only a few attain) have your authority to seek out theurgists, in order to receive at their hands the purgation of the "spiritual" soul at least, though not of the "intellectual." The result is, naturally, that since the vast majority have no taste for philosophy, you collect far more clients for those secret and illegal masters of ours than candidates for the Platonic schools. You have made yourself the preacher and the angel of those unclean spirits who pretend to be gods of the ether (*ciu.* 10.27).

The gods do not go away with philosophy. There is too much of the divine to fit into philosophical theories, and it keeps popping up in the most awkward places. Like the embarrassing involuntary movements of the body resulting from concupiscence (*ciu.* 14.16–17), awkwardly belying the myth of self-sufficiency in disobedience to God, so the gods reappear at the edges of philosophy, awkwardly belying the myth of the God hedged in by his own eternal knowledge. It turns out that, far from banishing myth, philosophy is addicted to myth. The project of carving out a pure sphere of intellectual control and self-purification depends upon giving the gods their due as the second-tier access to which lesser souls must resort for succor. As the one God is restricted by the uniqueness of history, and therefore is re-mythologized even in his abstraction, the gods reappear, demanding worship from those who cannot purify themselves by philosophy, and forcing those who supposedly can to pimp for them.

The Living Flame of Love

But the real God pays the price of history Himself, from all eternity, out of pure, active, and generative love. It is not just the thought that counts in this gift, but, as it were, the gift of creation, as a gift, is paid for. Instead of paying for His own transcendence with human misery, God "buys" created freedom with His blood, not out of any necessity, but because he is loving and manifests his power in weakness. Looking at the choices that free agents make in freedom, and trying to ask why, for example, some angels fell and others did not, we receive the answer (*ciu.* 12.10) that the ones who clung to God received the grace to do so, while the others did not. At face value, it seems as though this God is too involved, micromanaging everything, over-omnipotent, as it were, but the decision not to give auxiliary grace to the devil and his angels is at one and the same time the decision of God to suffer and die in history to redeem human beings from the evil the devil would cause. Pondering why the evil angels fell is the same thing as pondering why God was willing from all eternity to perfectly empty Himself, why God from all eternity had the unchangeable plan of His own self-emptying, and so had the eternal knowledge of Himself as a living, eternal holocaust of love.

Faced with any free action in time and history, we are face to face with the ultimate mystery, the love of God, amazing in its absolute *foolishness* from all eternity. God's foreknowledge of the devil's evil choice is the same as God's foreknowledge of his remedy (see *ciu.* 11.17), his own life, his own compassionate love which receives the many "set free from the domination of the demons … in a purification in Christ that is full of compassion" (*misericordissimam purgationem, ciu.* 10.27). There is nothing that can give an account of that love – it is trackless – *O altitudo!* – any attempt to track grace is an attempt to be less loving, to avoid, in self-justification, the sacrifice that love is and that love requires.

It turns out, unexpectedly, that God's eternal graciousness, His eternal plan or design, is the precondition for any philosophical account in which history is not sacrificed to God's transcendent knowledge of the world. Instead, God's eternal omniscience is an eternal sacrifice. For God to know everything, timelessly, eternally, immutably, is itself an act of supreme sacrifice. God is not intimidated by infinities because He is not afraid of giving up Himself. His love is not intimidated by even an infinity of infinite series to retreat into a self-enclosed protectorate of transcendence. From all eternity, He is aware of his own willingness to give up the most precious thing that exists – Himself.

Acknowledgments

An earlier version of this chapter was published by Cambridge University Press as Cavadini, J. C. 2014. "God's eternal knowledge according to Augustine." In *The Cambridge Companion to Augustine* 2nd Edition, edited by David Vincent Meconi and Eleonore Stump. Cambridge University Press. Reprinted with permission.

Notes

1   English translations of texts from *City of God* are taken from Bettenson (2003), though, in many cases, I have felt free to adjust the translation without noting the adjustments.

2   This topic has received excellent treatment in studies whose philosophical depth cannot be captured in a brief chapter such as this. A useful guide to the studies

of the issues raised by God's eternal knowledge, and its relationship to time as they bear upon the study of St. Augustine, can be found in O'Daly (1999), 135–150. The notes by G. Bardy et al. to Books 8–12 of the *ciu.*, in BA 34 and 35, are still indispensable in themselves, and offer a good guide to literature up to the date of publication, in 1959.

3   Famously, Augustine points out that the Platonists, in seeing in some way the Father and the Mind of the Father, as well as a third being between them, "see, to some extent, though from afar off and with clouded vision (*utcumque, etsi de longinquo, etsi acie caligante*), the fatherland in which we must find our home; but do not keep to the road (*via*) along which we must travel" (*ciu.* 10.29; cf. 10.23–24). They do see something, in the manner in which you can see something very far away and with distorted vision, but they could not give an account of the Trinity, the God who is absolutely free to love, to have a story and yet remain the true unchangeable God. Their pride distorts their vision because they have an investment in keeping God distant, so that their accomplishment in glimpsing him remains a marker of their prestigious wisdom. That is why they do not "recognize the grace of God through Jesus Christ," God drawn near to us. They "see" God, but do not "recognize" him.

References

Bettenson, Henry, trans. (1972) *Concerning the City of God against the Pagans*. Harmondsworth, Middlesex: Penguin Books (repr. 1984, 2003).

O'Daly, Gerard (1999) *Augustine's City of God: A Reader's Guide*. Oxford: Clarendon Press.

Index

Visioning Augustine, First Edition. John C. Cavadini.
© 2019 John Wiley & Sons Ltd. Published 2019 by John Wiley & Sons Ltd.